AF361406

Settling in the Hearts

Raphael Patai Series in Jewish Folklore and Anthropology

A complete listing of the books in this series can be found online at wsupress.wayne.edu

General Editor
Dan Ben-Amos
University of Pennsylvania

Advisory Editors
Jane S. Gerber
City University of New York

Barbara Kirshenblatt-Gimblett
New York University

Aliza Shenhar
University of Haifa

Amnon Shiloah
Hebrew University

Harvey E. Goldberg
Hebrew University

Samuel G. Armistead
University of California, Davis

Settling in the Hearts

Jewish Fundamentalism in the Occupied Territories

Michael Feige

Wayne State University Press
Detroit

© 2009 by Wayne State University Press, Detroit, Michigan 48201. All rights reserved. No part of this book may be reproduced without formal permission.

13 12 11 10 09   5 4 3 2 1

Library of Congress Cataloging-in-Publication Data

Feige, Michael.
    Settling in the hearts : Jewish fundamentalism in the occupied territories / Michael Feige.
        p.   cm. — (Raphael Patai series in Jewish folklore and anthropology)
    Includes bibliographical references and index.
    ISBN 978-0-8143-2750-0 (cloth : alk. paper)
    1. Gush emunim (Israel)—History.   2. Jews—Colonization—West Bank—Moral and ethical aspects.   3. Jews—Colonization—Gaza Strip—Moral and ethical aspects.   4. Land settlement—Political aspects—West bank.   5. Land settlement—Political aspects—Gaza Strip.   6. Religious Zionists—West Bank—Political activity.   7. Religious Zionism—Israel.
8. Arab-Israeli conflict.   I. Title.

JQ1830.A98G865   2008
320.54095694'0956953—dc22   2008037318

∞

Designed and typeset by BookComp, Inc.
Composed in Minion Pro

Contents

Photo section follows page 130

Preface and Acknowledgments

When asked why I delayed for so long in submitting the manuscript for this book, I answered embarrassedly with a joke: "Do you know the difference between a bulldog and a Jewish mother? The bulldog eventually lets go of the child." (In the spirit of these politically correct times, I need to add that I hope no Jewish mothers or bulldog owners were offended by that.) Now this caring Jewish mother (or Jewish father, an unjustifiably neglected category in jokes) is sending his child into the world.

The delay cannot be attributed only to my motherly or bulldogish tendencies, but has also much to do with the subjects of this research, the Gush Emunim settlers, being themselves, quite openly and admittedly, like Jewish mothers when it comes to their dedication to their beloved child—the land of Israel. They caress the land, kiss it, weep and mourn for its solitude, and fight fearlessly against anyone who wants to take it away from them. Part of my fascination with the group is their uncompromising passion, which is so rare in today's cynical world. Consequently, they are constantly involved in dramatic historical events, as every government attempt to send the army to evacuate resolute, strange-looking youngsters, growing sheep on a desolate hill in the desert of Judea, induces a full-blown argument over state and nation, land and history, loyalty and treason, possible actions and the cost of inaction, and the meaning of all this to celestial salvation. With regard to this book, every cutoff point is inherently arbitrary and makes me wonder whether I should wait until the current crisis is over. That, however, is exactly when the next crisis begins.

The enemies and the victims of the Jewish West Bank settlers would claim that I have my metaphors wrong. The loving mother has adopted, not to say kidnapped at gunpoint, a child that is not her own, a child that belongs to another grieving mother, who is rightly furious. They would claim that, rather than a Jewish mother, the settlers resemble more the bulldog, or possibly a rottweiler, taking into account the havoc they inflict upon their Palestinian neighbors and the dangers they pose to law and order in Israel. Portraying them as loving mothers obscures their violent nature.

In Israel, no social issue has entailed more intense conflicting feelings than that of the settlers fighting for Israel's appropriation of the territories occupied in the 1967 Six-Day War. In this book, I try to tread carefully and analyze from an academic perspective a charged political debate dividing Israel between Left and Right, defining identities and political affiliations—a perspective in which I have my own heartfelt opinions. Unlike most works on the conflict, I deal not with the political, but rather with the sociological and anthropological, trying to decipher the inner logic of the settler's adventure in the contested land they regard as being exclusively theirs. This necessitates close observation of who they are, what they do, what they write, and how they think.

I am indebted to my interviewees, mainly religious settlers, for opening their homes and their hearts and making this research possible. They were all forthcoming, kind, and hospitable, dedicating their precious time to long explanations and elaborate discussions. The fact that I disagree with their worldview was known to them, yet it never interfered with their willingness to articulate their experiences, thoughts, and feelings. In this intricate situation, I wish each and every one of them success, though I cannot extend that wish to their collective project. As for them, the personal and the public are inseparably entangled, so I am unsure how my contradictory blessings can materialize. My more modest hope is that they will find the book, including the parts that are critical of their actions and perspective, a fair presentation of their deeds, ideas, and passions.

Unless otherwise noted, translations are by the author.

This book is the culmination of two decades of research and combines ideas that were formulated through discussions with my teachers, colleagues, and students over a very long period. Thanking all would be impossible, and I want to apologize for the many I fail to mention.

My interest in the subject began in a course offered at the Sociology and Anthropology Department of the Hebrew University of Jerusalem by Gideon Aran many years ago. He contributed to my thinking and always pushed me to enter the field to experience my research matter firsthand—advice I pass along to any young researcher. I wrote my doctoral dissertation on the subject under the guidance of Don Handelman and Luis Roniger, and the dedication and insights of those two brilliant scholars enriched me and supplied me with surprising angles. My perspective was influenced by the innovative eye-opening ideas of Baruch Kimmerling, who passed away in 2007; his critical insights and supportive dedication are sadly missed.

In the past decade, I have been a member of the Ben-Gurion Research Institute, part of the Ben-Gurion University of the Negev. The heads of the institute—Tuvia Friling, Ofer Schiff, and Yehuda Grados—have supported my work spiritually and financially. My colleagues and friends at the institute have at times provided me a conducive working environment and at other times have sapped my strength with dramas and mini-dramas, about which I am not going to elaborate here. I thank Esther Meir and Zvi Shiloni, both great working companions and wonderful friends. So is David Ohana, with whom I enjoy arguing on every subject (apart from the need for long walks down the beautiful Zin Valley), yet his infectious enthusiasm and practical solutions, as well as our intellectual discussions, helped to sustain me in difficult times.

I have the great fortune of having as dear personal friends Barry Schwartz and Yael Zerubavel, two of the most stimulating, influential, and profound scholars on collective memory and political myth. I owe them a great personal and intellectual debt, and see my work as an implementation of their insights into new territories.

Jackey Feldman read the manuscript as a language editor, yet as a wise friend and a proficient cultural anthropologist his critical reading sharpened my understanding and boosted my confidence.

The editors at Wayne State University Press have been kind, patient, helpful, and utterly professional, making our cooperation a pleasurable learning experience. Dan Ben-Amos believed in my work, even when I thought that he should give up. Kathryn Wildfong and, later, Kristin Harpster Lawrence made the complex seem easy and clear, and led me confidently through the fascinating process of book publication. Work with copyeditor John Flukas was efficient, illuminating, and a true delight.

My wonderful family—Nurit, Galit, Noga, and Dana—are torn between their attempts to allow me time to work and wanting to see me more at home. As I maneuver within my dual career responsibilities as family man and university professor, I thank them for being there for me all these years.

And one more tribute before this Jewish mother/bulldog lets go: While I was working on this book, my parents-in-law, Shmuel and Esther Spector, passed away. They were devoted family and dear friends, and we miss them very much. This book is dedicated to them in loving memory.

Settling in the Hearts

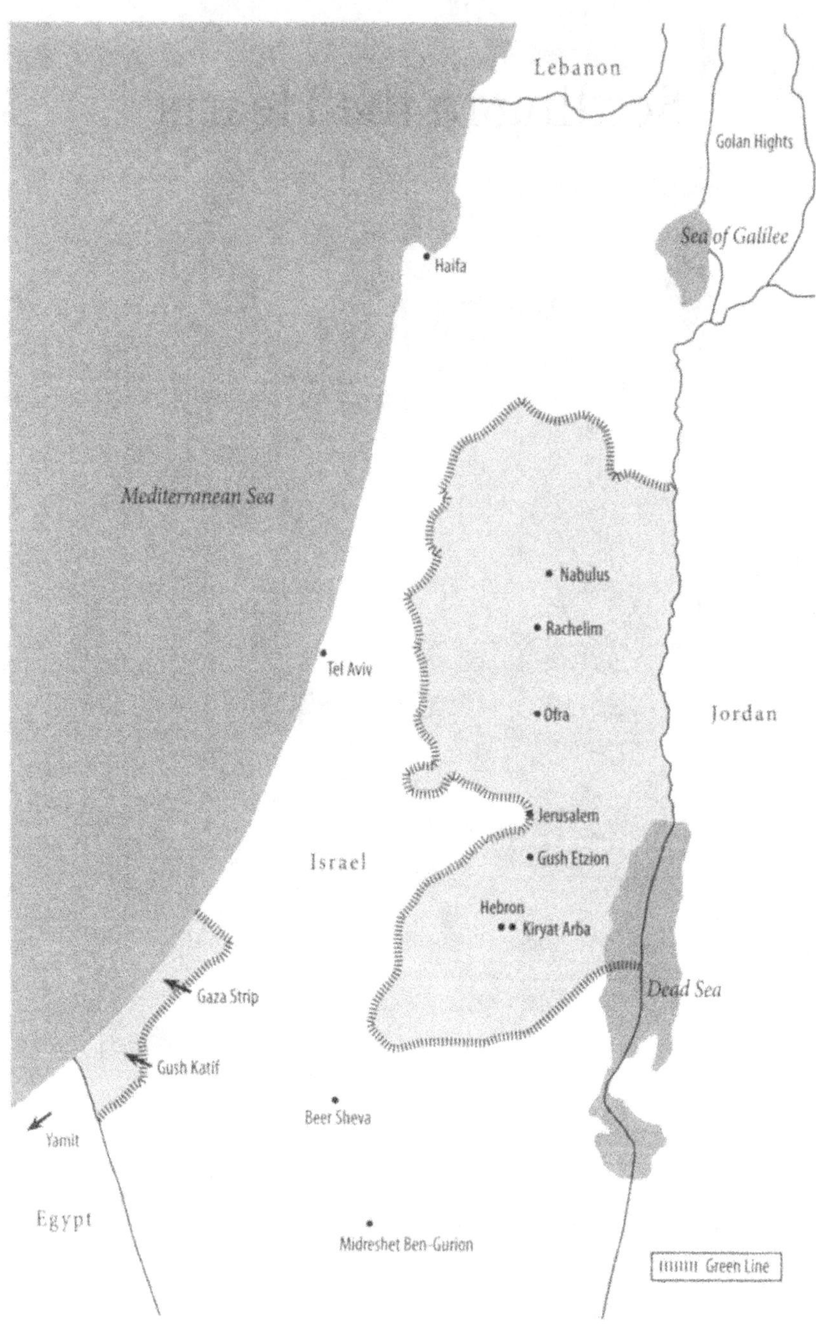

Lebanon
Golan Hights
Sea of Galilee
Haifa
Mediterranean Sea
Nabulus
Rachelim
Tel Aviv
Ofra
Jordan
Jerusalem
Israel
Gush Etzion
Hebron
Kiryat Arba
Dead Sea
Gaza Strip
Gush Katif
Yamit
Beer Sheva
Egypt
Midreshet Ben-Gurion
Green Line

Introduction

The Politics of Home and Death

On May 2, 2004, the Jewish settlers of the Gaza Strip were preparing for one of the most important days in their history. A plebiscite was to be held among the Likud Party members on Prime Minister Ariel Sharon's disengagement plan, which included the evacuation of all the settlements in the Gaza Strip and four of the most secluded settlements in the north of Samaria. Sharon suggested putting his plan before the members of the Likud because he was confident of his success within his own party. However, he grossly misjudged the organizational capabilities of the Yesha (acronym for Judea, Samaria, and Gaza) settlers: they reached most of the two hundred thousand voters in their homes and tipped the results in their favor. Sharon should have known better: more than others, he was responsible for the establishment and expansion of the ideological settlements. Had he not been the object of their rage and disappointment, he would have been proud to see the vigor they displayed. The settlers' supporters within the Likud Party arrived en masse to vote against the disengagement plan—against their own admired leader—while many supporters of Sharon's plan stayed home. The fact that Sharon is considered the father of the Gaza Strip settlement region made his defense of his program hesitant and unconvincing.

The drama of the plebiscite was overshadowed by another event. On the morning of that day, terrorists attacked near the exit of the Strip, on a road reserved for Jews only. Two Palestinians infiltrated the Israeli defenses and fired on a passing car, killing a pregnant woman—Tali Hatuel—and her four daughters, aged two to ten. The terrorists shot at the car and, when it stopped, closed range and made sure that all inside were dead. They were immediately killed by Israeli defense forces. The entire incident took less than a minute.

The murderous results were shocking even for a society used to frequent terrorist outbursts. Most of the Likud members had not yet voted, and the terrorist attack could strengthen the case of either side. On the one hand, it showed the dangers, if not the futility, of Israeli civilians' residing among 1.5 million angry Palestinians. The death toll among the Jewish settlers of the Gaza Strip was high indeed, and their evacuation might save the lives of settlers and of the soldiers guarding them. It could lead to reconciliation and, eventually, some kind of peace agreement. On the other hand, a withdrawal could be understood as a victory for terrorism and encourage its perpetrators. The slain woman, a resident of the Morag settlement, was an activist against the withdrawal, and, in a sense, a vote for the plan could be interpreted as a desecration of her memory on the day of her death. The demand to hold on, regardless of human cost, was central to the settlers' ethos, and, they claimed, should take precedence, especially when it was unclear which alternative was more costly in terms of human lives.

Hatuel and her children died, and their names joined the long list of settlers killed on the roads of Judea, Samaria, and the Gaza Strip in similar circumstances. Her convictions prevailed on that day. Likud voters opted for what they considered to be Hatuel's legacy, and any chance that Sharon might have had of winning the poll vanished. Because of the tragedy, there were no smiling faces after what was one of the greatest political victories in the settlers' history. In any case, all that did not matter: Sharon chose not to respect the results of the plebiscite and continued with his plan of disengagement and evacuation until its full completion. A little more than a year after Hatuel and her children died, their house was bulldozed to rubble.

That dramatic day in May 2004 epitomized the fate of the settlers throughout most of their history: standing fast against recurrent terrorist attacks and constant threats of eviction while struggling relentlessly for the support of the—at times hostile, at times sympathetic, usually apathetic—Israeli public. The settlers wished to construct their homes in the territories—private homes that would also be considered part of the national home, a return to the Land of the Bible—according to their religious belief. If, however, the term *home* conjures up images of tranquility and security, the settlers' newly established homes have little of those, as horribly exemplified in the murder of Hatuel and her four daughters.

Hatuel's friends swore that they would never forget her memory and desert their homes in the Gaza Strip. In Israel and abroad, many do not consider the settlements as legitimate homes, but see them as a colonialist project set in the midst of "native people," bringing with it agony, despair, violence, and injustice. While Israelis grieved the death of the family and were outraged at the violence against a pregnant woman and her small children, supporters of the Israeli "peace camp" were hardly surprised: to their mind, the Hatuel family had no business living in such a hazardous environment. She could only blame herself, moving into a war zone and bringing her little children along. They consider the settlers' cause both immoral and lost, dragging the rest of Israeli society into an everlasting cycle of violence.[1]

This book explores how a private and national home is socially produced, mentally constructed, and politically presented. The group analyzed is the Gush Emunim (Bloc of the Faithful) movement. The national home is what is internationally known as the "occupied territories," namely, the territories beyond the so-called Green Line, conquered by Israel in the 1967 Six-Day War and held by military and administrative rule ever since.[2] The protagonists see these territories as Judea, Samaria, and the Gaza Strip, referring to them with the acronym of "Yesha," which is also the Hebrew word for "salvation." Yesha is seen by the settlers as the holy ground that was the cradle of the Jewish people. To convince their many opponents both in Israel and abroad, the settlers' leadership and activists employ discursive strategies to construct Yesha as the true place of Zionism and Israel. They use similar strategies to construct their own sense of being at home. This book documents these strategies, as they are applied in various locations and contexts, in an attempt to understand how a sense of home is produced and reproduced in such a complex situation.

The subject of this research is the ideological settlers in Yesha, who arrived as part of the Gush Emunim movement or following its achievements.[3] The Israeli settlement in the occupied territories has been accomplished by numerous agencies and groups, of which Gush Emunim is just one. Of the approximately two hundred thousand Jewish residents of that area, most do not belong to this group.[4] Gush Emunim, however, was most consequential in the establishment of Israeli presence in the West Bank, bringing a clear ideology, impressive organization, political connections, and workforce with motivation, dedication, and commitment. Currently, most of the Gush Emunim supporters reside in the so-called ideological settlements on the mountain ridge of Judea and Samaria and are still the most active in the project of appropriating the land and struggling against territorial compromise.

This book concentrates on deciphering the basic meaning of the settlement project and the nature of the dialogue between the movement and Israeli society. After the movement's failure in stopping Israel's withdrawal from Sinai (see chapter 10), Rabbi Yoel Bin-Nun, one of the movement's foremost political and intellectual leaders at that time, coined a phrase that has been endlessly evoked ever since: "We have not settled in the hearts."[5] The question raised in this book is, how does a radical fundamentalist movement go about settling in the hearts of people? The understanding of how the movement constructs itself within the Israeli national context is, to my mind, the most important issue regarding Gush Emunim and its dialogue with the Israeli public.

The case of Gush Emunim holds great interest for followers of Israeli society, politics, and history, especially as it has not been researched extensively over the last decade. The connection between Israel and the occupied/liberated territories, with the millions of Palestinians living there, influences Israel's international standing, economic situation, and political discourse. How a determined minority group tries to establish a home in one of the most sensitive regions of the world is, therefore, an important part of contemporary Israeli history. More specifically, little research has been done on the effect of the dramatic historical events on the Gush Emunim settlers from the Oslo Accords until the Second Intifada and the disengagement plan. This book, covering a much wider historical perspective, beginning with the emergence of Gush Emunim, but also discussing the effect of the latest developments on the ideological settlers, is thus a novelty in Israeli academia.

The attempt of the Gush Emunim settlers to carve out a home for themselves in hostile terrain is relevant to important theoretical and historical issues. Generally speaking, Gush Emunim presents a case of connecting to the concrete in the age of the virtual, constructing place in the age of cyberspace, professing hypernationalism in an era of globalization, and embarking on a (by some definitions) colonial project at a time when multiculturalism and the elevation of the subaltern other are the order of the day. Furthermore, Gush Emunim stands in a very delicate place between Western modernity and religious fundamentalism, and its attempt to accommodate, perhaps even synthesize, two megaforces of the contemporary world may offer important insights for us all.

CONSTRUCTING PLACE IN THE POSTMODERN AGE: SOME THEORETICAL CONSIDERATIONS

Gush Emunim, an Israeli phenomenon of modern times, resists easy categorization, both with respect to Israeli society or to current sociological or anthropological theory. Whether one supports it or deplores it, Gush Emunim is a courageous attempt to withstand the winds of time, and in an age when "all that is solid melts into air" (Berman 1982), it tries to maintain a solid defiant position. Whether that attempt will be successful is still far from clear, but the endeavor reveals much about our conception of time, space, and identity both in Israel and elsewhere.

Gush Emunim is a religious-fundamentalist movement with a certain brand of messianism and an ultra-rightist political outlook. Its main declared aim is to bring the whole land of Israel within Israel's possession, and its main strategy is the construction of Jewish settlements on contested territory. It struggles for land against Palestinian Arabs with similar claims and against Israelis who think differently. If you would ask the Gush Emunim settlers to place themselves in the global system, they would favor Samuel Huntington's formulation of the clash of civilizations (Huntington 1996): they like to see themselves as standing on the frontier of Western, Judeo-Christian civilization, protecting it against the Arab and Muslim world. Ironically, Muslim fundamentalists concur with that depiction: they regard Gush Emunim settlers as the tip of the Western colonialist iceberg. Other formulations, originating mostly from "Western people" whom the settlers claim to be protecting, claim the opposite, and place them on the other side of the global divide. For the Israeli peace camp, the ideological settlers are seen as part of the fundamentalist phenomenon. For them, the settlers, like Muslim radicals, are religious fanatics that endanger the future of the region, if not Western modernity and the world. They call on moderate Palestinians to join forces with them to curtail the fundamentalists on both sides.

According to prevalent formulations of globalization, globalism is contested by localism: the great capitalist conglomerations find national, ethnic, and religious resistance to their penetration into particular markets.[6] The divide has been conceptualized through certain catchphrases such as Bernard Barber's *McWorld vs. Jihad* (1995) or Thomas Friedman's

The Lexus and the Olive Tree (2000). Although researchers have pointed out that the polarity may not be this extreme and, in actual encounters, global symbols take on local flavor, the binary conceptualization still potently structures our imagination. Placing Gush Emunim within this polarized world is a complex matter. On the one hand, as a fundamentalist movement, it vehemently opposes the homogenization and Americanization or, to use George Ritzer's term (1993), the "McDonaldization" of society. In this respect, Gush Emunim is on the side of jihad and the olive tree, and the believers are fighting a religious war against the evils of the modernizing and secularizing West in an attempt to connect to the ancient roots symbolized by the olive tree. The irony of using these symbols is, however, hard to miss: the settlers find themselves struggling against Palestinians, some of them dedicated to the idea of jihad, and in their attempts to take hold of the ancient homeland and improve their security, they have uprooted olive trees crucial for their Arab neighbors' subsistence. More importantly, in many respects, the settlers are clearly and manifestly part of the global world: in their use of technology, their education, and their participation in the labor force (like other fundamentalist groups in the Western world), as well as in their own self-perception. The settlers of Gush Emunim are not only on the battlefront between the global or the Western and its enemies, but also embody this dichotomy within their body and cognition.

In an age characterized by the changing meanings of space and place, time and history, Gush Emunim attempts to revive some classical conceptions. Late modernity and the postmodern age are known for the condensation of time and space, the high mobility of people and goods, the multiplication of actual and symbolic borderlines and the hybridism that these shifting, multiple borders produce, and the advancement of hyperreality and cyberspace (Harvey 1989; Giddens 1990; Castels 1996). All these have great effect on the settler movement and make up part of the context in which it performs; Gush Emunim, however, resists these trends, trying to reverse their historical direction. Their resistance is focused on the meaning of place. Against contemporary claims of deconstructing place and replacing it by border zones, and while proclaiming the fluid and hybrid nature of identity, the settlers assert their knowledge of the eternal truth of the people and the land. Gush Emunim is a nationalist movement in a postnationalist age, and an extreme territorial movement in a global, postterritorial epoch.

It might be argued that the local social environment in which the Gush Emunim movement operates—Israeli society—is one in which patriotism, Zionist ideology, and the ongoing conflict with the Palestinians have succeeded in repulsing the trends that deconstruct national identities in the Western world. Even in its local context, however, the movement can be seen as swimming against the current of trends within its home society. Gush Emunim arose as Israel was passing from a collectivist ideology to an individualized one—a phase marked by privatization of many of its national assets.[7] This process, which occurred in most Western societies, has been especially volatile in Israel, perhaps because it was marked by hostility toward the residue of the hegemonic socialist ideology of the early years of the state. With its collectivist ideology and claims to restructure the public good, Gush Emunim struggled against the prevailing tides of Israeli society.

When the bulk of research on Gush Emunim was conducted and written in the late 1980s, the main—some would argue, the only—issue on the Israeli agenda was peace and territories. Some still believe this to be the case: in a book he edited on the El-Aqsa Intifada (aka the Second Intifada), Adi Ophir (2001) claimed that, until the termination of the occupation, the Israeli Left can hold no other agenda. Today, with the expansion of the scope of Israeli social sciences, many claim otherwise. Israel is engulfed in a rapid process of globalization, which is supplemented and supported by a no less accelerated process of privatization, economic polarization, and sectorialization. Gush Emunim settlers are deeply entangled in these processes—processes which undermine the unique Jewish character of the state that the Gush Emunim believers hold sacred. Through its settlement project, Gush Emunim deepens the Israeli hold in the contested territories, thus impeding Israel's attempt to jump on globalization bandwagon.

Gush Emunim should be understood in the context of Israeli society and political regime as conceptualized by recent Israeli scholars. Oren Yiftachel (2006) has described Israeli society and state as an "ethnocracy," claiming that the Israeli social organization is structured so as to benefit the dominant Jewish ethnic group. Israeli democracy is limited in its ability to decide according to the interests of the demos rather than the ethnos. The Israeli occupation of the territories and, especially, the emergence of Gush Emunim are integral parts of the hegemonic logic of Israeli society, serving the interests of the Jewish ethnoreligious group at the expense of others. A different formulation was suggested by Uri Ram (2007), who claimed that, under the pressure of globalization, the Israeli identity is being polarized into post-Zionist and neo-Zionist poles. The first seeks to transcend Zionism and join the global world, whereas the other wishes to rekindle the Zionist spirit and stave off the culturally devastating effects of globalism. In these terms, Gush Emunim represents the neo-Zionist pole and emerged as part of the disintegration of the Zionist synthesis.

These two conceptualizations certainly hold much merit. What they may be missing, however, is the hybrid nature of Gush Emunim, straddling on the borderline between the global and the local. While in its ideology Gush Emunim is undoubtedly part of the fundamentalist reaction to globalism, and its aim is to strengthen the ethnocratic nature of Israeli society, in the lifestyle and aspirations of its supporters it is clearly part of the globalizing West. In what follows, I suggest why a closer examination of Gush Emunim has not yet been undertaken.

GUSH EMUNIM AND THE STUDY OF EXOTIC OTHERS

Surprisingly, no major academic book on Gush Emunim and the phenomenon of ideological settlement has been published either in Hebrew or in English for more than a decade. There is hardly any doubt that the settlement project is of immense geopolitical importance, and, in a sense, it has even changed the history of the Middle East by pressuring the Palestinians to reach quick agreement with Israel, and on Israelis to reconsider their interests in the occupied territories. Furthermore, in the last decade, the settlement project has been proven time and again as one of the most important issues in—many would clearly say obstacles to—compromise between Israel and the Palestinians. It stands to reason that Israeli academia, mostly supportive of the peace process and left oriented, would seek to comprehend the nature of this phenomenon. Although scattered academic works have been published on the settlers, hardly any attempt has been made to understand the phenomenon from an overarching perspective.

When Gush Emunim burst onto the Israeli political scene in 1974, attempts to decipher its meaning and significance abounded. In 1985, the first academic book, a volume edited by political geographer David Newman, was published, raising in its title the all-important question of *The Impact of Gush Emunim*. In 1991, books on Gush Emunim were published by two of the best-known researchers in the field: Ehud Sprinzak and Ian Lustick. An influential and comprehensive article was published that year by sociologist Gideon Aran as part of the celebrated Fundamentalism Project, supplying a historical and sociological overview of the movement. In the decade to follow, more books were published, but practically all were memoirs of Gush Emunim leaders (Segal 1988; Harnoi 1995; Shafat 1995). My own book, published in Hebrew in 2002, which compared Gush Emunim with its nemesis Peace Now, may be considered as a partial exception to this rule. In 2005, Idith Zertal and Akiva Eldar published a monumental work titled *The Lords of the Land* (with an English translation published in 2007). This book, however, only proves my point: It is overtly hostile to the settlers and examines how different Israeli institutions have succumbed to their menace. The lifeworld of the settlers and the internal logic of their project hold little interest for the writers, in comparison to documenting what they consider the damage the settlers have done to Israeli social fabric and civil identity (Zertal and Eldar 2007).

To appreciate the exceptional nature of this neglect, let us look at the rapidly developing field of collective memory. During the last two decades, numerous works have been published on the Zionist narrative: the great myths of Masada and Trumpeldor (Ben-Yehuda 1995; Zerubavel 1995), Holocaust remembrance (Don-Yehiya 1993; Segev 1993; Feldman 2002), commemoration of fallen soldiers (Sivan 1991; Azaryahu 1995), the phenomena of ethnic revival (Ben-Ari and Bilu 1997), the role of archaeology (Abu el Haj 2002; Hallote and Joffe 2002), the emergence of the "new historiography" (Silberstein 1999; Nimni 2003), Yitzhak Rabin's commemoration (Peri 2000; Vinitzki-Saroussi 2002), and so on. These works tackle the question of how Israel represents its collective past, and how these representations shape and are shaped by present politics, society, and culture. Although all of these representations are important, even crucial, to the understanding of Israeli identity, the elephant in the room is ignored. The sites of memory that have the most impact on the lives of Israelis are Hebron and Shechem (Nablus), whereas the most crucial debate on memory and identity centers on whether Israel is obliged, by the history of the Jewish people and the memories of wars and annihilation, to remain in Judea and Samaria. Israeli scholars researching memory and identity bypass these questions.

Two recent declarations have referred to alleged failures of Israeli sociology, each from a radically different perspective. Baruch Kimmerling (2003) has addressed the Israeli sociological community through the bulletin of its association and suggested a criticism "from the left." He decrees the absence of a developed sociology of military occupation. Kimmerling asserts that, as there is currently no higher priority, either theoretically or morally, than studying Israel's occupation regime, local sociology is betraying its calling by missing out on what defines the very essence of Israeliness today. Alek Epstein (2004)[8] published an article in the rightist journal *Azure,* claiming that, as a result of its leftist inclination, Israeli sociology neglects to study the plight of the settlers and other Israelis who suffer Palestinian terror. He claims that these are undoubtedly unique Israeli phenomena and that Israeli sociologists can provide substantial empirical and theoretical contributions by addressing them academically. Although the two writers address the issue from opposing perspectives, they are basically making the same claim—that the great drama of Israeli presence in the West Bank and Gaza Strip is not sufficiently attended to by Israeli researchers.

Why has so little of the energy of Israeli sociologists and anthropologists been invested in studying the group that is probably the most influential in determining the future of the state and the nation? There are some obvious reasons. One is that the West Bank—let alone the Gaza Strip—has become dangerous in recent years, especially since the El-Aqsa Intifada, and few people who do not live or work there, or who are called there for military duty, bother to visit, much less do research. Another reason is that most Israeli social scientists are politically alien, if not downright hostile, to the settlers and do not relish lengthy interviews with them. Endangering their life in order to research a group they strongly dislike is an experience that many Israeli researchers are willing to forego.

A further reason is that the settlers are not considered to be exotic enough. When I did my comparative research of Gush Emunim and Peace Now, I noticed the opposite tendency: while few thought that the intellectual and rather dry peace activists merited research, the study of the Israeli novelty of fundamentalists dancing on the barren hills of Samaria excited researchers. Consequently, Gush Emunim received academic attention in its formative years. Since then, the magic has faded while the politically animosity has remained, and the issues involved have become more volatile and, for many, more threatening. The fascinating, yet small, group grew to become 200,000 settlers in 145 settlements, whose representation by ministers and members of Knesset far surpassed their percentage in the Israeli population. The settlers, both leaders and activists, appear endlessly on television, their plight is told in the newspaper, their viewpoint is presented—possibly overpresented—in every possible media, and, like any novelty, they are becoming boringly repetitive. The basic scenario—where young religious settlers occupy a barren hill and claim that it is their sacred home, and several peace activists raise voices of protest against them while the Knesset deliberates issues regarding the Jewish right to the land and the danger to future peace prospects—by now has a tiring déjà vu character to it.

In a sense, the settlers fell victim to their own success: once their settlements became established and institutionalized, they became of little further interest and needed more intense provocation to catch the media's impatient gaze. The academic world is following suit and moves onto other subjects. New religious groups that have flourished in the social vicinity of Gush Emunim offer Israelis new venues to express spirituality and suggest to the researchers new, more exotic, though far less influential, subjects to study. Within Israel, some groups are receiving more academic attention not only because they are more exotic but also because they are considered to be connected to the major issues confronting Israeli society today. The conflict between Left and Right was once regarded as the most important conflict in Israel, dividing the nation into two opposing tribes (see Kimmerling 1984). Now, academic attention has moved elsewhere, and the issue of Israel's presence in the occupied territories is left behind, unresearched and undertheorized.

It is considered to be to the merit of Israeli sociology that it opened new fields of research that were either marginal or had been examined through overly traditional theories (Ram 1995). In the past decade, feminist theories and the study of gender issues became a pivotal subject of research; the study of *Mizrahim* (Jews of Oriental descent) was retheorized using the ideas of Foucault, Said, and Bhabha; the in-between identity problems of the Israeli Palestinians became the subject of intensive research; and the newly arrived guest workers attracted much academic discussion. What is common to these examples is that they enable social scientists to discuss general issues at the cutting edge of contemporary theorizing on gender, ethnicity, citizenship, and the postmodern condition. The West Bank settlers, to use a term from George Bernard Shaw's *Pygmalion*, are the "undeserving poor": their type of otherness is not appealing to the social scientists.

Critical sociologists and most anthropologists wish to fulfill one of the expectations of their field, which is to give voice to deprived people and to enable the subaltern to speak. Whatever else can be said of the settlers, and regardless of their own complaints on media neglect and bias, they are not voiceless. The opposite is closer to the truth—they are probably the most vocal and articulate group in Israeli society today. Since most social scientists do not sympathize with them and feel little inclination to give them more attention than they are already receiving, academic research on the group is regrettably lacking.

There are also theoretical reasons behind this neglect. A left-wing friend told me that there is not much point in studying the settlers' discourse: what difference does it make what rationales they provide for their colonial project and violent actions? The argument is that the viewpoint and ideological reasoning of the settlers are epiphenomena of greater social and political processes. The only reason why Gush Emunim settlers succeeded in their settlement project was because the Israeli state enabled them, backed them, partly financed them, and took international responsibility for their actions; all instead of crushing the phenomenon at the outset, as peace activists believe should have been done. The settlers themselves eagerly admit that they are only delegates of the state who are embodying the national interest as democratically determined; hence, both sides of the ideological divide downplay the role of Gush Emunim. If that is the case, perhaps, the argument runs, the ideological settlers are not very consequential in explaining Israel's presence in the West Bank.

Another claim popular with left-wing Israelis is that, although the settlers accentuate the sacrifices they had to make, their move to the occupied territories has in actual fact won them tangible resources. They received land at bargain prices, established exclusive communities of their own kind, and enjoyed years of tax exemptions and an opportunity to fulfill not only their national, but also their suburban, dreams. In national economic terms, the support that the state provided to settlers in the West Bank and Gaza Strip is tax money diverted to the well-being of an upper-middle-class community at the expense of the lower-class Jews and Arabs. That being the case, the Gush Emunim ideology can be presented as no more than a guise for a project that holds considerable economic benefits, and should be understood in terms of establishing and reproducing the status privileges of a strong social group.

Although, in my view, these claims have much merit and may support the conclusion that the settlers should receive fewer economic benefits, it does not mean that they do not deserve more academic attention. As research on colonial and postcolonial phenomena has shown, the ideological apparatus that stands at their basis is important to decipher. The issue should be understood in terms of what Max Weber referred to as "elective affinity": while rightist Israeli governments were looking for opportunities to hold the occupied territories yet lacked the workforce to do so, Gush Emunim supporters had "the right" (in both senses of the word) ideology and motivation. This coalition of interests between the political opportunity and the way it is addressed is never easy to achieve and should be examined empirically. The claim that Gush Emunim is no more than an epiphenomenon is a critical perspective on the settlers' statements and reflects a healthy suspicion toward their discourse, but is it sufficient reason for ignoring the study of the phenomenon itself?

There is one more reason why the settlers are less interesting now than they were before. Within the wide trend that has been dubbed "new history," "critical sociology," or "post-Zionism," a novel perspective was produced on the Israeli past. Some of the critical scholars see the Jewish immigration to Palestine, the 1948 war (which they will refrain from calling the War of Independence), and the expulsion of Palestinians as Israel's original sin. Israel is portrayed as a colonial state, and its moral claims and historical justifications are either ignored or proclaimed illegitimate.[9] In this academic context, there is little difference between the acts of the Gush Emunim settlers today and the very nature of the Zionist project and Israel's past appropriation of the land. This, incidentally, is what the settlers have been claiming all along—that their acts are a direct and unproblematic continuation of traditional Zionist practices, and that whoever criticizes them ipso facto reveals anti-Zionist positions. Although, in all probability, it was not the aim of the critical writers, accusing the "first Israelis" of the early years of the state of committing ethnic cleansing, of wide-ranging confiscation of property, and of holding racist attitudes toward Arabs and Oriental Jews, has taken the Gush Emunim settlers off the hook. When, for example, film scholar Ella Shohat (1998) adds the Jewish victims of Zionism (the Mizrahim) to its non-Jewish victims, she actually suggests diverting the focus of research and criticism from the settlers to what she defines as essence of the problem—the entire Zionist project.

Even if we accept the radical claims that Israel was created through immoral acts of needless atrocities (which I do not), it should be clear that, in history, no two events are identical, even if they appear similar. West Bank settlers' (so-called) colonialism is radically different from that attributed to Israel as a whole. And if either the construction of the Israeli regime or the plight of the Palestinians is motivation for research, it is difficult to understand what good would come of diverting one's eyes from the Gush Emunim settlers, as though they are irrelevant to the issue. The basic criticism of subsuming the critique of the Gush Emunim settlers under the larger critique of Zionism, however, is not moral and political, but purely intellectual. The settlers suggest a certain type of "being Israeli" that, while undoubtedly rooted in previous Jewish, Zionist, and Israeli formulations, cannot be reduced to them. Most Israelis do not agree with the Gush Emunim worldview, so the claim that "all Israel is Gush Emunim" is, at the very least, not helpful for understanding either the struggle over Israeli identity or the outcome of the Israeli-Palestinian conflict.

For numerous reasons that I have stated (and probably some that I have not), the study of Gush Emunim has advanced very little over the past decade or more. In this book, I wish to reconsider the literature on the subject, to update it where necessary, but mostly to suggest a novel way of understanding the phenomenon.

STUDYING GUSH EMUNIM: SOME METHODOLOGICAL CONSIDERATIONS

This book is a culmination of many years of research, starting in 1982, when as a young student at the Hebrew University in Jerusalem I wrote a seminar paper on "The Movement to Stop the Withdrawal in Sinai" (see Aran and Feige 1987) and did participant observation on the supporters of Gush Emunim, who flocked by the hundreds to the region to fight in that losing cause. My doctoral dissertation compared the two mass movements of the Israeli Left and Right: Peace Now and Gush Emunim (Feige 1996, 2002). This research allowed me insight into the inner workings of the settler project, but also supplied the perspective of Gush Emunim's foremost opponents. Much of the material for the current book came from that research conducted during the years 1991–95. Since then, I have continued to gather material on the ideological settlements. The last decade was a most dramatic one in the history of the Jewish settlement (actually, each and every period in that history is dramatic for some reason or another), and I followed the changes closely. My interest even ventures into the future: I participated in a project called "The Morning After," managed by Meron Benvenisti, which attempted to forecast how Israeli society would change following the achievement of a peace with the Palestinians, which would include the evacuation of settlements from the occupied territories. My contribution to the project was titled "The Morning After Looks at the Night Before" and concentrated on possible changes in Israeli collective memory following a peace agreement (Benvenisti 2002).[10]

The research for this book is inherently interdisciplinary. I have studied sociology and anthropology at the Hebrew University at Jerusalem. Working at the Ben-Gurion Research Institute at the Sede Boker Campus of the Ben-Gurion University, I am the only social scientist in a group that consists mainly of historians and have learned to respect their perspective. Anthropology has left me with a desire to tell the story through extensive or anecdotal ethnographies, which appear in numerous places throughout the book. My inclination toward historical thinking means that the specific ethnography is usually not the most important issue in any chapter or in the book as a whole, but is placed within a narrative that attempts to be inclusive. Anthropologists rarely remain within the confines of their chosen ethnography, and I see my field experiences as only part, though a crucial one, of the entire picture. In this book, ethnography serves as a means of grasping the deeper meaning of the settlement project—an opportunity to interview the people involved and a trigger for understanding documental accounts.

Apart from the ethnographic evidence, the research is based on extensive interviews,[11] movement publications, newspaper reports, and other types of material that can be clustered under the heading "visual anthropology." Since the religious settlement of Gush Emunim has grown, and now consists of dozens of villages, thousands of people, and numerous organizations, the material gathered for this research samples only a portion of it. As I could not research every individual settlement and all subgroups and historical cases (though they certainly merit further study), I chose to focus on the characteristics, processes, and examples that I felt most important for understanding the nature of the movement.

Some uses of the material deserve special mention. I have made much use of the newspapers and bulletins regularly published in the settlements because these publications reflect both ideological formulations and everyday life. First and foremost is the monthly *Nekuda* (meaning "full stop" or "dot on the map"), which first appeared at the end of 1979 and is published regularly to this day. *Nekuda* presents itself as the organ of the Judea, Samaria, and Gaza Strip settlements, and also as an expression of the political position of the Israeli Right. Other bulletins belong either to specific organizations or to certain settlements or regions. I should mention the two I used most frequently. One is Gush Etzion's *Gushpanka* (a play on words signifying "Gush" of Gush Etzion and "holding rights") and the other is *Et Ofra*, published regularly in the settlement of Ofra. These publications are internal organs that are not intended for the eyes of strangers. As Gush Emunim is a committed ideological group, most of the discourse with others is well controlled and not easy to penetrate. Some of these internal media of communication provide researchers with a glimpse into the inner working of the settlers' communities.

Another useful tool, though limited in its own way, is the critical gaze of the settlers' adversaries. Peace Now researched the settlements for its own political purposes. Their research is considered to be accurate and fair not only by the supporters of the peace movement, but sometimes also by the settlers themselves, who claim that the research is the act of defeatist Jews squealing on their own brothers to the authorities and the enemy. Furthermore, the settlers claim that the representation of the sociodemographic situation in the occupied territories as it is ignores both the historical perspective and possible future developments. For example, they claim that the fact that there are only fifty Jewish families in Hebron amidst tens of thousands of Arabs means that the Jewish presence has to be strengthened rather than abolished.

More data were produced during the 1980s by the West Bank Data Research Institute headed by Meron Benvenisti. Benvenisti's theory, which is presented later in the book, asserts that the Israeli presence in the territories is irreversible. Needless to say, this conclusion delights the settlers; thus, although he is hostile to the settlement project, his data are considered credible by all sides. A third group that works in the territories is *Betzelem* (In the Image of God), which is interested in issues of human rights and researches the behavior of Israeli authorities, the Israel Defense Forces, and the settlers. This group, which is highly esteemed internationally and has Israeli and Palestinian researchers, is considered by most Israelis to be part of the extreme Left. The settlers themselves, however, were not beyond appealing to Betzelem when they felt that the Israeli authorities had compromised their civil rights.

What is common to these reports is that they supply a generally reliable outside gaze on the settlements, yet say little about the nature of the phenomenon and the meanings it holds for the believers. To obtain a fuller view of the project, taking into account the settlers' viewpoint as well, these reports must be supplemented by other methods. The combination of outside reports and the settlers' discourse, as expressed in interviews and in their writings, jointly supplies what I hope is an even-handed account of the movement.

Another source of data has recently emerged from the settlers development of Internet sites in which they present their views. The virtual space is useful in deciphering the meanings of the actual place. Computer experts claim that these sites are technically undeveloped, but they are nevertheless of great use, especially in understanding how the settlers present themselves and what they deem important. The Internet is a legitimate tool of research today, but in this particular case it has special importance: The Jewish settlements are numerous and dispersed in hostile territory. Although the Internet cannot substitute for actual presence and observation, it facilitates research and enables easy access to basic facts and the settlers' presentation of self.

The Structure of the Book

The first few chapters of the book discuss the logic of Gush Emunim and the settlement project, the following sections present important examples of these principles at work, and the book ends with an exploration of the settlement project today.

Chapter 1 presents Gush Emunim as a sociological, political, and theological phenomenon, and serves as a necessary introduction to the rest of the book. The chapter first suggests a history of Gush Emunim and the ideological settlements, from its beginnings until today, and then raises the main issues organizing the discussion over the nature of the movement: How do we account for its origins? Is it primarily a political or religious phenomenon? The chapter concludes with a presentation of the ongoing academic discussion regarding the nature of Israeli presence in the territories.

Chapter 2 attends to the theological and nationalist connections of the movement to the land. My claim is that the connection is based on two different, complementary, and sometimes contradictory systems of thought. One is the theological, in which the land is divinely promised and settlement is a halakhic rule (rule of religious/divine law); the second is the national-historical, in which the rights to the land belong to the Jewish people because of its unique history. The historical spectrum that will be presented is a wide one: for various reasons, the ancient past, exilic times, and the Zionist return to the land all combine and contribute to the settlers' claims to exclusive rights to the land. The chapter concludes with one important reservation: although the importance of Jewish memory for Gush Emunim believers cannot be overstated, they still make distinctions and choices. They return to the Land of the Bible with modern technology, in search of the high standard of living that technology can provide, and bearing certain modern values, as well.

In chapter 3, I present the main method of occupying and appropriating land: namely, the settlement. It does the work both through its very presence and by making symbolic statements of belonging and returning. I shall discuss the vision that underlies the creation of settlements, the names given to them, their aesthetics, and the paradox that results from the realization of the grand vision of their mother movement.

Chapter 4 concentrates on the various practices that give space historical meaning. These have all been practiced frequently in Israeli history: archaeology, political marches, hikes, songs, and so on. As the religious settlers adopt them, the practices undergo certain changes, such as the adding of a critical subversive edge to them, at times directed against the nation-state that put them to such elaborate use. Furthermore, the settlers are dedicated to archaeology in a postarchaeological age and to national hiking at a time when Israelis are searching for other pastime activities.

Chapter 5 considers the way that the settlers encounter their most crucial conceptual and practical challenge: the Palestinian Arabs. Whereas the presence of the Jews in the Land of the Bible is well understood and conceptualized by the settlers, the presence of their local enemy is accounted for through various explanations: as the descendents of the biblical Ishmael and Hagar, as heirs to the Cossacks and the Nazis, and as a historical accident that has to be corrected. The chapter follows the changing place of the Arab in the settlers' worldview over time.

Chapter 6 discusses the effects of Palestinian terrorism on settler communities and the commemoration of the settlers killed in terrorist acts. Although the frequent attacks on the settlers deter Israelis from visiting, let alone moving, to the territories, the violent events strengthen the settlers' resolve to entrench themselves more deeply in the sacred land.

Chapter 7 presents a major example that pushes to the limit the various motifs mentioned thus far: the Jewish settlement of Hebron and Kiryat Arba. More than merely an example, Jewish Hebron is considered to be the center of the settlement project and to embody its meaning most fully. The chapter discusses the significance of the Cave of Machpela and biblical history, the 1929 Tarpat Massacre, the commemoration of the dead from within the community, and the place of the large Arab population of the city in the settlers' ideology. In conclusion, these historically resonating meanings are marshaled to try to explain the massacre committed by Baruch Goldstein in the Cave of Machpela.

After Hebron, in chapter 8 the discussion moves to the case of Gush Etzion. The uniqueness of this settlement region is in its connection to Zionist history and the Israeli military myth. This example enables us to see the similarities, tensions, and contradictions between the Gush Emunim version of history and the Zionist one, and to examine the dynamics between the two.

Next, in chapter 9, is the case of Ofra, one of the first and most distinguished of Gush Emunim settlements. The issue that I found most intriguing in Ofra is the playing out of the tension running through the book between the wish to be faithful to the fundamentalist decrees and the desire to remain an integral part of modern Israel. I shall examine this "boundary work" mainly through two practices used by the believers to represent their world: the political joke and the ritual.

One of the greatest traumas in the history of Gush Emunim was the Israeli withdrawal from Sinai because of the peace treaty with Egypt. The movement fought a futile battle against that decision and its implementation. The possibility that the evacuation of Sinai might serve as a precedent to Judea and Samaria was not lost on the settlers and directs their construction of the meaning of this event. Chapter 10 discusses this case, in which the settlers received a glimpse at the possibility of their project's demise.

Whereas chapter 6 discusses the basic principles at work in the commemoration of killed settlers, chapter 11 concentrates on one example: the murder of Rachel Druk and the establishment of the settlement Rechalim carried out by a group of women. Through this example, the crucial role of women in the religious movement is presented, and the meaning of feminism for the settlers' project is discussed.

Chapter 12 is dedicated to the emergence of a new generational group: the youth who grew up and were educated in the ideological settlements. The biblical sabras (native-born Israeli Jews) establish new outposts on barren hills of Judea and Samaria, and pose a challenge both to the Israeli authorities and to their parents, the leadership of the by-now established ideological settlements. Within this book, they represent the attitudes and behavior of those for whom the settlements are already a home in the sense of their having been born there.

The final chapter is dedicated to analyzing events that rocked the world of the settlers in the last few years: the Oslo Accords, the assassination of Yitzhak Rabin, the impact of suicide terrorist attacks in Israel, the building of a fence between Israel and Yesha, and the disengagement plan, culminating with the evacuation and destruction of twenty-two settlements in the Gaza Strip and northern Samaria. All of these events are analyzed from the perspective of the basic theme of the book: the quest to settle in the hearts of Israelis. All of these occurrences played a dialectic role of inclusion and exclusion of the settlers and their project as part of modern Israel.

Today, the settler project is locked within two conflicting and contradictory directions that became visible in the murder of the Hatuel family, presented at the beginning of this chapter: On the one hand, more than ever before, a wide consensus affirms that the isolated settlements, the ones in which most of the Gush Emunim population resides, will have to be removed, and a Palestinian state should be established. Statements to this affect are common not only among the Israeli Left, but also among those who were the main supporters of the settlement project. The fence that leaves the ideological settlements on the other side serves also as a metaphor of the failure of the settlers to convince the Israelis that Yesha is theirs for all eternity. Many Israelis see the disengagement plan and the evacuation of the Gaza Strip settlements as just the first step toward a more comprehensive withdrawal. On the other hand, with respect to national investment, growth, and development, the situation has never been better for the Gush Emunim settlement project. The terrorist attacks in the midst of Israeli cities, as well as those targeting the settlers, created new bonds of solidarity. Evacuation of the more established Jewish settlements never looked more remote from both the mind-set and the capabilities of the Israeli government.

Although the historical success of the Gush Emunim project cannot be assessed at this point, the importance of the phenomenon cannot be denied. Gush Emunim settlers have changed Middle East history and are a crucial factor in determining Israel's future, not to mention the Palestinian prospects of holding a viable state of their own. Their unique position betwixt and between Western modernism and religious fundamentalism, on the borderline, which is also the battlefield, between nations and civilizations, makes them a source of new perspectives on identity in today's world. Their dramatic story is crucial not only for the understanding of Israeli society, but also for confronting basic questions regarding communication in the modern and postmodern age: what does it take to settle in the hearts of people, and how does a resolute fundamentalist group attempt to achieve this goal?

1

Gush Emunim

History, Sociology, and Theology

THE DEBATE OVER THE OCCUPIED TERRITORIES

Gush Emunim spearheaded the most heated debate in Israeli politics—a debate that encompassed Israeli identity in all its complexity. The debate touched not only on questions of elections and political partisanship, but created two "tribes" of approximately equal size with radically different worldviews.[1] Gush Emunim was conceived as the quintessential representative of one of the sides and greatly defined and redefined the issues to be discussed. It formulated conclusive statements regarding two of the major divisions in Israeli society: the ideological and the religious. Before discussing the attributes of the movement, I shall present the context in which it operated.

Several weeks before the 1967 war, Geula Cohen interviewed David Ben-Gurion, Israel's first prime minister, then a backbench Knesset member. She asked him, "Mr. Ben-Gurion, what will you tell your grandson today when he asks you 'Grandpa, what are the borders of my homeland?'" Ben-Gurion responded, "Well, I will answer him, 'The borders of your homeland are the borders of the state of Israel as they are now. That is all.'"[2] Ben-Gurion, who, more than anyone else, determined Israel's borders during and following Israel's War of Independence, thus expressed the popular sentiment at the time: The labor of appropriating the land through occupation and annexation had ended, and Israel should now concentrate its energies and resources in securing its future and settling the relatively vacant Negev desert. The interviewer, Geula Cohen, who later became a leader of an extreme Right political party, pushed for the inclusion of the fuzzily defined Greater Israel within the debate over

Israel's borders. At the time, however, she represented only a small and powerless minority. Until the 1967 war, the dominant discourse affirmed the existing order and recognized the need for limiting the Zionist vision, accepting that the Jewish people had returned to its land to live there in peace within borders determined by historical contingency. The few who did not accept the existing borders were seen as eccentric nonrealists and were effectively marginalized in Israeli politics.

The 1967 Six-Day War brought the partisans of Greater Israel center stage as the question of Israel's borders became an open issue. The borders attained by the Israeli Defense Forces did not correspond to any mythological dimensions of the "whole land" of Israel: they did not, for example, include the east bank of the Jordan River, although they did include the Sinai, not considered part of the Promised Land. However, as enlarging Israeli territory now became an option, the argument over Greater Israel was applied to the territories that Israel controlled as a result of the war.

Two broad options were presented to the Israeli public. The first, later to be propagated by Gush Emunim, was to integrate the newly seized territories into the State of Israel; the other was to negotiate a compromise with whomever advanced sustainable claims to these territories, ceding them to secure the borders of pre-1967 Israel, possibly with minor alterations. The case for annexing the territories relied on two major understandings—the first regarding the nature of the adversaries and the second regarding the value of the bargaining chips. Many Israelis believe that the Arab states and the Palestinians would never agree to a lasting peace with Israel, whether out of deep-seated religious convictions, because of a concept of a pure Arab and Muslim Middle East, or because of long-term political reasons. Thus, any concession, they maintained, would serve merely as a stage in the overall plan to annihilate Israel. Furthermore, they claimed, the territories occupied in the Six-Day War should not be subject to negotiation, because of their religious and historical value for the Jewish people. Biblical sites that were the cradle of the nation, as well as the holy graves of the Patriarchs and Matriarchs, should be beyond diplomatic commerce. They are not to be seen as *occupied* territories but *liberated,* since, by their very essence, they belong to the Jewish people.[3] A third claim, rarely presented explicitly but instrumental in the continuation of the Israeli occupation, was based on the tangible benefits of holding the territories for the Israeli economic infrastructure: natural resources, a cheap Arab labor force, and valuable real estate.[4]

The strongest case for evacuating the territories, apart from the international community's rejection of continued Israeli occupation, was and is the political and moral consequences of ruling over a large Palestinian population in the territories. After the 1948 Israeli War of Independence, a relatively small number of Palestinians remained in Israel and received citizenship, while the rest either left or were evicted and barred from returning, thus becoming refugees. The 1967 war, on the other hand, did not produce major demographical changes. Hence, the presence of the Palestinians—including many refugees of the 1948 war—made the annexation of the territories a momentous, perhaps impossible, task. Furthermore, the price of occupation—terror, the decline in tourism, and the loss of Israel's moral and political stature in the world arena—might prove too heavy to bear. The claims that were voiced mainly by the Israeli Left were that such a move would undermine the Jewish and democratic nature of the Israeli state and would result in the establishment of an apartheid regime.[5]

Given their ambivalence regarding the nature of the territories, Israel's political leadership was loath to decide between the options. The occupied territories were left betwixt and between, in a state of constant temporality, and the attempts to break this stalemate became the single most important issue in Israeli politics for over three decades. Although Gush Emunim was, in a sense, a latecomer to this debate, once it entered, it changed the debate's basic contours.

In what follows, I explore the theories and conditions that led to the Gush Emunim's emergence, present the basic tenants of its ideology-theology, and explore the sociological and demographic complexity of West Bank settlement. In conclusion, I discuss various theories explaining the Israeli presence in the territories and the role assigned Gush Emunim within these explanations.

THE HISTORY OF GUSH EMUNIM

The 1967 Six-Day War is a good place to begin the discussion about Gush Emunim, though its roots run much deeper. This cataclysmic war opened the territories for subsequent settlement by movement activists and created the public atmosphere enabling the emergence of a religious-messianic movement.[6] Immediately after the war, the idea of Greater Israel was affirmed by a group of mostly secular public figures, including some of Israel's best-known authors and poets.[7] In the first year after the war, the National Religious Party (NRP) took the first steps to settle the Judea area of the territories: the "children of Kfar Etzion" returned to rebuild their village and a group, headed by Rabbi Moshe Levinger, settled in Hebron.[8] Meanwhile, other Jewish settlements were established with government assistance, especially along the Jordan Valley, in the Yamit region in Sinai, and on the Golan Heights, in order to retain these strategic areas under Israeli rule subsequent to peace agreements. These settlements were mainly secular.

In the early 1970s, the Alon Moreh *gari'in* (small settlement group; literally, "nucleus") was organized in order to settle in the vicinity of Nablus, while the Gush Emunim movement itself was formally established in Kfar Etzion in April 1974 as an ideological group within the NRP in the wake of the great trauma of the 1973 Yom Kippur War. Because of ideological differences and in order to reach wider audiences, ties with the mother party (the NRP) were subsequently severed. The link between the newly emergent movement and the Alon Moreh gari'in, on the other hand, was very strong because the members of both groups shared ideological and personal commitments. The Gush Emunim movement captured the attention of the Israeli public in the mid-1970s with demonstrations against Israeli territorial concessions following the Yom Kippur War and with continuous attempts to settle in the hills of Samaria.

The history of the movement can be divided into several partially overlapping periods.[9] In the initial formative-charismatic phase, the movement's activity was focused on demonstrations against agreements with Egypt, mass marches in the territories, and attempts, on the part of the Alon Moreh gari'in, to establish new settlements. After the eighth attempt, the gari'in received permission to settle, and another part of that group went on to form the settlement of Ofra. At that stage, the leadership of the movement was a small group, composed mainly of students of the Merkaz HaRav Yeshiva, joined by a few secular activists.

The second period began with the change of government in 1977. Prime Minister Menachem Begin began his term of office with the declaration "there will be many Alon Morehs." The Israeli government, however, proceeded to conduct peace talks with Egypt while curtailing the establishment of more settlements as a result of international pressure. Gush Emunim succeeded in establishing more settlements and began a process of institutionalization. The settling agency Amana was established in 1977, and the Yesha councils, a body representing the heads of councils in Judea, Samaria, and the Gaza Strip, was established in 1980. Some of the former leadership figures found formal roles within newly formed local governments, and local leaders began to assume leadership roles in the movement.

The third period, which began with the struggle against Israeli withdrawal from Sinai in 1982, was characterized by concomitant crisis and institutionalization. The withdrawal from Sinai, on the part of a government seemingly dedicated to the idea of Greater Israel, was a major blow to imagined future prospects of the West Bank settlements.[10] Subsequently, in 1985, the *Jewish underground,* a group of settlers that had targeted Palestinians and had planned to blow up the Temple Mount mosques, was discovered.[11] When its leaders and activists were found to be important members of Gush Emunim, this revelation brought about heated internal debates and jeopardized the movement's standing among the Israeli public. Throughout the period, the settlement project gained in power and political influence, whereas Gush Emunim as an organization ceased to exist. It was replaced by various settler organizations, some ad hoc and some permanent.

The fourth period began with the Palestinian First Intifada on December 1987, whose most violent events were directed against isolated ideological settlements on the hilltops of Judea and Samaria. The settlers retaliated, and numerous violent encounters occurred between them and their Palestinian neighbors.[12] While the settlements continued to increase in population, they found themselves under consistent physical attack and had to realign to maintain their momentum.

A fifth period started with the Oslo Accords. Certain areas in the occupied territories were handed over to the Palestinian Authority, and weapon-bearing Palestinian police patrolled in close proximity to the settlers. The threat of evacuation became eminent. Two focal points of this era were the massacre of twenty-nine Palestinians in the Cave of Machpela in Hebron by Kiryat Arba settler Baruch Goldstein, and the assassination of Prime Minister Yitzhak Rabin by Yigael Amir, who, though not a resident of a settlement, was sympathetic to their cause and found friends and supporters within the settlements.[13]

The last period begins with the Second Intifada in September 2000. While the hallmark of that intifada is the murderous suicide bombings in Israeli cities, over 95 percent of terrorist attacks have taken place in the occupied territories, targeting settlers and the soldiers guarding them. Consequently, growth of the ideological settlements has slowed somewhat, while some of the secular and less ideological settlements have been partially abandoned and are on the verge of collapse. An emergent phenomenon is the dramatic appearance of the young second-generation settlers nicknamed "the youth of the hills," who attempt to settle in outposts (*ma'ahazim*) on virgin areas in the territories.[14] The crisis of the last period culminated with the disengagement plan, the evacuation of settlers, and the destruction of twenty-two settlements in August 2005.

It is much too early to provide any conclusive statement on the continuing history of the settlements; it is even difficult to discern whether their history can be characterized as an astounding success or a great failure. The stages and chronology that I have suggested are part of a history in the making. Given the constant political upheavals and peace initiatives, it is clear that the dramatic history of the ideological settlers of Gush Emunim is far from over.

EXPLAINING THE ORIGINS OF GUSH EMUNIM

One of the most engaging questions about Gush Emunim is the account of its origins. Most researchers cite the Six-Day War, which renewed the contact of the Israeli public with Jewish sacred spaces and aroused strong messianic feelings within the national religious camp. The Yom Kippur War was also seen as important, insofar as its effect on popular moral resulted in a national value crisis. That war resulted in a loss of credibility of Israel's most trusted institutions, such as political leadership and the military, and an erosion of faith in the ability of the nation to achieve its aspirations. The sense of crisis invited radical groups, including Gush Emunim, to advance their case.

The explanation for the rise of Gush Emunim in terms of the Israeli value crisis and anomie is compelling and popular among both researchers and followers. Movement activists explicitly claim that the movement aimed to return the Jewish Israeli collective to the Zionist route, following the trauma of the Yom Kippur War. This corresponds with theories of social movements connected to the name of Neil Smelser (1962). Based on Talcot Parsons's structural-functionalist paradigm, Smelser sought to explain how social systems returned to a state of equilibrium after social changes. He distinguished between two types of movements: norm oriented and value oriented. The first emerges from a generalized feeling that social behavior is deviating from the accepted social values; the second suggests a total overhaul of all components of the system, from high values to everyday practices. Gush Emunim would probably fall under the category of value-oriented movements, because it suggests a massive transformation of all aspects of Israeli existence. It defines itself, however, as a norm-oriented movement seeking to return the Israeli system to its original path following a crisis in the Israeli social system in the wake of the war.

While the value-crisis hypothesis may well account for the opening of a window of opportunity for social movements at that time, it does little to explain why the movement that emerged arose from the national religious camp. Thus, the anomie explanation must be coupled with a historical account of the changes that enabled that camp to capitalize on the historical opportunity.[15]

Researchers of the national religious camp claim that the crisis addressed by Gush Emunim was actually the success of secular Zionism and the establishment of the Jewish state. The drama of national salvation was, to the disappointment and surprise of observant Jews, performed by nonobservers. Between the secular pioneers, on the one hand, and the ultra-Orthodox, on the other, young religious Zionists felt second best: they were neither the vanguard of the nation nor the paradigm of religious commitment. Their frustration was fueled by their conviction that the Zionist project was divinely orchestrated. In the view of the national religious adherents, secular Zionists had ignored the divine basis of the Zionist urge, whereas the ultra-Orthodox were in error in not seeing the Zionist enterprise as part of the process of divine redemption. The Six-Day War, followed by the crisis of the Yom Kippur War, gave this camp the opportunity to correct what it saw as the blindness of other groups in society.[16]

In his research on the origins of the leading Gush Emunim group, sociologist Gideon Aran (1986) identified a group of young of religious Zionists called *Gachelet*. In the early years of the state, the group arrived at the Merkaz HaRav Yeshiva, where it encountered Rabbi Kook the Son. Developing the writings of his father, Rabbi Abraham-Itzhak HaCohen Kook, Kook the Son presented them with an ideology that placed the victorious Zionist project within a religious framework and assigned his followers a privileged position with respect to other groups. This encounter of an enthusiastic young group, the message of the yeshiva, and the historical opportunity provided by the Six-Day and Yom Kippur wars, helps explain why the movement emerged in the form that it did.

Political scientist Ehud Sprinzak (1993) pointed out that, in many respects, Gush Emunim is not as revolutionary as it may seem, insofar as

Israel has a long "tradition" of illegalism justified by the sacred national cause. Gush Emunim joined a respected lineage of groups that committed acts that were illegal but considered socially legitimate. For example, the celebrated Palmach unit (a paramilitary unit) of the late 1940s was notorious for its pranks, yet its contribution to the national effort was highly valued and acclaimed. According to Sprinzak, Gush Emunim built upon this deep disrespect of formal legalism prevalent in Israeli society. Furthermore, Sprinzak points out that Gush Emunim is not revolutionary even from the perspective of the national religious camp. In their ideology and religious practice, there is little difference between the Gush Emunim believers and the rest of the national religious public. Although Gush Emunim founded new settlements in the territories, the religious communities within Israel serve as the bases from which the groups leave for their missions and provide logistic aid and moral support (Sprinzak 1981).

Sprinzak's claims are only partly convincing: it may be contended that Gush Emunim illegalism is of a different nature than that of groups such as the Palmach, and that the difference between Gush Emunim settlers and the more general national religious group should not be downplayed. Sprinzak, however, is undoubtedly right in insisting that the movement cannot be understood outside of its historical and social context. Gush Emunim arose from a complex combination of continuities and transformations, both within Israeli culture and society and specifically within the national religious camp.

Gush Emunim Theology and Ideology

The source of Gush Emunim's ideology is found in the writings of Rabbi Abraham-Itzhak HaCohen Kook, as interpreted by his son, Rabbi Zvi-Yehudah HaCohen Kook, and taught in the Merkaz HaRav Yeshiva in Jerusalem. The students of the yeshiva and their disciples generated the leaders and activists of Gush Emunim and have provided theological legitimacy for its political action throughout its history.

Rabbi Kook the Elder was the first Ashkenazi chief rabbi during the British Mandate years and was the one who founded the still functioning institution of the Chief Rabbinate. Although he grew up in ultra-Orthodox circles and never declared that he did not belong to that camp, he became an important spiritual leader of the national religious camp and maintained good relations with many secular intellectuals.[17] He died before the establishment of the state, and his teaching had fallen into partial oblivion. His yeshiva became marginal among the religious institutions of Jerusalem until the young Gachelet group revived it. The extent of Gush Emunim's devotion to the teachings of Rabbi Kook is a matter of debate. Gideon Aran stresses the novelty of the Gush Emunim project through the use of the idiom "Kookists" to portray the group (Aran 1991). However, some of the most important principles of Gush Emunim can be seen as a continuation of the teachings of the movement's mytho-historical father.

One of Rabbi Kook the Elder fundaments was that the redemption has already arrived and can be seen with the naked eye. According to him, Zionism was a visible proof of the divine decision to return the people of Israel to their land. The disciples of Merkaz HaRav then incorporated the Six-Day War and the Yom Kippur War into the divine historical scheme, presenting them as stages in the process leading to full national and cosmic redemption. A second principle found in the writings of Rabbi Kook is the sacredness of the entire land of Israel. The borders of the Promised Land should be determined through halakhic deliberation rather than historical contingency or diplomatic negotiation. The redemption of the people is intricately connected to the redemption of the land, with the final goal being the gathering of the entire people of Israel in Greater Israel, living according to precepts of the Torah. While Gush Emunim theology includes the three inseparable components of land, people, and Torah, for political purposes the struggle over the land has to take precedence.

Gush Emunim is defined by its leaders and supporters as a Zionist revival movement: they claim that the true nature of Zionism is religious-messianic, and that celebrated Zionist urge for "normalization"—to be like all other nations—is a surrender to forces foreign to Judaism and a denial of the true essence of Zionism. The Jewish people, they claim, should realize its destiny by reconnecting itself to its roots in time and space; only then will it be able to fulfill its unique role in world redemption.

Within this perspective, the Zionist movement and later the State of Israel hold a special place as worldly expressions of the divine redemptive process. According to Gush Emunim believers, the state is not merely a secular organization, but the expression of God's will. As part of the divine promise, the existential nature of the state is characterized by its historical necessity and its essential sanctity, irrespective of the actions of its citizens; furthermore, the actual citizens and their elected leadership may act in contradiction to the sacred nature of the state—for example, by deciding to withdraw from parts of the sacred land or evacuating Jewish settlements. In such cases, as Ehud Sprinzak has observed, their actions may be considered as legal but illegitimate. Conversely, those who break state law in order to halt a withdrawal are acting illegally but in accord with the true nature of the state. In the eyes of the believers, it is the sanctity of the state that limits the rights of its citizens to make historical decisions based on a democratic majority when it conflicts with imperatives deriving from the sanctity of the land of Israel.

Rabbi Kook endowed the secular—at times even antireligious—pioneering project with religious legitimacy and sanctity even when not acknowledged by the actors themselves. Although the supporters of Gush Emunim are reluctant to follow his footsteps and accord religious value to their secular—let alone left-wing—adversaries, they see themselves as representing the inner truth of Judaism and Zionism and as understanding the true meaning of the State of Israel. The fact that secularism is still dominant, and—many would claim—growing in power, poses a theological problem for those who see the state as a stage in divine salvation. The sanctity of the state has become a hotly debated issue among the ideological settlers, especially after what they consider to be the betrayal of the land in the Oslo Accords.

This, however, is not the only issue dividing the supporters of Gush Emunim. Political scientist Ian Lustick (1991) has formulated the fault lines as follows: What is the locus of religious authority after the death of Rabbi Zvi-Yehudah Kook? What are the territorial limits of Greater Israel? What are the pace and the political dynamics of the redemption process? What should the policy toward Palestinian Arabs be? How is the notion of peace defined and conceptualized? These questions delineate various strategies on the road to achieving religious redemption through possession of the greater land of Israel.

The Gush Emunim ideology has been criticized both from within and without the religious camp. For the moment, I postpone discussion of the competing rights to the land and the direction of Israel's future while focusing on two criticisms of the role of Gush Emunim from within the religious camp. Gush Emunim believers claim that they understand the true divine intentions and can see beyond the veil and interpret God's will. According to Rabbi Kook's assertion, this divine will is self-evident to anyone who opens his or her eyes. Religious intellectual Yeshayahu Leibowitz predicted that, once the messianic bubble burst, the leaders of

Gush Emunim would be the first to follow "that Messiah," meaning Jesus Christ. Although few would agree with such a radical assertion, Aviezer Ravitzky, one of religious Zionism's foremost intellectuals, expresses great worry over the Gush Emunim's concept of sanctity and messianism.[18] Reflecting on Leibowitz's statement, Ravitzky poses these questions: What would happen to traditional Judaism in case the Gush Emunim project fails? Would this also entail the denial of the partial success and religious worth of the establishment of the—albeit limited—Jewish state? How could the Gush Emunim believers be so certain that the Messiah has arrived, and that the Third Temple would be the last? Ravitzky worries that the powerful and popular messianism of Gush Emunim might endanger the future of traditional Judaism.

In a celebrated article, author Haim Be'er (1982) claimed that Gush Emunim is a Canaanite phenomenon. The Canaanites were a small intellectual group that promoted the development of an Israeli identity determined by geographic location rather than Jewish historical traditions. Although Gush Emunim is indeed committed to Jewish tradition, Be'er claims that, in consecrating the land, Gush Emunim unwittingly promotes a fetishism of place—of soil, rocks, and trees—not unlike the Canaanite pagans of ancient days. This may result in the forsaking of other, more spiritual and profound, Jewish principles. Beyond the more immediate criticism of Gush Emunim's practices of adulation of the land, Be'er questions the possible implications for basic Jewish beliefs. Like Ravitzky, he examines the long-term significance of the choices made by religious Judaism and forewarns that the focus on settling the land may transform and impoverish Judaism as we know it.

GUSH EMUNIM: A MESSIANIC OR A POLITICAL MOVEMENT?

Ravitzky and Be'er, who have strong affinities with the national religious camp, seek to salvage the camp from what they regard as the harmful deviation of Gush Emunim. Secular writers raise other questions grounded in sociological theory rather than theological deliberations. There is apparently no question that Gush Emunim is a religious-messianic movement. Janet Aviad (Odea 1977), a sociologist and later one of the leaders of Peace Now, was the first to apply insights from the sociology of religion to analyze Gush Emunim systematically as a religious phenomenon. Acclaimed author Shulamit Hareven (1977), also a future member of Peace Now, vehemently criticized Aviad's thesis. To Hareven's mind, Gush

Emunim was merely one more reflection of the Israeli Right, whose political claims are commonly robed in religious lingo. Thus, critical research should be able to penetrate through the religious cover terminology to decipher the "real" motivations at stake. She claims, "Gush Emunim is not a religious group by any definition. It holds no different ritual, it has no different beliefs, and does not demand of its members any special behavior or change of personal characteristics. Gush Emunim is a political group" (105).

The answer to the question of whether religion is an active force determining political behavior or merely an ideological guise hiding materialistic interests of colonization is one of the most important—yet illusive—issues in understanding the movement. For example, Aviad visited the settlement of Ofra and reached the conclusion (somewhat contrary to her previous claim) that the institutionalization of the movement demonstrates that the radical messianic urge has diminished with time (Aviad 1991). Another distinction, contradictory to Aviad's contention, is that between manifest and latent levels of activity. When left-wing author David Grossman visited Ofra, he was presented with a specter of banal normal living. He wrote that, while in everyday life and political actions the movement presents its more moderate political side, the engine that propels it, and that is rarely exposed to the Israeli public, is radically messianic. He attempted to decipher the logic of his hosts in the following way: "It is difficult for me to connect the pleasant people I met in Ofra with the obliquity of those who chant the words of the prophet Isaiah, 'Take counsel together and it shall come to naught,' but they are the same people . . . I saw them on one of their calm days. Almost in their slack days. Not in the season of their messianic heat. Not at a time of 'high messianic tension,' but it lies in wait for them always, like a disease" (D. Grossman 1988, 51–52).[19]

These perspectives presume a clear-cut difference between rationalism and messianism, secular logic and religious behavior. Gideon Aran (1991) claims that the uniqueness of Gush Emunim is its fusion of religion and politics. The synthesis between religion and politics is bidirectional: a demonstration and lobbying in the Knesset are defined as religious acts, whereas prayer and Torah learning are considered political tactics. The religious practices are "modern magic" that recruits God for the solution of earthly problems, whereas settlement is considered to be a ritualistic act. Thus, the defining of Gush Emunim as religious or political is rendered irrelevant because the movement itself obliterates the differences between the two realms. Aran, however, still gives precedence to religious transformation in explaining the emergence of Gush Emunim because the fusion of the political and the religious is a religious dictum in the eyes of the believers.

Gush Emunim's Sociology and Demography

Gush Emunim began as a group of national religious youth, graduates of the religious education system and of Bnei Akiva, the religious youth movement. Many of them served in Yeshivot Hesder, which combines Torah study with army service. An early research paper demonstrated that, in the first ideological settlements, a small but essential nucleus was affected by the writings of Rabbi Kook and the education it received at Merkaz HaRav, whereas the great majority reported that they were motivated by belief in the sanctity of the land and the need to halt evacuation through settlement. Many mentioned convenience, quality of life, and the high level of education as their reasons for moving to the newly established settlements (Weisburd and Waring 1985).

Although the movement consisted mainly of religious Israelis, it also targeted secular right-wing supporters. In the intellectual movement that preceded the rise of Gush Emunim, the secular element was the great majority. This group, however, never succeeded in recruiting mass support for the idea of a Greater Israel and soon declined in face of the more committed religious followers of Gush Emunim. Few of the secular supporters found leadership positions in the new movement, and most supported Gush Emunim from afar. For Gush Emunim, a movement that claimed to represent the true will of the people, the coalition with secular groups was of utmost ideological and political importance. To attract a secular following, Gush Emunim had to find temporal solutions to a basic dilemma: the emphasis of the strong religious determinant in their worldview would alienate many secular Israelis, some of whom were strongly antireligious. Stressing the common political goals, on the other hand, would dilute the motivation and zeal of religious supporters, who were the great majority of the movement activists. The movement's strategy was to navigate between these two poles while trying to elicit secular support without losing its religious core.

Gush Emunim's basic assumption was that, once the settlement project took hold, the rest of the nation would become engulfed in popular enthusiasm and join in. When in actual fact the Israeli government began to implement a settlement program in 1981, it had little to do with changed values among the Israeli population: settlement was based on capitalistic principles, economic incentives, and the promise of a better life (Shafir 1985). The residents who arrived in the larger towns and new communities in the territories could not be considered as continuing the ethos of Gush Emunim: most were nonreligious, and their main, sometimes sole, motivation for moving to the occupied territories was economic.

The differing social and political motivations of Jewish settlers in the West Bank can be plotted onto three north-south strips on the map. The easternmost strip consists of the Jordan Valley settlements—mainly agricultural settlements—belonging to the kibbutz or moshav movements. Most to the west, close to the Green Line (the 1949 Armistice Line) and Israeli urban centers, are relatively large settlements that house those who sought to improve their quality of life. In the middle, on the hills of Judea and Samaria, are the ideological settlements. That is also where the majority of the Palestinian population resides, in a string of large towns and cities (ranging from north to south): Jenin, Nablus, Ramallah, East Jerusalem, Bethlehem, Halhul, and Hebron.

The Gush Emunim settlers evolved, to a large extent, as a distinct group within Israeli society, with distinctive symbols, including manners of speech and an informal dress code. Geographers have found what they define as "demographic rift" between the ideological settlers and the rest of Israeli society, which is reflected through a myriad of institutional realms and political attitudes (Goldberg and Ben-Zadok 1983). The distance and solitude of the hilltop settlements, their shared experiences and ideology, are accompanied by differences in political interests. In many ways, however, the ideological settlers are indiscernible from other Israeli citizens. The settlers are an integral part of the Israeli economy, politics, communication and, perhaps most important, the military. While many settlers do their reserve duty in the vicinity of their homes, most young religious settlers join the army enthusiastically and serve with nonreligious soldiers within general units.[20]

Among the new members of the ideological settlements, many are new immigrants to Israel, mainly from the United States and France. An early study depicted American immigrants as the most moderate among the settlers (Waxman 1985), but episodic evidence from recent years indicates that this is no longer the case. Another prominent group is the ultra-Orthodox (*Haredim*). Although many of them come to the settlements for economic reasons and to escape demographic pressures within their

Jerusalem and Bnei Brak neighborhoods, most of them support Gush Emunim wholeheartedly. Furthermore, some Haredi and national religious camps have formed a hybrid group with some settlements of its own (Y. Sheleg 2000).[21]

On the margins of Gush Emunim, we find a proliferation of radical and often eccentric religious and political groups. Best known was the currently outlawed Kach group, once headed by Meir Kahane, that supported the expulsion of Palestinians and the Judaization of the state, and that included many Gush Emunim supporters.[22] Other new Jewish religious movements find a welcoming environment in the occupied territories. Most of these groups combine new religious ideas with political extremism.

The Gush Emunim ideological settlers are thus a minority among the Jewish residents of Judea and Samaria. While the number of Jews living in these areas is not easy to determine, there are currently over two hundred thousand: less than half of them are religious and, of them, less than half belong to the Gush Emunim group in some way. Some 3.5 million Palestinians live in the occupied territories, 2 million of them in the West Bank. In the Gaza Strip, before the August 2005 evacuation, approximately 8,000 Jews occupy 20 percent of the land, in the midst of 1.5 million Palestinians.

ISRAELI PRESENCE IN THE TERRITORIES AND THE IMPORTANCE OF GUSH EMUNIM

Gush Emunim has left its mark on the map of the most contested territory in the region, and therefore it would hardly be an exaggeration to claim that the movement has changed the history of the Middle East. Although Israelis and others still propose withdrawal and Israeli evacuation of the territories as a solution to the Middle East conflict, the possibility of carrying out such a policy has been severely hampered by the presence of scores of militant Jewish communities in strategic points on the contested terrain. If the aim of the movement was to render the evacuation of the territories difficult, it has succeeded. Ironically, the proof of this was the Oslo Accords, when the area ceded to the Palestinian Authority was chopped up into a bizarre archipelago to accommodate to the needs of the settlers. It is ironic in a different respect that the very existence of the settlements accelerated the negotiation process because Palestinians felt that they were losing land with the passage of time. Gush

Emunim has thus affected the time-and-space perspective of the Israeli-Palestinian conflict, sometimes against their own interests of perpetuating Jewish control over the land and crushing Palestinian claims.

Surprisingly, some of the theories devised to explain the prolonged Israeli presence in the territories have attributed little importance to Gush Emunim. Though most researchers were hostile to the movement's project, they accepted its claim that the Israeli occupation and settlement of the West Bank should be understood from the perspective of Israeli interests rather than as a whim of an eccentric radical group.

The best known of these theories was developed by Meron Benvenisti, geographer and former vice mayor of Jerusalem, who noted Israeli economic interests, the military presence, and the penetration of an Israeli urban center into the territories as the key factors accounting for the occupation. The cognitive question of whether Israelis viewed the territories as belonging to Israel was, for him, of secondary importance. His conclusion, formulated in the mid-1980s, was that the link developed between Israel and the territories was so tight that a "second Israeli republic" was inadvertently created—a unified sociopolitical unit that included Israel and the territories it occupied. Thus, the conflict between Israel and the Palestinians has now become an internal conflict between two ethnic groups within the same political unit. His famous claim was that Israel has passed the point of irreversibility, which renders the debate regarding the future of the territories obsolete and irrelevant (Benvenisti 1995). After the Oslo Accords, Benvenisti had to rethink his position, but he maintained his claim that the place of the occupied territories vis-à-vis Israel should be understood in light of economic interests and geopolitical facts rather than ideological positions and agreements between political elites.

In a similar vein, sociologist Gershon Shafir (1985, 1996) analyzed the connection of the State of Israel to the territories in terms of a colonial enterprise. In his formulation, the former Zionist pattern, which he calls "pure settlement colonization," gradually changed after 1967. The new pattern being formed in what he considers a neo-Zionist regime resembles "plant colonialism," in which the "natives" are considered inferior to the new settlers. His view stresses the economic interests involved, both in classic Zionist settlement and in the new settlement of the occupied territories.

Both Benvenisti and Shafir concentrated on the material aspects of Israeli presence in the territories, and, whereas Benvenisti drew clearly negative conclusions regarding the possibility of withdrawal, Shafir did not preclude the possibility of decolonization. Sociologist Sami Smooha (1986) chose a different venue, analyzing the symbolic and cultural aspects of Israeli occupation. His conclusion was that the territories are not part of the Israeli mental map, and hence an ideology of annexation cannot be accepted in Israel. The occupied territories are already "the other." Over time, he suggested back in 1986, a synchronization of mentality and presence will be achieved, and Israel will withdraw from the territories.

In conceptualizing the Israeli presence in the occupied territories, sociologist Baruch Kimmerling (1983, 1989) pointed out the difference between presence, ownership, and sovereignty. Using the term *frontier*, as applied by Fredrick Turner to the westward expansion of the United States, to understand the connection between Zionism and land, Kimmerling stressed the process of land acquisition and the strategies of legitimation of Zionist presence throughout the last century. For him, the occupied territories are a new frontier, a place under the control of Israeli army, with a growing civilian presence, yet not within its legitimate sovereign rule.

While most researchers tried to conceptualize the connection between state and territory, a group of scholars, affected by postmodern and postcolonial theories, obliterated the difference altogether and conceptualized Israel, on both sides of the Green Line, as an occupying entity. Adi Offir, Hanan Hever, and their companions established a small political movement called The 21st Year and suggested a new understanding of the place of the occupation in the Israeli psyche. The occupation, they claimed, has become part of everyday Israel and now structures the Israeli social and cultural orders. Terminating the occupation thus entails an all-out revolution in the way Israelis think and act, and the extraction— not only of the settlers—but also of the occupation from the minute details of mundane Israeli life. This conceptualization complements in a sense Benvenisti's theory: both show how the occupation restructures Israeli life and mentality and thereby defines Israel today.[23]

Ian Lustick (1993) suggested a dynamic framework of the link between state and territory through a comparative analysis with other cases of colonization and decolonization. He proposed a three-staged model of "the territorial construction of the state," in which he examined options of expansion and contraction of territorial boundaries. One stage is the "incumbency stage," in which it is relatively easy for a state to disconnect itself from a certain territory, that is, to engage in a process of decolonization; the cost may be a change of government, but not the destabilization of an entire political regime. Lustick's second stage in called the "regime stage," in which evacuation of territory results in violent protest and a real threat against the regime itself. The third stage is the "ideological-hegemonic stage," in which the territories are so much a part of the national map that leaving them is beyond the people's political imagination. Between these stages are thresholds to pass. The challenge encountered by movements of territorial annexation is how to move their societies through the stages and past the thresholds until the nation's possession of the territories becomes an unproblematic cultural given. Using Antonio Gramsci's (1971) theory and terminology, Lustick inquires as to when such a hegemonic state is achieved.

According to Lustick, who developed his theory in the 1980s, Israel is trapped between the thresholds in the regime stage and thus unable to decide whether the occupied territories are an indivisible part of the national body or should be exchanged for peace. His judgment of the situation, which can be claimed to hold still today, is less important than his conceptualization of the options of the state and the political movements within it. For Gush Emunim, Lustick's formulation is mainly a game plan. It reminds us of Rabbi Yoel Bin-Nun's assertion "We have not settled in the hearts" as an expression of the settlers' interest in moving the State of Israel beyond a crucial threshold that will make the evacuation of the settlements a practical impossibility and cognitively unthinkable.

This book is an attempt to confront this question: How are the ideological settlers of Gush Emunim seeking to plant their project in the hearts of their compatriots, and what are the challenges they will encounter along the way?

2

Space, Place, and Memory
in Gush Emunim Ideology

In the history of Gush Emunim, there is a cherished myth of creation, remembered by the believers with fondness, admiration, and amazement. On Israeli Independence Day 1967, a month before the Six-Day War, the old Rabbi Zvi-Yehudah HaCohen Kook, head of Merkaz HaRav Yeshiva in Jerusalem, held his annual speech. Among the various yeshivas of Jerusalem, Merkaz HaRav was the most enthusiastically Zionist, and, unlike in other yeshivas, Independence Day was a day of celebration. At one moment, the voice of the rabbi broke and he uttered the following words: "Where is our Hebron—aren't we forgetting it? Where is our Shechem, and our Jericho, where are they—forgotten? And all the other side of Jordan—it is our . . . Every region and every piece of soil that belong to the God's land—are we allowed to forsake even one millimeter of it?"

At the time, his words were seen as the incoherent mumbling of an old man, but within a month they were reinterpreted as prophecy come true. The Israeli army had occupied most of the places mentioned by Rabbi Kook, and many of the young yeshiva students who attended the event at Merkaz HaRav were among the warriors and, with their own eyes, saw what they regarded as the fulfillment of their rabbi's words. For a messianic movement such as Gush Emunim, this story was hailed as a *hierophany*, an encounter with the sacred, a moment of birth, and undeniable proof of the truth of their mythohistorical interpretation.

The sermon is a good starting point for understanding the intricate nature of Gush Emunim's commitment to the land because the sermon informs us of both the nature and the importance of memory. In the sermon, there is an implied tension between memory in general and the memory of certain events and places in particular. Although this tension is not always acknowledged or accepted, it is basic to the dynamics of contemporary fundamentalism and its connection to its social environment.

The importance of memory to the Gush Emunim project cannot be overstated. The movement's name, *Emunim,* which means "loyalty to the past," was adopted with clear and declared awareness of its meaning. Movement activists define Zionism as an answer to the call of the ages. As a fundamentalist religious group, memory and loyalty to the past are of the very essence of the movement; as a Jewish movement, this fact is even more pronounced. The Jews have been dubbed the "people of memory," and the importance of memory in Jewish ritual and everyday life is immense. Furthermore, Gush Emunim is also a nationalist movement, and Jewish nationalism—Zionism—stresses the importance of the past as much as other national movements—in light of its conflicts with other streams within Judaism and with the competing national movement of the local Palestinian population, perhaps more so.[1] As a revival movement within both Jewish religion and Israeli nationality and as part of the national religious camp that ideologically synthesizes the national and the religious, the importance of memory for Gush Emunim is tremendous.

There is still another reason for the central place of memory in the movement's ethos—a reason that some critics would regard as primal. Gush Emunim sought to settle a land populated by Palestinian Arabs, who are considered to be the native inhabitants in the eyes of most observers, including many Israelis. The image of nativeness and authenticity is crucial to the Palestinian argument. To convince people that the territories are not "occupied" but "liberated," and that they belong to the Jewish people, Gush Emunim has to counter such claims by redefining nativeness and authenticity, stressing the importance of long-term memory, and claiming that ancient Jewish presence gives them prior rights to the land. This does not entail, however, that this use of memory is merely a shallow manipulation; the great importance of memory drives Gush Emunim supporters to settle in Yesha, while their settlement acts oblige them to stress even further the importance of memory, creating a vicious cycle in which social identity and practical interest intertwine inseparably.

Memory, for the movement's activists, is not merely a charter of rights to territory. It is an overarching principle that constructs the position of the movement vis-à-vis the rest of society and determines its critical positions vis-à-vis modern Israel. The problem of contemporary Israeli society, according to Gush Emunim believers, is that it does not remember the ancient past legitimizing its existence and even tends to forget its own heroic past of the last few decades. The fact that Israeli society is ambivalent regarding the future of the territories is, for the believers, proof of the shallowness of Israeli historical roots. A "healthy" nation, so claim the believers, should never forget its history and tradition. Settler David Hantshke (1996) writes of "common Israelis," "It is a public detached from all connection to its origins; it lives as a herd without direction the life of the moment without a past, and hence without a future beyond its own nose; a post-cultural public" (29). Here, the line divides the Israeli public into those who remember and those who forget. Rabbi Shlomo Aviner (1980) writes, "The nation forgot who and what is was and, consequently, she does not understand the value of the Land of Israel. The Land is understood as hundreds of kilometers that pose an external means for our existence rather than something linked to the very essence of our life; because of the terrible crisis we do not know what our life actually is" (11).

The words of Rabbi Zvi-Yehudah Kook reflect this loyalty to the idea of memory. The rabbi lamented that he and his followers, and with them undoubtedly the rest of Israeli society, may have forgotten the places sacred to the Jewish people; he may also have implied that they had forgotten the very need to remember—the urge that defines them as part of the Jewish people. Although he did not suggest going to war to capture new (or old) sacred places, he certainly wanted to revive the commitment to their memory. It is easy to see how the subsequent occupation of the territories would be comprehended as a miraculous event and why the followers of the old rabbi will be averse to any territorial compromise.

After mentioning specific places, the rabbi then states a more general principle, namely, that the people of Israel may not relinquish a single millimeter of the land. Two principles are at work here. One is the meta-historical principle that sanctifies the land by virtue of the divine promise to the people of Israel. The other is that specific places are more sacred than others because of their mythohistorical role in the Jewish past. Although those principles are not necessarily contradictory, there is a potential for tension here—if not for "true believers," then certainly for the rest of Israeli society and, as a result, for the movement's dialogue with its social environment. If a certain hill in Judea is less sacred than Hebron, could it not be forsaken in order to keep a more sacred place? The Israeli public, at least parts of it, can comprehend the religious and historical importance of Hebron or Shechem, but what about other dots on the map? What about Ramallah or Kalkilia, Palestinian towns unmentioned in Jewish past? Are they included in the rabbi's prophetic sermon?

The tension implied in the rabbi's words has accompanied Gush Emunim throughout its existence: the believers are committed to mythical boundaries determined by divine will, while concentrating their efforts on places where there is a better chance of constructing a national home. Thus, during the Lebanon War, Yoel Elitzur (1982) of Ofra posed a question: suppose that a Jew residing in the city of Sidon in Lebanon decides to make *aliya*—to immigrate to Israel—and moves to the southern city of Eilat. Most Israelis would define his act as a return from exile to the land of Israel. However, according to the halakha, he would be leaving Israel, because the promised borders of the land include Sidon and exclude Eilat, regardless of today's political boundaries.

Elitzur posed his question whimsically, but Rabbi Ya'akov Ariel was dead serious when he joined the troops of the Israeli Defense Forces (IDF), which entered Lebanon in 1982. He showed soldiers that, according to the Bible, Lebanon was part of the greater land of Israel, thus arousing national outrage. The soldiers were furious, because they hoped to finish the war soon and return to what they considered their home, on the other side of the international border. For the rabbi, when they were in Lebanon, they were in actual fact returning home. "I did not talk about a settlement plan in southern Lebanon," apologized the Rabbi; "The ear cannot withstand a noise so loud."[2]

These anecdotes illustrate the inner contradictions and dramatic choices that underlie Gush Emunim ideology. This chapter explores the Gush Emunim discourse connecting the Jewish people to the land, and, in particular, the rationales that tie the settlers to the Land of the Bible. I attempt to decipher the ideological apparatus that underlies the labor of constructing a national home. First, I outline the general religious precept of settling the land and its radical implications for the established Zionist ethos. I then examine the temporal consciousness and historical narrative that characterize Gush Emunim but that derive from secular Zionism. I present two significant examples showing how believers understand and adopt the national holidays and how they conceptualize the most traumatic event in Israeli history: the 1973 Yom Kippur War. I conclude with a crucial reservation to the importance of memory to Gush Emunim believers: they live very much in the present, and learn how to balance their priorities and make compromises. This is what makes Gush

Emunim so interesting as a border phenomenon between Western modernity and its greatest nemesis: religious fundamentalism.

METAMEMORY AND METAHISTORY

Any discussion of the importance of the past in determining the sanctity of space must begin with religion, and the most important principle in the belief system of Gush Emunim is the divine promise that the people of Israel would return to the Holy Land. According to the believers, God's promise gives the Jewish people exclusive rights to the land, and therefore the "true believers" of Gush Emunim understand their actions as the fulfillment of a religious precept: a *mitzvah*. A crucial point emanating from this idea is that Jewish history as such, and history in general, does not render political property rights in the present. In other words, the connection between the people and the land is metahistorical: it precedes history and constitutes it. The most authoritative memory is the commitment to the covenant that binds God and the people of Israel.

Unlike other cases of ethnic nationalism, for Gush Emunim the right to the Jewish land is not seen as acquired by virtue of birth.[3] Rather, it is the Promised Land, in which the people of Israel are supposed to arrive, rather than the land from which they have set out on their journey. This is a well-acknowledged principle of Jewish thought, as Aviezer Ravitzky (1991) formulated it: "[The Jewish people do] not come from the land, as an autochthonic nation born from the soil, but rather goes to the land, arrives in her and makes her his homeland" (1). Consequently, the land does not belong to the Jewish people in the same unproblematic way that—to cite the example regularly presented in Zionist debates—France belongs to the Frenchmen; there is always a *differance* (rift) between the nation and the land. The meaning of the covenant is that while the Jewish people can never relinquish their rights to the land, they can be evicted from the land or return from exile, dependent on their deeds or on the ripeness of cosmological circumstances. In any case, the relation of the Jewish people to its soil was never unproblematic. History (apart from the mythical event of the covenant) does not grant the people the right to the land, but it can provide a lesson on the correct national behavior that will assure and guarantee continuous Jewish existence in the land.

In a 1975 interview, Hanan Porat, one of the political and spiritual leaders of the movement, tried to explain the uniqueness of the Jewish people. Other people, he claimed, assimilated after being detached from their homeland. They did not conserve a notion of *return*, let alone *aliya*. Porat mentions that the biblical precept to Abraham was "go forth from your land and your birthplace and your father's house to the land I will show you" (Genesis 12:1). To uphold the word of the Lord, Abraham is obliged to forget and forsake the primordial attachments that make other people into nations, as is expected today from a Jew who "makes aliya." Porat (1975) criticizes David Ben-Gurion, Israel's first prime minister, for trying to ground the connection of the people to the land in historical memory. The Israeli Declaration of Independence, which Ben-Gurion wrote and read proudly, begins with the following words: "Eretz-Israel was the birthplace of the Jewish people. Here their spiritual, religious and political identity was shaped." Porat claims that these constituting words are plainly wrong: the people of Israel were created outside of their land, in the desert, and the land was a promised image, not their natural habitat. He goes on to claim that, had Ben-Gurion been correct in his assertion, the Jews would not have held the right to return to the land:

> The historical reason, in its literal sense, is not relevant. If two millennia ago there were Jews here—does that give us any rights? Will the Vikings come and demand rights to Scandinavia or England? Will the descendents of the Tatars, the Mongols, and the Vandals claim rights to the Far East? These things do not hold water, not morally and not in their inner logic. The uniqueness of the Jewish people is that their connection to the land is metahistorical. They create history and are not just derived from it. (4)

In pitting himself against Ben-Gurion, Porat rejects the secular Zionist view that presents the Jewish return in terms taken from modern nationalism. For Porat, Zionism is qualitatively different from other nationalist movements because it is a religious return based on divine logic.

The metahistorical dimension, as explained by Porat and as held as self-evident by the Gush Emunim believers, is the most radical and uncompromising component in the movement's ideology. Whereas the debate between the Right and the Left in Israel is basically a *secular* argument regarding the optimal strategy for Israel in a changing world, Gush Emunim's metahistorical view defines the debate as a *religious-theological* one focused on the fulfillment of God's will. This conceptualization transforms all members of the opposition into heretics in the original religious sense of the term. Compromise and withdrawal are no longer a viable political option, but a severe religious transgression. Furthermore, Zionism called for autoemancipation of the Jew, placing the Jewish people, rather than God, center stage in the drama of national redemption. Gush Emunim opposed this notion; for them, even the so-called secular pioneers, let alone the religious believers of Gush Emunim, are agents of a divine redemption. Beyond the seemingly secular processes of history lies a deeper truth in which God's unfolds. Although Gush Emunim may not have attempted to remove the Jewish people from history, it certainly brought God back in, and through the front door.

The metahistorical element is most prominent in spurring political action in places that have little historical Jewish resonance. For example, when Daniella Weiss (1986) of Kedumim explained the need of her settlement to expand, she said, "I decided that it is time to go to battle without hesitating, not for territory of the nearby army camp—that is in Jewish hands anyway—but on the barren hills north of the village that await their redemption." The hills to the north were awaiting redemption by virtue of being there, not because of any historical event that occurred on the site. Rabbi Moshe Levinger has often expressed the idea of the metahistorical sanctity of the land: he calls the believers to redeem the qasba (market) of the Arab town of Kalkilia, where there is no claim of prior Jewish settlement. Through this seemingly absurd assertion, he expressed that redemption of the land has little to do with historical facts—the question of its Jewish or, in the case of Kalkilia, Palestinian Arab history is irrelevant.

BUYING ZIONISM WHOLESALE: HISTORICAL MEMORY

The nostalgic remembering of days gone by is foreign to the thinking of the religious Zionist camp. Whereas secular Zionism framed its return in terms of the basically Christian concept of resurrection, the religious Zionists had little use for this imagery. For them, divine redemption was a promise for the future, and, although some biblical verses promised a return to former glory, the religious Zionists did not take the promise literally. Historian Yosef Salmon (2004) remarks that, while secular Zionism can be seen, at least partly, as oriented toward the past, religious Zionism is mainly oriented toward the future. Gush Emunim's turn to nostalgic romanticism and territorial nationalism can be seen as a revolutionary transformation of the historical consciousness of the religious Zionist camp.

As Rabbi Ariel said, "The ear cannot withstand a noise too loud." Settling in the town of Kalkilia was never a viable option for Gush Emunim supporters and never presented as a plan for implementation. To endear the settlement project to the Israeli public, movement speakers focused on locations with resonance in Jewish history, such as Hebron, Gush Etzion, and Alon Moreh. Rabbi Shlomo Aviner (1990) presented the idea in the following way: "Even he who is outside of religion but still possesses healthy Jewish feeling understands that a people has to be loyal to its land. It is easy to understand that a people without its land is a dead people and a people without its entire land is a crippled people" (49). In turning to a broader public, Rabbi Aviner appeals to what he considers universal national sentiments, which may have been rooted in religious feelings but is currently seen as autonomous from them.

Gush Emunim adopted key symbols from secular Zionism and transformed them into parts of its own ethos. In this book, numerous such examples are cited and discussed. Perhaps the one of greatest importance is, ironically, the adoption of the Zionist historical consciousness. In the Zionist conceptualization, history is divided into three stages: the golden age of the ancient past, when the Jewish people lived on their land; the long era of exile, in which the physical absence was accompanied by national degradation; and, finally, a glorious return, embodied by the national movement (for example, see Zerubavel 1995). This three-staged schema is adopted from modern nationalism and appears in similar fashion in other national movements. It is part of the definition of Zionism as a secular movement that transforms the Jewish temporal consciousness.[4]

In traditional Judaism, time in exile is understood as circular, and redemption is portrayed as a divine process that is the object of prayer but not direct human intervention. Zionism politicized the notion of redemption by introducing the nation as active agent in the process and replacing the role of God with that of the nation. Gush Emunim absorbed this conceptualization, adapting it to the thinking of a religious movement. The three-stage structure of history was appropriated in its entirety. In what follows, I examine the three periods of the historical narrative and concentrate on points of similarity and departure from the established Zionist narrative.

STAGE ONE: THE ANCIENT PAST

The followers of the movement revere early Jewish history, which in its earliest part is biblical, whereas later parts are described in various ancient texts, both religious and secular. This history begins with the Patriarchs and Matriarchs as portrayed in Genesis, moves on to the conquest of the land from the Canaanites by Joshua Bin-Nun and the Judges, and continues with King David and his dynasty, the House of David. Beyond these events presented in the Bible, the wars of the Hasmoneans during the Second Temple period are also remembered. Antiquity ends with the destruction of the Second Temple by the Romans and the last stand on the Masada, and later the Bar Kochba revolt. The compilation of all these elements makes up the mythohistory of the Jewish people of the First and Second Temple periods.

The Bible has had a strange fate in Zionist history.[5] Secular Zionism enthusiastically appropriated the book from its traditional context. For traditional Jews, the Bible was for centuries a sacred—but little studied— book, whereas the hermeneutic and legal literature, such as the Mishna and the Gemara, was more consequential for everyday life. Zionism isolated the Bible, granting it an unprecedented position of privilege as the book that depicts, with considerable accuracy, the history of ancient Israel. The later additions, containing centuries of Jewish wisdom, were discredited and neglected because of their connection to exilic existence and their religious connotations. Furthermore, from the entire corpus of the Bible, only a few books were selected, mainly those that were associated with the military occupation of the land and the period of the early kingdom, while the great prophets were studied because they presented a universal Jewish morality.

The centrality of the Bible to the emerging civil religion was greatly enhanced by Israeli first prime minister David Ben-Gurion, who held Bible classes at his official residence. The Bible quiz, starting in Independence Day 1958, was hailed as a national solidarity ritual. However, soon afterward the book began to lose its cherished place in the hearts of secular Israelis, and today Israelis know substantively less than their parents about the content of the book that legitimized their national quest.

Gush Emunim, as Aran (1993) has correctly observed, appropriated the Bible from secular Zionism rather than from traditional Judaism. Thus, the religious settlers view the Bible not only as a religious text, but also as a historical book, representing events as they actually happened. Unlike for secular Zionists, for the religious believers, the Bible still retains its sanctity. Thus, it not only depicts a historical narrative, but also imbues that narrative with sanctity. The Gush Emunim believers still savor the Mishna and the Talmud, and the Bible does not replace them in the hearts and the schools as it did for secular Zionism.

The Bible is omnipresent in the settlers' world: many of their villages have biblical names, as do their children, who tend to be Bible experts. For a long time, the winners of the Bible quiz have repeatedly been young religious boys and girls mainly from the settlements. Bible classes, which have fallen from grace in the secular schools, have, in recent years, been revived in the national religious ones, with new textbooks and teaching methods. The settler's political discourse uses biblical idioms intensively. As the settlers debated controversial issues, they resorted to biblical examples. Sometimes, biblical heroes are personified in daily life. Hanan Porat claimed that a withdrawal from territories was like spitting in the face of the Matriarch Rachel, who is awaiting the return of her sons, whereas, in abstaining from settlement, the State of Israel is telling Rachel that she should wait two thousand years more. The tears of a personified Rachel become, in Porat's words and in the mind-set of the settlers, something to be reckoned with in taking political decisions.

Biblical discourse is also reflected in the charter of the settlements, such as Beit Horon, established in 1977. In this text, we see the stories of the Hasmoneans, associated with the site, appear in this text, and biblical language is used throughout to refer to contemporary events. Through their charter, the settlers wish to show that they are returning not only to the Land of the Bible, but also to its universe:

> Be strong and brave for you shall give as an inheritance to this people the land which I have promised unto their forefathers to give unto them (Joshua 1:6). Today . . . we ascend to the land, we the pioneers of Gush Emunim, to renew the Jewish settlement in Beit Horon on the road leading to Jerusalem from the valley of Ayalon. We, the great-grandchildren of the Maccabees take possession of the land in the place where Matathias the Hasmonean and his sons defeated the foreign ruler and the Hellenizers and expelled them from the ancestral heritage and purified the sanctuary. This privilege was first granted in the thirtieth year of the renewed independence of Israel, as the Likud government rules the land, following the generation of destruction and revival. Through this deed, we proclaim the renewal of the tie between the people of Israel and the land of Israel. (quoted in Shafat 1995, 288–89)

The emotional attachment to the Bible adds power and impetus to the commandment of settling the land. The connection to the Bible-as-history adds a romantic flavor to the movement. The return to the land of Israel is conceived not only as an abstract religious precept, but as an answer to the wishes of the people who lived and acted on the sacred land in the past. Although the divine decree can theoretically be implemented anywhere in the land of Israel, the historical narrative informs the believers as to where they should settle and what historical event resonates through their acts. They return to Hebron like Abraham, reside in Tekoah like the prophet Amos, and live in Beit Horon where the Maccabees have fought. As the early Zionists were also enchanted by the Bible and ancient Jewish history, through their attachment to these stories the settlers see themselves imitating, at times even emulating, both: the Hebrew settlers of ancient times, as well as the first Zionists, whose national feelings were also guided by their careful reading of the Bible.

STAGE TWO: THE CURSE OF THE EXILE

In their appropriation of the Zionist historical metanarrative, Gush Emunim supporters also absorbed the negation of the Jewish exilic existence into their ethos. The Zionist goal of concentrating the people of Israel in their ancient land entailed a discrediting of all other possible lands and existential options. The homelands from which the Jewish immigrants arrived were defined or redefined as temporal ports on the route that would eventually lead back to the true home: the land of Israel. Thus, the ethnic histories of the various Jewish ethnic groups, including their languages and rituals, were negated. Immigrants from Eastern Europe refrained from speaking Yiddish, whereas those from Muslim countries shut their windows when they listened to Arabic music.

The moral connotation attached by Zionism to the act of immigration is depicted by the use of the word *aliya,* meaning "ascent," to signify arrival in Israel; leaving Israel, on the other hand, is called *yerida,* meaning "descent." The transformation from what was considered as the weak and cowardly "old Jew" of the exile into the brave heroic "new Jew" of the new land was not only geographic, since, according to the Zionist ethos, Jews could remain old or exilic even in the land of Israel (e.g., the Haredim). Conversely, in certain historical conjectures, Jews could act in an exemplary manner abroad, as witnessed by the rebellions in the camps and ghettos during the Holocaust. The change is basically a mental and cognitive one of the Jews discovering their true self and thus fulfilling their destiny in the land that awaited them. The ultimate proof of the futility of Jewish life in the exile is the Holocaust, in which defenseless Jews were butchered by the millions. According to Zionist belief, the possibility of another Holocaust is eminent because of the inherent abnormality of Jewish existence in exile.[6]

Since the establishment of the state, and especially over the last few decades, the powerful trope of the negation of the exile has lost much of its import, as have other Zionist symbols. The emergence of new ethnicity and the growing importance of Holocaust memory, as well as the opening up of Israeli society to the processes of globalization, changed the understanding of exile in Israeli culture. The symbol, however, enjoyed a second awakening among Gush Emunim believers. As in other cases, Gush Emunim appropriated the essence of this important principle while adding meanings of its own. Here, too, they adopted and adapted symbols that were declining among the secular population that first developed them.[7]

As a settlement movement dedicated to appropriate land, the negation of the exile became a central theme in the writings of Gush Emunim leaders and especially in their rabbinic texts. Rabbi Kook the Son taught his students, "The air of the exile is stupefying, full of the filth of the influence of other foreign cultures, which blocks the course of our lives and our ideals."[8] His students learned the lesson. Rabbi Eliezer Waldman wrote, "The land of Israel as a whole is a mountain of belief, a peak and height of belief, whereas the lands outside are an abyss of darkness of heresy and weakness, darkness of the lost path. All belief in the divine mission is linked to the belief in the land of Israel" (Aviezer 1985, 594). In response to a person who wanted to leave the country out of fear for his life, Rabbi Aviner (1990) responded, "Fear belongs to the curse of the exile [. . .]. In our land we return to our strength and fear nothing, we fear only our Creator" (82).

Exile, in these citations, is still the great evil, but for reasons somewhat different than for secular Zionism. In the land of Israel, Jews can live among themselves without pressures to assimilate into a non-Jewish environment. Living in Israel is a mitzvah, and those who fulfill it become better Jews in the religious sense. These motifs were not part of secular Zionist reasoning. The basics, however, are present in these sources: the encounter of the Jews and their ancient homeland unleashes powerful forces that propel them toward an active history—one they cannot experience in exile.

Negation of the exile is a complex and multifaceted phenomenon. For the immigrating pioneers of early twentieth century, it was an organizing principle, though they had tight connections with friends and family members and deep affection to the world they left behind. The second generation, the first to be born or educated within the Zionist community in Palestine (the sabra), had little firsthand knowledge of the rich Jewish life in exile, so their negation was less informed and more absolute. The Gush Emunim settlers, as religious Jews, have a deep appreciation of Jewish existence in exile. Thus, their position is basically ambivalent. After all, they are committed to the Jewish past, and the memory of the previous generations studying Torah in the yeshivas of Poland and Lithuania is dear to their hearts. Thus, while they appreciate the Jews who make the leap, leave their exilic life to fulfill what they consider the most important of religious precepts, living on the land of Israel, the Gush Emunim settlers' affinity to the observant Jew across the sea may at times be greater than to the secular—at times antireligious—Israeli who happens to live in Tel Aviv.

Although the settlers' actual view of exile is complex, the trope of exile itself remains unequivocally negative. The settlers endlessly use the term *exilic* to denigrate their Israeli adversaries, who, to their mind, are less faithful to the land than they are. For them, those who reside in the coastal plain and criticize the settlers reveal, through actions and words, the weakness of their character and their fear of what the gentiles may say, which attest to their exilic personality. Ironically, it is primarily the Zionist Left, who invented and developed the dichotomy between homeland and exile, that is depicted by the settlers as holding an exilic mentality. For example, the Peace Now project researching and disclosing the facts regarding the settlement project is seen by the settlers as the act of frightened exilic Jews who want to squeal in order to find grace in the eyes of the gentiles.

The powerful trope of exile is directed not only against the Israeli Left, but also against the entire secular Zionist project. Zionism is based on two rationales: the first is the saving of the Jews from the dangers of homelessness, and the second is the return to the land of the fathers. Gush Emunim settlers invariably accentuate the second and downplay the first. For them, the full return to the true place is the basic logic behind the Zionist project, and the dangers of diasporic existence cannot serve as sufficient justification for the return. Running away from the perils of Russia, Germany, or Morocco does not constitute a positive agenda and leaves the Jews with no further role in history other than mere existence.

In the eyes of Gush Emunim supporters, the secular Zionist project did not succeed in realizing what they consider the true significance of return, and the concentration of Zionist settlement in the coastal plain rather than in the historical terrains of Judea and Samaria is evidence of this failing. The movement is far more critical toward contemporary Israel, claiming that it had forsaken its roots and betrayed the logic of its existence. In a sense, the movement sees itself as replacing the tired and powerless Zionist movement. Hillel Weiss, a literary scholar from Kedumim, has criticized the Israeli culture of forgetfulness and suggested his movement as a replacement (H. Weiss 1994):

> We have bought from you the whole of Zionism wholesale. You ran away from Zion, escaped from Zionism, left history and the precepts of the ages to us, and we carry them with love, hug and kiss them, clean the dust off them, and keep a place of affection for you in our heart, notwithstanding the anger and disappointment. We know that without you we would not have been what we are today, and because of that we thank you, thank you forever. You have dried the exile out of our bones and have absorbed it back into your bones.

At important political junctures, however, the movement resorts to exilic imagery, particularly to present the settlers as victims. Whereas secular Zionist leadership of the early years of the state portrayed itself as sovereign and heroic, and avoided presenting itself as suffering, helpless Jews, the Gush Emunim settlers often frame their complaints and demands in exilic terms. When they face eviction from their settlements, they usually choose the strategy of passive resistance to avoid violent encounters with the army. They speak of their struggle in terms of the sanctification of the name of God, a strategy adopted from the repertoire of medieval European Jewish existence (Wolfsfeld 1984, 1987).[9] Whenever there is a case of conflict between the settlers and the state and army, the exilic idiom is reproduced. Exilic terms are used in two directions. First of all, the Israeli government is portrayed as exilic, as unprepared to implement its sovereignty in the land of Israel, and as afraid of what the gentiles may say. Second, the settlers themselves are compared to Jews persecuted solely because of their wish to preserve their identity. While the settlers stress their chosen identity as new Jews proud to return to their homeland, their existential situation often evokes among them exilic imagery.

The working of this imagery, however, should be understood as a political use of the potent trope of the negation of the exile. As the settlers evoke exilic role play, positing themselves as the persecuted Jews and the

Israeli government as the hostile gentiles even while the government plays the part of the scared Jew, they liken their situation in Israel today with that of the Jews of the Diaspora. Their claim—be it implicit or explicit—is that, ironically and tragically, the Israel in which they live gives rise to exilic situations that contradict its ethos and its promise.

STAGE THREE: THE ZIONIST MYTH

Alongside the appropriation of the ancient past and the negation of the exile, Gush Emunim fondly adopts modern Zionist and Israeli mytho-history. At an early stage of Zionist history, some of the Jews in Palestine became figures of mythical proportion. These were the ideological pioneers of the early immigrations, especially the second and third aliyas, and the fighters of Tel Hai, the War of Independence, and other IDF battles.[10] All these heroic stories and many more are now either criticized by Israeli "new historians" or are slipping into oblivion as Israel becomes a postideological—or, as some would claim, post-Zionist—society. The settlers lament this situation and embrace Zionist and Israeli heroism as proof to the greatness of the Jewish people in their homeland, preserving the memory of these heroes better than any other group in Israeli society.

Of all the various heroic stories appropriated by the settlers, the most revealing and politically charged—and for many the most infuriating—is that of the pioneers of the second and third aliyas. In their first pamphlets, the settlers claimed, "There is a straight line leading from Tel Hai to Alon Moreh." Through the trope of the early pioneers, they connect themselves, as latter-day pioneers, to the most sacred founding myth of the Israeli society, which until now was claimed by the left-wing kibbutzim. The pioneers may enjoy the greatest symbolic capital of all groups in the Israeli public. Thus, if Gush Emunim can be seen as the truthful heirs of the fathers of the nation—and not as their monstrous mutation, as their rivals would have it—then their project must be viewed as an integral part of mainstream Zionism.

The question of whether the Gush Emunim settlers are present-day pioneers is a matter of political opinion and has little to do with historical evidence. Some points of comparison, however, shed light on the nature of the settlement project. The most important difference is the sociopolitical context. The early pioneers acted before the establishment of the state and assumed some of the state's functions, such as settlement and defense. The Gush Emunim settlers encounter the collaboration and/or opposition of the state apparatus, and some critics have pointed out that their acts of defiance undermine the legitimacy of the state they cherish. The fact that the "arbitrator" between the settlers and the Palestinians is the Jewish state, not the Ottoman Empire or the British Mandate, changes the moral standing of their position.

There are, however, important similarities. Like the pioneers, the settlers went to live on a dangerous frontier to fulfill their ideas of a better society.[11] Both groups regarded themselves as avant-garde, hoping that others would follow once they "saw the light" or realized the success of the colonization project. Both groups' self-understandings can be considered as either inspirational foresight or condescending and elitist. Both ventures are also open to the same criticism—that of removing the best young forces from society and throwing them into a costly adventure in the peripheral wilderness. Hence, doubt and conflict are always an integral part of such ventures, though the settlers were criticized more than their cherished predecessors.

Although the pioneers were secular and the Gush Emunim settlers are religious, both groups can be described as religious in different ways. The socialist pioneers were striving for a better world, and a bureaucratic state was seen by them as diminishing their dream. The Gush Emunim settlers also aspire for higher values, and the mundane life of tranquil civility is seen by them as a compromise of the promise of national salvation. Both groups stand in a Nietzchean opposition to the banality of everyday life and to the understanding, most popular among Israelis, that the accomplishment of the state is the denouement of the historical cycle of the Jewish people. This is best exemplified through the structure of the settlers' national calendar.

NATIONAL HOLIDAYS AS A SEMIOTIC SET

National holidays are the temporal embodiment of historical concepts (Connerton 1989). Gush Emunim settlers share most secular or religious holidays, as well as their interpretations, with the rest of Israeli Jewish population. There are, however, some crucial differences in their comprehension of history that are well illustrated by the way they celebrate their holidays. I shall concentrate on the Israeli "month of memory," between Passover and Independence Day, to show where the settlers' historical consciousness diverges from the general Israeli understanding.

The series of commemorative days—Passover, Holocaust Memorial Day, Memorial Day for the fallen soldiers, and Independence Day—form a semiotic set: while each day has its own significance and tells a meaningful historical tale, their ordering and proximity encode Jewish history according to Zionist historiography (Handelman and Katz 1990). These days lead from the divine promise of the land, through the exile and its most horrific manifestation, the Holocaust, on through war and sacrifice to the denouement of national redemption. In a relatively short period, Israelis get an intensive lesson in their sanctioned history, transmitted by affect-producing rituals. Through the month, the Israeli Jews identify with and reassert their loyalty to the narrative that renders national meaning to their lives.

Turning to the settlers' calendar, Passover, as a religious holiday, is celebrated in basically the same manner as by Jewish Israelis of other social and political groups. The same can be said of the days of national commemoration. Unlike the ultra-Orthodox (Haredim), however, the national religious group has absorbed these days into its calendar and imbued them with sanctity. Rabbi Zvi-Yehudah HaCohen Kook claimed that standing for the fallen IDF soldiers during the siren is a holy mitzvah in memory of holy men, whereas other rabbis have even issued a halakhic decree that requires standing during the siren (Arend 1998, 211). Both secular and religious Jews act similarly during these days of remembrance, though religious Zionists tend to add some religious attributes to the secular practices.

Regarding Israeli Independence Day, the picture is somewhat different. Although the day had sacred meaning for Israelis, it did not receive—unlike preceding memorial days—a sanctioned and binding form. There were attempts to formalize the day, for example, through military parades, national song contests, the Bible quiz, or even family gatherings around a meal consisting of symbolic food and the reading of the Declaration of Independence. None of these enjoyed lasting success because Israelis preferred other forms of celebration—actually recreation—such as street entertainment and picnics. Lately, television has also become a focus for Independence Day. In short, there is no collective decree demanding that Israelis celebrate the day in one way or another or even mention it at all.

The national religious camp had more success in formalizing the holiday, and the Gush Emunim settlers followed suit. The settlers are also extremely critical of the lightheartedness toward the day among their secular compatriots. The Gush Emunim supporters follow the ways of Rabbi Zvi-Yehudah HaCohen Kook, of whom it was said that he would watch the Independence Day military parade in with great joy, saying that the tanks, guns, planes, and uniform of the IDF are the dress of the High Priest and serve the most holy of religious precepts.

The day has assumed a religious meaning. Three rabbis from the settlement of Ofra suggested how the day should be celebrated by the settlers. They understood Israeli Independence Day as the "cornerstone marking the great hand of God that was revealed to us." They suggested appropriate prayers alongside secular attributes such as raising the flag. However, they also suggested turning the flag raising into a religious mitzvah: the Chief Rabbinate should decide who exactly is supposed to hang the flag where and when, as well as the exact size of the flag. The seemingly secular day is to assume religious meaning: "Promoting the name of Israel, the IDF and the land of Israel is done through everyday things. Hiking, marching, celebratory mitzvah meals, army parades and so on." They conclude by stating that such festivities annul required traditional acts of mourning for the dead.[12]

In comparing Gush Emunim with the other Israeli Jews, however, the greatest difference relates to Jerusalem Day, which is celebrated on the day Jerusalem was reunited in the Six-Day War. This day falls several weeks after Independence Day and, although part of Israeli secular calendar, it has lost almost all meaning for most Israelis. Attempts to revive the day for the Israeli general public have failed miserably: a few hike by foot or travel by car to Jerusalem, but most would not even mention the day. The reason for the failure of this day to assume a meaningful niche in the overburdened Israeli national calendar is probably the problematic political situation of Jerusalem and the subsequent reconsideration of the consequences of the Six-Day War. A further reason may be that religious Zionism, mainly the Gush Emunim faction, has appropriated the day as its own and, in the minds of many, has politicized it to the extent that others are unwilling to participate.

For the national religious camp, Jerusalem Day is celebrated with a mass pilgrimage to the holy city, the waving of flags, and dancing in the streets. Traditionally, there is a walk from the Merkaz HaRav Yeshiva to the Wailing Wall, replicating the walk of Rabbi Kook on the liberation of the city. The celebrations come to express the special place that the city holds in the camp's worldview, and the importance of the day derives from the meaning of the Six-Day victory in the settlers' collective memory. Gideon Aran (1987, 430) explains, "Each year, on Jerusalem Day, Kookism celebrates the event that, more than any other, made Zionism afraid of the fulfillment of its own dream" (see also Aran 1988).

The religious settlers see Independence Day and Jerusalem Day as part of a semiotic set: while each has its own meaning, their combination generates additional meanings. Independence Day founds the sacred framework and structure of the state, whereas Jerusalem Day is the day of return to the holy sites in Jerusalem and the land of Israel. Jerusalem Day thus fills independence with meaningful content and marks a higher level on the ladder of spiritual elevation. Whereas Independence Day symbolizes the body, Jerusalem Day symbolizes the spirit of the nation.

Here lies the great divide between the historical consciousness of Gush Emunim and that of the general Israeli public. For Israelis who do not grasp the holiness of Jerusalem Day or have misgivings about the consequences of the Six-Day War, the calendarical representation of the Zionist narrative peaks with Independence Day, which is a symbolic conclusion to the horrors of the Holocaust and the great sacrifices of the national wars. Positioned at the end of the semiotic set, Independence Day stands as the epitome of the Zionist solution to Jewish history. As such, it creates a problem for secular Zionism. If independence closes historical circles, what is there to aspire to once the long-sought independence has been achieved? Ironically, Independence Day—as it is positioned in the yearly cycle—defines a post-Zionist Israel that has fulfilled its destiny and has no further historical role to play beyond its own existence. Many Israelis will not accept the analysis presented here, because in their mind Zionism has further roles to fulfill, and I tend to agree. However, the structure of national calendar transmits a powerful imagery of finality and completion, and posits a challenge to those who wish to renew the Zionist ethos.

The settlers have no such problem because for them Independence Day stands in the middle of a process, leading to a yet higher stage that is closer to full national redemption. Not only do they celebrate the achievement of the state, they also pay attention to the content that it holds, which for them is represented by Jerusalem Day. The independence of the state is only one stage among many in the national ascent to greatness.

Although few Israelis would take notice, Independence Day, which seemingly represents national solidarity and the accomplishment of mutual goals, teaches us of the deep divisions within the celebrating Jewish-Zionist community. It symbolizes the great difference between the narratives, as the end of one is merely a stage for the other.

WAR FROM A METAHISTORICAL PERSPECTIVE: FROM YOM KIPPUR TO THE INTIFADAS

The Israeli Independence War and the Six-Day War played a crucial role in the worldview of both Gush Emunim and the larger Israeli public. For a movement that is dedicated, even obsessed, with the question of land, the two wars that have formed current Israel's boundaries of control are understood as miraculous events. This raises the question of how the believers understand war as such. The most important challenge here is the 1973 Yom Kippur War, which for many Israelis is understood as the quintessential war and as the greatest national trauma in Israeli history. It did not expand their territory significantly, and most Israelis remember it through scenes of human suffering and death rather than as a glorious victory.

The Yom Kippur War against the armies of Egypt and Syria took the Israeli government, army, and public by surprise. It was riddled with failures in preparation and management, and caused alarm and even panic among Israel's leaders. The death toll of more than 2,600 was the largest that Israel has suffered since the War of Independence. Following the war, Israel's international standing declined drastically, and it was forced to concede territory, while the economy took a long time to recover from its devastating consequences; some would say it is still recovering today.

While, on a private level, the war was a traumatic event in the lives of many Israelis,[13] its collective representation marks it a watershed in Israeli history. Charles Liebman (1993) attempted to explain why the war induced mass sentiments of depression. The answer would seem obvious enough: the great number of dead, the failures before and during the war, and the disappointment with the political and military elite. Liebman, however, focuses on the lack of redemptive narrative framing the war. He reminds us that the war began catastrophically for Israel but ended with what could easily have been interpreted as a glorious military victory. There were great acts of courage and heroism that could have been accentuated to boost national pride and moral. And the war could have been defined as part of a long-term process of reconciliation and acceptance into the region and hence as the price that Israel had to pay for a better future. Depression, Liebman suggests, is a narrative decision—one among several options.

Liebman goes on to explain why, to his mind, Israeli society chose one interpretation of the war over all others. The promise of the Six-Day War was of more security, better economic well-being, and greater Jewish immigration. The Yom Kippur War, on the other hand, accentuated the existential threat looming over the nation and its dependence on foreign aid and diplomatic support. Rather than Israeli heroism, the war was constructed in terms of Jewish suffering, especially because this was in accord with the growing global politics of identity. Lastly, Liebman discusses the term *mechdal* (failure through inaction), which came to define and symbolize the war. According to Liebman, the war was defined as a sorry mistake—a deviation from the hegemonic Zionist ethos valorizing perpetual action over inaction. Hence, it could not support an uplifting interpretation.

Liebman was a national-religious Jew of moderate dovish political attitudes who was critical of the Gush Emunim ethos. His in-between position enabled him to map different possibilities for conceptualizing the war in collective memory, and his analysis can shed light on how Gush Emunim leaders and activists could reinterpret the war. He rightly noticed that the interpretation of the war as failure is only one possibility among other alternatives. Gush Emunim proved him right by suggesting and adopting another one, more in line with its own political and religious viewpoint.

As explained in chapter 1, the Yom Kippur War is crucial to the emergence of Gush Emunim. Although the Six-Day War was indeed most important in the ethos of the movement, it was only after the Yom Kippur War that the movement was established and began to act in public. This was no historical accident. The political crisis caused by the war opened a window of opportunity to the young leaders who established the radical movement. Israeli control of the occupied territories was threatened as some land in the Sinai desert and the Golan Heights was relinquished in agreements immediately after the war. Among the first actions of Gush Emunim were demonstrations against American Secretary of State Henry Kissinger as he attempted to negotiate a truce based on Israeli territorial compromise.

The importance of the Yom Kippur War, both for Israel and Gush Emunim, was hardly reflected in writing. By contrast, we find much written about the Six-Day War because it was considered a miraculous event that enabled the return of the Jewish people to the holy places; the Lebanon War erupted in 1982, at the height of the movement's activities, and therefore received much mention; and the two intifadas, which directly affected the safety and well-being of the settlers, generated rich discussions about settlement and the "other."

That little is written on the Yom Kippur War does not mean that it is peripheral; the opposite is probably true. The war was absorbed into the movement's ethos in ways that countered its subversive potential. Gush Emunim located the Yom Kippur War firmly within the Jewish and Zionist metanarratives, making it an integral part of the redemption process. The believers claim that there are ascents and descents on the long road to salvation, and that the war does not shatter the pervious historical understanding. Paradoxically, the war strengthens that understanding by exemplifying the inevitable suffering along the road to the final goal. Not that the Yom Kippur War was not traumatic to the young religious soldiers that fought in it along with their secular friends. Rather, since it was not constructed as a national trauma by the movement leadership, it does not appear as a trauma in the scarce accounts of the warriors themselves. Although this might be seen as an attempt to hide or repress the magnitude of the trauma, it is also part of an even larger metahistorical narrative that encompasses the war and gives it reassuring meaning. For the Gush Emunim believers, unlike for most secular Israelis, the war was part of the historical and cosmological order of things. Thus, no collective crisis ensued.

Few religious soldiers discussed the war and their war experiences in any detail, and, when they did, the trauma they may have experienced remained well hidden. As publicist Robik Rosenthal (2001, 42) discussed the most impressive book to come out of the national religious camp on the war, Haim Sabato's *Teum Kavanot* (1999; English translation, *Adjusting Sights*, 2003), he remarked, "War has no dimension of horror. A war without blood, without mutilated bodies; the Torah passages and faith in their applicability cover it all."[14] An atypically vivid account was presented by one of the leaders of Gush Emunim: Hanan Porat (1988, 105). He describes his near fatal injury in the Sinai battles:

> I was left lying, naked, in a pool of my own blood, under the canopy of the sky in the midst of a bombardment. My army buddies pulled me to a makeshift trench and desperately called on the wireless for an armored vehicle to come and take me. I felt the blood quickly oozing out of my

body . . . My life was leaving me as I, gasping for breath, sank deeper into a sea of darkness. I was certain that this was my final hour. I said to myself—my fate was decreed! I had already parted in my mind from all my relatives and friends, my father, my mother, my wife, my son . . . Then, suddenly, I heard in the darkness, from a long way off, music playing softly: "A hymn for the Sabbath day," and above me, peeking at me to revive my soul, was "Something invisible yet certain as light."

Even when Porat provides a detailed description of his war experience, it is encompassed within a national-religious narrative and includes mythical components rarely found in other Israeli war stories. He is saved by what can be described as an evocation of the holy Sabbath and a revelation of a divine nature, described using the words of the secular poet Rachel. Porat's war experience is not traumatic in the sense that it leads to a break with his former existence; rather, it serves to reassure his belief in his former world.

In the thinking of the warriors that are part of the Gush Emunim community, the big picture and the metanarrative are more important than the suffering and loss of the individual. When a soldier is interviewed about his war experiences, he expresses his feelings as follows:

A man going to battle must think for himself the grand thoughts, not the little thoughts . . . The vision has to be a general one. At the end of the day, this is a struggle required for the people of Israel. If the people of Israel needs this struggle, of what significance am I and my life? I cannot measure it by my private life. Even if we have regrettably many casualties in war, it is not as significant as the destruction or non-destruction of the nation. Of course we suffer the injury of every soldier and son. Each one is an entire world unto himself. But that will not determine whether the nation will rise or fall.[15]

Since the leaders and supporters of Gush Emunim saw themselves as being able to encompass and comprehend the wider historical picture—the great perspective of national rebirth and divine salvation-they felt obligated to pass this insight on to the rest of society, who defined the war as a traumatic crisis. The narrative of the movement's beginnings starts with the depressed nation and continues with the new spirit that the enthusiastic religious youth instilled in the nation as a whole. According to one semimythical story, immediately after the war two religious women went to Prime Minister Golda Meir and told her that they could offer hope to depressed people through new settlement in the ancient national land. Gershon Shafat (1995, 11), one of the movement's first leaders, who opened his book *The Settlers* with a chapter called "Birth Out of Pain and Chaos," writes, "Several weeks after the Yom Kippur War, from within the downtrodden mood all around, against the sadness of an entire nation that has no one to show him the light, with a broken leadership and a depressed people nurturing each other, there crystallized in us the need to do something." Evidently, Gush Emunim presented itself as having the desire and the ability to solve the national trauma, and, naturally, its members did not see themselves as traumatized. This accords with the general perspective of "true believers" (in Gush Emunim as in other fundamentalist movements), who regard themselves as holding the key to eternal truth and assume the role of enlightening others.

The influential rabbinical discourse further strengthened the normalization of war—this one and others—in the national narrative. War was defined as part of a process that could be understood only in its entirety. Rabbi Eliezer Waldman, head of a yeshiva in Hebron and one of the most influential spiritual leaders of Gush Emunim, wrote on war and on the redemption process:

> We regard the state of Israel as the beginning of our redemption. It is possible that some expect that the redemptive aspect will be perfect, and they do not understand why it does not reveal itself immediately as perfect. They wonder how descriptions of world peace coexist with the wars, misery, and victimhood that are the absolute opposite of the desired good and the pure. This way of looking, this anticipation of the hope of the beginning of redemption, stems from a lack of knowledge and understanding of the process of redemption . . . On the one hand, war is accompanied by destruction and killing, and, on the other, the power of the Messiah is awakened . . . The world is in the process of the awakening of messianic forces and hence the evil must be uprooted.[16]

In his understanding, war and suffering are an integral part of the quasi-organic revitalization process of the Jewish people on their sacred land. The divine nature of war precludes the possibility of understanding it as a shattering trauma. Rabbi Ya'akov Filber (1989, 237) takes the point even further:

> As in every generation, they arise to destroy us. Again there was an attempt to wipe out the name of Israel and as always, God Almighty, this time

through his messengers the IDF soldiers, saved us from them . . . The future will reveal what divine providence wished to tell us through this war; is it a punishment for ancient transgressions . . . or was God concealing his face from us? . . . This war brought many of us to think deeply about the nature of the people of Israel and exemplified the people's unique fate in the history of nations.

The suffering of the people of Israel in the war is similar to other events in the long Jewish history in that it has a divine origin and falls into a well-established narrational pattern. The appropriation of the war from its secular context is, in a sense, a reversal of the Zionist proverb of "returning the Jews to history" and breaking with the period of exile. From this perspective, the war is merely one more disaster befalling the Jewish people throughout its history. The Israeli soldiers are the happenstance messengers of salvation rather than active subjects with a will of their own. The experience of war, rather than shattering former existence, actually reassures the truth of Jewish suffering; the traumatized soldiers and bereaved families can be consoled by their plight being the same as that of their cherished forefathers throughout Jewish history.

To conclude, the Yom Kippur War was defined by the Gush Emunim leadership and supporters, including by those who actively fought in it, as an integral and logical part of the long war for the land of Israel. It may have been more tragic and hard-fought than others, but, if we define trauma as a break in the normal order of things, then the war was not traumatic. It was framed as a normal part of Jewish history, bestowed on the people because of its unusual destiny and sacred role, and part of the process of redemption. If there was an individual trauma, it is barely noticeable behind the hegemonic movement discourse of the political and spiritual leaders.

While such a stand can easily be understood in terms of Jewish continuity and religious beliefs, it can also be interpreted as an attempt to counter a deeply repressed trauma. The Yom Kippur War enabled the believers a glimpse of the possibility that their vision would not materialize, because of defeat on the battlefield and Israeli concessions. More importantly, the war showed the believers what they interpreted as a frightening model for national and individual disintegration and defeatism. Their choice—of understanding the war as a normal occurrence—can be seen as a means of countering the disruptive effects of the war. If the war was an integral part of the historical process of Jewish redemption, it is not traumatic and should not lead to what the settlers consider as hasty and unnecessary retreats.

This was also the case with the Lebanon War: the settlers wholeheartedly supported Prime Minister Menachem Begin and Defense Minister Ariel Sharon against the peace protests of the Left. The picture, however, changed in many respects during the two intifadas. For the first time, elaborate accounts began to appear either of encounters with raging Palestinians or of the horrors of terrorist attacks inside the settlements. The narrative was modified in response to the new type of warfare as the horrors of war reached the homes of the settlers. Two of the following chapters are dedicated to the comprehension of the place of the Palestinians within the historical narrative and the impact of terrorism on the settlers' community.

MEMORY AND COMPROMISE

This chapter demonstrates the totalistic nature and extent of Gush Emunim's commitment to the Jewish past. The believers, however, do place limits and boundaries to their allegiance to memory and tradition. The supporters of Gush Emunim see themselves as firmly entrenched in the modern world aligned with a secular Israel; thus, they attempt to negotiate the various components of their identity in response to the different contexts in which they are involved. The mythical return suggested and implemented by Gush Emunim activists is, as they admit, a partial one.

The settlers, including the staunchest "true believers," acknowledge the limitations of reproducing the past. First, the sacred books do not describe the past in enough detail, and the secular sciences such as history and archaeology cannot provide a definitive conclusion as to its true nature. The believers understand very well that the formulation of an accurate representation of the past is beyond their powers; hence, they seek to represent the values and ethos of the past and to be loyal to tradition as they understand it.

Second, even if they could reproduce a certain past era, they are not committed to a single period only. They realize that biblical time is composed of numerous epochs, from nomadic existence to the Davidic kingdom, and that their attempt at recreation is, at best, an inaccurate collage. In few cases, a more accurate reproduction of ancient life is possible and even greatly esteemed: in some remote settlements, residents try raising sheep, while a few eccentrics even live in caves. However, even these attempts should not be understood merely as reproductions of biblical life, because they are influenced by New Age or Far Eastern religions (as discussed in chapter 11).

Some—probably most—settlers will deny that they seek to reproduce the biblical era. By their definition, they are not much different from other Israeli Jews who accept the premises of Zionist ideology and attempt to return the Jewish people to their homeland. Yoel Bin-Nun (1994, 93), for example, claims that there is a common mistake in the understanding of the Gush Emunim concept of the entire land of Israel: each political camp has positions that it won't surrender regarding where the final borders of Israel should pass, and the difference between Gush Emunim supporters and the Israeli Left is basically quantitative. He adds that, according to the halakha, much of the entire land is not under Israeli rule today, and, although some dreamers in Gush Emunim argue that these areas should be returned to the possession of the Jewish people, they do nothing to implement their dream.

The role of demarcating where the shifting lines between living in the present and returning to the past falls mainly on the shoulders of the rabbis. Rabbi Avi Giser of Ofra gave me an example of the complex meaning of the return: the Maccabees are heroes worthy of emulation, but this does not mean that today's believers hold the right to reenact their deeds, such as killing those who turned to Greek—that is, universal—culture (*mityavnim*). While this example shows that the settlers make clear distinctions in their worldview between past and present, even more convincing differences can be seen in their lifestyle. The settlers live in modern homes, use modern utilities, hold modern occupations, and dress in a modern fashion, all against the backdrop of a landscape that they define as biblical. Their project is an attempt at introducing principles of fundamentalist religion into everyday life, which is basically regarded as modern. Examples of settlers' compromises with modern life may be found everywhere, largely because they are not defined by the believers as compromises.

This chapter has presented the principles treasured by the settlers—principles that define their project. But we have seen that it would be a grave mistake to define the settlers as anything but modern and totally committed to modernity (even if they are highly critical of the shallowness and alienation that characterize modern culture). In that sense, they are no different from most fundamentalist phenomena in the West, which combine modern technology and culture with traditional values.[17] The tension between the overlapping commitment to the past and the present creates tensions for every fundamentalist group. The fundamentalist enclave is usually a community of believers that isolates itself from the secular modern world to ensure the continuation of tradition.[18] The case of Gush Emunim is the opposite—that of a modern enclave planted within a traditional setting of Arab villages. The next chapter discusses the symbolic meaning of the Gush Emunim settlement.

3

What Is a Settlement?

Presence, Images, and Aesthetics

THE SETTLEMENT AS SIGNIFIED AND SIGNIFIER

The greatest symbol and most important resource of Gush Emunim is the settlement, the "rurban" village strategically located on the hills of Judea or Samaria. It broadcasts to its environment, to the rest of Israeli society, and to the world that the Jews have returned to the land to stay. The grand ideas and messianic designs of the settlers assume the concrete form of houses and communal relations in an enclave setting.

The Gush Emunim settlement aims primarily at creating geodemographic facts that will prevent any territorial compromise on the part of Israeli government. As such, it raises the Israeli price—financial, moral, or political—of any agreement. Over the past thirty years, the network of settlements in the West Bank has proven to be the most valuable resource of the Israeli Right. This has been proven time and again, as border negotiators and fence builders devised ingenious ways to circumvent, bypass, or include them. In other words, the most important attribute of the settlements is their "thereness"—their defiant existence.

For the Israeli right wing, the settlements are living proof that the hawkish worldview not only enjoys popular support, but is backed by people willing to act according to their ideology. For Gush Emunim, the settlements also create well-institutionalized bases of power that enable the mother movement to continue its struggle with greater intensity, more resources, and better intelligence. The construction of a settlement creates new jobs in administration and education, which are filled by movement supporters and activists. The settlement network enables the idea to survive and prosper years after the movement organization has ceased to exist. Significantly, the organization that assumed the political functions of Gush Emunim is the Yesha council, which represents the settlements. Logistically, the settlements supply the personnel, machinery, tools, and know-how for further expansion. They are enclaves grooming the next generation of settlers in a totalistic atmosphere favorable to the movement's messages. Their very existence generates expansion: they require safe roads, nearby army camps, public buildings, and open spaces for further development. Events that occur in or around the settlements—such as death of settlers at the hands of local Palestinians—become triggers for further political action. The settlement project has institutionalized the Gush Emunim ideology, granting it renewed life and a set of vested interests.

The creation of a viable and thriving community in the contested territories was a challenge adopted by the Gush Emunim movement with impressive and surprising success. When, in 1976, Rabin's government accepted the Kadum compromise enabling Gush Emunim to build its first settlement, Rabin stated that the settlers would remain on the hills for a few weeks and then return home. The settlers sought to prove him wrong and demonstrate that successful Jewish communities can thrive in the unfavorable terrains of Judea and Samaria. Thus, the very existence of the settlement project is proof that the alternative national program suggested by the fundamentalist group is indeed a viable option for Israel.

The creation of a settlement is tied inseparably to Jewish religious law and memory. It is a fulfillment of the mitzvah of settling the land, which believers regard as obligatory, irrespective of historical circumstances. It is a symbolic reenactment of the conquering of the land in ancient times and a reproduction of the pioneering Zionist practice, which has gained mythical status in Israel. Furthermore, the settlement represents the defiant nature of the Gush Emunim project and hails what the Gush Emunim believers see as their best qualities, such as perseverance and loyalty to the land. If we take the settlement of Alon Moreh as an example, its name, taken from the Bible, points to the divine promise and the Jewish link to ancient Shechem throughout the ages. In Israeli contemporary symbolism, however, it has a secondary connotation that represents the struggle to open Samaria for Jewish settlement. This meaning was most apparent when Prime Minister Menachem Begin, in his first statement after assuming power in 1977, declared that there shall be many Alon Morehs: he transformed the name of the specific settlement into a generic name for all settlements.

The settlement is a statement of belonging to the land. It manifests the Gush Emunim presumption of shaping Israeli destiny; concomitantly, it represents a partial withdrawal from general society. The settlers atop the hills of Judea and Samaria are secluded from the rest of Israeli society by their choice of residence. Gideon Aran (1991) expressed the duality and ambivalence of the settlement by calling it a countersociety:

> Gush Emunim's society operates alongside Israeli society: half dependent and half independent, apart from the public and the establishment but competing with it and aspiring to lead it. The Jewish fundamentalist enclaves, especially the settlements, are ghetto-like, with all the advantages this allows for leading a religious life in a secular world. At the same time, the settlements are both a bridgehead for assault and a model of an alternative life-style. Gush Emunim is more than just an intellectual current or pressure group: it is actually a countersociety. (304)

In what follows, I present and analyze some of the symbolic aspects of settlements as countersocieties. First, I discuss the idea of the *communal village*—especially how it allows the settlement to define its own meaning. Second, I examine the typical names that the settlers give their villages and the logic behind the creation of the new map. Third, I discuss the semiotics of the settlement itself as a Jewish enclave atop a hill surrounded by wilderness and hostile Palestinian Arabs. Next, I examine one of the most important and impressive rituals of the settlers: the political march. Apart from its being a political tour de force, the march defines the settlements as national symbolic centers. Last, I discuss the significance of the creation of the settlements for the concept of *homecoming* that is so central to Gush Emunim ideology.

The Communal Village

The Gush Emunim settlements are planted communities: they were established through the willful acts of visionaries and designers after much deliberation and through a political and administrative process. That is the case with most other Jewish settlements throughout Zionist history, contrary to most Arab villages, which were established and grew based on local available resources and population pressures without government planning. Hence, the construction of the Israeli settlements was always much more than merely finding a place to live for a growing population; it held national meaning and entered into political debates. In this respect, Gush Emunim settlements resemble other types of rural settlements in Israel, such as the kibbutz or the moshav. The creation of a Jewish presence in an area served territorial claims and was an uncontested Zionist dictum that the plough granted rights and marks the borders of the Israeli entity. Therefore, the act of settlement lent esteem to the ideological movement establishing it, and religious Zionism had its own set of kibbutzim and moshavim, established prior to the Gush Emunim settlements.[1] Gush Emunim thus followed a well-established Zionist practice.

In other respects, however, the Gush Emunim settlements are unique in the landscape of Israeli rural settlements: previous settlements were considered to have intrinsic value as special types of human organization that radiated their influence across Israeli borders. The kibbutzim were seen as an important social experiment, and their attempt at sharing production and consumption and restructuring family functions was viewed with great interest and anticipation around the world. At the peak of its glory, the kibbutz was considered a substantial Zionist contribution to communal thinking, and similar experiments were attempted elsewhere in the world. Establishing a presence on the land, while certainly an important national goal, was not considered as sufficient justification for creating a new community, and therefore a revolutionary socialist content was conceived as essential for life in the kibbutz.

The new Gush Emunim settlements, following the experience of the kibbutz, sought an ideological and bureaucratic definition for their type of existence and opted for communal villages. In this type of settlement, the residents usually work elsewhere and share neither production nor consumption. The communal village is much like the modern suburb, and the workers leave each morning and return at night. This arrangement was preferred because of the rough terrain, which does not enable intensive agriculture; the proximity to Israeli urban centers; and the social makeup of the residents, most of whom are white-collar professionals and semiprofessionals. Gush Emunim targeted mainly city dwellers who would not have arrived had the settlements demanded a transformation of lifestyle and the redistribution of property.[2] Developing local industry would have been costly and time-consuming. Thus, whereas the kibbutzim demanded the redemption of man (which is one reason why they remained small and exclusive), the Gush Emunim settlements strove for the redemption of land and accepted all normative families passing a screening committee.

Unlike the kibbutz movement, Gush Emunim has little to say about social and economic relations and the structure of communities, beyond a general penchant for religious communal life. The religious decree and political will to settle the entire land of Israel are much stronger than any urge to transform Israeli society. This is not to say that the settlements do not have a distinct religious nature, and the wish to live within a religiously observant community is an important motivation for moving to a settlement (Weisburd and Waring 1985). A secluded religious community can offer a fuller religious experience than a regular Israeli city—the rabbi enjoys more authority, the gates to the settlement are closed on Shabbat, and the semiotics of the environment are controlled. The settlements, however, cater to people who arrive with certain worldviews and, unlike the kibbutz, do not presume to change them, let alone change the world.

Although the social structure of the settlement is not ideologically motivated, a handful of supporters propose the Gush Emunim settlement as a model for Israeli society and maybe even the rest of the world. Unlike in the kibbutz, however, ideological goals are not part and parcel of the basic makeup of a settlement, but rather reflect individual decisions on the part of some residents who wish to define and live in an exemplary community (as we examine in a chapter 9 dedicated to the settlement of Ofra). Furthermore, some settlers see the lack of ideological content in the structure of the villages as an adaptation to the needs of the day. They claim that, while the kibbutz was good for its time, the communal village is an innovative solution for the individualistic modern person. Yoel Bin-Nun expressed the universal vision of the communal village: "The only solution to the deterioration of the modern city is the communal responsibility of small neighborhoods . . . In this respect, we can be pioneers of the Western world."[3] This vision never materialized. If the secular kibbutzim failed to transform Israeli society and the world in general, neither did the religious settlements.

To increase the Jewish presence in the contested terrain and to attain a critical demographic mass, Gush Emunim settlements sought not to infringe on the personal liberties of those who wished to join. Numbers became more important than other ideological concerns. The Gush Emunim leadership was most explicit about this (Y. Sheleg 1986):

> From the outset, we talked about the fact that Samaria will be a success
> when people will move here for exactly the same reasons they move from
> Netaniya to Hadera [two cities in Israel]. I am not sorry about the decline
> in ideological tension. It is clear that things cannot remain at the same
> level. In order for a settlement to become normal, it must not consist of
> idealists alone. Idealists are usually difficult people and there have to be
> some normal people. (19)

The Gush Emunim settlers strove for villages they could consider as
normal and therefore opted for the communal village, which allows each
individual to do as he or she pleases. The Gush Emunim settlements are
considered a novelty in Israeli society, but only with regard to location.
Among the religious Zionist community, they are seen as one option
among several potential places to reside. Settlements could thus concentrate on their principal goal, which is to Judaize the land. The settlements
were able to accumulate such rich symbolic significance because in one
important respect—the transformation of the individual who resides in
them—they have none.

On Names and Maps: The Born-Again Landscape

The settlement project can be partly understood as an attempt to reproduce the ancient, former, or sacred map of Judea and Samaria.[4] Naming
new places is a well-known way of establishing a sense of homecoming,
and Zionist settlement used this method extensively long before Gush
Emunim. Many of the names given to cities, towns, and rural villages
in Israel represented the connection of the glorious past to the heroic
present of a people returning to its ancient homeland. Some names were
taken directly from the Bible, either as names of ancient locations (for
example, Eilat and Hazor) or simply as names borrowed from the biblical repertoire (for instance, Petah Tikva and Rosh Pinah). Other names
express the general concept of Zionist return. The name Tel Aviv, for example, signifies the old and the new conjoined: *tel* means "archaeological mound," whereas *aviv* is "spring"; the entire name is an inventive
translation of Theodore Herzl's book title *Altneuland* (1941). Other
names commemorate great world leaders (for example, Kfar Blum, after
the French prime minister), known Zionist figures (for instance, Herzlia)
or fallen soldiers. Kiryat Shmona (City of Eight) commemorates in its
name the battle of Tel Hai and the eight who died nearby. After the estab-

lishment of the state, many deserted Arab villages became Jewish towns, and their names were changed, at times totally (for example, Halsa became Kiryat Shmona, and Um Rashrash became Eilat) while, at other times, the Arabic name was hebraized (for instance, Ein Chud became Ein Hod).[5]

The Gush Emunim settlers encountered a similar challenge in giving "correct" names to their settlements and almost invariably preferred biblical or ancient names. Giving the new settlements old names had a clear political function: it was a way of signaling to Israelis, Palestinians, and the rest of the world that the Jews held prior rights to the land. Through their ancient names, the settlements skip over millennia of history and declare themselves to be older and more authentic than the Arab villages that surround them. Beyond the manipulative dimension of these naming practices, giving a settlement a biblical name reflects the essence of Gush Emunim as a cultural project dedicated to returning to the Land of the Bible. This strategy declares that the settlers are identical with, or at least a direct continuation of, their biblical forefathers.

For the settlers, the settlement project is *grosso modo* an attempt to reproduce an imagined ancient geography. Aside from the individual meanings of the names given to settlements, the map in its entirety manifests the return of the people to the land. To be sure, this map never existed in such form before; there are acknowledged mistaken identities, names taken from different historical periods, and numerous modern names. All that, however, makes little difference to the settlers: the map they created represents the Jewish return to the ancient land, "trivial" historical mistakes notwithstanding. Although they are fundamentalists in their worldview, they are not overly obsessive about achieving precise authenticity.

In re-creating the ancient map, the settlers are also reproducing and reenacting the occupation of the land in biblical times. They see themselves as the people of Israel returning to the land of Canaan, to Hebron and Shechem as did the Patriarchs, and to Jericho and Gibeon as did Joshua. Although movement members might reject its Christian overtones, Judea and Samaria could be termed a *born-again landscape* in two senses (Jackson 1980). First, the landscape is supposed to redeem, now that it has been returned to the way it was before its true nature was buried beneath other maps, whether of gentiles or of modernity. Second, the territory is born again in the religious sense; it becomes Judaic again, accentuating its sacred nature. The land is considered to be Jewish in its essence, and the Gush Emunim believers take upon themselves the role of purifying it and restoring it to its former glorious state.

By giving Hebrew and biblical names to the land, the settlers in effect reproduce the Zionist practice no less than the practices of the biblical Patriarchs and Joshua. The differences, however, should not be overlooked. Secular Zionists certainly defined their immigration to the land of Israel as a return to the Land of the Bible, but not in terms of the reproduction of an ancient map. First and foremost, they did not return to Judea and Samaria, the ancient cradle of the nation, but rather to the Coastal Plain, which in ancient times was populated by mainly other ethnic groups such as the Philistines. The creation of a new map is best signified by the construction of Tel Aviv adjacent to the ancient city of Jaffa. The celebrated secular Zionist settlements were the kibbutzim and moshavim, such as Degania and Nahalal, whose location had little to do with historical memories. Israel's first prime minister David Ben-Gurion's vision of making the Negev desert flourish pointed away from reproduction of biblical themes.

Gush Emunim, while showing great appreciation for the former Zionist settlement effort, proposed a radically different perspective: it presented a tentative ancient map and suggested the establishment of settlements whose names bore prior meaning. A Jewish settlement called Beit El (Bethel), for example, is worthwhile not by virtue of its current population (other than their being Jewish), but as a reproduction of a town that once existed in approximately the same place. One cannot imagine an idea more foreign to the mind-set of the socialist pioneers, but Gush Emunim is a movement that takes the idea of return much more literally. "What did the hearts yearn for for two millennia?" asks one of the first Gush Emunim leaders (Simon 1986, 44); "For Degania and Netaniya or for Beit El and Shiloh? And what did the Jews dream of in the darkness of the exile—of Ceasaria and Herzlia or of Shechem and Hebron?"

The creation of the settlement project on the hills of Judea and Samaria constructs a territorial hierarchy in which the Coastal Plain, where secular Zionism chose to settle and the majority of Israelis now reside, is of less important symbolic value than the biblical land on the hills overlooking the plains. If the new Gush Emunim map is one of memory and devotion to the past, the map of the rest of Israel becomes a map of forgetfulness and oblivion. The hills of Judea and Samaria are not only the geographic, but also the moral and historical, high ground, whereas the plains are populated by Jews less devoted to lofty values.

At times, this concept is expressed outright. Yoel Elitzur (1980b), the most prominent among the settlers who bear the name-war upon their shoulders, laments what he considers as the historical oversights of secular Zionism, which

> neglected ancient names and preferred instead names denoting a memorial or a monument to some deceased Zionist leader (with all due respect to their memory, these names are often meaningless for generations that follow). There is no need to give examples for this "interment" of the historical land of Israel; all one needs to do is to travel the Sharon Road or the Judea Coastal Plains, the Jezreel Valley or the Zvulun Valley, and look at the signs pointing the way to places with names such as Sirkin, Citron, Warburg, and Vitkin—who were doubtless men of great renown in their generation, yet whose commemoration has turned entire districts of an ancient, yet living, land into a modern cemetery. (12–13)

Elitzur, however, is not only critical of the Zionist settlement in the Coastal Plain, but also of his own friends when they are not faithful to the principles of returning to the correct names of the land. When the movement presented its settlement program in 1976, the question of settling in the right place was marginal compared with more important considerations, such as establishing a Jewish presence at strategic points, near central highways and on controlling hilltops. The program document stated, "Secondary considerations for the placement of settlements [. . .] the proximity as much as possible to sites of historical Jewish importance" (Shafat 1995, 308). This issue became of great importance, however, once the Jewish presence was established, and there was a need to determine its meaning.

Few settlements were established with the express aim of being in the exact spot where the biblical forefathers had lived. Hebron (which is discussed in chapter 7) is the most significant example, but Alon Moreh is also significant as the first Gush Emunim settlement group (*gare'en*) that sought to settle in, or as close as possible to, the ancient city of Shechem (Nablus). The settlement of Shiloh was established near the original site, discovered in archaeological digs. A unique case is Susia. The existence of that ancient Jewish town was unknown in Jewish sources, but was discovered in archaeological excavations. The new settlement of that name was based on scientific findings. In any case, the settlers are not free to decide on the names chosen: the National Naming Committee of the Prime Minister's Office has that responsibility and considers various factors. The settlers, however, being well acquainted with the territory and its history, play a significant role in the decision, even if at times that involves heated debates with the committee.

On the current map of Judea and Samaria, one can find many settlements with biblical names, including Efrat, Gibeon, Michmash, and Tekoah, among others. Some have adopted biblical motifs without replicating biblical names. The group that established Karmei Tzur, for example, originally wanted to name their village after ancient Beit Tzur, but the National Committee refused because the site was not definitively identified. The name chosen reflected the presence of vineyards (*kramim*) in the area and its proximity to the ancient site. A settlement in Samaria is called Yakir, a new name, after the word "beloved"—*yakir*—which in Jeremiah 31:19 refers to Efraim, in whose tribal domain the settlement was established. The first group of Alon Moreh, not allowed to enter Nablus, settled for a place they called Kedumim. Literally, *kedumim* means "ancient," and there is a Palestinian village named Kadum nearby. However, in this case as in many others, Kedumim refers primarily to the place of memory in the mind-set of the settlers.

Other names have little or no connection to ancient Jewish history and sometimes retain vague links to other histories. The settlement Nofim is thus called because of the beautiful view it has (*nof* means "landscape" in Hebrew), and Karney Shomron (literally, the "Horns of Samaria") connotes a nearby mountain with two summits. Barkan is a hebraization of a Byzantine name. The National Naming Committee decided that the settlement should be called Beit Aba, in commemoration of right-wing Zionist leader Aba Achimeir, but the residents refused to accept the name, so the committee was forced to change its mind. Interestingly, Zionist memory, which had great import in naming practices within Israel, was not supported by the local residents and lost the day. On the other hand, the Ali Zahav settlement was first called Yoezer, after a Jewish sage who lived nearby in ancient times; this time, however, the residents wished to commemorate Aliza Begin, deceased wife of Prime Minister Menachem Begin, and their request was granted. This is a rare case of the settlers allowing Judea and Samaria to serve as a "Zionist cemetery."

There are also examples of settlements that take after the local Arabic name. Nili resonates with Zionist history: it was a Jewish espionage group during the First World War. The settlement by that name was built near the Arab village of Na'alin. The settlement of Ofra arrived at its name deductively. An Ofra appears in the biblical text, but knowledge of its original location had not survived through the ages. As the group of settlers searched for a suitable name for their village, they realized that the nearby Arab village is called Taibe. The word *ofrit* in Arabic means "demon," so, to avoid bad luck, the locals changed similar sounding names to *taibe*, which means "good." All that was left for the settlers to do was to reverse the process. Although they assumed that they found the right spot, after years of further research the residents of Ofra (Elitzur among them) concluded that they were mistaken and that the biblical Ofra lies elsewhere. They treated the affair jokingly, never seriously considering a change in their settlement's name.

The one case in which the principle of not turning Judea and Samaria into a "Zionist cemetery" is consistently and systematically broken is in commemorating those killed in terrorist attacks. The National Naming Committee battles insistently against the settlers on this point with some success and frequent failures. A settlement by the name of El David was erected in the Judean desert to commemorate David Rosenfeld, murdered by Arabs when standing guard at a nearby archaeological site, and Eli Presman, who was killed in battle in Lebanon. The committee refused to accept this name, even though it had a biblical sound to it, because of the principle of fairness: why should one murdered Jew receive the honor of a settlement in his name and another one not? The committee suggested an alternative, Nokdim, meaning "shepherds," and the residents accepted willingly, sensing that it was a "correct" name for the region.

The settlement Beit Haggai was erected south of Hebron in memory of six yeshiva students killed in Hebron in 1980. In this unique case, the village was built by the friends of the victims; usually the burden of memory, especially when building a new settlement, is collectively shared. For the group of young yeshiva students, naming the settlement after their dead friends was only of secondary importance: they were willing to accept other options, but were eventually given a hilltop and an opportunity to pick a name of their choosing. The chosen name, Beit Haggai, is an acronym of the names of the murdered yeshiva students. The Naming Committee, however, refused to accept this decision and, after much deliberation, renamed the settlement as Haggai, after the biblical prophet. When asked, the residents of the settlement smile knowingly: they are all expert Bible students and, to the best of their knowledge, the prophet lived and acted in a different region altogether. Today the settlement is known as Beit Haggai, and its historical connotation is well known to the settlers in the region, though not to many other Israelis. In this case, it was the history of the settlement project itself that was engraved on the map of Judea and Samaria.

The struggle to name places accompanies the act of settlement in its attempt to appropriate the land; it is, however, sometimes turned against the settlement project itself. Yoel Elitzur (1980b) was furious at the decision naming Efrat, a religious community in Gush Etzion: "We must find her real name and not confuse future generations with two versions of the land of Israel" (13). He presumes that the place has a *real* name—one that is revealed rather than decided. The case of Anatot near Jerusalem raises a more delicate issue. The name, chosen by the residents themselves, was declined by the Naming Committee, its proximity to an Arab village by the name of Anata notwithstanding. The committee suggested the name Almon. Anatot was preferred by the residents because it was the birthplace of the prophet Jeremiah. To their frustration, Gush Emunim leaders agreed with the Naming Committee and left the residents to fight on their own. This case raises questions regarding the inner contradictions of radical fundamentalism: who is more *radical* (meaning "going to the radices," the root of the matter) and who is more *fundamentalist* (meaning "returning to the fundamentals")—those who want to live in the town of the great prophet or those who insist on the town's being built in the what they consider right place? The residents, however, continue to call their place Anatot, ignoring the decisions of the formal national organizations.

The Naming Committee decided to call the settlement known as Neve Tzuf by the name Halamish. This time, the residents insisted on Neve Tzuf, and the settlers' leadership backed them against the authorities. Yoel Elitzur (1985) supported their cause: "Halamish is a historical name; a city by that name existed in Talmudic times in the Bashan [. . .] and it will be a pity not to renew it in its original place" (22). However, to do so, Israel would have to occupy Syria, where ancient Halamish once stood. Elitzur's words cannot be interpreted as a suggestion to declare war immediately against neighboring countries to fill the holes in the settler's born-again map, but it does allude to their long-term objective and hints at the possible meaning of full redemption.

THE SEMIOTICS OF SETTLEMENT AND OCCUPATION

After discussing how settlements are named, let us examine the appearance of Jewish settlements and their symbolic import. The ideological settlement, usually set on a barren hill overlooking its surroundings, expresses messages both to their residents and to Palestinians and others who see them. Here I will propose a semiotic analysis of the settlement in its geographic context, referring and building upon the work of two Israeli architects, Eyal Weizman and Rafi Segal (2002),[6] who presented their insights in an exposition in a museum in Vienna (May 2002) and in an exhibition in Berlin (July 2002).

Settlements have a typical life span and are often personified in the settlers' discourse as human beings, growing from childhood to adulthood (in the settlers' concept of the settlement life span, death is not a viable option). Some of the settlements arise by government decision, whereas others start as nonauthorized outposts that gradually receive legitimation and become institutionalized. Although the houses are complete in some settlements before the residents enter, in most—86 percent of the settlements of Judea and Samaria—a temporary camp precedes construction. The future residents live at the new site in various types of shelters, including old Jordanian houses, army barracks, old police stations or, most often, mobile homes. The erection of a temporary settlement pressures the government either to authorize the deed or to hasten construction work. The temporary settlement serves important political functions and is usually not dismantled when the fixed settlement is established, but used for public institutions or to absorb new families. Some of the mobile homes are moved to the next settlement site.

The temporary mobile home became an important symbol embodying the nature of the Gush Emunim project, especially the idea of the movement as an avant-garde moving from one hill to the next. The mobile-home outpost communicates anxious temporality: it is under the threat of eviction by the Israeli army in case of a government negative decision and is a prelude to the village that will soon be established on roughly the same spot, freeing the mobile home for further use in the next outpost. Caravans star in the lore of the settlers as a sign of pioneering bravery and commitment (Shvut 2002a): "Families who have left large apartments in the city resided in one room or shack of 12 square meters, without an indoor toilet, without running water, without a stable supply of electricity, without a grocery store" (176).

Settlements—with the possible exclusion of the very first ones—are built according to similar principles and share certain visual features. Looking at a photo, it is difficult to establish in what settlement the photo has been taken. The settlement sticks out of its environment, usually as a human presence within a desert or among barren hills, or as a regimented structure adjacent to scattered Palestinian houses. The settlements bring a novel, highly modernistic architectural element to the region in which they are located. While their names declare their commitment to the biblical tradition, their construction certainly does not.[7]

Gush Emunim settlements are usually located on high ground, overlooking their surroundings. The land traditionally occupied and cultivated by the Palestinians was mainly in the valleys, and, as there was no organized land register for the area, Israel claimed legitimate rights to confiscate uncultivated land. The result was that the West Bank was divided vertically, with the hilltops virtually annexed by Israel, while the lower areas remained in Palestinian hands. This meant that the settlements were isolated from one another, and Jewish regions could usually not be formed contiguously. It also meant that the presence of the settlements arrested any possibility of creating a continuous and contiguous Palestinian space, and thus, as some commentators claim, a viable Palestinian state.

As a natural element, the hilltops have determined much of the settlements' architectural designs. The settlements are built in concentric rings—round or elliptical—following the topographic contours of the specific hill chosen. The lots for residential buildings are of equal size and located in long chains on the perimeter, in a sense protecting the public buildings in the middle on the hilltops. Basically, the settlements strive for a perfect circle, but due to the restraints of the specific sites, both in terms of available land and the morphological contour, the result, as Weizman and Segal (2002) conclude, is an arbitrary "anti-form." However, in comparison to the Palestinian villages and refugee camps, the structure of the settlements is clearly visible and extremely regimented.

The concentric roads create, in a sense, a fortress atop a hill, not unlike the Crusader fortresses nearby. The organizing social principle of the *communal village,* including a long acceptance process that ensures that those who join will be socially similar to those already within, strengthens the enclave nature of the settlement. Weizman and Segal (2002) define the settlement contours as an architecture of claustrophobia. The gaze of the residents living in the perimeter houses (which applies to most homes) is directed two ways: outward and inward. Both gazes reflect the need to guard the settlement against its hostile environment and strengthen the image of a fortress. The gaze is also a means of controlling the Arab activity of the lower lands. Weizman and Segal, who define the settlements as optical devices, express this notion: "The fantasy of the private home serves the urge for military control, and the simple act of homeyness, wrapped in a cosmetic mask of red roofs and green lawns complies with the geopolitical goals of territorial control" (51).

Until recent years, many of the settlements, for ideological reasons, had no fence around them; the settlers claim that it is the Palestinians who should be behind fences, and a fence is an articulation of the boundaries of Jewish presence on the land—one that the settlers are reluctant to make. Choosing to live in places that interrupt Palestinian space leaves the settlers extremely vulnerable to enemy infiltration, and settlers have often been killed in their homes. Since the defense of the settlements is not based on walls, fences, and other physical obstacles, they must rely on the gaze—on the ability to use the higher ground to see attackers from a distance.[8] Some of the violence against the Palestinians, perpetrated either by the army or by the settlers themselves, are meant to create an unobstructed view from the vantage point of the settlements or the roads leading to them.

The chain of settlements located on the highest hilltops also creates an unobstructed line of vision between one another. The mutual gaze can be understood as an additional way of watching each other's back, but it also supports the comforting notion that they are not alone. What was said before about the symbolic relations between Judea and Samaria and the Israeli Coastal Plain applies here as well—the settlements hold the geographic high ground over the Palestinians, which can be understood as metaphorically pointing to the moral high ground.

The landscape seen from the windows and balconies in the settlement homes is not only beautiful, but also reflects the complex, dialectical situation in which the settlers find themselves in their secluded enclaves. From many of their homes, the settlers have a panoramic view of what they define as the Land of the Bible, the reason for their arrival. The pastoral view of olive trees and stone buildings is marketed and commodified in attempts to sell houses in the settlements, but is highly dependent on the Palestinians remaining inside the orientalist haven created for them. Once the danger of uprising and terrorism grows immanent, the pastoral landscape becomes sinister. The olive trees can be either part of the pastoral biblical scenery and, hence, a precious resource, or a hideout for terrorists and, as such, a liability that must to be removed. As long as the Palestinians are too weak or disinclined to object, without a political will of their own, they are part of the landscape. Once they object to remaining an inanimate part of the scenery, the harmonic picture is transformed. Instead of being viewed for aesthetic pleasure, they are seen as gazing back, as a menace that one must guard against.

The settlement is placed within a certain environment that is viewed dialectically: on the one hand, it is the "right" landscape for those who want to return to the biblical world, whereas, on the other, it is dangerous enemy terrain that must be conquered and civilized. The same can be said of the physical landscape of the desert or the barren hills that surround the settlements. The settlements express the return to antiquity, but they themselves harm the environment, cut roads through the pristine landscape, and defile the virgin image forever.[9] The settlers are therefore entangled within an ironic paradox of authenticity: the closer they get to the authentic, the more they participate in ruining it and substituting it with the contours of the modern Israel from which they retreated. The illusive Land of the Bible always eludes their grasp.[10]

The settlers conceive of their settlements as utopic enclaves or islands in a hostile environment. As they proudly display and present their villages, the gate is hailed as a locus of cognitive and esthetic transformation, as a switch from the dangerous to the safe, from the desecrated to the pure, from wilderness to culture and cultivation. Witness this example of the coupling of aesthetic beauty with a communal utopia and a sense of time standing still:

> As we rise and approach Yitzhar, the air becomes clear. You reach the roof of the world and you imagine yourself in another place and time: young women walking barefoot [. . .]. Near the buildings that the Nahal [army unit] has left, there is extravagant gardening in an array of colors, and young men are still hoeing and pruning even if the clock hands show that work time ended long ago and it's time to be with the family.[11]

Such descriptions appeared in numerous settler publications, expressing what, to the mind of Gush Emunim activists, was their greatest success. It is a paradoxical success because it negates the concept of returning to the Land of the Bible and presents the area outside of the settlements as hostile and dangerous. The relation between the secure inside and the feared, yet desired, outside is an important focus in settler discourse. They are challenged to break free of their own creations—the Jewish enclaves in which they feel comfortable and relatively safe—and to impose these same principles on the entire space around them, be it the occupied territories or Israeli society. Their success in constructing the settlements led to a vested interest in keeping and guarding what they achieved, and they are troubled with the prospect of having to settle for partial redemption. I next discuss one practice of displaying sovereignty over the outside—the political march—whereas in the subsequent chapters I discuss several other strategies, such as the hike or the illegal outpost.

THE POLITICAL MARCH AS PILGRIMAGE

One of the best-known and most popular of the settlers' strategies is the political march. These marches take place on certain dates in the settlers' calendar, on national holidays (for example, Sukkoth and Independence Day) and local holidays (for example, Samaria March and Hebron Day), as well as special walks to certain places under current political debate. This demonstration march has a certain pattern: whenever possible, there are several routes—among others, normally one for families and one for competitive sports; on the road, there are locations where the marchers can find information and guidance; at the point of arrival, a rally takes place, including speeches and an artistic performance; hiking, sightseeing, communal bonding, and political indoctrination are all combined. The marches attract families, yeshiva students, schoolchildren, and youth movement members, and it is an opportunity for secular right-wingers to display their sympathy for the basically religious settlement project. The marches are not only political, they are also educational and good entertainment. Gershon Shafat (1995) wrote,

> [The aim of the marches] is to learn of a region that the hikers do not usually visit, to connect to the beautiful landscapes of our land, to crystallize young groups that will eventually create settlements, to display those who think of settling in Yesha, to show force against the government, to gain the sympathy of the general public for a positive enterprise that exemplifies the connection of the people to its land. Only those who walk in the marches can understand the great satisfaction felt by the marchers of all ages, among them old people and children and even babies in their strollers. (156)

One of the main differences between the settlers' marches and those of other political groups is that space and place are central to the political show of power. Unlike marches in cities—for example, by union workers—the settlers use the marches to establish their claim to contested territories. Their message is invariably the same: a certain place belongs to the people of Israel and should not be compromised. The marches express the idea that the true center of the land of Israel is in Yesha, and that the essence of Zionism is settlement of the land.

In this sense, the political march is a type of pilgrimage. Anthropologist Victor Turner (1978) expressed the idea behind pilgrimage as travel to the "center out there," the symbolic center outside of the everyday realms of life. The settlers' pilgrimage is meant to make the sacred center an everyday center—to converge the two centers—by creating a Jewish community on the spot or by strengthening the community that already lives there. The center of the pilgrimage is not, therefore, a single fixed "center out there," but rather a shifting reference point that gains its sacred status by displaying the essence of Zionism at that spot, in the form of Jews clinging admirably to their land against opposition. For the settlers, the place where the march is headed portrays Zionist values at their purest. In the Independence Day march to Gush Katif in the Gaza Strip (1994), the purpose presented in a pamphlet was "to see the implementation of the Zionist vision in agriculture, settlement, education and security, to gain encouragement and spiritual strength, to strengthen and be strengthened."

Because the "center out there" constantly shifts, the land in its entirety is consecrated. The actual place is, in a sense, arbitrary and conjectural: the settlers travel to a concept or idea of the true Zionist place—one that can be (and should be) located anywhere in the land of Israel. The pilgrimage travels in loops: Kiryat Arba settlers would march to a place such as Nezarim in the Gaza Strip (when it still existed), and, on the following occasion, the residents of Nezarim would complement their friends and march to Kiryat Arba. The pilgrimage is thus detached from the specific place and demonstrates the idea that it is worth marching to the land of Israel in its entirety.

Because the destinations of the marches are the settlements, the walk is usually an uphill climb. Thus, marching to the settlements is an act of elevation, and the physical effort becomes a metaphor for the political one. The participants feel the strain and the thrill of the ascent from the valley, where they walk through Arab villages and through field, forests, and barren lands, up to the physical and symbolical peak, where Jewish presence and flourishing modern existence rule supreme. Through their march, the settlers symbolically reenact the essence of their national project: ascendance to true national and religious salvation.

The Dialectics of Settlement and Memory

Throughout the history of the Zionist project, success has brought about crises of ideology. Once the basic goals behind the great idea have been realized, the question of what comes next inevitably arises. Thus, after the emergence of the state, Zionism entered into a long crisis that continues to this day. New goals had to be formulated, and while their roots may be found in the Zionist ethos, they usually gained prominence as makeshift solutions sought to keep the Zionist flame burning. Post-Zionism was, in a sense, born the day that Zionism fulfilled its primal mission, which was the establishment of the Jewish state. The same can be said about the Kibbutz movement, whose crisis was far more severe. Once the kibbutz concept was fulfilled, the question of preserving the idea through different environmental changes arose, leading to a full-fledged crisis and the end of the classic kibbutz as a viable option in Israeli society.

Constructing settlements was the prime object of the Gush Emunim movement; once that mission is completed, or at least partially realized, the question of what comes next arises. The problem has not yet arisen in full force because the settlement project is young, constantly under attack, and understood as a project in perpetual construction, but, nonetheless, its newness is gone. Questions of institutionalization, battle fatigue, and the challenges that face the second generation are growing prominent. More importantly, the settlements are the implementation of a vision and a dream. What is to become of the ideology once it materializes in the actual world? Rabbi Shlomo Aviner (1980) has lamented the fate of the grand idea: "What has happened to Gush Emunim and to the redemption movement is what is described in *Orot HaTshuva* [a book by Rabbi Kook the Elder] about the great idea that descends from above in order to be implemented in reality, and in the process loses its beauty and is perceived in a petty, partial, and immature way . . . The body disguises the soul" (11).

The settlement project enters a new stage, in which it becomes a reality and bears its own developmental logic. For Gush Emunim leaders and activists, the dream has, at least partially, come true. Those who wanted Judea and Samaria to become the true home could see young children and, later, adults who know no home but the settlements. The continuous contention over the legitimacy and the very existence of the settlements, however, has accentuated their status as Israeli outposts on remote hills in hostile territory that are undergoing a process of growing Palestinization. The sense of home, so dear to the settlers, is compromised time and again. The questions that the settlers set out with still trouble them today: what does it mean to be at home, and how can such a feeling be created and sustained? I conclude with the words of a publicist who laments the problems of the settlers' home-creating strategies. In his mind, the settlers still have much to learn and a long way to go before they will create a feeling of home, and that process has little to do with the opposition against them (Sorek 1997):

> Our brothers, the veterans of the workers' settlement [meaning the kibbutz and moshav], who for years we have seen ourselves as following, developed a real relationship toward their plots (which they inherited from the Arabs). He who respects this world makes it his home. The result is an entire culture of Israeli romanticism whose songs we love to sing. Such songs have yet to issue from our midst. Because we believe in ideas, words, books, and ideologies, the little secrets that may be learned only from life itself, the quietude of village wisdom, the humble connection to nature and unarticulated life—all these we have yet to learn, and all these are part of settlement, which means the return to the land in the most basic way. (74)

The creation of the settlements as havens is one challenge facing the settlers. Keeping in touch with the rest of their surroundings, where Palestinian towns and refugee camps dominate the landscape, is a further challenge. The strategies of symbolically appropriating the land is the subject of the next chapter.

4

"Our Forefathers' Footsteps"

Studying the Land

The Truth That Lies Beneath

The Gush Emunim settlers are convinced of what their sacred texts teach them: that the territories where they live are the eternal possession of the Jewish people and belong to them and them alone. When they look at the terrain around them, however, the landscape they encounter is problematic. While the barren hills, traditional (Arab) villages, and olive trees are images that they can cherish and appreciate as biblical landscape, Arab cities and towns, refugee camps, and even Israeli army barracks deface the biblical image. The settlers search for strategies to bypass the semiotic elements that are, from their perspective, difficult to digest, in order to experience a land with which they can identify completely. They want to construct a gaze that will pierce the alien landscape and cement their desired bond with their ancient forefathers.

This problematic of connecting to the essential land beneath the unassuming surface has a long history in Zionism. The Zionist movement has struggled to appropriate the land symbolically, devising various strategies for endearing the land to the people. Although the Zionists were certain that the land justly belongs to them, they still had to create a sense of homecoming among masses of immigrants and instill love for the homeland among the young. This was done through a set of practices, among them archaeology, hiking, folk songs, and board games, to name a few.[1] The Gush Emunim settlers took after the Zionist tradition and tried to adapt these practices to new spaces.

The religious settlers, however, encounter two problems that their predecessors did not. First, in a period that some call post-Zionist, and most will agree is postideological, many practices have lost their nationalist significance. Archaeology has lost its former magic, and Israelis have abandoned the educational hikes. Israeli folk songs remain popular, but few written anymore connect the people to the land. Board games, which enabled children to "walk" the land, were replaced by other alternatives and eventually by computer games. The settlers thus appropriate practices that for most Israelis have long lost their charm and persuasiveness.

Second, for most Israelis, the status of the territories where these practices are applied is ambivalent. The Israeli peace camp favors separation and withdrawal and resists attempts by the settlers to endear to the Israeli public what they see as occupied territories. Others might agree that Israel should keep the territories, but feel that, given the presence of millions of Palestinians, a process of cultural appropriation is inappropriate. Many feel threatened and even terrified by the masses of Palestinian Arabs and disenchanted by the barren hills. Altogether, Gush Emunim settlers find few clients excited by tours of Judea and Samaria; few parents outside of their camp are prepared to send their children on hikes to Hebron and Shechem, and meagerly few Israelis are eager to learn of new discoveries about the past of the contested regions.

In this chapter, I present and analyze the settlers' methods of transforming Judea and Samaria into the established Jewish homeland, not only for those who are already convinced, but also for the general Israeli public. The adoption of traditional Zionist practices by a religious fundamentalist movement arouses intriguing questions. Sometimes these practices initially have been declared by secular Zionists as substitutes for religious practices, whereas some of these practices embody secular reasoning in their essence. For example, archaeology was conceived by secular Zionism as a link to the ancient past, bypassing the religious implications of the biblical text. It is surprising that some of the leaders of Gush Emunim are among those who are most intensively and enthusiastically involved with such research to the point of establishing institutions to disseminate knowledge.

I present the practices of symbolic appropriation of the land used by the Gush Emunim settlers, concentrating on the most important one: biblical archaeology. I examine the adaptation of basically secular practices to a new religious context and conclude with a discussion of the functions such practices serve for the settlers. First, I shall show the nature of the phenomenon through an example taken from a town within the boundaries of pre-1967 Israel.

WHEN IS PURIM TO BE CELEBRATED?

In an article published in *Tehumin,* a journal of halakhic law, Rabbi Nathan Ortner (1988), the rabbi of the city of Lod, suggested a halakhic change that should apply to his city. He sought to establish in Lod the custom of reading the Scroll of Esther on the Jewish holiday of Purim on the fifteenth day of the Hebrew month of Adar, as is the practice in Jerusalem, rather than on the fourteenth of the month, as is practiced in the rest of the country (1). He claimed that Lod had existed on the same place since the days of Joshua, and thus, according to the Jewish law, Purim should be celebrated on the earlier date. This special occasion is called *Purim Demukaffin* or *Purim Dekrachin,* meaning "the Purim of cities encircled by walls." In support of his claim, Rabbi Ortner quoted Talmudic lists of cities that had been destroyed in ancient times, and noted that Lod was not mentioned among them. He used argumentation commonly accepted in rabbinic discourse and referred his readers to Holy Scriptures and the evidence presented by well-known rabbis.

Rabbi Ortner sent his conclusions to other known halakhic experts, including the two Israeli chief rabbis, but, although they commended him for his research, they were reluctant to grant him his wish.[2] They were, presumably, unwilling to sanction the claim that the modern city of Lod is a direct continuation of the ancient city. This meant that the residents of Lod, most of whom are secular, would celebrate one of the most popular national holidays on a day different than that of other Israelis (apart from those in Jerusalem).[3] But the rabbis were deterred by another issue: accepting the law would endorse the view that the Zionist return was, indeed, the true one and that the religious authorities should endorse the deeds of the secular state. That, however, was exactly the claim of Gush Emunim.

Yoel Elitzur (1988), lecturer at the Hebrew University and resident of the settlement of Ofra, added a very different voice, representing the logic of Gush Emunim. He is one of the most important among a group that I henceforth refer to as *settler-researchers.* In this case, he supported Rabbi Ortner in the same journal, yet used truth claims that were until then rarely found in religious writings in Israel. His article reviewed descriptions by Jewish, Muslim, and Christian pilgrims; he compiled a chronological history of the city; he scrutinized the archaeological evidence based on professional reports; and he supplied a map, something that the other rabbis did not imagine necessary, to show that modern

Lod indeed stands on the location of the ancient one. He did examine the halakhic stand and the claims of tradition, but only as part of broader research, and without rendering them privileged truth status as was common practice among university researchers. His concluding words returned to the religious discourse: "As discussant before sages, I am honored to submit this tract for the review of our rabbis who sit in judgment; from them shall go forth the Law" (380).

Elitzur's introduction of scientific methods into religious discourse is typical of Gush Emunim settlers' discourse and is a novelty, maybe even a revolution, in halakhic reasoning. When Rabbi Ortner (1988) ventured into historical and geographic reasoning, he pointed to the ancient graveyard in Lod as evidence for the ancient town's location in the same spot. He explained, "According to the *Hevra Kadisha,* who are experts in these things, the tombs belong to the age of the Amoraim" (342). In other words, he deferred to the religious authorities in charge of burial; clearly, he was either unfamiliar with secular archaeological research or considered it untrustworthy. The radical potential of Elitzur's suggestions is evident: in his mind, the religious authorities do not hold all or most of the relevant knowledge of the past, and secular historians and archaeologists could and should be trusted and consulted.

The question of the exact location of Lod is of great importance to Elitzur and his friends in Gush Emunim for religious as well as national reasons. Zionism is defined as the return to the land, and the placement of the land's boundaries and central locations are crucial issues for a credible act of return. The argument regarding the true date of Purim conceals a much deeper issue, which goes to the heart of the meaning of return. The celebration of Purim on the fourteenth of Adar is a day of remembrance, characterizing the Diaspora or exilic existence, whereas Purim of the fifteenth symbolizes the return to the cities of ancient days and the continuation of life within them. Elitzur (1988) notes in his article that "on the crest of Lod it is written 'and the sons shall return to within their borders.' These borders are not solely material borders; the return is also to the land of Israel and to its sanctity and precepts" (378).

While establishing the legitimacy of their own return, the Jewish settlers disqualify Palestinian claims based on the Palestinian protracted presence in the area. The case of Lod is representative. Although Lod was populated by Arabs prior to 1948, Elitzur (and the other rabbis) see that as irrelevant for the establishment of the city's present identity. Researchers like Elitzur do not disregard past or current Arab presence, and they even use their knowledge of it to reconstruct the map of the ancient land. However, in their view, Lod is an entity transcending its residents of whatever nationality or religious affiliation. What is true for Lod is no less true for other places in the whole land of Israel, including those beyond the Green Line: they are all considered to belong to the Jewish people by divine promise, regardless of the specifics of their history. Historian and Kiryat Arba resident Yosef Sharvit (1985) claims, for example that it is wrong to talk about the "Jewish quarter of Hebron," or a "Jewish quarter" in any other town in Israel for that matter, because Hebron is essentially Jewish even if most or all of its residents are not. The term "Jewish quarters" implies a limitation to Jewish existence on the land, which for Sharvit and his fellow settlers is unacceptable. Such a concept can exist only in exile, in places that are not inherently Jewish.

Researching the Land of the Bible

The return to the land of Israel, if done properly, entails a commitment to research that will link what is written in the Holy Scriptures with elements of reality from the close vicinity of the settlers. A small but important group of religious settlers engage in Land of Israel Studies, a combination of historical, archaeological, botanical, and zoological studies that uses the Bible as a starting point. Their main goal is to examine the biblical stories in their geographic and historical context; the result, as we have seen in the case of Elitzur's study of Lod, is a synthesis of secular and sacred bodies of knowledge. The logic underpinning these studies, like the logic of the entire settlement enterprise, stems from the perception of the Bible not only as a sacred text, but as a literally accurate history book. What is written in the Bible is seen to be true not only in the moral sense, which is self-evident for a religious community, but also on a purely factual level, as reliable evidence of actual events. From this standpoint, settlement and studies are two sides of the same coin, as both aim to create a tangible manifestation of the holy text in the daily life of the present. Furthermore, both aim at enriching the spiritual life of the believers through reaching and touching the lives of the ancient men and women who lived in the days of the Bible.

There is a radical, even revolutionary, element in the settlers' researching the Bible in its own context and tying it to the land on which its stories took place. The Jews are called the "People of the Book" and have survived through the ages with the sacred texts as their "movable territory." The revolutionary edge of settlers' research is therefore aimed not only or especially at secular Zionists, who have long accepted the Bible as foremost a secular history book, but mainly toward the traditional religious establishment. In Israel, ultra-Orthodox Jews (Haredim) rely solely on the texts and do not accept scientific methods that aim to establish the truthfulness of the biblical stories. They are engaged in a long and bitter struggle against the archaeology establishment over the issue of grave digging (Aronoff 1986; Weingrod 1995; Hallote and Joffe 2002).[4] For the rabbis of religious Zionism, the acceptance of secular sciences, with their potential for secularization, is a great challenge as the rabbis seek to synthesize the traditional and the modern. These rabbis have accepted and propagated the idea that the Bible grants them legitimate rights to the land; this, however, does not prove that the new settlements are the same as their biblical predecessors. Thus, for example, Rabbi Zalman Melamed rejected Yoel Elitzur's suggestion that Purim be celebrated for two days in Rabbi Melamed's settlement of Beit El, because he considered the assertion that modern Beit El is a direct continuation of ancient town as too radical.[5] This indicates how the rabbinical halakhic system, which resists scientific discovery, continues to exist alongside innovative views that combine Torah studies with secular science.

Rabbi Israel Ariel's two-volume atlas of the biblical borders of the land of Israel demonstrates the differences between the two rival types of knowledge. Rabbi Ariel can be placed strictly within the traditional rabbinical establishment, which takes exception to the settlers' research, although he zealously supports the settler cause. He defines the atlas he laboriously compiled as "research" and links it to the "heart's desire" of Rabbi Kook the Elder to see science studied inside the yeshiva. Rabbi Ariel (1988) criticizes secular scholars for minimizing the importance of the study of the land of Israel and claims that "the science of the land of Israel in general calls for new research from geographic, biblical, historical, archaeological and other angles" (12). He defines his sources as "tradition and Kabbalah, as they have been handed down from generation to generation." Ariel dismisses as "medieval alchemy" the accepted method of using Arabic village names to identify biblical sites. He thus thinly disguises both his disdain for modern scientific method and his reluctance to grant the slightest value to the Arab presence on the land of Israel. He does not reject archaeological findings in principle, but does not believe in their potential to produce new and relevant insights into biblical studies. He uses archaeology only when it supports the evidence brought by tradition or to provide illustrations in the margins of the atlas text. The spirit of today's critical archaeology, as discussed later in this chapter, is evidently unknown to him or alien to his thinking.

Researchers such as Elitzur and his friends function according to completely different assumptions. They use a combination of Jewish sources, archaeological findings, and the names of Arab villages to establish the identity of a site. They quote both halakhic and scientific sources, adopting the pattern of substantiation that is accepted in the academic world. Rabbi Ariel's concept is strictly hierarchical, with religious sources enjoying irrefutable credence, whereas the settler-researchers promote a critical dialogue among fields of knowledge that should, ideally, lead to harmonic unison. Indeed, Rabbi Ariel does not refer to their research findings and they rarely scrutinize his research.

Here we see a manifestation of the differing perceptions on the appropriation of the land. Rabbi Ariel and other traditional rabbis rely on divine promise and halakhic precepts in determining the rights of Jewish people to the land; in this, they have unquestioned authority over the camp of believers. The national religious camp, however, has one leg planted firmly in the modern, scientific, and technological world, and the advantages of scientific reasoning are well known to them. As religious observers, the new researchers accept the halakhic reasoning without question, but also try to find proof of the ancient existence of Jews on the land from other sources. This is a development of great importance to religious thinking, but it also holds great significance with regard to possible dialogue with the secular world. Whereas the rabbinical apparatus is closed to secular Israelis, the researchers use explanations that resonate more among the secular public and are linked to established Zionist methods of land appropriation. The researchers' links to fields of secular knowledge make them much more sensitive to changes in discursive patterns in Israel and give them some say in the state educational system and school curriculum, especially with regard to Bible studies. The use of modern Western sciences to underpin claims to the land is an expression of the perceptual revolution that produced the Gush Emunim movement, which is directed both toward secular Israelis and toward traditional halakhic Judaism. To be sure, this by no means entails their acceptance by left-wing secular Israelis, but it does make the challenge more intense—perhaps more threatening—to those who criticize the movement from the perspective of Western rationalist thought.

A SYSTEM OF RESEARCH AND TEACHING

The field of Land of Israel research has developed its own houses of study outside the yeshivas. Seminaries (*midrashot*) aimed at promoting research of, and hiking within, areas within Judea, Samaria, and the Gaza Strip have been established in numerous settlements, such as Kedumim, Kfar Etzion, and Kiryat Arba. Field schools, affiliated with the National Association for the Protection of Nature, were founded in Ofra, Susia, Alon Moreh, and other settlements. This entire system is completely state and public run, and, from the administrative aspect, is part of a national network of institutes promoting knowledge of the country's geography and rendering services to schools on field trips. The system gained momentum during Zvulun Hammer's term as minister of education. As a member of the National Religious Party, he was sympathetic to the project and appointed Yohanan Frid, a Gush Emunim founder, as commissioner (see Sprinzak 1991, 134). Past heads of these institutes included some of the best-known settler leaders: Hanan Porat of Kfar Etzion, Yoel Bin-Nun of Ofra, and Noam Arnon of Kiryat Arba.

Like the parallel academic knowledge system, the Land of Israel Studies is based on a hierarchy of producers and consumers of knowledge. At the apex of the pyramid are a number of esteemed researchers who combine a thorough knowledge of academic and religious sources, and are usually also innovative entrepreneurs. They compile the body of knowledge and establish the institutions that develop and disseminate it. Some of the researchers study in university departments, whereas others come from the benches of the yeshivas, but usually both will have extensive knowledge in both fields of knowledge. Centers of study are formed around seminaries or field schools in the major ideological settlements. In an introduction to one of the numerous collections of articles published by the settler-researchers, Ze'ev (Zabo) Erlich (1985) wrote, "The authors of these articles are all residents of Ofra, the first Jewish settlement in the area, now celebrating its tenth anniversary. The authors maintain a network of open discussions and extensive commentary on various topics. They constitute a sort of open seminary for sharing ideas" (5).

Further down in the system are the field school and seminary teachers and guides, who learn the knowledge, master it, and pass it on to the numerous groups that arrive at the settlements. Much of the guidance and teaching activity falls on the shoulders of young women of the National

Service (an alternative to military duty for religious women), who are trained within the system itself. All of the top researchers are men—a sign of the gender differentiation within the national religious intellectual elite.[6]

Israeli schoolchildren of all age groups are the main target audience for these institutions. After the First Intifada broke out, the circle of participants dwindled down to the religious school children and finally to the children of the settlements themselves. Another group of consumers are religious adults from within and outside the settlements, who come to spend the Shabbat in an atmosphere of study that includes lectures and hiking. The activities of the system combine the dissemination of knowledge with the declaration on the part of the consumers that they are committed to the ideology that the teachers represent.

Adopting Biblical Archaeology

The researchers' expertise is interdisciplinary, while maintaining a unique link to biblical archaeology. The settler-researchers follow the discoveries of professional archaeologists with great interest and use their findings in their attempts to decipher the connection between the terrain and the sacred texts. They do not maintain an actual intellectual dialogue with Israeli professional archaeologists, as the academic experts do not appreciate the settler-researchers' interpretations, to say the least. Their research parallels that of established science and selectively adopts its findings while maintaining a critical distance from it. They have no desire to replace the professional practitioners, and, since they have no academic credentials, they are not allowed to conduct excavations; instead, they wish to direct Israeli archaeology informally toward assuming the role that they feel is its essence—proving the biblical claims of truth and illuminating the historical and geographic context of the Bible's stories. Hence, they may sometimes suggest excavating in localities mentioned in the Bible or protest the lack of research on sites they deem important.

The settlers' interest in biblical archaeology should be understood against the backdrop of the general Israeli interest—some would say, obsession—in the early years of the state. During the 1950s and 1960s, biblical archaeology was considered part of Israel's "civil religion" (Liebman and Don-Yehiya 1983) and was even portrayed as the "national pastime" of the newly established state. Excavations of Hazor, Masada, and the Judean desert caves were headline news events; professional archaeologists, most notably Yigael Yadin, became culture heroes; academic conferences of the Israel Exploration Society attracted audiences of thousands, among them top political leaders; and coins, stamps, and other national symbols expressed the national interest in the field.[7] However, by the 1970s the popular enthusiasm for archaeology declined, and today few nonarchaeologists follow new developments in the field with interest.

Most important, professional archaeology in Israel is in the process of constructing a historical narrative incongruent with the one portrayed by Zionism and radically different from that suggested by Gush Emunim settlers. The historical narrative accepted uncritically by Zionist ideology was taken from the Bible: the Israelite tribes conquered the land of Canaan and established a unified kingdom that survived until it was divided into two kingdoms. This story was not only taught in Bible lessons in the Israeli education system, but also in history lessons, as an undeniable truth. Gush Emunim, as a religious and nationalistic movement, took this historical narrative to be self-evident.

Professional biblical archaeologists in Israel and abroad, however, were quick to spot that excavation evidence does not agree with the biblical story.[8] In fact, even the so-called national archaeologists, such as Yigeal Yadin and Yohanan Aharoni, cast doubts on the biblical narrative. By now, hardly a single professional archaeologist accepts the biblical narrative regarding the beginning of Israelite presence in the land of Israel as reflecting actual historical occurrences. Thus, for example, it was found that the stories describing Joshua's conquest of the land could not possibly be true. Time differences exist between the destruction of various ancient towns, whereas some of the towns described in Joshua were not inhabited when Joshua was to have roamed the land. From a different angle, excavations have revealed evidence of massive Egyptian presence in the land of Canaan at that time, something not mentioned in the Bible. In other words, while it was expected that biblical archaeology would prove the truth of the biblical stories for the benefit of the Zionist narrative, in actual fact it undermined them. For this and other reasons, professional archaeologists either withdrew or were gradually demoted from their high national status.

Moreover, beginning in the late 1970s, Israeli social and humanistic sciences developed a critical view toward the national endeavor. The so-called new historians questioned the validity of other parts of the Zionist narrative, as did critical sociologists (Pappe 1995; Ram 1995; Silberstein 1999; Nimni 2003). An integral part of the criticism of the Zionist narrative was the claim that the sciences were applied for nationalist purposes, thereby compromising, even betraying, their social and moral calling. By the time of the appearance of Gush Emunim, Israeli sciences were unwilling to be dragged uncritically into national projects, let alone by an ultranationalist religious group.

The settler-researchers found themselves, to their sorrow and anger, faced with an academic world that refused to accept their scientific agenda or give credence to their interpretations. The settler's interest in biblical archaeology arose decades after the waning of Israeli mass interest in the subject. One can see their interest as mimicry, perhaps the adaptation of a successful nation-building practice and its reapplication on new terrain. The settlers' use of biblical archaeology, like other Zionist practices, serves to neutralize criticism against them, because they claim that there is in fact no difference between the deeds of the Gush Emunim settlers and those of the first Zionist colonizers. Another explanation for the reappearance of archaeology as a nationalist practice is in the similarity of situations. Whenever a new community tries to establish itself in a land already occupied by others, issues of legitimacy entail, and archaeology can help in constructing a useful past. Following this logic, the fact that Israelis in general stopped relying on archaeology to strengthen their sense of home may mean that they have reached a certain comfort and security in their feeling of belonging—one that the Gush Emunim settlers are still struggling to achieve.

The similarities between past Zionist interest in digging the land and today's Gush Emunim settlers' interest are, however, misleading. One difference has to do with the meaning of redemption and return. Zionism of earlier times was conceived as a return of the Jews to the land of Israel *in general,* not to any specific place. Zionist settlement efforts were invested in sites not occupied by Arabs, sometimes outside the boundaries of the historical or halakhic land of Israel. Sacred places, such as Hebron and Shechem, were neglected by Zionist Jews during the first stages of their colonization project. Gush Emunim, on the other hand, aims to return the people of Israel to *The Place*—Judea and Samaria— where the mythic history of the people began. Consequently, the general national movement was interested in biblical archaeology, or "Jewish archaeology," as such. The places it excavated and studied were not necessarily associated with the mythic cradle of the nation, though Jewish themes were usually preferred. The settlers, on the other hand, are interested in biblical archaeology in its strict sense: uncovering the truth of the Bible itself, in the places where the most dramatic biblical events occurred and in locations contested directly and bitterly with Palestinian Arabs.

Another basic difference has to do with the function of archaeology in Israeli civil religion. Before and during the early years of the state, archaeology was seen as a kind of substitute for religion. Historical roots in the land, discovered by a scientific discipline, were conceived as replacing the divine promise to the chosen people and thus supporting the Zionist project. In the eyes of the religious settlers, archaeology has a radically different use. For them, it serves to enhance their religious beliefs and their force. They adopt a secular-scientific practice to battle the secularization process, not to find their place within it.

During the early years of the state, national archaeology can be seen as an uneasy and fragile alliance between a disciplinary science and a national movement. Archaeologists rarely compromised their professional ethics, nor were they specifically asked to do so (A. Elon 1994, but see Ben-Yehuda 2001). While national leaders such as David Ben-Gurion (the first prime minister) and Yitzhak Ben-Zvi (the second president) eagerly asserted that archaeology proves Zionist claims to be true, they did not intervene in the actual research programs of the profession, nor could they explain in what way pottery or human bones found in excavations proved the Israeli cause.[9] For the Gush Emunim settlers, who usually have no strong disciplinary background, nationalism and archaeology are tightly connected, and the digging into the relevant past to strengthen present national identity is much more pronounced. For them, archaeology has a mission, which is nationalistic and romantic rather than academic. Gush Emunim's interest in archaeology is limited to *scriptural fundamentalism*, namely, proving the biblical truth claims, finding the exact spots on the map mentioned in the holy text, and understanding phenomena that are described there in their geographic context. Their "science" is contextual and pragmatic, searching for specific answers to questions originating from their particular religious worldview. Hence, they have little interest in other fields of archaeology (prehistoric, for example) or in the archaeology of other regions, ethnic groups, and religions.

The Zionist movement, and later the State of Israel, had much to gain from autonomous archaeologists enjoying high esteem in the academic world. A national movement takes pride in the "genius" of its people, and such respect cannot be achieved under terms of a totally controlled science. For archaeology to be able to play a national role, it had to be presented as impartial and professional. This is not the case with the settlers' research. They do not belong to an international network of practitioners, and their research has a much more limited scope. They try to find scientific proof for the truth claims of the Bible and want to impress Israel's professional archaeologists with their case. However, Israel's academic world is only the sideshow: the real clients for this type of archaeology are the Israeli general public and the settler community itself.

Israeli historian Ya'akov Shavit (1997) differentiated between "greater" and "lesser" archaeology. He claimed, "In Israel (and elsewhere) . . . 'archaeology' never meant only sites, ruins, or the various material findings. It meant 'greater archaeology': an archaeology that renders new pictures of the past, a new concept, and a new narrative of history" (51). Professional archaeology, however, soon retreated into specialized institutions and concentrated on "lesser archaeology," namely, the demands and limits of its academic field. As such, it developed, or at least suggested, a critical perspective toward the very founding myths of the Zionist narrative, which it helped to establish at an earlier phase. Gush Emunim settlers are interested solely in "greater archaeology," and the profession as such does not interest them much. They wish to "de-professionalize" Israeli archaeology or, in other words, to detach it from its universalistic pretenses and reconnect it to the nation-building process. In their mind, this fully accords with strict scientific ethics because it will move the discipline closer to fulfilling its real calling, which is uncovering the truth.

The Feeling of the Land

Israeli archaeology is not the only role model for the settlers' research: the settlers with a penchant for biblical archaeology identify most profoundly with the Protestant researchers who traveled through the land in the nineteenth and early twentieth centuries, Bible in hand, in an effort to identify biblical sites.[10] For these researchers, as for the settlers, archaeology is a mystical experience of great emotional intensity. Living in the Land of the Bible, with an awareness of the ancient Jewish life that once existed in that very same place, and with findings sand artifacts from ancient days within arm's reach, combine to create excitement and even exaltation.

The researchers "live" their field of research and "sense" whether their claims are correct. They travel its roads, see its sites, and combine the experience of daily life with research. In an anecdote told during a conference in 1993, Yoel Elitzur took the experiential component in research to its extreme: if one does not burst into tears, it is a sign that the place has been mistakenly identified.

> Here's a personal story . . . A few years ago I guided a group of hikers in Ein Giv, that is, Givon. I stood above the very deep excavation there and explained to the group what it was that I saw there . . . One girl sat alone, looking at me . . . I approached her, and she said, "You must know, I'm very disappointed; when your father guided here we all cried. He showed us and guided us at the Pool of Givon, told us how war develops, how we must be wary of it, and we discussed it" . . . Why can't I make people cry? . . . It has always been very difficult for me to be absolutely certain that I am actually standing next to the Pool of Givon.

Finding the inner truth of the territories is part and parcel of the existential project of the Gush Emunim supporters. They see themselves as moving to reside on holy ground, in conflict with the Arab population and their supporters within the Israeli society. Their true, and perhaps only, lasting coalition is with their mythical forefathers who walked the land in biblical times and left some traces there beneath the earth. Archaeology is thus an identity-forming practice par excellence.

ACTING AT THE EDGE OF THE ACADEMIA

Gush Emunim researchers found themselves in opposition to the academic establishment in Israel. Most Israeli archaeologists and historians wanted nothing to do with the newcomers and criticized their conferences and publications harshly. By their definition, the settlers' "science" was no more than ideology, thinly veiled with academic lingo. Asked to write a critique of a book of articles based on one of the conferences for the academic historical journal *Cathedra,* Mordechai Zelkin (1994), a professional historian stated, "The collection in question. . . . bears witness to a regrettable attempt to present the readers with a collection of scientific articles while concealing the tendency underpinning some of the articles and the entire editorial approach" (153).[11]

Settler-researchers have their own scores to settle with professional archaeologists and voice their claims in terms of professional academic ethics. They claim (most inaccurately) that academia readily trusts all kinds of ancient texts, such as the writings of Josephus Flavius, while disregarding the Bible as a sufficiently reliable historical document. According to them, archaeologists who deny biblical truth harm their own professional integrity. It is also claimed that many Israeli researchers avoid researching Judea and Samaria for political reasons and thus evade their national calling and miss an opportunity to make great discoveries. Although the settlers do not wish to appropriate the archaeological discourse from its established practitioners, they do argue that Israeli archaeology should redefine its goals and social position. They demand that the archaeologists return to their historical role of assisting the Zionist project in connecting people and land. In short, they suggest a "re-Zionization" of archaeology.

There is usually little, if any, dialogue between settlers and professional archaeologists. Encounters do occur when paths collide, especially during a high-profile excavation in a known site within the settlers' realm and whenever an institutional setting enables such encounters. The question of the altar at Mount Ebal near Shechem (Nablus) is a case in point. The professional archaeologist who conducted the excavation there, Adam Zertal from Haifa University, claimed that he had found an altar from the period of Joshua, whereas most Israeli archaeologists sharply criticized his interpretation (cf. Kempinski 1986 vs. Zertal 1986). The settlers, thrilled to find a professional archaeologist who concurred with their conceptions, backed Zertal wholeheartedly; in a sense, he became "their" archaeologist. He is invited to their conferences and treated with much respect as a cultural hero, somewhat like their own version of Yigael Yadin, the national archaeologist-hero of the 1950s and 1960s. The fact that most professional archaeologists go so far as to ridicule his interpretation only shows, in their mind, how prejudiced the establishment is against the settlers' worldview and against the "true" interests of the profession.

Yoel Bin-Nun accepts Zertal's claims and explains in detail why, according to biblical sources, the edifice found at Mount Ebal is indeed a Hebrew altar from the time of Joshua. Bin-Nun then has to contend with other findings discovered in the excavations, primarily the presence of the bones of animals whose use as offerings was prohibited by the Torah. Zertal, linking his research to current theories, claims that this indicates a link between the religion of Israel and the earlier Canaanite religions, thus implicitly challenging the religious dictum that the Torah was God-given. Bin-Nun does not accept this outright attack on the biblical narrative, especially when it appears in the writing of virtually the only archaeologist who may be linked with the settlers' cause. Bin-Nun

(1985) explains these findings in an alternative way, claiming that "there is insufficient basis here for such a far-reaching interpretation, that fallow-deer and roebucks were sacrificed at any time" (142).

Zertal's findings hold a central place in the promoted tour of the area of Shechem and are presented to visitors as proof of ancient Jewish presence and the truth of the biblical narrative. The findings are described in a guidebook published by the Samaria Seminary, and the tale of the discovery of the ancient altar is related as a story of adventure and religious revelation. The archaeologist becomes an epic hero:

> On the thirteenth of October 1983, most of the doubts in the logical heart of archaeologist Adam Zertal fell away . . . it is not completely clear what it was in the huge area that ignited his imagination . . . but his experienced eye picked up the fine, consistent note that made all the difference . . . Zertal: "I remember it as if it were only yesterday . . . suddenly the light broke forth . . . I immediately opened to the book of Leviticus where the altar was described." (Maudlinger 1987, 12–15)

The author goes on to discuss the significance of the discovery and expresses his disappointment with its critical reception and the mistaken impression it made in Israel and throughout the world: "The altar's features correspond exactly with the biblical passage's unique and specific description! The discovery of America and man's first step on the moon are nothing in comparison" (15).

The case of the altar on Mount Ebal was a dramatic example of the encounter between the settlers and established archaeology, which intensified once the settlers found a rare crack within the professional facade. Their success could be only partial because, as a professional archaeologist, Zertal was totally committed to the ethics of archaeological excavations and posed the settlers some tough questions.[12] Needless to say, his enthusiastic acceptance by the settlers did little to enhance Zertal's position or credibility among his fellow practitioners.

A more institutionalized setting for such encounters is the annual conferences on Judea and Samaria research that began in 1991 and continue to this day. These conferences are held at the College of Ariel, which is affiliated with Bar Ilan University. Ariel is a large settlement on the western slopes of the hills of Samaria, and the college caters to students in various fields of science from both the settlements and the wider region of the Coastal Plain, on the other side of the Green Line. The conferences are officially defined as part of a scientific discourse unrelated to political ideology. The organizers of the conferences have invariably preferred chairpersons who are well-known researchers unaffiliated with the settlers' political camp.

The conferences can be understood as part of a normalizing discourse that reproduces the basic assumption that Judea and Samaria are "neutral" regions whose investigation can be isolated from the political context. They promote their own banality, as merely "another regional conference" within the borders of Israel, where experts discuss questions of a purely academic nature. Publicist Meron Benvenisti (1992) commented critically in his article "The Wretchedness of Academia," "These 'innovations in research' do not address the issue of more than a million Palestinians among whom the scientific researchers have settled. The demography, economics, society, and political views of the Palestinians are irrelevant."

A large portion—more than half—of the conference is dedicated to natural sciences, such as the typical fauna of the region or the amount of rainfall on the slopes. A small part is dedicated to current political issues from an academic perspective. One or two sessions are dedicated to archaeology. The lecturers and the audience are mostly settlers, and occasionally amusing mistakes arise when the situation is not recognized as being basically a settlers' event, such as the geographer who decided to use the conference to present and develop his plan of dividing the region's airspace between El Al (Israel's national airline) and Air Palestine (still nonexistent). His listeners, mostly hard-core settlers who fight any attempt to share control over land or air with anyone, smiled at his squirming to explain to them the advantages in his thesis.

In another, much more telling, incident, two researchers, professors Israel Bartal and Yossi Ben-Artzi, refused an invitation to present papers at the conference, citing the location and goals of the event as the reason. Bartal and Ben-Artzi are central figures in research on the history of Zionism and of the settlement of the land of Israel (for example, as editors of the acclaimed historical journal *Cathedra*), and are well known and respected by the settler-researchers. Their refusal to enter into a dialogue with the settlers was interpreted by the hopeful newcomers as a slap in their face by the representatives of the Israeli scientific establishment. In their refusal, Bartal and Ben-Artzi expressed their opinion that science cannot be detached and isolated from the context in which it is produced and disseminated. College director Ya'akov Eshel (1992) published their refusal in *Nekuda,* claiming that they violated the principles of scientific ethics.

The levels of the lectures on archaeology are diverse: some are quite professional and would be accepted by other university conferences; others demonstrate enthusiastic attempts to force the archaeological evidence to comply with the Bible; and still others start from a question originating in the Bible and proceed examine it by using scientific tools. I will provide some examples of the last type, which is the trademark of settler research. Arye Burstein attempted to clarify patterns of tending vineyards in various regions and formed his question as follows: Where was the biblical vineyard of Navoth located—in Samaria or in the Jezreel Valley? Although his question was taken from the Bible, his answers relied on conventional scientific methods. Meir Bar Ilan searched the Bible and other ancient sources for the meaning of text he intended to present to the public: the motive for his search was to clarify the Torah portion written on the stones at Mount Ebal. He summed up a lecture presented in strict academic language with a phrase taken from halakhic discourse: "We may deduce from this: The writings in this chapter refer to curses and curses alone." Zabo Erlich used aerial photos, maps, and colorful arrows to analyze Joshua's entry into the land. He referred to principles of modern warfare and compared the biblical event to the battle of the Suez Canal in the Yom Kippur War.

The unique meaning of the researcher-settler enterprise was distinctly and dramatically expressed in Zabo Erlich's lecture at the 1995 conference at Ariel. Gabriel Barkai, a professional archaeologist from Tel Aviv University, chaired the session on ancient archaeology. Erlich lectured on the location of Gan Uza, mentioned in the Bible as the burial site of a number of kings from the House of David. He reviewed brief previous proposals for identification of the site, including that proposed by Barkai himself in a study published in the 1970s, and presented them on a map. Erlich found the proposals unsatisfactory and searched the Bible for additional clues. He combined the route taken by Saul in his pursuit of David with the path of the Holy Ark from Beit Ye'arim to Jerusalem—both stories that mention Gan Uza—and located what he claimed to be the exact point of intersection of the two paths—the valley of Hinnom in Jerusalem. His work was, in words taken from a previous gathering, "to lay out the biblical verse on the map."

At this stage, Erlich added to the analysis an unexpected dramatic surprise. *Voila,* at the precise point of intersection, Barkai himself had excavated a magnificent grave, but had interpreted his findings differently. Erlich summed up, "The geographic analysis that supplements the biblical analysis is further clarified and explained by the archaeological findings, which in our opinion were not interpreted in enough depth; they shed light on details hidden in the biblical text."[13]

The central figure in organizing these conferences is Zabo Erlich, and it was he who invited Barkai to chair that session in the first place. It was he who constructed the framework in which he compared his view to that of the professional archaeologist who sat next to him. Thus, before the eyes of the admiring settler-researchers, he contrasted two alternative approaches to the national role of archaeology in Israeli society. On one side sat a representative of professional archaeology who was out of touch with his real mission, which was the discovery of the biblical past and the active participation in appropriation of the land. His detachment from his true calling could be deduced from his incorrect identification of the tomb he had found. On the other side was the representative of the settler-researchers—he had adopted the findings from the excavations but set them in a new interpretive framework by using a careful reading of the biblical evidence. In this microencounter, set up by Erlich, the settlers' research was declared to be victorious. The professional archaeologist sat there quietly and somewhat amused; as he told me afterward, the lecture was most selective regarding evidence, and he did not consider it a threat to his professional reputation.

The Educational Hike: Learning How to See

In the previous chapter, I discussed the political march, where the settlers "climb" from hostile surroundings into their enclaves, thus demonstrating that they hold the higher moral ground. The educational hike does the opposite: one leaves the enclave in order to "dominate" space that is not under everyday Jewish rule. The hike is a visit to the land that lies outside the Jewish enclave, and it relies extensively on archaeological finds and insights. The expert settler-researchers mark spots, and the settler children, guided by adults, walk there to enhance their attachment to that spot and to the route that takes them there. Meanwhile, they make the statement that all the land is theirs. Anthropologist Robert Paine (1995b) joined the settlers in one of their guided walking expeditions and reported the following in his field notes:

> We stand on a Samarian hillside . . . Our guide is from a *yeshiva* . . . in Judea. What I see laid out in the landscape before me is, to my left and

along a stony elevation, an Israeli settlement of white cement bungalows with red-tilted roofs; and in a fold of the valley in front of me, a sprawling Palestinian village with its mosque.

I turn to listen to my guide. The landscape he "sees" apparently contains neither the settlement nor the village: what he is telling us to "see" is the site where Jeremiah was born and where the Maccabees—just across the valley before us—fought and defeated a Roman legion [*sic*]. In directing our eyes to these sites, he refers us to "over there, by that hip of boulders" and "beyond those gnarled trees"; neither village nor settlement are used as orientation points. (161)

Educational hiking is another popular secular Zionist practice that was appropriated by the settlers. Sociologist Saul Katz (1985) researched the hiking system developed by the Zionist community in Palestine during the 1920s. He remarked that the guide is defined as an educator, not as an entertainment agent; the guide initiated a process of deneutralization of the landscape; that is, its transformation through interpretation into a national landscape. The hike is supposed to create a quasi-religious experience, and the ideology that motivates the hikers is resocialization, in the sense of reowning something that was theirs all along. All these components are evident in the settlers' hikes, which, as mentioned before, are an integral part of the national Israeli system that preceded it.

There are, however, differences that entail from a religious group's use of a basically secular national practice. The hike, apart from being considered beneficial for the body and the spirit, a way of crystallizing (*gibbush*) a school class,[14] and a method of developing healthy national feeling, is seen as holding religious value, as a means to present the glory of God's creation to children. A booklet on the subject explains, "Human wonder brings man to heights of faith that may not be attainable without looking at nature" (168). This concept of uniting with nature reminds one somewhat of the Hasidic connection with the environment, but is basically far removed from most concepts of traditional Judaism. The Haredim (until very recently) would not go on hikes so not to waste study time. For the Gush Emunim settlers, as for the secular Zionists before them, the hike is an integral part of study, especially study of the Bible.

Teachers, guides, and students of the Gush Emunim camp appreciate the concept of the hike and present its importance as self-evident. To their mind, just as the chemistry teacher has a laboratory, so a Bible teacher should use the laboratory of the land of Israel. One of the teachers complained to me that few children outside of the settlers' realm use the unique opportunity provided by Israeli control of the biblical land in order to enrich their study:

> There is no doubt that education in the country today performs a momentous injustice. They teach children the Torah, especially in secular but also in religious schools. The first place they talk about is Shechem. Today it is a little difficult to get into Shechem, but reaching the view from Mount Grizim is easy and not dangerous. There we can show Shechem and explain where the historical event occurred. But they don't take them there, and the children think that it is somewhere beyond the mountains of darkness [. . .] Where else in the world is there a place where it is possible to have children who read the Bible visualize how it looks? Meanwhile, only our children are privileged.

What exactly is shown in such a trip overlooking Shechem? Currently, Shechem is a large Palestinian city whose residents prefer the name Nablus; the visiting children are required to look beyond the visible Nablus of the present and see the biblical Shechem of the past or maybe of the future. In any case, the hike removes the objects they encounter along the way from the present and constructs a way of seeing that points to a different reality, considered to be deeper and more inherently true. Extracting the sense of the authentic from the array of objects that are in the field of vision is the mark of a good guide, for the religious settlers as for anyone on a trip.

In an interview, one of the best-known guides explained this to me, reflecting Robert Paine's experience from a different perspective:

> I take the group on a hike and finish it in the vicinity of Anatot, and it doesn't matter if it is ten kilometers north or south [. . .] I stand there and I say, "Guys, now we are going to pray *mincha,* and, think about this, Jeremiah sometimes mentions the Temple and the afternoon ritual offerings [. . .] And now we're going to say this prayer, everyone to himself; just remember that the prophet Jeremiah lived around here." This is after a day in which they received intensive [classes on] Jeremiah and receive intensive [classes on] the desert. [. . .] The *mincha* prayer that day is totally different [. . .] He then feels that his great-grandfather, someone from his lineage, is praying with him.

Some motifs in this quotation merit attention. The guide does not know where exactly Anatot stood, but it does not matter to him. He produces the experience of praying with Jeremiah on whatever spot the group is in at that moment, as long as it is near enough to be credible. His ritual is not a special one in itself—it is the daily prayer of *mincha,* which he does not change. What he does is transform the experience of the known prayer through creating a new context. This is one example of the difference that Judea and Samaria makes in the everyday life of the observing Jew: it would seem that the daily prayers can be performed anywhere and that their substance does not change. Their sacred nature derives from their being eternal, above and beyond the specific context of their performance. Gush Emunim revives the ancient rituals through placing them in a historical and geographic setting.

Another motif worth noticing is how religiosity, nationalism, and science are all interwoven into one harmonic whole, and that learning about the desert is no different than studying Jeremiah. All learning concerning the land of Israel is sacred, and reading the Bible is also learning something relevant about the land. The group is integrated with the desert and with the prophet, and, in what may be considered more surprising, each individual is supposed to connect with his private ancestors, who in all probability lived in exile. In his prayer, the hiker represents generations of Jews who probably would have wanted to have this experience but were not fortunate enough.

In the quotation, we can also see the great importance of the guide in constructing this meaningful experience (albeit in an account supplied by the guide himself). On the ground are numerous elements that were not there in biblical times, and the guide's narrative has to recreate the biblical world in the minds of his group. In this respect, the Arab towns and the Jewish settlements pose similar problems: they were not there and therefore should not be seen during the hike. The hikers "cannot see" Arab Ramallah, because it was not there during the days of the Patriarchs. They also use the new Jewish settlements only for their facilities: when it comes to reproducing the biblical world in a hike, the current Beit El or Michmash cannot replace the ancient sites. The students, whether young children or adults, are requested to bracket the present and look for signs of the past. A good guide is supposed to be able to create such an experience, and an attentive body of students should comply and be emotionally affected.

Two more motifs should be mentioned with regard to the hikes. One is the unavoidable, and sometimes desirable, friction with the Arabs along the way. Like the Zionist hikes of the pre-state days, the hikes are a way of declaring ownership and a sense of home, which is, ideologically, a decree to venture into Arab space. Unlike other Israeli hikes, the physical challenge of long walks in dangerous terrain is somewhat subdued in the settlers' hikes, partly because the national content is deemed to be of greater importance than building the body. Walking through Palestinian villages, however, entails its own dangers. Although secular parents have severely criticized the educational school hikes, and taking physical risks is no longer accepted in Israeli hikes today, many parents of settler children unhesitantly accept that their children will march through the qasba of Hebron or the fields of a hostile village. Usually, mandatory armed escorts secure the hikes, but violent events have indeed occurred, with Jewish hikers injured or even killed. From my experience, there is a tension between the children, who want to vandalize Arab property along the route, and the guides and teachers, who, either for educational purposes or out of broader interests, try to restrain them.

Furthermore, whereas the guides and teachers use the hikes to reinforce educational values, the children have their own agendas, which include the release of school tension and harassing the teachers. Some children approach the hike with the solemn attitude expected of them, but others are more absorbed in playful relations with their friends. Beneath the formal world of the hike is an uncontrolled informal world. Although the settlers' educational system has obvious success in transmitting the values of Gush Emunim to the next generation, the second-generation settlers grow up to be somewhat different than their parents —much more adventurous and individualistic. I mention the results of the settler's educational practices in chapter 11, where I discuss the "youth of the hills."

OTHER USES OF THE LAND OF ISRAEL STUDIES SYSTEM

The settler-researchers supply the settlement project with sites and tracks for hiking, names for settlements, and other benefits. Conducting research, suggesting walking routes, and arguing with one another and with secular practitioners can be considered the occupation of an intellectual elite associated with the political elite of the settlers. Antonio Gramcsi (1971) remarked about the importance of "organic intellectuals" in the establishment of cultural hegemony, and the settler-researchers fulfill this role. The impact of this system, however, is not always apparent. For example, the "two Yoels," Elitzur and Bin-Nun, both who were residents of Ofra at the time, argued over the exact route of the Eastern Way mentioned in the Bible. Their debate occasionally appeared in publications and was mentioned in lectures, but most settlers paid little attention to this minute discussion; many never heard about it. Thus, we should examine the social role of the research project more closely.

The most obvious use for Land of Israel Studies is political argumentation. Although a broad group of experts may give presentations or lead hikes to practically any place in the contested territory (or any region in Israel, for that matter), there are specialized experts for each and every region. The researchers can suggest a seemingly endless supply of sites with some Jewish past awaiting its salvation through settlement. Each settlement in practice is always just a fraction of the full potential of locations awaiting Jewish return and revealed by the settler-researchers. When movement spokespersons present their case for a certain area, they are well acquainted with its geography and its place in Jewish history and tradition, and they can discuss the latest archaeological research conducted in the area. Land of Israel Studies can use the depth gained from scientific expertise to support the shallower political argument.

Here is one example: When former left-wing minister of education Shulamit Aloni claimed that the Tomb of Joseph was actually a relatively recent tomb of a local sheikh, the head of the council of Samaria, Benni Katzover, replied, "I have a more than a reasonable basis to assume that archaeologists have misled you, in view of the facts that I shall now disclose."[15] He went on to submit historical evidence for the antiquity of the site, based on the work of the settler-researchers. What he was claiming was that, contrary to the opinion of the minister of education, Jewish presence at the Tomb of Joseph is not an arbitrary abuse of Palestinian rights that is based on irrational religious beliefs, but a fulfillment of a Jewish right, well documented in historical records.[16]

The knowledge about possible sites for settlement has served the settlers well. Even before the establishment of first settlement, young Gush Emunim supporters went on field explorations, and some located spots for their future homes on those hikes. Ron Shechner, former head of the Mount of Hebron council, explains how he decided to locate his settlement, Beit Yatir: "One day I went hiking in the Mount of Hebron, and it hit me. . . . We saw Lutzifar fortress and we knew: this is the place where we shall live."[17]

However, more important than the practical uses of the accumulated research is its symbolic value. Archaeology and fundamentalism share a similar "metamessage": the truth sought does not lie on the surface. Beneath the visible landscape and sociodemographic realities lies a deeper, more genuine stratum. Archaeology, which brings the past to the surface and places it in a present-day framework, serves as a metaphor for the way fundamentalism relates to its environment. Through the use of archaeology, the settlers convey an important message both to Israeli society and to themselves: that the harsh realities of the present are a thin layer covering the great truths that connect the people to the land.

When we examine the practice and metaphor of archaeology, we see how it connects and disconnects the settlers from various real and imaginary groups. It creates a double connection: The first is with the mythic patriarchs and ancient kings, who left their remnants for them to be found; the other is with fellow Jews both in Israel and elsewhere, who share ownership of the same recovered past. On the other hand, digging deep—in a true or metaphorical sense—is a political statement of radical disengagement from the neighboring Palestinians, whose social landscape is thus defined as detached from the true nature of the sacred space. Through archaeology, the settlers define who they are and who they are not.

The first and foremost function of settler archaeology is to prove the privileged rights of the Jews as being first on the land, especially vis-à-vis the centuries-old Arab villages' claim to authenticity. A settler in Hebron told me why, to his mind, there is no basis for Palestinian archaeology: whenever an Arab lifts a stone, there is a Jewish stone laughing at him from beneath it. For him, this was ultimate proof, supporting the divine promise, that the land belongs to the people of Israel. His claim, however, was inaccurate. When Palestinian archaeology did emerge, it searched for ancient Canaanite culture in order to advance the narrative that, even in biblical times, the Palestinians were first on the land. Yasser Arafat even used his biblical knowledge to mock the Jewish historical narrative by claiming that, when the sons of Jacob went to Egypt, the Canaanites—in his terms, the Palestinians—chose to remain in the land of Canaan. The Palestinians learned the national use of archaeology and ancient texts from other national movements, especially (and explicitly) from Zionism. They could have easily learned it from their neighbors and enemies, the Jewish settlers nearby.

5

Hostile Visitors

The Palestinians in the Settlers' Worldview

ON BECOMING NATIVES

The overriding aim of the settlers is to be defined as *natives*—those who belong to the land and to whom it is nonreflexively taken for granted the land belongs. That is the how they understand their position, and their goal is to convince others that this is actually the case. However, in the eyes of many Israelis and most non-Israelis, the place already has its natives: namely, the Palestinian Arabs who have lived in "authentic" villages and towns there from time immemorial. The settlers' discursive strategy is therefore oriented simultaneously in two directions: to proclaim their position as representatives of Jewish memory and history in the place, and to explain and rationalize the symbolic (if not physical) dislocation of the Palestinians from that same place. This is a complicated task for numerous reasons, and here are two of the most important: First, the settlers, proud of their Western appearance, find it hard to evade the associations of their project with colonialism, considered a primeval crime. They look too modern to pass as natives, but are reluctant to efface their Western appearance and identity. Second, the settlers sympathize deeply with the symbolism of the traditional Arab villages. Walking the land, they see in the pastoral Arab presence a reminiscence of the biblical past they hold so dear.

I joined a group of settlers on one of their hikes across the fields of Samaria. I was following some young yeshiva students who were walking, chanting, and dancing when they came across an old Arab woman, dressed in her traditional attire, who was walking her donkey. One of them blocked her way and asked her whimsically, "For how much for your

112

vehicle?" while his friends laughed at his joke. The woman responded with a loud curse, well understood by the Jewish group. The yeshiva student halted in surprise and raised his hand to hit the woman, but his friends hastily stopped him. "Why did she say that?" he asked, partly in wonder, partly in complaint. "What did I do to her?" The event, however, was immediately forgotten by the cheerful group as they hurried on their way, and the woman continued walking her donkey.

Although one can debate endlessly whether the settlers should be defined as victimizers or victims, as colonialists or homecomers, this moment summons up past colonial situations. It is an expression of colonial power versus subaltern resistance, of Western condescension versus local pride—and the settlers' presence in the territories generates an endless flow of similar events. One of the strongest criticisms of the settlers is that, regardless of their own attitudes toward the Palestinians, their project raises the potential for immoral acts being perpetrated by the settlers themselves or by those expected to safeguard them.

We see that while the Jewish settlers and the Palestinians may—to the chagrin of both sides—share the same space, they do not share the same "place," and the logic of one place assumes the obliteration of the other. The young yeshiva student met the Arab woman in a pastoral landscape of plowed fields and vineyards. Beyond treating her as a national enemy, he regarded her as ludicrously primitive and defined the difference between them based on their technology—specifically, the kind of vehicle used. The national divide may have provoked his jesting—he would hardly have spoken that way to an old Jewish woman—but the content of the joke had more to do with tradition and modernity. He does not feel that he has an obligation to civilize the Arab woman, because she does not belong to his people, and, furthermore, her backwardness is politically convenient and in line with his cultural presuppositions. The national conflict appears in another form: the yeshiva student assumed that even if the woman did not accept his right to march through her village and fields, the power differential between them should have prevented her from reacting.

In the yeshiva student's mind, she was anchored in a passive role rooted in orientalism, traditionalism, and patriarchy, as well as occupation, all of which should have ensured her silent compliance. He himself was occupied with the dynamic and energetic actions of settlement, nation building, and self-redemption, which allowed him to march proudly through her village. While his time was progressing, hers was standing still. The docile oriental Arab had a place in the settlers' world, but the enraged, politically aware Palestinian woman had none.

To his surprise and dismay, the woman responded by talking back. He found his assumptions either wrong or obsolete: the woman had undergone "Palestinization" and encountered him in a basically symmetrical national conflict. With her symbolic gesture, she became like him: the Palestinian woman with the donkey became as much a symbol of national struggle as the Jewish settler with the gun.[1]

The symbolic conflict between the young settler and the Arab woman charges the encounter with deep meaning. The two debate definitions of authenticity and, hence, their respective rights to the land. The settlers claim that their rights are based on divine promise, a glorious history, and centuries of devotion, even if they no longer resemble the people of the Bible and did not physically reside on the land for the past two millennia. The Palestinians base their claim on their decades of residence, apparent in their houses, attire, and labor. The condescending jest of the young yeshiva student reveals a deep anxiety: The Arab woman is far more similar to the people of the Bible, and she uses the same means of transportation. The "joke," ironically, subverts the legitimacy of the settlers by stressing how far they have deviated from their biblical role models. To stretch the metaphor, as a symbol of ancient attachment to the land, what and how much are the Jewish settlers ready to pay for that donkey?

The encounter between the settler and the Arab woman was not supposed to become a dialogue, since dialogues between the settlers and their Palestinian neighbors are quite rare. Their "inside" joke was part of the juvenile group's overall victorious happy feeling derived from their victorious march. The response from the woman who was the object of the joke was unwarranted. Her reaction surprised the group, creating tension by undermining the boundaries of the exclusive discursive group: suddenly, an old Arab woman, uninvited to participate, had raised her voice, refusing to remain the passive object of others' jokes. It's no wonder that the other marchers intervened to pull their friend away from the encounter: they did not wish to engage in a meaningful discussion—even a violent one—with the woman because that might make her a subject whose comments were of consequence. By refraining from further interaction, they were, in a sense, implying that they did not notice the insult, or that an old Arab woman's words should not be taken seriously and, thus, that the traditional role of the old woman was as strong as ever. Walking on and swallowing the insult was the settlers' way, in this particular case, of preserving their discursive boundaries or, in other words, of conserving their right to discuss the future of the land and the fate of its inhabitants without the vocal participation of its Palestinian residents.

Most of the motifs in settlers' discourse about the Palestinians were apparent in this brief ethnographic episode. The presence of Palestinian Arabs on the contested territories and their insistence on their national rights are the most troubling issues that the settlers must address. The settlers can well explain the purpose of their own presence on the land, but the Palestinian presence is, in a sense, a mystery to them that calls for conjectures and theories. The previous chapter dealt with the elaborate research system examining the land and what lay beneath it. When it comes to understanding their Palestinian neighbors, it is safe to say that the settlers know very little of their neighbors' history, demographics, and aspirations, and substitute various beliefs and stereotypes for research. Time and again, they have expressed surprise when faced with Palestinian rage and searched for ways to comprehend it. In what follows, I present the various rationalizations that, in the eyes of the settlers, give meaning to the existence of uncompromising "others" on the land that is supposed to return to Jewish possession.

The Gush Emunim view of the Arabs has to respond to the ideological challenge, as well as to the practical problem of residing near a large, potentially or actually hostile population. It must be remembered that the settlers' discourse about the "proper" place of the Arab takes place within a violent context and has developed in response to hostile encounters in which settlers have killed and been killed. The discussion of the settlers' perspective, which accentuates the violence that they have absorbed, should not obscure the violence that the settlers have inflicted on their neighbors. Although I shall begin with the general concepts regarding the meaning of the presence of others on the Holy Land, I shall also present the actual violent relationship between the two conflicting groups that culminated in the years of the Second Intifada.

The Palestinians as the "Other" for Zionism and Gush Emunim

Gush Emunim's treatment of the Palestinians has to be understood against the backdrop of the Zionist relation to the Arabs over the years, which is itself based on Western images of the Orient. As stated before, the settlers have appropriated many of the symbols and values of secular Zionism as part of their religious ethos. The place of the Arab as the ultimate "other" was also adapted from secular Zionism, including some of the methods of either confronting or ignoring the intricate issues involved.[2] Basically, their situations were similar: communities of immigrants who moved to reside on a land inhabited by natives who violently resisted their arrival. Both the early Zionists and the Gush Emunim settlers may have had economic considerations that supported their move, but their settlements were primarily legitimated by an ideology of homecoming. Both came, according to their worldview, to what they considered an empty land or, rather, a land whose residents had no political rights and therefore little moral ground for objection to the act of homecoming. Both saw themselves as representing the values of the West in the East, of modernity in a traditional setting, while simultaneously criticizing the West for its decay and shallowness. And both had a commitment (albeit not the same one) to the Bible, which framed the meaning of return and the status of the local Arabs. It's little wonder that we find great similarities between the views of the Palestinian Arabs of Gush Emunim and the early Zionists.

However, there are also important differences. The context of the early twentieth century can hardly be compared with that of the late twentieth century. Early Zionists acted within the confines of Ottoman rule or the British Mandate, against an Arab community that enjoyed the same rights that they did, whereas Gush Emunim operates under the auspice of a Jewish state that rules contested territories. The settlement of Westerners among native people isn't accepted any longer by the international community as it was in the time of the early Zionists. The religious-messianic world of Gush Emunim was never part of the Zionist ethos, and biblical precepts, such as the obligation to settle everywhere on the land or to treat the Arabs as *gerim*—the halakhic term for "resident aliens"—was never seriously debated by Zionist leaders. Dov Schwartz (1997), a researcher with a National Religious ideology, wrote, "The intellectuals of religious Zionism seemingly had easy ideological work with respect to rights to the land. They did not need to employ apologetic tones, historical or political utilitarian, in presenting the crucial place of the land of Israel in Zionist action. The presence of the Arab people did not lead adherents of religious Zionism to doubt the sovereignty of the people on its land" (13). Perhaps most importantly, the secular Zionist movement and the liberal Israeli state could reach agreement and compromise with the Arabs nations and the Palestinians, including territorial concessions, whereas Gush Emunim, because of its political extremism and religious zealotry, could accept no compromise.

Over the years, a gradual process took place within the Israeli public in which the Arab gradually ceased to be the menacing other and became a partner in negotiation. This process was by no means unilinear, and the Second Intifada revived primeval fears. From a wide historical perspective, however, the menacing connotations of Arabs for Gush Emunim settlers grew just as the Arabs' threatening position was declining in the rest of Israeli society. Gush Emunim initiated its demonstrations against the Israeli government over the interim peace negotiations with Egypt and Syria, and continued to protest the attempts at reconciliation with the Palestinians. As the Arabs increasingly became possible negotiation partners for most Israelis, the Gush Emunim settlers did their utmost to perpetuate the Arabs' status as ultimate others. The settlers see their role as constantly reminding the Israeli public of the long history of the conflict by showing how menacing and hateful the Arabs actually are.

The Palestinian as an Authentic Primitive

Like the Zionist settlers that preceded them, the Gush Emunim settlers see no inherent conflict between themselves and the individual Arab, as long as he or she is not attached to a movement seeking national rights. They display examples of personal friendship and compassion. One of the first *Nekuda* issues displayed a picture of a settler helping an old blind Arab across a road. Elyakim Haetzni, one of the settlers' leaders from Kiryat Arba and a lawyer, helped individual Arabs deal with Israeli authorities. A resident of the Neve Tzuf settlement explains, "You can say that their [the Arabs'] lives have changed completely since we arrived, because their standard of living has risen substantially. They have never earned as much . . . Their mentality has changed, too: they dress differently, behave differently—our effect on them has been considerable" (Ben-Pazi 1988, 69).

In general, the settlers reproduced the old Zionist stand that has strong orientalist undertones—that the arrival of Jewish settlement benefits the Arab natives, so the natives should be thankful. According to the settlers, accepting and approving the Gush Emunim project are in the interest of the local Palestinians, primarily for economic reasons. Rabbi Zalman Melamed (1988) suggests a different concept: since the settlement is part of a divine process, objection is sacrilegious, and the

Muslims, who share the same God, should be the first to realize that. He says, "We must explain this to them. They must be partners in the redemption process of the people of Israel, not fight it. Quite the opposite, they bring disaster upon themselves through their current behavior; not physically, but mentally and morally" (11).

Accepting the Arabs is possible as long as they remain isolated individuals who do not demand national rights. For the Palestinians to remain so, it is preferable that they stay "simple" *fellahin* ("farmers"), as they presumably were for generations and as befits their nature. Their Palestinization—namely, their demand for political rights—counters the interests of the Jewish settlers, but also, as the settlers see it, counters their self-interest. From the settlers' perspective, it is not "natural"—let alone beneficial—for Arab villagers to align themselves with the national movement and rise up against the Jewish neighbors that bring prosperity to their villages. Often, when villagers become hostile, the settlers attribute the behavior to a small group of manipulative agitators who abuse the kind nature of the Arab *fellah* for political purposes. As a Jewish resident in the Muslim quarter of the Old City of Jerusalem explains, "When the agitation started, there was a change in their behavior. We feel they are possessed by hatred and depression. All at once they stopped meeting our eyes. They are easily agitated by the threatening force of a minority that overpowers them, they are frightened and hateful" (Ben-Pazi 1988, 109). Here, the orientalist concept of the childlike native with no will of its own is unmistakable.

Accordingly, Gush Emunim solutions for the conflict and their understanding of the status of local Arabs depoliticize and denationalize the Arabs. The Arabs may remain on the land for as long as they stay in their pristine "authentic" situation without objecting to the Judaization of the entire land. Gush Emunim has never openly resorted to the radical solutions of the extreme Right—the transfer of the Palestinians from the land—though doubtless many activists would not object to the implementation of a solution by ethnic cleansing. The typical Gush Emunim solution hints at the possibility of population transfer, not as a mass solution, but reserved only for those who refuse to accept Israeli presence and sovereignty; namely, the presumably relatively small and identifiable group of agitators. Rabbi Dan Be'ri (1985) suggests what he regards as autonomy, which includes the Palestinian citizens of the state: "We must clarify to them that while we have the power they will not receive any sovereignty in our land. Citizenship is for the sons of the Jewish nation alone: we should render them the status of *gerim,* autonomous as much as possible. If they display hostility—[we should] evict them from the land or fight them honorably." The halakhic term *gerim* suggests placing the Palestinians in a status conceived by religious rather than state law.

A children's book by Emuna Elon (1988) displays the relationship between a settler boy from "Ramat El" (a thin disguise for the author's settlement Beit El) and a Palestinian boy, Fatchi, from the refugee camp of "Jisafon" (Jilabun). The Jewish boy learns of the lifestyle of his friend and the history of his people, including the deportation from his former village, and they become friends in the shadow of the national conflict. The story ends with an ironic twist: the Arab child Fatchi, with the assistance of his Jewish friend, finds a treasure, which belonged to Fatchi's family, near the mosque in the former village where there is now a kibbutz. Unsurprisingly, the kibbutz members oppose the actions of the settlers and hold leftist views that morally contradict their residing in homes built on the ruins of an Arab village.

The Arab boy intends to use the money to build a better future for himself and his family outside of the land of Israel. Meanwhile, he lectures the kibbutz members: "Now I know that the Arabs have many lands and the Jews have only one land. Allah has created it for you. If we take this land—where will you go?" (82). The book is empathic toward the Arab boy (who has conveniently converted to Zionism) and proposes that the settlers learn their neighbors' culture and lifestyle. It concludes with a solution to the private problem of Fatchi and his family (emigration) while offering the Palestinians no collective solution.

The Arab boy's lecture exemplifies another important point: according to the settlers, deep in their heart the Arabs know that justice is with the Jews returning home. A boy from a refugee camp can tell the story to the guilt-stricken kibbutz members better than any representative of Gush Emunim. The reason why the Arabs know that which the Israelis are unsure of is that the Arabs have not been tainted and contaminated by modernity and secularization, and "simple" traditional people easily recognize the eternal truths of life and time. Whereas in Elon's story a boy holds this knowledge, usually the settlers attribute such understanding to old Arabs. A resident of Alon Shvut tells of a young Arab shepherd who resents a settler's demand that the boy move his herd from a fenced area. His old father tells him, "The Jews settled on a land that never was ours" (Ben-Pazi 1988, 51). Possibly (assuming the settler's account is credible), the father was trying to avoid a violent confrontation that he could not hope to win, but his words touched a favorable chord in the settler's heart because he cites them as a true expression of Arab understanding.

The religious settlers often confront their rabbis with questions regarding relations with Arabs. This is another difference from secular Zionists, who allowed no intermediaries, certainly not religious authorities, to explain the presence of the Palestinians. When Rabbi Shlomo Aviner (1990) was asked whether meetings with Arabs should be commended and initiated, he replied,

> It is a good idea, in order to increase peace, to meet the Arabs who live in the land of Israel, but only on the condition that it will be based on the truth; namely, that they recognize the fact that this land is ours, this state is ours, and that we have taken no state from them, nor do we owe them any state. If they recognize this, it is good to meet them and, if they don't, then they are liars, and we have no dealings with liars. (67)

According to Aviner, an Arab who claims national rights to the land is neither a Palestinian nationalist nor a proud patriot; he is not even deluded. He is simply a liar because he, along with all his compatriots, know that the Arabs hold no rights to the land. The early Zionists never made such claims regarding the Palestinians, although they, too, hoped that the Arab national movement would not take hold.

Being a natural native, the Arab "senses" the truth of the Jewish claim. He can comprehend the deep devotion of a people to their land—something that is lost on the modern and postmodern man of hyperspace and rapid mobility. Ironically, the settlers see the Palestinians as sharing their worldview: while they stand against the Arabs on one—shallow and superficial—level, they believe them to be partners in a deeper struggle against fellow Israelis—a struggle common to all who share devotion to tradition. Therefore, it is not surprising that, in Elon's book, the Palestinian refugee boy knows what the kibbutz members have long forgotten: that he must be loyal to the land given to his people by God. He should therefore also recognize that he and his people do not belong to the land.

An interesting, yet atypical, story relates to Rabbi Menachem Fruman (1993) of the Tekoah settlement and his attempts to create links with Muslim religious leaders. In his reasoning, the religious leaders of both sides should meet because they have a better chance of reaching an agreement than political leaders. To the queries of his friends and the skepticism from all sides of the political spectrum, he answered,

It is important to stress that, in a Jewish-Muslim religious dialogue, the fact that the Jewish side is linked to the idea of a Greater Israel is not a problem. Quite the opposite. In a religious dialogue, I, as a man of Greater Israel or, more specifically, a settler, have much to discuss with the Palestinians. The attachment to the land that characterizes the men of Greater Israel and most of the Arabs is a potential basis for coexistence. He who conceives of himself as living within the context of his traditional culture will be able to respect the attachment to the land and the culture of the other. (43)

The possibility of conceiving of a religious peace stems from a basic principle shared by both religions: It is God who owns the land and He can give it to the believers. Fruman suggests a depolitization of the land—a declaration that, because of its sacredness, both religions should share control.

Fruman found no support among his fellow settlers, including the rabbis of his own camp: he was criticized harshly in his home settlement to the point of being evicted, and the Muslim fundamentalists he met were also not enthusiastic about his plan. Fruman himself maintained his rightist views and supported harsh measures against Hamas leaders, including the killing of his interlocutors from Hamas, Sheikhs Ahmad Yasin and Abdul Aziz Rantisi, by the Israeli Defense Forces. His marginal views are nevertheless important because they show an inventive development of the logic of Gush Emunim. For Fruman, the Palestinians are first and foremost Muslims, just as, for him, the nature of the Jews is basically religious. His solution bypasses political Palestinian representation because militant political representation fails to grasp the true nature of the people: basically, the "authentic" Jews and Arabs can reach an agreement based on their mutual understanding, common to true believers, of the nature of the attachment to the land and their standing before God. Unlike Fruman, most settlers found no point in discussing the rights of the Palestinians, neither as a nation nor as part of a religion, and the Palestinians never accredited the settlers with any rights worth discussing.

THE PALESTINIANS AS TEMPORARY SOJOURNERS

According to the settlers' view, the land belongs to the Jewish people, and the Arabs have no true claim to be discussed, negotiated, or compromised. The Arabs, like the Romans or Crusaders before them, are only temporary sojourners in the home of others. Rabbi Yitzhak Shilat (1988) writes,

> We did not invite the Palestinians to come and reside in our land: they penetrated and invaded it, as foreign nomads, when we were not home. Only because of the compassion that lies deep in the soul of our people did we not evict them from here and allowed them to live peacefully and quietly in homes they built on our historical land. To this generosity they reply on each recurring occasion with cries of "itbach el-Yahud" ["butcher the Jew"] . . . For those who do not wish to live with us in peace, our verdict is this—that they be sent away to their people and their ancient lands. Had they any self-respect, they would have gone there by own free will. (48)

Since they are visitors—and it is unconceivable for the rabbi to think that they do not realize what they are—they have other places that they can call their own ancient homes. The settlers were very late in using the term that the rabbi uses—"Palestinians"—to designate the local Arabs, because it implies a certain acceptance of their rights to the land.

Gush Emunim settlers see the Arab world as threatening the return of the Jewish people to their homeland mainly for reasons of religion, anti-Semitism, and greed. While they realize the differences between various groups within the Arab world and among the Palestinian people, they tend to see them as a unitary whole, without relevant subgroups. The Palestinians are, according to the settlers and the Israeli Right in general, an integral part of the Arab people and not a nation in their own right. The Israeli Arab citizens are basically similar to their brothers who are not Israeli citizens. If the whole land of Israel includes both sides of the Green Line, it stands to reason that the fate of the entire Palestinian population under the rule of Israel should be the same.

The view of the Arabs is a mirror image of the basic ideology of Gush Emunim: they are "whole" just like the land of Israel is "whole" and the people of Israel are "whole." Differentiation, especially regarding the Palestinians who are Israeli citizens, divides the land, as well as its people. Differences among factions of Palestinians, such as those between secular nationalists and extreme Muslim fundamentalists, also receive scant attention. If any subdivision is analytically useful for the settlers, it is the one between the common man or woman, who are pastoral and non-political and willing to live in peace with the Jews, and the militant agitators, who are usually a minority and act against the true interests of their people and the divine course of history. Israeli political and territorial concessions are dangerous because they encourage extremists and enable them to lure more common Arabs into a circle of pointless hate.

The interests behind the inclusive view of the Arabs are apparent: if the Palestinians are no different than other Arabs, then the Palestinians belong to a powerful nation and not to a relatively small group of mostly refugees, and their claim to the land is petty and greedy. The Arabs, as the settlers never tire of mentioning, already have twenty-two states that may be considered homelands. Apart from rejecting Palestinian national claims to the land, and pitting the small Jewish nation against hundreds of millions of Arabs or Muslims, this view also absolves Israel of moral responsibility toward the Palestinians. Their larger national family, the Arabs, can and should take care of them, and their claim to someone else's home is morally flawed. According to Gush Emunim, there is no "Palestinian problem," and if that nonproblem were to be "solved" through a Palestinian state and Israeli concessions, it would endanger the future of Israel and compromise the eternal rights of the Jewish people. The settlers stress that the conflict is a perennial one based on absolute religious values that preclude any possibility of compromise.

The discourse about the Israeli Arabs, though the settlers rarely encounter them, is important.[3] Gush Emunim supporters claim that the Arabs have little right to participate in Israeli political life and practically no right to participate in the discussion over basic issues determining the future of Israel, such as arguments regarding peace, territory, and the future of the settlements. They are seen as a fifth column, potential traitors, loyal to Israel only when convenient, and never to be trusted. According to Gush Emunim, Israel is and should be an ethnocracy: a state dedicated to the public good of one ethnic group and actively participating in social conflicts in favor of the sacred ethnos rather than the demos (namely, the entire body of citizens).[4] One of their main arguments against the Oslo Accords was that, since they were passed by the Israeli parliament only with the support of the Arab parties, they were illegitimate.[5]

Author Mira Kedar (2002) of Ofra tried to understand why, at the outset of the Second Intifada, the land that had waited faithfully for the Jews to return and had not accepted any other nation's permanent presence, had produced a second nation once the Jews had decided to return. The eternal rights of the Jews are, for Kedar, undeniable, as is the newly conceived nature of the Palestinian people. Just as she believes that the Jewish return has divine meaning independent of the will of individuals, so, too, has the Palestinian emergence and their violent uprising. What, she wonders, is the divine role that God has allotted the unwelcomed intruders? Here are her conclusions:

> The Palestinians are the clouded mirror that the God Almighty has set before us—with the murderous inclinations and their moral decay and so on—[God says,] "Here, have a look: this is what a people that cleaves to the land of Israel as ordinary people look like; look, if you insist on building here a state like all other countries." (49)

After years of living side by side with the Palestinians, Kedar cannot merely dismiss them as passing overnight visitors and seeks to account for their function in the divine order of things. They still are visitors, but not accidental ones. Again, her explanation takes no account of Palestinian demands and regards the Palestinian people as manipulated objects of God's will. She does not suggest a dialogue with her neighbors: rather, she understands their existence as part of the most important of dialogues, which is that between the people of Israel and God, as another test that the people have to pass. Like other groups of gentiles, their meaning stems from their role as a mirror for the Jewish people in the divine plan.

THE PALESTINIANS AS GENTILES

In addition to the argument that the land is not the national home of the Palestinians and that they should not be considered a nation, other historical argumentations are often applied. The Palestinians are compared to hostile anti-Semitic gentiles, and the vivid imagery of pogroms and the Holocaust is often evoked. As is the case with the difference between theology and the history (see chapter 2), historical images are believed to have more effect on the Israeli public. If many Israelis insist that the Palestinians are indeed a nation, the settlers want to show that the Palestinians are like other nations that persecuted Jews in the past and therefore deserve little sympathy.

When a clash between a group of settlers who went hiking in the fields of Samaria and some Palestinians from the village of Beita ended in violence, with one settler girl and two Palestinians dead, the following letter was published in *Nekuda:*

It seems that somewhere, in bygone days, we have already seen those rabid, murderous faces of the villagers of Beita, and the sound of the galloping horses of Chmielnitzki's Cossack hordes echoing in our ears. And from the depth of oblivion, the drunken cry of the ravishers and murderers of the Jews of Kishinev suddenly arise. Like a pack of wolves summoned from the depth of the forest by the scent of blood, they darted out of the taverns of Kiev and emerged from the darkened alleys of Marrakech.

Yes! Yes! To smash the Jew's head! To shatter his skull because you are a Jew! And so the evil weeds of the village of Beita replaced the unbridled savages of the beer cellars of Munich. And in place of the evil weeds uprooted from the banks of the Vitula, new fruit ripened on the terraces of the backward village, rotten as always. (Naor 1988, 16)

This example is rare in its extreme language and historical elaboration, but reflects the attempts to present the Palestinians within a meaningful framework adopted from the traumatic Jewish past. The Beita residents are uncritically associated with the enemies of the Jews of bygone days and in various exilic situations. The events that led to this letter were far more ambivalent than the letter implies: the act of hiking through an Arab village was anything but an innocent stroll through the countryside, and accounts differ as to the guilty party: there were victims on both sides, unlike in historical pogroms; the only one armed was the Israeli guard, and some claimed that it was he who shot the Jewish girl accidentally; and the villagers gave refuge to the frightened settler girl hikers. In retaliation, the Israeli army blew up some of the houses in the village, giving rise to claims by left-wingers that it was Israel committing a pogrom against the subjugated Palestinians. Israeli public opinion was divided over this issue, and the letter used strong metaphors to impose one contested interpretation of the events over all others.

The letter reveals some interesting points regarding the settlers' historical consciousness. Jewish history is considered to be unified: not only is there no difference between the killers in Beita and other killers throughout history, but no distinction is made among killers in various historical contexts. The main metaphors are taken from the Eastern Europe pogroms, the Holocaust, and the ordeal of the Moroccan Jews, creating a homogeneous history. Although the Beita incident takes place in the Jewish homeland, the basic structure of the narrative is clearly exilic.

That, however, is exactly the point that the writer is trying to make, which constitutes the operative logic behind similar use of historical metaphors by the settlers. The land of Israel is assumed to be the place of salvation and redemption, where Jewish history is to be transformed into a heroic and victorious one. To the declared dismay of the settlers, they find that the exile is as relevant to them as it was to their forefathers. The tension between the definition of salvation and dire reality is a potent discursive strategy. It is usually aimed at the Israeli government, which, through its impotence, allows the fearful exilic conditions to exist in the land.

Numerous examples place the Palestinians in the position of the generalized national nemesis. As the women of Kiryat Arba entered Beit Hadassah in Hebron, Miriam Levinger made this promise, using loaded Holocaust imagery: "Hebron will no longer be Judenrein." Violent actions by the Palestinians are constantly referred to in terms of pogroms. One of the first volumes of *Nekuda* (no. 122) to be published after the outbreak of the First Intifada bore the caption "Brothers, there's a fire in the land," referring to a Yiddish song sung in the Kraków Ghetto and later adopted in Israeli Holocaust remembrance ceremonies. A writer in an earlier *Nekuda* volume expressed the eternal unity of the enemies of Israel: "In every generation they arise to kill us, and therefore every generation has its Amalek. Our generation's Amalek is expressed in the Arabs' demonic hatred of our national revival in the Land of our Fathers" (Zeruya 1980).

The settlers' logic, therefore, runs in two ways: the Palestinians hold no collective rights to the Promised Land, and, if someone still insists on treating them as a nation with territorial rights, their horrendous deeds should be taken into consideration. While the first claim encounters the claims against the settlers that they are strangers to the land, the second counters increasingly common moral claims that the settlers, and with them the entire Israeli occupation structure, assume the historical role of the violent gentiles. According to this equation, the Palestinians become today's Jews, persecuted through no fault of their own. Yeshayahu Leibowitz angered many when he applied the term "Judeo-Nazis" to the reality of the occupied territories; Moshe Zimmerman, historian of the German past, called the youth of Hebron "Hitlerjugend"; and a retired Israeli officer said that the knitted skullcap is the Israeli equivalent of the Nazi armband. Less radical historical analogies appear constantly in Israeli media: Palestinian children with stones in their hands while standing against Israeli tanks remind many of the story of David and Goliath, but with the Israelis, who claim to be descended from David, in the role of Goliath.[6]

On the public stage, the settlers counterattack the moral argument by trying to convince the public that their situation resembles the plight of the Jews throughout history. Over the years, however, the stage and the players have not remained the same, and some accumulating changes are worth noticing.

Changes in Perspective

The settlers' understanding of the Palestinian presence in the territories has remained basically the same for thirty years, but some nuances are beginning to appear. As the settlers began to know the Palestinians somewhat better, historical metaphors and halakhic formulas were no longer sufficient to give meaning to the presence of unrelenting enemies on the sacred land. The two most important novel perspectives were contradictory, appeared in different social locations, and indicate two directions that the question of the "other" may take in the future. The first is represented here by men, and the other by women. Without further research, we cannot estimate whether the gender difference holds much meaning.

The first direction that is increasing in legitimacy is simple hatred of the Palestinians, based on years of their violent objection to the settlers' project and unrelated to elaborate theological explanations and deliberations, historical examples, and biblical metaphors. Two reasons can explain the recent emergence of open hatred. The first is despair of possible accommodation, and the understanding that, unless a radical solution is imposed, the settlers may find themselves evicted from their homes. Consequently, ideas that once belonged to the radical fringe now appear openly on the pages of *Nekuda*. One Ofra resident writes,

> Terrorism is defeating us because we do not dare articulate openly what the heart already knows: that only a large-scale eviction of Arabs can overcome terrorism. We have already tried peaceful coexistence by means of great concessions and failed, tried the military option and failed. The third option—that of recapturing the entire territory, will also fail ... only when we shall dare to consider eviction out loud shall deterrence return and will it be possible to live here, not just die here. (Sorek 2002, 42)

Many, however, do not even bother to suggest other failed options. Palestinian terrorism is enough reason for them to hate. A second reason is the emergence of a new generation of settlers, as is discussed further in chapter 11. Whereas the older settlers who began the settlement project are bound by the religious worldview and Rabbi Kook the Elder's philosophy, the younger generation has intense experiences that construct its perspective. A young settler expressed himself regarding revenge:

> It is a legitimate thing. A warm heart is a legitimate thing. You arrive at the funeral of a murdered victim, and you feel as if you have arrived at a funeral of someone who died of old age. Everything is so organized and pleasant . . . You must not mention Arabs, as though they are not involved. The call for revenge is a message that we are human beings. (Shafran 2002, 26)

For this young man, a warm heart is turned toward his fellow slain Jews while coldhearted revenge is reserved for the Arabs. In his view, the settlement project and the funeral practices are part of a heartless and formalized establishment that lacks the true spirit that leads to emotional action. These emotions are declared in the passage to be legitimate, warranted, and positive. The traditional Gush Emunim establishment, however, still exercises power through the Yesha council, and, while talk of revenge is prevalent and violent acts toward Palestinians are commonplace, the settlers' establishment condemns them. This establishment is equally unresponsive to the other trend, which entails some first, hesitant voices suggesting greater compassion toward the plight of the Palestinians.

In the 1980s, celebrated author David Grossman, a harsh critic of the settlement project and one of the more eloquent representatives of the peace camp, visited the settlement of Ofra. In his dialogue with the settlers, he raised a question that, to his mind, received no answer: how can it be that the settlers cannot see the suffering of the Palestinians who wait at roadblocks for hours each day? He wondered about the difference in the concept of time: for him, and he assumed for the settlers as well, time is a precious commodity, whereas for the stereotypical Palestinian it is supposed to have little significance. The Palestinians are considered to be part of the unchanging Orient, so their time stands still and holds little value. Grossman (1988) asks how is it possible that the settlers cannot see the "other," even though he or she is easily visible waiting at the roadblocks?

On one level, a simple answer to Grossman's query is readily supplied by the settlers: for the goal of Jewish national salvation and personal security, others may have to suffer, especially those who are hostile to the presence of the Jews in their homeland. According to the settlers, the suffering of the Palestinians is, therefore, their own fault. On another level, there is no answer: the settlers look at the Palestinians who wait at the roadblocks for hours while they pass easily, but they do not "see" them. *Grosso modo,* this selective gaze has not changed, and expressions of sympathy toward the national enemy are rare, although some developments do deserve mention.

Over the years, the values of Grossman and his fellow liberal Israelis have slowly filtered into the sensitivity of at least some of the settlers, even though there is still little sympathy for Palestinian political aspirations. Hayuta Deutch of the Neve Daniel settlement writes, "On my way I passed two Palestinians, tired from their day of work, waiting at the intersection on the way to Nahalin, the nearby Arab village. They, too, want to get home. They raise their hands to hitchhike, but they don't mean that I should stop."[7] She sees the Palestinians—it is important for her to point out to her readers that she can *see* them—and they are not Cossacks or Nazis but daily laborers. She understands the situation as composed of two communities that share the same space yet are alienated from each other.

Author Mira Kedar (1999), in one of her stories, gives names and personal traits to the Palestinians, and describes a complex relationship between them and the storyteller. The Palestinians arc building her home as news arrives of a terrorist attack:

When Amad said that there was one killed [. . .] and several injured, I did not know whether the dead person was ours or theirs but I did not ask or anything, either because I was embarrassed to ask or because at that time, and in the way that Amad told it, it did not really matter. The one killed [. . .] is dead to his mother and father, his wife and children, his brothers and sisters, his male and female friends regardless of whether he is ours or theirs [. . .] A fellowship stood between us that day, a friendship over one matter, like an island of peace within a time of war. Before they returned to Rantis, I asked Hasan to call me once they reached home so that I would not worry. Within less than an hour, he called and I said Baruch Hashem El-Hamd Alla ["Bless the Lord," in Hebrew and Arabic]. And I called Amad to thank him because he had called me from his house and was worried. (75–76)

We can choose to be critical or skeptical toward the concern of the writer for her Palestinian workers and claim that the sympathy she expresses toward them veils the continuing oppressive relations between the sides.

After all, the Palestinians are building her house on land they claim to be their own and are paid less than minimum wage. However, it would be a mistake not to notice the change in tone: it was never the habit of the settlers to sympathize with Palestinian victims, and any attack on Jews was seen as a crime of mythic proportion. The universal humanistic claim of the author that—albeit for that moment—she did not care about the nationality of the dead, and her willingness to accept the Palestinians into the metaphorical family of grief, are indeed radically novel in settlers' writing.

Here and there, we may also find reflexive criticism of the years of misguided attempts to decipher the nature of Palestinian existence on the land. Hesitantly and subtly, insights from the criticism by the Israeli peace camp penetrate the settler's discourse, legitimated by its being expressed by people on the inside. In an article in *Nekuda,* Hayuta Deutch (2002) reflected on the mistakes she thinks were committed by her friends:

> From their perspective, [the Palestinians] are under occupation, and this perspective—their perspective—I have missed. We have missed. I go back to look at that mythical sentence—"We have not settled in the hearts"—and I see that it missed the crux of the matter, which is the reason [why we have failed]. We were blind to the moral cause that negated our right to trample the honor and rights of the person who lives on his land, even if he is a Palestinian. It is his land in a simple sense, even if it is my land in a more complex sense. (60)

The famous image from Sabastia, December 1975, after the Kadum compromise was announced, and the Israeli government agreed to the establishment of the first Gush Emunim settlement. Movement supporters are dancing, carrying leaders Hanan Porat and Moshe Levinger on their shoulders. (Photograph by Moshe Milner. Courtesy of the National Photo Collection, State of Israel.)

The establishment of a new settlement: Alon Moreh. Most Gush Emunim settlements started with mobile homes and makeshift solutions that became part of the lore of the place. (Photograph by Herman Chanania. Courtesy of the National Photo Collection, State of Israel.)

An aerial view of the Elazar settlement. The regimented uniform houses, along the perimeter roads, overlooking their surrounding areas, can easily be seen. (Photograph by Herman Chanania. Courtesy of the National Photo Collection, State of Israel.)

Children walking in a new settlement (Pe'erim). Since the settlement project was criticized for being no more than a shallow political statement, the development, sustenance, and even symbolic declaration of mundane everyday life held great importance for the settlers. (Photograph by Moshe Milner. Courtesy of the National Photo Collection, State of Israel.)

Settlers and visitors marching in front of the monumental building of the Cave of Machpela in Hebron. The sacredness and political centrality of the place made it a locus of settler identity and a site of ongoing violent clashes with Palestinians. (Photograph by Sa'ar Ya'akov. Courtesy of the National Photo Collection, State of Israel.)

This tree located in Gush Etzion was seen from afar and thus symbolized the desire to return and rebuild its settlements after its destruction in 1948. When that happened following the 1967 war, the tree became the symbol of Gush Etzion and literally turned into a monument as it was filled with cement. (Photograph by Refa'el Yaniger; from the *Hebrew Wikipedia.*)

The settlement of Ofra, constructed in 1976, became one of the centers of the settlement project and the place where many of the Gush Emunim leaders reside and its major institutions were created. (Photograph by Herard Reogorodetzki. Courtesy of the National Photo Collection, State of Israel.)

The clash between the army and Gush Emunim protesters barricaded on the roof-
tops of Yamit, April 1982. The problem faced by the Gush Emunim supporters was
how to show devotion and set a high price for future evacuations without alienating
the general Israeli public. (Photograph by Tal Or Beni. Courtesy of the National Photo
Collection, State of Israel.)

A female soldier evacuating a child. This picture especially was popular among the settlers because, to their minds, it exemplified how traumatic evacuations can be, not only for those evacuated, but for the evacuators as well. This picture and other depictions were seen as bridging the rift after the bitter clash between soldiers and settlers. (Photograph by Tal Or Beni. Courtesy of the National Photo Collection, State of Israel.)

The Yamit Yeshiva at Neve Dekalim, in Gush Katif at the Gaza Strip, commemorated the destruction of the town of Yamit. The monumental building is structured in the shape of the Star of David, with one point buried in the ground. Students and visitors symbolically enter a Zionist space that was abridged by the evacuation from Sinai. The building was destroyed in the 2005 disengagement from Gaza, thus suffering the same fate as the town it commemorated, destroyed in 1982. (Photograph by Michael Yakobson; from the *Hebrew Wikipedia*.)

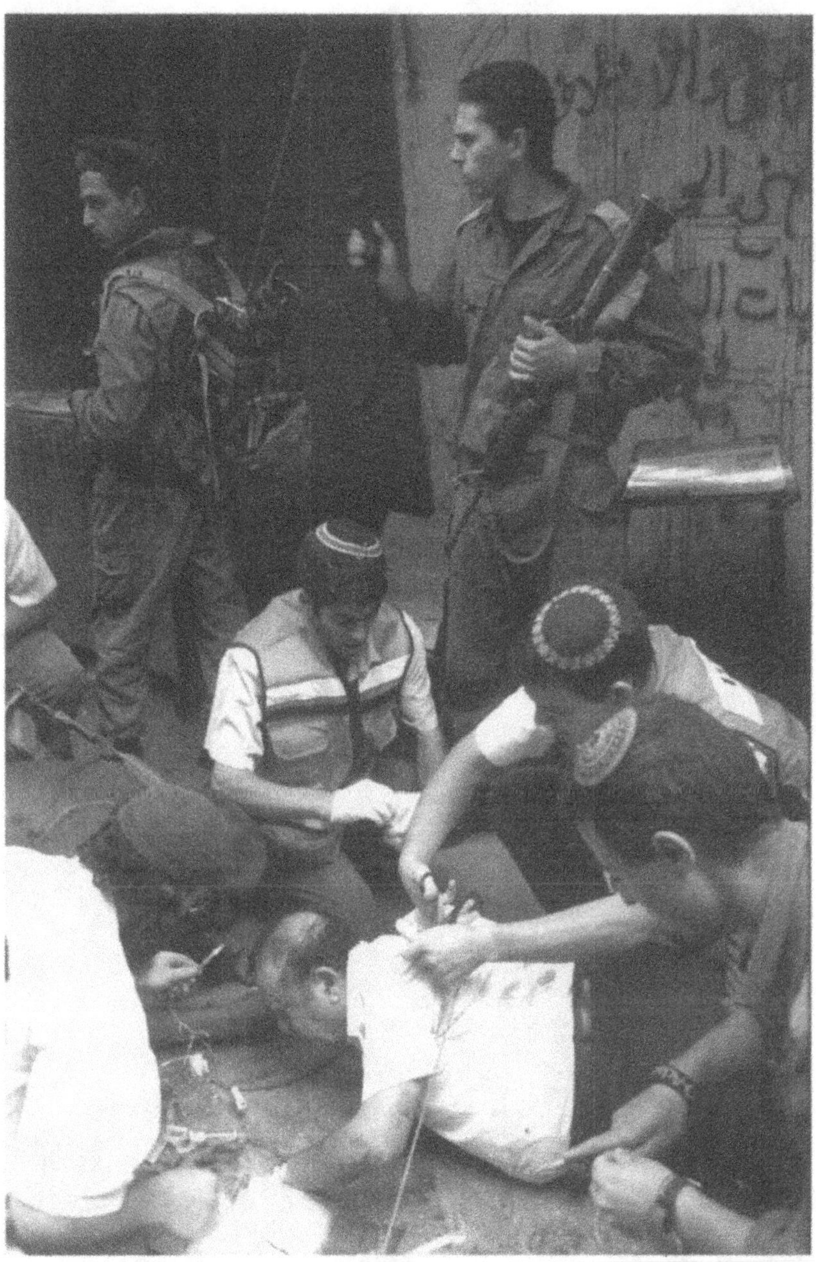

Over the years, and especially during the two intifadas, terrorism became a constant in the settlements. Paramedics are treating and saving the life of settler Nissim Gudai, a stab-wound victim in market of Hebron, with soldiers guarding the scene. (Photograph by David Silberman. Courtesy of the National Photo Collection, State of Israel.)

With the growing threat of violence and terrorism, segregative measures were introduced to protect the settlers. Here is a children's bus on a Gaza Strip road leading to Gush Katif. The road is reserved for Jews only and protected by walls on both sides and by a tank. (Photograph by Moshe Milner. Courtesy of the National Photo Collection, State of Israel.)

Religious girls hold hands near the Western Wall in Jerusalem, in a human chain extending all the way to Gush Katif, in a demonstration against the disengagement plan. Their clothes are covered by bumper stickers protesting the plan. (Photograph by Amos Ben Gershon. Courtesy of the National Photo Collection, State of Israel.)

A destroyed house in Gush Katif. Such scenes of destruction represent the nightmare hanging over the heads of the Gush Emunim settlers, both because of the private tragedy and because of the national implications of evicting Jews. Such scenes revive historical memories of exile and powerlessness. (Photograph by Michael Yakobson; from the *Hebrew Wikipedia*.)

Following Palestinian terrorist attacks, Israel has built a fence around the West Bank, and a high wall dividing western and eastern Jerusalem. Civil rights organizations were critical of the effect this had on the Palestinian society and economy. From a different perspective, the construction of walls and fences place the Jewish settlers outside of a main symbol of Israeli boundary. (Photograph by Jacob Rask; from the *Hebrew Wikipedia*.)

With the pressures to halt the construction of further settlements, young settlers went to build and live in illegal outposts. This photo shows the Gilead Ranch in Samaria. The Israeli government and the settlers' establishment leadership are ambivalent toward the phenomenon, both criticizing their illegal actions while supporting the settlers and supplying their basic needs. (Photograph by Michael Yakobson; from the *Hebrew Wikipedia*.)

With the aging of the initial Gush Emunim leadership, the future of the settlement project rests in the hands of the younger generation. Growing in different circumstances, while experiencing intense political strife, lawlessness, and terrorism, they hold different values from their parents. (Photograph by Daniel Maleck Lewy; from the *Hebrew Wikipedia*.)

6

When a Home Is Not a Home

Terrorism and Its Effects

Terror, Perseverance, and Jewish Vengeance

An editorial in *Nekuda* addressed the issue of the Arab who kills Jews:

> This is the Jewish vengeance, this is the Jewish answer to the Arab killer, from the early days of Hebrew settlement until this day: you came to uproot, both plants and human beings, and you wound up building and planting—with your murderous and devastating hands—the continual life project of the people of eternity. Your very act of murder will open a well of life in that same place of murder; your act of uprooting will bring about beautiful gardens and fields, will build the house of life for the people of Israel.[1]

This quotation expresses the settlers' urgent need, after repeated tragedies, to explain the dire physical and psychological consequences of terrorism to the Palestinians, the general Israeli public, and, probably most importantly, to themselves. The explanation never varies—death and destruction shall bring the opposite: life and further construction.

Increasingly, terrorism has become the central defining experience in the lives of the Gush Emunim settlers. The threat of violence, first from Palestinian terrorists infiltrating from outside the territories and later from neighbors, has restructured the lives of the settlers in important ways. In this chapter, I discuss the consequences of living under the constant threat of terrorism, and the way that the experience was conceptualized to enable the continuation of everyday life and prosperity.

PALESTINIAN TERRORIST AND THE SETTLEMENTS

Palestinian terrorism against Israel has a long history, starting in the days before the establishment of the Israeli state. In the early 1950s, Palestinians from across the borders tried to infiltrate Israel, either in an attempt to return to where they had lived until 1948, or to steal, or kill Israelis. Their actions led to what historian Benny Morris (1993) has called Israel's border wars. After the 1967 Six-Day War, the Palestinians realized that the Arab armies could not liberate their homeland and resorted to terrorist attacks on Israelis in Israel and abroad. Israel retaliated through diplomatic measures and military operations. As the Palestine Liberation Organization (PLO) became more established and was subjected to international constraints, it entered diplomatic negotiations with Israel, and one of the terms of the Oslo Accords was the termination of violence as a means of managing conflicts. Although Israelis debate whether the Palestinian Authority endorsed or condemned it, terrorism against Israeli citizens, especially settlers, did not stop and, with suicide attacks, reached even new heights. The settlers never tire of mentioning that they are not the first or the only victims of Palestinian terrorism, but, in their case, the onslaught has unique characteristics and is more intense; thus, it has become a formative experience.

At the start of the settlement project, attacks by Palestinians were relatively rare, and the few incidents in which Israelis were shot at were perpetrated mostly by Palestinian infiltrators. The first attacks against the Jewish community in Hebron resulted in the 1979 killing of Yehoshua Saloma. A year later, six yeshiva students were killed in front of the Beit Hadassah settlement in Hebron. In the mid-1980s, a rise in the violence against settlers led to retaliation in the form of Jewish vigilantism, hailed by some of the settlers and abhorred by others.[2] Apart from attempts to blow up the mosques on the Temple Mount, the Jewish underground targeted Arabs, with revenge and deterrence as its prime motivation. The capture and trial of its activists triggered a heated debate among the settlers regarding the limitations of force and the role of the state vis-à-vis its citizens.[3]

The First Intifada was mainly a Palestinian popular revolt that involved rioting and stone throwing, but by the early 1990s there were numerous incidents of settlers killed by firearms. In the settlers' protests against the Oslo Accords, their main slogan was "Don't give them guns." The suicide bombings that began in 1994 targeted Israeli population centers inside the Green Line. In the period between the start of the First Intifada (December 1987) and the start of the Second Intifada (September 2000), 490 Israeli were killed, 55 of them settlers, or 11 percent—four times their percentage in the general population.[4]

In the Second Intifada, the Palestinian civil rebellion was crushed early and lost its momentum, but extremist Islamic factions such as the Hamas and the Islamic Jihad, along with the secular Tanzim, continued the battle through suicide bombings in Israeli cities and by targeting settlers on the roads and in their homes. Although the horrendous affects of the suicide bombings are the best-known feature of the era, most of the attacks on the settlers took the form of shooting from hideouts at Israeli vehicles, and infiltration of the settlements to fire with various weapons at the settlers. Between September 2000 and August 2003, 162 settlers were killed in terrorist acts within Yesha, which is 20 percent of the 852 Israelis killed in that period and half of the total number of dead within Yesha (soldiers and civilians). There were 2,200 incidents of Israeli vehicles fired upon, in which 100 people were killed. Bombs exploded near passing cars 1,090 times, killing 64 Israelis. Forty-three Israelis were killed when terrorists infiltrated their settlement. Altogether, more than 95 percent of the Palestinian terrorist attacks were aimed at the settlers. By July 2003, there had been more than 17,000 violent attacks on Israelis within the area of Yesha, or approximately one terrorist act per ten settlers. Most settlers in the ideological settlements on the mountain ridge of Judea and in Samaria and Gush Katif of the Gaza Strip have encountered Palestinian violence more than once, and all have heard shots and explosions outside their homes.

The settlers' homes, schools, and villages became unsafe. Terrorists appeared at family gatherings, in the parents' or children's bedroom in the middle of the night, or on the roads of the settlements. Family and friends stopped visiting the settlements even for special celebrations. Although the sense of normal life was shattered by suicide bombings throughout Israel, the effect on the settlements was more profound: the homeyness they wish to communicate to the Israeli public was undermined by the insecurity of their homes.

The problem of the settlers is exacerbated because the Palestinian organizations, when trying through agreement or unilaterally to reach a truce, have declared that the targeting of settlers is legitimate and thus not covered by any pact they might reach among themselves or with the Israeli government. Even when condemning terrorist acts within Israeli cities, the Palestinian leadership was reluctant to condemn attacks on settlers. Defined by the Palestinians as Israeli soldiers rather than civilians, the settlers—including women and children—were considered fair game. What enraged the settlers most was that some Israelis made similar distinctions: after two settlers were killed at the Bracha settlement, publicist Yair Lapid commented that, since he could never comprehend the logic of their life, he could not feel enraged by the circumstances of their death.

Terrorism directly affects the lives of settlers, but some of the effects, as the words of Lapid insinuate, are indirect: as Palestinian terrorism claimed more lives of nonsettlers inside the Green Line through suicide attacks, the settlers were pushed into an apologetic position. The question of the causal connection between the settlers' actions and indiscriminate Palestinian terrorism was one of the most sensitive in Israeli civil discourse, partly discussed but mostly silenced. The opponents of the settlement project placed much of the blame on the military occupation and in particular on the settlers, claiming that the oppressive living conditions of the Palestinians drove them to extreme measures. They even called the Second Intifada "the War for the Peace of the Settlements."[5] The reply by the settlers and their supporters was that withdrawal and compromise would only prove to the Palestinians the success of their murderous methods and invite more bloodshed and further withdrawals. They also pointed to the years of violent encounters and terrorism preceding the establishment of the settlements. All of this is secondary to their basic claim that, in the struggle for Jewish rights to the land, the existence of Palestinian terrorism has little bearing on the main issues of religious and historical rights; if anything, it only confirms the superior moral position held by the Jews.

An examination of the settlers' publications demonstrates the traumatic effects of terrorism in everyday life. Some of the tragedies hit entire families, such as the killing of four members of the Gavish family in their home at Alon Moreh: husband, wife, son, and grandfather. An especially disheartening trauma is the number of cases in which both parents have been killed, leaving some children orphans. Consequently, in many settler homes, it has become common practice to leave the house in separate cars. The settlers reported discussions and decisions in the family of what to do if one of the parents were killed. Women related that, based on the chance they might be killed, they took extra care to leave their house clean and orderly before going to work. A settler wrote about security concerns gradually dominating his thinking and behavior: first they installed special car windshields to protect against stone throwing; then the car became a mini–army headquarters with communication technology and tracking devices. They then bought a handgun, which they hid under a jacket—even when attending weddings. Eventually, they openly carried an M16 rifle at all times (Wasserman 2001, 54).

In the past, when ideology rather than necessity directed behavior, settlers were reluctant to have a fence, regular or electronic, surround their settlements, claiming that it would symbolize that their presence in the territories is ghettolike and exilic. Currently, nearly all settlements want an electronic fence, and only budgetary constraints keep the government from meeting the great demand. The same logic applies to bypass roads. As these roads were constructed, following the Oslo Accords, the ideological settlers debated whether they should use them. Their claim was that these roads bypass Palestinian towns, thus obliterating civil Jewish presence from parts of the land. With the increased danger of terrorism, even the most devout settlers chose to travel on the safer bypass roads. The segregated roads solution, however, inadvertently created its own problems and tragedies: Palestinian terrorists soon discovered that, since there was little chance of mistakenly killing Palestinians on these roads, they could concentrate on ambushing the cars on them.

The settlers' project found itself faced with the most trying problem of its existence as it became clear that the safety and security of its adherents could not be guaranteed. The success of the project relied on non-ideological Israelis who sought to improve their standard of living, but, to the chagrin of the ideological settlers, residents of the smaller secular settlements were the first to demand that they be evacuated and compensated, and some of their villages were on the verge of becoming ghost towns. Some Israelis, mostly religious, became even more committed in the face of the deteriorating security situation and decided to join the settlements to strengthen them. In fact, during the 1990s, the number of settlements, especially the ideological and the ultra-Orthodox ones, grew, with some even doubling in size. Overall, terrorism accentuated the division among those who were committed, those who were stuck where they did not want to be, and those who decided that Yesha was too risky a project to consider joining.

On the symbolic level, the settlers looked for a way to include the victims of terror in the national narrative without undermining the settler cause. Here again, the settlers resorted to traditional Israeli practices, though they made some necessary adjustments. In the sections that follow, I outline the Zionist practices that served as the foundation for the settlers' own practices.

COMMEMORATING THE DEAD IN ISRAEL

Among the elements of Israeli civil religion, the commemoration of war dead has immense emotional power and visible presence, rivaled only by the memory of the Holocaust. As Israelis grieve together by standing during the siren on the Memorial Day for the Fallen, the Israeli "imagined community" of national solidarity is visible for all to see. The physical connection to the historical plight, represented by the "presence" of the absent soldiers, is a marker and measure for belonging to the Israeli community.

Commemorative practices for those who died in service of the nation began in the early twentieth century[6] and were epitomized by the heroic figure of Trumpledor, killed in 1920 at Tel Hai (Zerubavel 1995). The War of Independence, with its six thousand Jewish casualties, was another point of reference for the emerging culture of bereavement. In Israeli culture, the sacred status of the war dead has been meticulously preserved and nourished. Memorial Day is regarded with utmost solemnity. A substantial part of Israeli popular culture—poems, songs, literature, plays, and film—is dedicated to the memory of the fallen soldiers, and the Israeli symbolic landscape is replete with places that commemorate them. Monuments abound on roadsides, city central plazas, and kibbutz lawns—more relative to both the size of the population and the number of fallen soldiers than in any other place in the world. Towns and agricultural settlements are named after dead warriors. The families of the fallen soldiers receive benefits from the state and hold a central symbolic place—some would claim even a suffocating one (Shamgar-Handelman 1986; Zerubavel 2003). The dead are nationalized in the sense that the entire nation claims them as family, and restrictions are placed on private commemoration. The fallen are the most potent and sacred of Israeli symbols.

The centrality of the fallen in the Israeli ethos is bound up with the concept of sacrifice, best symbolized through the Akeda: the binding of Isaac, in which Abraham follows God's command and brings his son Isaac to sacrifice, but God substitutes a lamb in Isaac's stead. In the modern Israeli version, through their decision to immigrate to Israel, the fathers brought their children to the altar, but their children were not spared. The dead soldiers became the sacrificial lambs.[7]

Israeli memory culture underwent major changes over the last few decades, starting with the Yom Kippur War, through the Lebanon War, and on through the two intifadas. The bereaved families gradually became more bitter and confrontational toward the government and the army and constituted a political presence to be reckoned with. Families insisted on more private expressions of bereavement; for example, the right to deviate from the formal text on epitaphs on soldiers' tombstones. Most important, however, especially in the context of this chapter, have been the changes in the categories of the sacred fallen. The 1973 war was the last great conventional war fought by Israel. Since then, most of the dead of the Israeli-Arab conflict were killed either as civilians in terrorist attacks or as soldiers in guerilla warfare or accidents. The heroic soldier, killed while storming an enemy post, has practically vanished from Israel's contemporary military history. The changing demographics of death called for a corresponding change in the practices of bereavement.

The randomness of terrorist victims threatened to erase the all-important symbolic hierarchy of Israeli society: among the dead were guest workers, tourists, Israeli Arabs, women, and children, whoever happened to be in a bus or a café at the unfortunate time of a terrorist attack. The celebrated soldiers of yesterday—male, young, Jewish, and mainly of Ashkenazi origin—were quickly becoming a minority among the dead. The question soon emerged as to whether a teenage girl, who died in an explosion while having coffee at a restaurant, should receive the same privileged treatment as an air force pilot whose plane was shot down. Since a disproportionately high percentage of the dead were ideological settlers, the question of inclusion and exclusion into the highly esteemed group of war casualties became extremely sensitive: have the settlers, through their victimhood, become the new Israeli heroes?

"What Kind of Father . . .": Commemorating the Dead in Ideological Settlements

Ideological settlers being killed in terrorist attacks give rise to "second-order memories": they settled the land in order to fulfill the decrees of Jewish memory and became objects of memory themselves. Rendering meaning to the deaths of their fellows was one of the most intricate and important challenges that the settlers took upon themselves: it had to relate both to Jewish religious traditions and to established Zionist practices. Moreover, the very success of the settlement project depended on the ability of the settler leadership to persuade others that they were there to live and prosper, not to die at the hands of Palestinian "natives." Although living dangerously could lure some adventurous settlers and would not deter the "true believers," it was bound to scare off most families, especially those not committed to Gush Emunim ideology.

The settlers commemorate through various practices, some of which express their grief and religious beliefs and some—sometimes the same ones—that express their anger at the government for not doing enough. Among the more religious traditional practices are the writing of Torah scrolls and their presentation to a synagogue, and the editing of religious books in memory of the deceased. These practices, however, are easily converted into political action: for example, the meaning of a processional presentation of a Torah scroll to a synagogue is determined by the location of the settlement and the speeches delivered on the occasion. However, some of the practices that commemorate settlers killed in terrorist acts are novel and overtly political. In these cases, the memory of the dead is recruited to strengthen the settlers' cause. First and foremost among these practices is the establishment of new settlements named after the dead.

Some of the settlements can be called *monument settlements,* based on the logic of their establishment and the name given them. The settlers claim that they follow a long chain of Zionist tradition by naming settlements after their dead friends. One of the settlers' periodicals wrote,

> "What shall we tell the children?" one of the women of Kfar Darom cries as the coffin is lowered into the grave. We shall tell them, "After the eight that fell at Tel Hai—Kiryat Shmona was built. After Yosef Haim Brenner was murdered by vicious killers—Giva't Brenner was built. And we shall build Yad Yair and Rechalim and Kfar Dror and the Giva't Rabbi Biran." So we shall not be ashamed when the orphans will ask, "Why did our father die?" We will be able to say, "So that the land could be built; so that you and all the people of Israel will be able to live securely."[8]

The two historical events mentioned occurred in 1920 and 1921—the saga of Tel Hai, led by Yosef Trumpeldor, and the killing of the well-known author Haim Yosef Brenner. Their names were given to the development town of Kiryat Shmona, erected in 1949, and Kibbutz Giva't

Brenner, built in 1928. Both namings were not a response, in the sense that the Gush Emunim settlers understand it—the towns were built years after the events, and their names expressed respect and grief, not defiance, deterrence, and retaliation. Brenner was a revered Zionist writer, and the kibbutz movement had good reasons to name one of its communities after him. This is one of many differences between the settlers' commemoration and secular Zionism's treatment of its heroic dead—a difference never acknowledged by the settlers.

Another, more crucial, difference is in the cultural discourse surrounding the event. Bereavement led the Zionist pioneers to contemplate the heavy sacrifice they and their children had to make for the fulfillment of the Zionist dream, as symbolized through the Akeda story. Many of the settlers' dead were young, and their arrival was their parents' voluntary decision. It was far more voluntary than in the case of the earlier Zionists, many of whom, though ideologically minded, also escaped harsh living conditions, anti-Semitic persecution, and, at times, even annihilation. The motif of the Akeda, in the Zionist sense, is practically nonexistent in the writings of the settlers; their recurring claim is that the sacrifice only strengthens them in their just decision to take their children and move to the contested land. Some of the more ideological leaders even claim that, to display confidence in their cause, Jews should travel everywhere, opening their car windows wide and challenging the Palestinians to dare hurt them. In their logic, only this will prove to the Palestinians that the Jews are here to stay and convince them to desert their murderous ways.

When the daughter of one of Gush Emunim's leaders, Menachem Felix, was shot and killed from an ambush on the road, her father went to Jerusalem and protested with his friends that it was unsafe to drive the roads of Samaria. His anger was clearly directed toward the Israeli government, and his decision to move to a violent contested territory, exposing his daughter to the dangers of the Samaria roads, was never doubted neither by himself nor by his friends, all of whom had either family members or close friends who had been killed. According to the settlers' ideology, to even allow this thought, so central to the secular Zionist ethos, to creep in their minds is sacrilegious. This is partly due to their belief, as a religious community, that calamity comes from God, and, hence, parents' decisions are not at fault as long as they concur with the will of God. It may also reflect a great legitimation anxiety: the Gush Emunim settlers hear endlessly from their secular opponents that the settlers are to blame for the trouble that befalls them, as well as for many other security, economic, and social ills in Israel. For the ideological settlers, accepting the blame is unthinkable.

During the years of the Second Intifada, the articles in *Nekuda* describing visits to newly established havens had virtually disappeared and had been replaced by visits to terror-stricken communities. Over that period, roughly half of the covers of *Nekuda* were dedicated to terrorist victims. The writers always looked for a positive angle; namely, the strength of the residents who had just witnessed the violation of their private space, or the resolve of the settlers to persevere. In the stronger religious communities, the story is invariably an uplifting one. After a terrorist entered a house in Alon Moreh and killed four people of three generations in the same family, Meira Dolev (2001), writer for *Nekuda*, described her visit to the place:

> During the first days, it seemed as though there were voices of collapse. Those who had left for the holidays did not want to return, and those who had not left wanted to leave immediately, not knowing for how long, and in a whisper the word "leaving" is heard time and again. But "such a disaster can lead in opposite directions," someone told me . . . "Either to a fall into the abyss or to growth." And gradually it turned out that she was right, and that the people of this mountain are as strong as its rocks. And with all the difficulty and the pain, and without ignoring the bereavement, they drew strength from reserves—reserves that it is scarcely believable that they still possess after so many disasters and terrorist attacks and the everyday coping with gunshots and explosive devices and anxieties and loss and longing, and in the village roads new voices are heard. (2)

Losing a settlement to terrorism, for the religious Gush Emunim settlers, is not considered an option, even though the mountain-ridge ideological settlements are hardest hit. It is indeed an option, though, for the less ideologically inclined secular settlers. The difference between the two communities was apparent in the case of Chomesh, a secular settlement in north Samaria.[9] In 2000, there were fifty-four secular families in the village. Within ten days in June 2001, in three different events, three residents were killed in terrorist attacks on the road leading to the village. Within the next few days, half of the residents left. None of them succeeded in selling their apartments, and few managed to rent for a pittance. Visitors stopped arriving, and mechanics and suppliers refused to answer calls from Chomesh. Soon all the utilities, like the grocery, day-care center, and medical center, collapsed.

Many of the secular settlers expressed despair. A woman said, "The people here are great . . . but for me this is the end of the story. If I am offered compensation, I'll get up and go. There is no future in this place. Chomesh is a difficult place, for adults like me and for children." A former resident also said that, for him, the story was over: "It is not worth human lives. We do not have the power to cope. The Palestinians have won." Secular settlers, who were attracted by the quality of life in the settlements, can frame their experience as a bad business decision and remake their lives someplace else. The Gush Emunim devotees, believing that the Jewish return is God's will, cannot accept the possibility of failure, neither for themselves nor for neighboring secular settlements.

Accordingly, religious families started arriving in Chomesh, led by Menora Chazani-Katzover, daughter of settler leader Benny Katzover. The deterioration of the settlement was arrested. The secular families remaining in the settlement were very appreciative, and great effort was made to enable the two communities to coexist. For example, the local swimming pool had special hours for men and women, to cater to the needs of the religious group, and special hours when mixed couples were allowed, according to the wish of the secular residents. Chazani-Katzover, a film producer by profession, documented her arrival on film, in which she reflected on her experience:

> Sometimes I think that we are being put to the test here, that God wants to send us redemption, but from up there He asks himself, do they really want this land? What are they ready to do for her? And what does He see? That we have left the Tomb of Joseph. I want to raise my hand. I am here! I came to Chomesh! I want the land! . . . Sometimes I do not know if we will withstand the test.

Her test is not unlike the Akeda, God's trial of Abraham. In Zionist memory, the guilt is transferred to the fathers who, through their act of immigration, hold the responsibility for their sons killed in battle. The "hero" of the story, the thinking and deliberating subject, is the father. In the case of the settlers, Chazani-Katzover's father was responsible, more than most, for bringing Jews to the contested territories. However, unlike in the case of secular Zionism, the father is not a subject who bears the responsibility, and expressions of remorse about settling in the midst of hostile Arabs are absent from the settlers' discourse. The "hero" of this Akeda is God. In any case, the sacrifice was in vain, because Chomesh became one of the four settlements in northern Samaria to be evacuated in August 2005.

Consider the next quotation by a young settler describing his feelings after an attack on a yeshiva that claimed the life of his friend. His words attest to the settlers' view of terrorism as cruel fate that is inexplicable based on history:

> For me the intifada has weakened my faith somewhat. Some months be-fore the start of the intifada I went to Poland, and I returned to a state under terrorist attack. I feel that God does not care for us. He exists and He runs the world, but He does not care. Every day He sends a terrorist to kill His sons and daughters. What kind of father abuses his children like that? (Zilberkland 2002, 39)

The words of this young student reveal his great frustration arising from the feeling that he and his friends—who are faithfully carrying out the words of God and are the chosen and favorite sons—are treated in such a manner. Mentioning Poland is most revealing in this context: the speaker was among the many Israelis who travel to Poland as part of the deep Israeli commitment to the memory of the Holocaust. The great theological question raised by the horrors of the Holocaust is where God was when his chosen people and innocent children were slaughtered by the millions—a question that led to a widespread crisis of faith. The young yeshiva student associates what he conceives as the arbitrary death of his friends with the Holocaust, and his conclusions lead to theological doubts. His statement implies that the hate of the Palestinians is unprovoked by the settlers or by Israeli policy, but, like the Holocaust, is a calamity that has struck innocent victims. His conclusions, therefore, lead to questioning his religious belief rather than his political convictions.

The ordeal of the settlers in Yesha is a unique occurrence of terrorism on a massive scale against a community. It has hardly been researched enough, partly because, as I stated in the book's introduction, most Is-raeli scholars are reluctant to conduct research about the settlers, and many claim that the settlers enact a type of terrorism on their Palestin-ian neighbors that is as cruel, if not more so, than the terrorism they suffer themselves. Regardless of moral deliberations, there is a theoretical and practical question here for which it is still too early to suggest a full answer: from sociological, psychological, theological, and other aspects, how does a community confront terrorism on a massive scale? This question may be of great relevance during the twenty-first century, and the Yesha settlers' experience holds important lessons in this regard.

The widespread feelings among the settlers is that they will remain in Yesha regardless of Palestinian terrorism, that their project is a just and moral one, and that the great sacrifices they endure should not lead to moral deliberations or political doubts. These convictions, however, have to be produced and reproduced, stated and restated, with each new terrorist act. In chapter 11, I elaborate on one example to demonstrate how the closure of subversive meaning is accomplished.

7

Jewish Hebron

Fathers, Sons, and Sacrifice

Among Hebron Jews, national memory rules supreme. Hebron and nearby Kiryat Arba, claim the settlers, are where Zionism can be witnessed in its essence: a small number of dedicated Jews, obeying the biblical decree and the provisions that history has imposed upon them, have returned to the place of their forefathers to struggle against those seeking to evict them. A visitor to Kiryat Arba first encounters a large sign: "Kiryat Arba, a Zionist political settlement; as it is oppressed, so shall it flourish." The sign proclaims the town as a political-ritualistic enclave standing defiantly against two "oppressors": hostile gentiles and deluded Jewish Israelis.

Hebron is not a typical Jewish settlement. It encompasses all the motifs and components discussed in the previous chapters and pushes them to their extremes. In the settlers' version of the national geobody, Hebron is the heart, the most important and indispensable part; in comparison, all else is inconsequential. According to the book of Genesis, it is the burial place of the Patriarchs and Matriarchs of the nation and the first possession of the Jewish people in the Holy Land. The Cave of Machpela is the most sacred religious holy site in Judea and Samaria, second only to the Temple Mount and the Western Wall in Jerusalem. King David made Hebron his capital city before capturing Jerusalem. A small Jewish community had resided in Hebron under restrictive conditions for centuries until most of its people were massacred and the remainder expelled in 1929 (the Tarpat massacre). The return to Hebron and the plight of the new settlers there have entered Gush Emunim lore, adding to the sacred aura of the place.

Unlike in other settlements, in Hebron the Jews live in close proximity to the Palestinian population. This leads to constant friction and, consequently, a relatively large number of terrorist victims. In addition, Hebron is constantly threatened with evacuation, increasing its importance as the lynchpin of the settlement project. Not that the residents of Kiryat Arba and Hebron are any different from other settlers; they are a proud part of the Gush Emunim project and have more than their share of radicals and extremists, although some other settlements far outdo them in this respect. What distinguishes Hebron is that the concentration of so much history and memory in such a restricted area makes its situation volatile and extremist.

This chapter examines Hebron both as a case study and as a sui generis example. While Hebron illustrates all the principles discussed earlier, the sacred center has its own logic, different from that of other settlements. I shall try to decipher the symbolic code of Hebron, focusing on its most important points: the town of Kiryat Arba, the Cave of Machpela, the memory of the Tarpat massacre, the return to the homes of the former community, and the commemoration of terrorist victims. Hebron as a whole, however, is larger than the sum of its parts. It is like a symbolic enclave with its own rules and logic. To employ Pierre Nora's (1989) celebrated terms, while in other places there are *lieux de mémoire* (places of memory), Hebron is a unique attempt at creating an all-encompassing *milieu de mémoire* (community of memory). The identity-forming past is everywhere, part of everyday life, and the basis for future hopes. Hebron also has its present, though, as a relatively poor development town. I will explore the intricate relations between the symbolic Hebron as sacred *axis mundi* (world axis) and the quotidian Hebron as a backward development town. The final part of this chapter suggests a symbolic interpretation for the most infamous incident in Hebron since the Jews returned in 1968: the massacre by a Kiryat Arba resident of Muslims praying in the Cave of Machpela.

The New Jewish Settlement in Hebron: A Brief History

During the Six-Day War in June 1967, the town of Hebron was occupied by the advancing Israeli army.[1] Soon afterward, shortly before the 1968 Passover holiday, a group of religious Zionists, headed by Rabbi Moshe Levinger, arrived for the holiday, renting rooms in the local Park Hotel.

Afterward, the group remained, demanding that Jews be allowed to return to the ancient holy city. Eventually, the Israeli government conceded, consenting to build a new town, Kiryat Arba, close to Hebron. The settlers, who had until then lived in the Hebron military compound, moved to Kiryat Arba in 1972.

When Gush Emunim was established in 1974, the new town became its main stronghold. Some of the young leaders of the movement received their higher education in the yeshivas of Kiryat Arba, and the residents actively participated in the movement's demonstrations and acts of defiance. In 1979, Miriam Levinger, wife of the settler's leader, headed a group of women who took over Hadassah House inside the densely Arab populated city. This was the first step in the establishment of Jewish enclaves within the city. In 1980, six yeshiva students were murdered by Palestinian terrorists at the entrance to Hadassah House. In response to this and other murders of settlers, the Israeli government authorized the construction of a Jewish neighborhood within the city of Hebron. Two other major events in the turbulent history of Hebron were the exposure of the so-called Jewish underground, which had planned to blow up the mosques on the Temple Mount and kill Palestinians; and the murder by Baruch Goldstein of twenty-nine Muslims praying inside the Cave of Machpela. The leader and some members of the "underground" were residents of the Kiryat Arba and Hebron, as was Goldstein, a Kiryat Arba resident. In agreements reached between Israeli authorities and the Palestinian Authority, Hebron was divided between Jews and Arabs, as was the Cave of Machpela.

Today, the populations of Kiryat Arba and of the Jewish enclaves in Hebron number about five thousand and five hundred, respectively. Although, politically, Kiryat Arba is the largest of the Gush Emunim settlements, sociologically it is somewhat exceptional. Whereas most settlements are defined as "communal villages" and all wishing to join must be screened by an acceptance committee, in Kiryat Arba there are no restrictions on Jews wishing to join, and consequently the population is more heterogeneous. It comprises a mix of Jews of various ethnic origins and levels of religious observance, including a substantial group of non-religious Jews and new immigrants. The town is also the center of the ultra-rightist Kahane (Kach) movement.

Owing to the large number of children per family and its relative isolation from Israeli economic centers, Kiryat Arba is one of the poorest towns in Israel. Many residents were attracted by the low cost of housing and came to stay. Kiryat Arba suffers from negative population selection: the better-off families migrate to the more upscale neighborhood of Ramot Mamre in the north of the town, whereas the ideologically motivated prefer to move into Hebron, and the young tend to leave for new settlements. Most of the residents work in education, administration, and light industry, with many working in Jerusalem or in nearby settlements. Kiryat Arba serves as a regional economic and educational center for the area called Southern Mount Hebron that consists of ten new settlements.

Overlooking Hebron: Kiryat Arba as Substitute Place

From a symbolic perspective, Kiryat Arba has always been seen as a substitute for the "real thing"; that is, the city of Hebron proper. Even its founding fathers, who, one would assume, would be proud of the town they established, define their own actions as a compromise with the Israeli government's policy of Arab appeasement. Kiryat Arba was built as a neighborhood of the larger Hebron, and the concept that guided the planners was that of Nazareth Ilit, the Jewish city built (to quote the title of Dan Rabinowitz's 1997 book) "overlooking Nazareth." The Kiryat Arba leadership never settled for the segregative concept of "overlooking Hebron." Thus, while the name Kiryat Arba is a biblical one endowing it with a certain sanctity, its close proximity to Hebron undermines its attempts at achieving autonomous symbolic status.

Many of the most strongly ideological families moved into Hebron as soon as they had the chance, thus expressing their ambivalence toward Kiryat Arba. The first to do so were the women who took over Hadassah House. In their first proclamation, they stated, "When we went to live eight years ago in Kiryat Arba . . . [i]t was a compromise of accommodation with the government. Our wish was and still is Jewish settlement within Hebron." Miriam Levinger, leader of that group, said, "We started at the Park Hotel and later the Government Building, intending to settle in Hebron, but we settled for Kiryat Arba, which is actually Hebron, but not really living within the City of the Patriarchs."[2] Years after the construction of Jewish enclaves inside Hebron, a yeshiva student still lamented, "Fifteen years have passed since the erection of Kiryat Arba and still the Kirya is here and Hebron is there."[3]

Kiryat Arba and Hebron are dialectically related to each other as center and periphery. Hebron is the symbolic center that renders meaning to

Kiryat Arba. Kiryat Arba, however, is the location of secular power, has a larger population, and, in general, serves as a link with the rest of Israeli society. The true believers are expected to move into Hebron eventually, where the sanctity (and danger) is greater. Relations between the Hebron–Kiryat Arba complex as a whole and the rest of the Gush Emunim settlement project are similar; here too, we find a symbolic center and a more affluent and somewhat more secure and consensual periphery. This logic can be extended in concentric circles to the settlements vis-à-vis the rest of Israel and to Israel vis-à-vis the rest of the world. At this time, Hebron is considered to be the center of centers, and Kiryat Arba is important, indeed, but in an ambivalent location in respect to the center.

Kiryat Arba relinquished the burden of carrying the torch of memory as the settlers' center of action was pulled toward the Cave of Machpela and the homes of the butchered Jews of the pre-1929 community. Kiryat Arba itself contains several memorial places, the most infamous among them the tomb of Baruch Goldstein, located in the garden commemorating Rabbi Meir Kahane. The two places are associated with the extremist Kach movement and are regarded with ambivalence by many residents of Kiryat Arba, as well as by other settlers. The marginal symbolic status of Kiryat Arba with respect to Hebron, coupled with its relative proximity to the holy places, gives the extremist groups space to thrive.

The Cave of Machpela: The Center of Centers

The Cave of Machpela is an ancient monumental building, where, tradition asserts, the three Patriarchs and three of the four Matriarchs are buried, as detailed in the book of Genesis. Other traditions mark this as the location of the gate to the Garden of Eden and the place of the eventual arrival of the Messiah, who will first revive the Patriarchs, considered to be merely asleep. The arrival of the Israeli army at the cave during the Six-Day War was seen by both religious and secular Jews as one of the most exhilarating moments in a war full of grandeur. The cave, however, was very soon appropriated by the religious settlers and totally neglected by secular Israelis. In the last two decades, the only secular Israelis to visit the cave have been the soldiers guarding it, and the rare tour group.

For the Hebron settlers, the cave became the core of their identity, whereas other settlers arrive frequently on pilgrimages. A rabbi who is not a resident of Hebron, wrote, "It is clear to all that the sanctity of the

city is linked with the Cave of Machpela and to those who sleep in Hebron [the Patriarchs and Matriarchs]. For us, the field with the cave is the
center of the city. For us, the city is worthless in comparison with this
grave site" (Rosen 1974, 11). A resident explained, "The Cave of Machpela is the center of our life . . . The cave is the point of convergence of
heaven and earth; it possesses all the spiritual and earthly power, which
together create great perfection: a Hebronian perfection."[4]

The importance of the cave as a symbol is evident in almost every
home and building in Kiryat Arba (as elsewhere in Judea and Samaria).
Pictures of it adorn many walls, and it is the chosen topic for numerous
artworks, some realistic and most allegorical, and the emblem for most
public institutions in town. Even the wine bottled in Kiryat Arba is called
"Machpela" and bears the cave's imprint on the cork. The cave is the preferred place of worship, especially for the celebration of life-cycle events.
Even when a wedding is not held in front of the cave, the wedding invitations will usually bear its picture. The link of the settlers to the cave is
also reinforced through research. Using textual analysis and archaeological findings, two local researchers have concluded that the cave is "in the
right place."

The settlers exhibit an emotional attachment to the cave. Some say
that they do not leave Kiryat Arba for better circumstances elsewhere
because of their wish to stay close to the cave. The cave is personified: it
"talks," it "cries," and, most of all, it is "happy" to see the return and loyalty of Jews. The cave remembers what occurred in Hebron—events to
which it stood witness. A schoolboy published a poem in one of Kiryat
Arba bulletins: "I told her tell me, tell me, the Cave / Why are you sad?
What has happened to you? / And she said in a quiet voice / I have just
remembered the massacre of Tarpat"[5]

The Cave of Machpela, beyond its unique meaning for the settlers
in Hebron and elsewhere, is one of the many pilgrimage sites scattered
across the land of Israel and is visited by many with personal problems
who believe that the sleeping Fathers and Mothers can bring wealth,
happiness, marital success, and good health. Most of these holy sites
throughout the country are associated with the new ethnic revival and
the reemergence of the cult of North African zaddikim (saints). These
are mostly found in or around development towns, where many of the
lower socioeconomic classes of Mizrahi Jews reside. The sacred sites lend
prestige to the peripheral towns, making them symbolic centers. This
may be one reason for their establishment and success.[6] Whereas the cave

endows a generally poor town with esteem that attracts a flow of pilgrims with the ensuing economic benefits, in the case of Hebron and Kiryat Arba the sacred place existed previously and determined the choice of the location for the establishment of a settlement.

Unlike the residents of the development towns, the residents of Kiryat Arba and Hebron are mainly Ashkenazim of national religious affiliation. For them, the cave is sacred, not because the holy men and women buried there can perform miracles, but because it symbolizes the roots and essence of the nation. When these residents pray, they do so for political as well as religious reasons, accentuating their presence in a contested site; their entreaties will mostly be for national salvation rather than personal health or success. They were, however, quick to take advantage of other types of commitment to the cave, including the ethnic revival in Israel. On major holidays, busloads of pilgrims arrive at the cave, and the two understandings of an Israeli sacred site, the national religious and the Mizrahi religious, are combined. While this mass manifestation of popular attachment to the site strengthens the settlers, it also strengthens the phenomenon of new ethnicity and ties together the interests of two of the phenomena that most strongly challenge the ethos of secular Israelis.

The cave also differs from the new Mizrahi holy places in another important way: whereas the mushrooming of holy places of Mizrahi zaddikim should be understood in the context of the troubled history of Mizrahi immigrants in Israel and their problematic connection to their peripheral place of residence, the Cave of Machpela must be understood within the context of the Israeli-Palestinian conflict. As the Patriarchs are sacred to Islam, the cave is holy for the Muslims as well. Consequently, the explosive struggle over the cave is both national and religious and therefore has a tense uncompromising nature. It goes to the heart of the settlers' demands to determine the true history of the land. They like to show a caricature of one Arab saying to the other, "We must not give in! Tomorrow they will claim that Abraham, Isaac, and Jacob were Jewish!" In other words, if the cave is not under Jewish control and if Muslim Arabs still hold the keys, Jewish history cannot be redeemed.

The cave narrates the conflict between Jews and Arabs along certain lines. Each clash evokes, on the part of the settlers, a historically loaded discourse built upon the dichotomy of exile and salvation. Stories abound of *talith* (prayer shawl)-wearing Jews dragged through the mud and beaten on their way to prayer and of Torah scrolls desecrated. The term used invariably is *pogrom*, taken from the exilic context. In such depictions, the Arabs assume the role of the malicious gentiles, and the government—though Israeli—assumes the role of the indifferent or hostile authorities. In their narrative strategy, the settlers contrast the anachronistic exilic situation with the political aspirations of a Jewish Hebron. The purpose of Zionism and the establishment of the state of Israel, as they see it, is to eliminate such situations of Jewish powerlessness and negate the exile; yet, they argue, under the defeatist Israeli government, such events occur, even in the most sacred of sites: the city of the nation's fathers and of King David. This definition of the situation, as exile within the sacred home, goes a long way toward explaining the settlers' motivation.

At present, the cave is divided between the two angry religious communities. Cases of violence on both sides are frequent, having culminated in the Goldstein massacre. The intensity of Jewish hatred toward the local Palestinians is attributed by the settlers to the massacre of 1929. For the Jewish population, this is an unforgivable historical crime that annuls any rights of the Hebron Arabs to the site.

Tarpat as the Hebronian Holocaust

The complaints of Israeli soldiers trying to keep the peace in divided Hebron provide the Israeli press with a steady flow of stories on the tense relations within the city. One soldier, who initiated a photo exposition in Tel Aviv describing the difficult moral situation in which the soldiers find themselves, told the following tale: Settler girls played near his position at the "Gross Plaza" in Hebron when an old Palestinian woman passed carrying grocery bags. The girls picked up stones and threw them at her. When the soldier demanded why they were doing that, the girls answered, "How do you know what she did in Tarpat?"[7]

The 1929 massacre or "Tarpat" (after the Hebrew acronym for the year 5689 according to the Jewish calendar) is a founding experience in the identity of the Hebron Jews. A peaceful Jewish community lived in Hebron for centuries under restrictive laws, yet well integrated into the social and economic life of the city. The outbreak of the Arab-Jewish conflict in Palestine made Jewish life in Hebron precarious: in 1929, an Arab mob killed sixty-seven Jews, and the British authorities evicted the rest. The communal institutions, such as the synagogue and cemetery, were desecrated and pillaged, and the houses were given to new Arab dwellers.[8] After that, Jews did not return to live in Hebron until the present settlers arrived.

The current community regards itself as a direct continuation of the previous, destroyed community and defines the crime committed by the local Arabs decades before its own arrival as one inflicted upon itself. The tragic events served to legitimate their arrival in Hebron and their penetration of the Arab-populated city. As Rabbi Levinger entered Hebron, he immediately demanded that the murderers of Tarpat be sought out and brought to trial. The settlers brought with them a Torah scroll that had survived the massacre and was to be given only to the Jews returning to Hebron. In general, Tarpat supplied the historical framework and supported the narrative of the arrival of Rabbi Levinger and his group in the city.

The settlers have reinstated the memory of Tarpat, claiming that it should hold historical importance for modern Israel. Actually, they attempted to revive a memory that had been dead for decades. Unlike other dramatic events in the turbulent history of Jewish presence in the land of Israel, and contrary to numerous major events of the Jewish-Arab conflict, the Hebron massacre has slipped into collective oblivion. Its date was never declared a formal day of bereavement or remembrance in Israel, and it did not even enjoy informal status anywhere. This oblivion has much to do with the non-Zionist nature of the pre-1929 Hebron Jewish community. It had tried to save itself by relying on British Mandate forces and good neighborly relations with the local Arab population. It acted in ways defined by the Zionist ethos as nonheroic and exilic, unworthy of national commemoration. An indication of the peripheral nature of the Tarpat story is the difficulty the remnants of the community encountered in raising money for a memorial book. By the time they succeeded, Rabbi Levinger and his fellow settlers were already in Hebron, adding their own chapters to the Hebron narrative (which were indeed included in the memorial book) (Avisar 1970).

Is the association between the new and old communities manipulative or does it reflect an actual "authentic" emotional bond? It is not easy to disentangle the politics of identity to reach the motivations underlying it. Clearly, the identification with a peaceful community, and innocent victims of unprovoked violence, has benefits for the settlers. In their eyes, the perpetrators of such a hideous crime have lost their moral right to object to the return of the Jews to Hebron—a right that was dubious in any case. "They ask us if we are afraid to live in Hebron," says a woman settler: "Those who should be afraid are the Arabs who have not yet apologized for the great massacre."[9]

But the presence of Tarpat for the Jews in Hebron is everywhere. It is taught in schools, written about passionately in local bulletins, and used extensively in internal political discourse. Government decisions against the settlers are criticized as "Tarpat all over again." Some of the survivors of the massacre have returned to live in Kiryat Arba, whereas others have transferred their rights to the new settlers. The small and diminishing group of Tarpat survivors has been important for the sense of genealogical continuity that it has bestowed upon the settlers. The survivors have been asked endlessly to tell and retell the story of the massacre and have been treated with utmost respect.

In the settler's narrative, the massacre was the main reason for coming to Hebron in the first place, both personally and collectively. When Haggai Huberman (2002b) tells the story of Kiryat Arba and Jewish Hebron, the subtitle of his article is "Erasing the shame of Tarpat." Ze'ev Hever is one of the leading figures in the reestablishment of Jewish presence in Hebron. In one of the settlement's internal publications, he, somewhat awkwardly, described the three major duties that the people of Israel have in Hebron: erasing the shame of the *hurban* ("destruction," another term laden with exilic connotation) of Tarpat, reversing the failure of the former community to return to Hebron, and reestablishing the continuity of life in Hebron.[10] Obviously, none of these goals have much to do with the well-being of the current residents of Kiryat Arba or Hebron; they are all different ways of making the same point—that the role of the new community is to replace the old one, inherit its history, and settle its scores. Subsequently, the success of the settlement is defined by the relief it brings to those who remember Tarpat. A resident explained his feelings about living in Hebron:

> I grew up in the shadow of the fear and terror that emerged whenever the story of the Hebron murder was told in my home; I developed an allergy to the name of Hebron . . . Today I find it difficult to get used to the simple fact that I live in the city of the Fathers. Not one day is routine. Now happiness has replaced that awful fear. Every regular day becomes a holiday: a day of victory for the forces of life over the forces of death.[11]

Jewish transformation motifs are prevalent in foregoing quotation—from darkness to light, from destruction to construction, from exile to homecoming, from death to life—all taken from traditional Judaic prayers and texts. The telling of the narrative is important, though the actual facts are dubious: it is doubtful how many Israeli Jews, religious or secular, grew up in the shadow of fear and terror because of Tarpat stories. However, many Israelis did grow up under the impact of a greater calamity whose effect on Israeli identity has been acknowledged and explored extensively.[12] When the Hebron residents think of Tarpat, their immediate analogy is the European Holocaust. The national religious sector places the Holocaust at the center of its identity, as do the Hebron settlers. The memory of the Holocaust supplies the common language in which to speak of Tarpat in a way that is meaningful both to the settlers and to other Israelis.[13]

Idioms appropriated from Holocaust discourse dominate the discourse of the Tarpat massacre. One can even say that, for its Jewish settlers, Tarpat is the Hebronian Holocaust. The terms used to describe the Tarpat horror are those used to describe the violent events in Europe that peaked with the Holocaust: such as *praot* (riots) and *hurban* (destruction). The narrative that the settlers tell bears many similarities to that of the Holocaust: in both events, the evil expressed is satanic and incomprehensible, evidence of a basic unchangeable trait of the killers; annihilation of Jewish existence and memory is an integral part of the crime; the locals betrayed their peace-loving Jewish neighbors, which—in light of Jewish history—was only to be expected; some "Righteous Gentiles," few in number, saved Jews even at considerable risk to themselves and deserve acknowledgment; commemoration of the history of those murdered, as well as the deeds of the killers, is a sacred moral obligation; and the perpetrator community must pay reparations, even if this will never erase the memory and its responsibility for the crime. For the settlers, there will never be a "new Germany," nor will there ever be a "new Arabic Hebron." The settlers assume the "never again" position expressed by many Israelis in relation to the Holocaust, and regard the success of their endeavor as an act of defiance against their tragic history. As in the case of the establishment of Israel, the past tragedy of Hebron imbues political action with deep morality, which can easily deteriorate to wholesale legitimation of violence.

Just as Yad Vashem in Jerusalem commemorates the Holocaust, a museum in Hebron commemorates Tarpat. A dark room contains miniature pictures of the victims and broken gravestones leading down into a hole. There are also large pictures of the horror, and visitors are spared nothing. Another artifact is a gravestone with a swastika painted over it—the act of a Hebron Arab—showing, in the eyes of the settlers, the affinity between the two calamities. The museum confronts the same basic problem of commemoration so acutely evident in the case of the Holocaust: as the number of actual witnesses dwindles over the years, telling and retelling become crucial in the battle against the attempts to diminish the extent of the horror. The museum is part of an attempt to pass the burden of remembering on to the younger generation. Due to the extensive socialization and the recurring acts of Palestinian terrorism, one can say that the settlers of Hebron tend to regard themselves as survivors of Tarpat.

While the Cave of Machpela engenders a religious discourse of exile and redemption, Tarpat supports a moral and legal discourse. The settlers' wish to persecute the murders of Tarpat did not materialize, but their demand to return to places that had belonged to the former community and had been owned by Jews was honored. This is not their only rationale for penetrating the heavily populated town, but it provides great legitimation for the endeavor. Here we see one of the crucial flaws in the analogy with Holocaust remembrance: the Jewish community of Hebron insists on returning to live in proximity to the community whose members it defines as murderers. Whereas the so-called Zionist solution after (and before) the European Holocaust was to leave exile and return to the national homeland, the settler's solution is to transform Hebron from a locus of exilic reality to a mark of the homeland.

REBUILDING THE LIFEWORLD OF THE FORMER COMMUNITY

Even more than in the Zionist ethos, *return* is the key symbol of the settlers of Hebron, and it tends to be extremely literal. The memory of Tarpat created a context of concrete places with documented pasts, where it became possible to strive for a reversal of the historical fortunes.

The ancient Jewish graveyard of Hebron was the first locus of symbolic value with which the settlers reidentified. It was identified and restored, with special attention devoted to the plot where the dead of the Tarpat massacre were buried. Instead of leaving the cemetery as a relic, the settlers' logic dictated reopening it for dead from their own community. A mythological drama of a biblical nature ensued. The first to die in Kiryat Arba in 1975 was a baby, the firstborn of the Nachshon family, named (not surprisingly) Abraham. The settlers brought him to be buried in the ancient graveyard over the objection of the Israeli soldiers guarding it. As the history-mythology of the story goes, the mother, named (obviously) Sara, carried her son's body in her arms past the soldiers to the graveyard and buried it there with her bare hands, saying, "If God has taken from me the son that was born in Hebron and circumcised in Hebron—this son shall open the cemetery for us."

The symbolism of this act is stressed by the Jews of Hebron because it resonates endlessly with the history of the place. For example, the first purchase in ancient Hebron was when the Patriarch Abraham bought the Cave of Machpela in which to bury his wife Sara, whereas, in the modern-day version, the mother Sara brought the child Abraham to burial. The event connected three points in time: the ancient Patriarch, the dead community that had used the cemetery, and the new community. The name Hebron is etymologically derived from *chibur,* meaning "connection." Hebron connects the dead and the living, as well as man and God, and its name was probably given to it because it was an ancient necropolis (place of burial). The story of the burial of Abraham Nachshon is so important in Hebron's mythology because the essence of life in Jewish Hebron is intimately connected with death, burial, and remembrance.

The next stage in the return to the places of the former community was the reconstruction of the Avraham Avinu (Our Father Abraham) Synagogue. The ruins, which were near the Arab market, had been used as a rubbish dump and as goat and sheep pens. The great gap between its past grandeur and its present dismal state was an important motivation for reviving it as an active institution. In their reconstruction, the settlers turned to research, using old pictures and aerial maps. Significantly, once the synagogue was reconstructed, the old Torah scroll was returned to its original place, and the synagogue was handed over to the Sephardic community. Although the majority of the present community is Ashkenazi, the logic of return meant that things would have to be the way they were before the breach of Tarpat.

The synagogue and the graveyard, the house of life and the house of death, are most important in the life of a practicing religious Jewish community. This was, however, only the start for a broad project designed to return to Jewish hands all the buildings that belonged to the former community. The settlers also reclaim residential homes, mostly by buying them from current Arab owners, while complaining that the houses have actually been bought twice: once by members of the former community and once by the new settlers. As the Jewish community inside Hebron grows, old houses are purchased and new houses are built. The expansion of Jewish Hebron creates new points of friction with the Arabs, who become more hostile toward the settler's project as it increasingly threatens their homes and daily routine.

The restoration of the old structures to their former use creates a unique situation that takes the concept of collective memory and commemoration to great extremes. The new settlers find themselves living in the city of the former community, next to the same neighbors they define as potential and actual murderers. They live in the same houses, sometimes in the same rooms, where their predecessors were violently butchered. They use the same synagogue that holds the same Torah scroll, and they bury their dead in the same graveyard. Thus, the new place merges with the old one, and the new settlers ritually assume the identity of the murdered members of the former community. They do not live in the shadow of the memory but rather live the memory itself, transforming themselves, metaphorically, into shadows of the past. Perhaps the words of Miriam Levinger, who reentered Hadassah House, present this concept of the present-past best of all:

> On the first Saturday evening after we returned to the Hadassah House, yeshiva students came and danced under the windows of the building. At that moment, we felt as if the souls of the murdered of this place had come and gathered with us at the window to see what was happening, and rejoiced with us at the sight of Jews dancing on Saturday evening in the streets of Hebron. I wanted to calm them and say to them, "You can rest, you have waited for many years, now we have returned. What was in Hebron in the past is what will happen in the future. For ever more."[14]

Levinger did not realize how right she would prove to be. Within a few months, six of these yeshiva students were killed in a terrorist attack in front of Hadassah House. Not only were their lives a continuation of the lives of the murdered Jews of the former community, but they died in the same way. The Jewish residents of Hebron, who dedicated their lives to the commemoration of a former community, now had to search for ways to commemorate the members of their own community.

COMMEMORATING THE VICTIMS OF TERRORISM

Monumental history in Hebron is an ongoing venture, creating a dialectical pattern in the relations between space and memory: An event occurs somewhere in Hebron and thus sanctifies that spot. This engenders commemorative acts and attempts at creating a permanent presence. This presence in turn, while being defined as retaliation for the initial act of violence, encourages further Palestinian violence. Thus, memory and appropriation of space go hand in hand.

Hebron settlers suffer from Palestinian violence more than settlers in other places because of the relatively high friction between the communities and the more immediate and intense threat that the settlers pose to the local Arab population. The memory of Tarpat generates, among the settlers, intense emotional feelings toward the Arabs in their proximity, which other settlers do not always share. The residents of Kiryat Arba were overrepresented in the Jewish underground, and their main motivation was to retaliate against Arab terrorist acts (Medoff 1986). Significantly, in Haggai Segal's book (1988) on the history of the Jewish underground written from the perspective of one of its members (himself a resident of the Ofra settlement), the first chapter is dedicated to the murder of the six yeshiva students in Hebron, an event that is portrayed as a major motivation for those who joined the clandestine group. Terror is an everyday possibility in Hebron, and commemoration of its victims is an important part of the Hebronian symbolic world.

Of the numerous commemorations in Hebron over the years, I will concentrate on two: one because it was the first, and the second because I observed it firsthand.

The first of the settlers to be killed in Hebron, in 1979, was a yeshiva student named Yehoshua Saloma. All the components of settler commemoration were already present at that time. Rabbi Eliezer Waldman (1980) spoke at the funeral and connected the death to the renewed life and new beginnings: "The blood is calling us to release the chains of the Jewish settlement in Hebron, chains that disable Jewish life at the place of the murder" (3). Mourning was an integral part, not only of the story of the killing, but also of the connection with further development of Jewish Hebron. The invitation to the commemoration ceremony read "The entire community, men, women and children, are called to join us in our sorrow and grief, and to take part in Israel's return to Hebron." Commemoration included a demonstration, prayer in the Cave of Machpela, and a tour of the sites of the former community, especially "the houses and institutions that are meant to return to the people of Israel."

A monument was erected at the place of the murder, and, once a year, the teachers and students of the yeshiva where Saloma studied come to conduct a ceremony. Since the monument is situated in a predominantly Arab public space, it is often defiled despite the fence built around it. The settlers view this situation with great anger and pray for the day when they will be able to safeguard the monument properly. Here we can see the dynamics of Jewish communal expansion: the monument that commemorates a past victim may tomorrow become the basis for further infiltration.

In 1993, another yeshiva student, Erez Shmuel, was killed on his way to the Cave of Machpela. The place where he was killed was immediately renamed Erez Alley, and a placard was placed on the wall. At the shivah (seven-day mourning ritual), two Israeli flags were placed on the spot so that it resembled a national memorial. Rabbi Waldman, the student's teacher, commenced a long hunger strike at the commemorative site. At the mass rally held during the shivah, political and religious leaders declared, once again, the connection of the murder to the rebuilding of Hebron. Dov Lior, who held the office of the Rabbi of Kiryat Arba, linked the death of Erez Shmuel to national goals in the following way: "Erez died as an envoy of this community, for the right of our people to walk freely in our land." Death in Hebron is never devoid of meaning: it is always connected somehow to the greatness and suffering of the past and to the promised salvation of the future.

Hebron has its "sacred map," with special pilgrimage and tourist routes and attractions. The map combines places associated with various histories: the ancient one of the Patriarchs and kings, the Tarpat one, the markers of new Jewish presence, and the location of murderous acts against the settlers. A walking tour in Hebron, organized by Midreshet Hebron, is also a tour through history. Erez Alley, which is the starting point of the tour, already has its own mythology, including the dangers of walking to the cave, the murder, and the commemorative acts. As is the custom with mythic tales, Rabbi Waldman's hunger strike grows longer with every retelling of the story. I once witnessed the amused soldiers who safeguard the tour correct the tour guide about the length of the hunger strike.

Visiting Erez Alley on the way to other attractions lends the tour its meaning; the visitors assume the role of yeshiva students wishing to enter Hebron to connect with the roots of their identity. Through symbolically replicating his act, they demonstrate that terrorism has failed in its attempts to deter Jews from their continuing attempt to complete their journey into Hebron. Moreover, by beginning the tour from a place of commemoration of a yeshiva student, the visitors are reminded that the current residents of Hebron are also heroes of mythical stature, on a par with their mythical fathers. According to the settlers' narrative, Hebron is a place where heroic history is being made and commemorated, produced and reproduced, at the same time and through the same acts.

The Arabs of Hebron in the Settlers' Eyes

I joined a group of settlers on their tour around Hebron. We were guarded by soldiers and moved through the streets of the partly deserted town. The few Arabs who were sitting in front of their shops looked at us with a gaze filled with hatred. Although the only weapons in sight were held by the soldier guarding us, it was, nevertheless, a frightening experience, and not only for me. The settlers started singing "settler songs" at the top of their voices. This singing, as far as I could tell, fulfilled two functions: first, it showed the Arabs that Jews are unafraid to walk the streets of the town they consider to be theirs, and, second, it helped in confronting the fear of a situation in which a small group of Israeli Jews march under army protection in a city heavy populated with hate-filled Palestinians.

Some seventy thousand Palestinians live in Hebron, with many more residing in the neighboring towns and villages. They separate the Jewish community and the Jewish urban centers of Jerusalem and Beer Sheva. Basically, the stereotypes held by Gush Emunim about the Arabs, as presented in chapter 5, hold for Kiryat Arba and Hebron as well, but this case has some unique characteristics. Whereas, in other ideological settlements, settlers seek to manifest their presence inside Palestinian villages while residing at a safe distance from them, in Hebron, the sacredness of the holy place, combined with the political mythology of Tarpat, necessitates a more complex and elaborate concept of the status of the Arabs. The Hebron Arabs possess both much more of a history and menacing presence than the Arabs in other places. According to the settler's worldview, their own presence in Hebron is self-evident, whereas the Palestinian presence is not merely a practical problem but a theological dilemma, a historical anomaly, and a moral outrage.

Two seemingly contrasting images dominate the settlers' understanding of the Arab presence in the sacred city. One is an orientalist viewpoint of the natives as enchanting, yet violent, primitives who, with special care and education, can be taught to see the truth. From the settlers' perspective, the Hebron Arabs are a special kind of savage whose ancestors can

be traced to the Bible and whose actual parents participated in an unforgivable crime. The other image somewhat resembles that of the Wild
West. The settlers see themselves as civilized people arriving in a wilderness populated with hostile natives. It makes little difference whether
the Arabs are inferior or equal; they are an immutable enemy, and all the
settlers can do is hold them at bay.

Let us start with the first image, in which the settlers assume a social-
izing mission that attempts to save the Hebron Arabs from their moral
backwardness (not unlike the "white man's burden" of European colonialism). In Hebron, the settlers used to define good neighborly relations
between Jews and Arabs as a goal, a viable possibility, and an ideal. This
may derive from the evident demographic weakness of the settlers, but
it also holds important ideological significance. Rabbi Levinger stressed
the reeducation of the Arabs from the moment he arrived: "We are helping them to free themselves from their education toward extermination
wishes . . . We are purifying them of the atmosphere of murder and ac-
customing them to a peaceful atmosphere."[15] His vision was "The Arabs,
though they may object at first, will get used to the men, women, children, shops, Hebrew signs, Hebrew names, Israeli mail . . . and to the
Israeli flag and Israeli sovereignty!"[16]

The *real* Arabs, according to some of the settlers, are those described
in the Bible, and Rabbi Levinger accentuates the point by calling them
"Ishmaelites." The settlers regard with wonder that the Cave of Machpela
serves two nations and religions, both descending from the same mythic
father buried there. That does not imply that they would yield an iota of
what they believe to be their exclusive rights to the cave, but in the background is always a glimmer of returning not only to the place, but also
to the social relations of the biblical era that are part of the place. At the
aforementioned rally in memory of Erez Shmuel, the father of the murdered settler recited a poem in Arabic through the loudspeakers that was
intended for the Arab residents of Hebron. He said that their mother
Hagar of the book of Genesis is now ashamed of her sons for the murder and for refusing to live peacefully with their relatives, the Jews.

Orientalist conceptions can be seen also in the surprising respect that
the Arabs sometimes "enjoy." As mentioned in chapter 5, since the Arabs
in general and the Palestinians in particular are viewed by the settlers as
inherently premodern people, they are seen as truly and profoundly com-
prehending the meaning of divine promise and love of the land—things
long forgotten by the modern and mostly secular Israeli population.

According to the settlers, both populations not only share space in Hebron, they also share the same basic understanding of the situation—the rightful return of the Jews to Hebron. Both can differentiate between good and evil, even if the Arabs have chosen the wrong path.

A resident told me that the Arabs watching the sight of Sara Nachshon bringing her son Abraham for burial in the Jewish graveyard could not understand why the Israeli government and army would prohibit it. He asserted that no Arab in his right mind could understand the sick mind of the Jews, not doing what is obviously right. A book commemorating the six yeshiva students killed in 1980 states, "In Hebron they [meaning the Arabs] knew that the Jews have come home. To tell the truth, they knew better than we did" (Aviezer 1985, 23). The Arabs of Hebron also expected, according to the settlers, to be severely punished for the Tarpat massacre when the Israeli army entered Hebron, and were surprised when they were not. The settlers and the Arabs, they maintain, while entangled in a battle of life and death on one front, share an understanding of what is important in life, unlike secular modern Israel with its propensity to forget its own roots in history. The Arabs, however, are deceitful insofar as they refuse publicly to accept the rights of the Jews and their responsibility for crime of Tarpat.

Following this reasoning, the settlers criticized the decision to build a new town, Kiryat Arba, instead of being allowed to establish their community within Hebron. They complained that Kiryat Arba was built as a Jewish ghetto, whereas their wish was to become regular citizens of the town, well integrated into its economic and social life. The reeducation of the Arab population of Hebron would be impossible without a sustainable presence alongside the settlers' chosen students. In the settlers' way of thinking, distancing them from Hebron encourages incitement of the tranquil Arabs against the settlers.

Even though Jewish enclaves have been established inside Hebron, the settlers and Arabs are strictly segregated, and breaching the lines is seen as a hostile act. The Israeli Defense Forces that protect the settlers and their visitors who want to tour Hebron also find themselves protecting the Palestinians from the rage of the settlers. Landscape semiotics are also radically different: the settler architecture is modern whereas the Palestinian is traditional Middle Eastern. In addition, all municipal facilities, such as transportation, commerce, health, and education, are separate. A settler and an Arab resident of Hebron will never wait in the same line for service. The settlers in Hebron receive their supplies from the outside rather than from their Arab neighbors. Even the maps that they hold are different: the settlers name sites in accordance with Jewish history and their own martyrology, whereas the Palestinians have their own names for the same places. The Hebron agreement between Israel and the Palestinian Authority has placed a formal seal on the reality of segregation by dividing the city between the two hostile communities.

The institutionalization of segregation symbolizes the total failure of the settlers to transform the Arabs according to the settlers' wishes. Although the Arabs are still patronizingly seen as premodern, the settlers have forsaken any pretense of reeducating them. The hostility of the Arabs is sometimes understood as a lack of gratitude toward the good intentions of the returning Jews, and as a manifestation of their alienation from the attempts to place the Arabs in the symbolic order chosen by the settlers. The redemptive urge has been reduced, and revenge is much more prominent in the settlers' frame of mind.

Symbolic acceptance of Arab rights as individuals or as a collective is much less a part of the settler's discourse today. Arab presence is seen more as a historical accident—a result of contingency rather than divine or historical rights. They are only passersby in a city that belongs to others. For a community that places a high premium on remembrance and historical rights, this is tantamount to delegitimation of present Palestinian existence. Without an anchor in ancient history, the only relevant history that applies to the Arabs is Tarpat and the terrorist acts directed against those defined as the rightful owners of the place.

In the rally after the death of Erez Shmuel, the difference between the Jewish presence and the Arab presence was made very clear. One of the speakers called on each member of the crowd to stop on their way home at the place where the murderers emerged from the ruins and take out a stone until no stones would be left. Stones create houses and also symbolize them. The speaker implied that, while Jewish ruins are to be preserved and rebuilt, Arab ruins have no such mystique and should be demolished. For the settlers, the Arab house, especially if it is used to hide terrorists, does not hold the same sanctity and rights to exist as the Jewish house. Yet, Arab houses dominate the landscape and fill the view of most windows in Kiryat Arba, let alone the Jewish enclave in Hebron. From their bedroom windows, the settlers can see that Hebron is still not theirs.

Many examples can be presented of how the overimposing Arab presence is denied and repressed. In photographs in publications aimed at bringing new residents to Kiryat Arba, the Palestinian population is not mentioned and Arab houses are whited out. A girl wrote the following "historical" description of the mythic founding event of her community: "The city of the Patriarchs is desolate, the houses are broken, the stones are gray. No living sign in the dry desert. Mice and rats celebrate and insects multiply. Cats howl and big wild dogs wander around like wolves, whining from hunger and thirst. Then, one day in the year of 1968, Rabbi Levinger said, 'Can I hire your hotels for seven days?'"[17]

In the girl's story, Hebron had neither a history nor a civilized existence prior to the arrival of Rabbi Levinger and the Jewish settlers. The hotel seemingly materialized when Rabbi Levinger knocked on its door. The description brings to mind images of the Wild West and the American frontier. Rabbi Levinger, nicknamed "the sheriff of Hebron" by both his supporters and opponents, presented this image as he ran (unsuccessfully) for a seat in the Israeli Parliament. Levinger and his friends have assumed a new role in Hebron—not as educators, but as guardians and upholders of the law they brought with them—a law that has no consideration for the interests of the local Palestinians and that is related ambivalently to Israeli law and order.

The intense pressure of the settlers, coupled with the explicit or reluctant backing of the army, had catastrophic results for the Hebron Palestinians. Following the Goldstein massacre, the two communities were divided and protected from each other. Within a few years, the Hebron market and its surroundings witnessed a mass migration, and large areas were practically emptied of Arab residents, who could see no future in residing near the incessant pressure of the Jewish settlers. Not surprisingly, Hebron is the only place in the West Bank where a massive evacuation of a Palestinian population took place. In the city area that is today under direct Israeli rule (20 percent), there are five hundred Jews and thirty-five thousand Palestinians. A review in an Israeli television documentary stated, "The Jews enjoy a high standard of leaving, freedom of movement, and a rich spiritual life. The Palestinians are ghostly figures living in a continuous hell of barracks, checks, searches, movement restrictions, and constant badgering, without any real protection."[18]

A Concentrated Reality

The description of some of the many religious and historical sites in Hebron portrays only part of the picture. Hebron is conceived by the settlers as a whole greater than the sum of its parts. Every site has several complementary meanings that explain why it is sacred in itself and how it is connected to other places and other stories. Each story is also a metaphor, and the stories are easily interchangeable. The entirety of Hebron is represented in each of its parts. Yossi Sharvit (1985), a historian living in Kiryat Arba, expressed the recurring circular pattern of Hebronian history: "One should know and recognize that we add our stones to the ones built by our fathers. We do not start something new but add layers to the fortress walls built through the ages . . . All the links join to form a long chain garlanding the hills of Hebron, adding the memory of ancient days to the passion of renewal" (145).

For example, in addition to the Patriarchs, the Cave of Machpela commemorates the members of the former subservient community, who were permitted to climb only to the seventh entry step outside the building to pray, as well as the glorious and tragic history of recent times. Archaeological research, conducted by the settlers themselves, adds new stories; the symbols may incorporate new events and render them meaningful. The Avraham Avinu Synagogue commemorates both the Patriarch Abraham as well as the former community that was wiped out in Tarpat; later, the heroic story of its reconstruction was added. In the synagogue, tour guides tell of a Saturday night some centuries ago, when one man was lacking from the ten needed for minyan (ritual prayer group of ten). A stranger joined who turned out to be Abraham himself, visiting the synagogue named after him in the city where he is buried. Mythology is condensed into symbolic legend and concentrated in the sacred site.

Since Hebron is, so to speak, a forest of symbols where each act resonates through the ages and each place bears numerous narratives, a general sense of holiness emerges from the accumulation of the sacred and the historic. Many residents describe their relation to Hebron in terms of mystical experience. Elyakim Haetzni, a secular resident, tells his story: "Hebron is part of our genetic code. Once my genetic needle pointed toward Hebron, I felt an electric shock. In Hebron, I feel for the first time at home."[19] One of the residents explained to me that he came to live in Hebron because of the sound of the name "Hebron" when he says it. Another resident wrote, "Sometimes, when the wind is howling in Hebron and Kiryat Arba, it seems as if you can hear King David crying."[20]

The return to history and the merging of "social time" with "monumental time"[21] has important consequences for the daily management of the community. Hebron has a past to which its residents are dedicated and holds a utopic future; it does not have a concept of the present. The head of the municipality explained why internal politics in Hebron is actually national if not metaphysical: "The most trivial things in the life of the town, such as the cemetery or synagogue, become complex in Kiryat Arba. . . . That's what happens when the cemetery is the Jewish cemetery of Hebron and the synagogue is the Cave of Machpela. . . . What differentiates Kiryat Arba from other municipalities is Hebron."[22]

Hebron is seen as a ritual place where Jewish and Zionist history is condensed and played out repeatedly. The story of Hebron includes the same motifs as the national narrative of Zionism: a great past of ancient fathers and glorious kings; a long period of exile, with Jews wishing and praying to return; a Holocaust demonstrating how fragile Jewish existence without sovereignty can be; and, finally, a triumphant return accompanied by great human sacrifice.

Unlike most secular Israelis, however, the settlers of Hebron live close to, and some actually within, their symbols of good and evil. A visitor from another settlement stated, "The residents of Hebron do not live in another reality, but they experience the Yesha reality in different doses. It is a concentrated reality."[23] In the eyes of the Hebron settlers and their supporters, their experience is more real and clear. Everywhere in Israel, the Jewish logic of return to the ancient homeland despite violent resistance is the same; the difference is that the Hebron settlers realize this truth and see it in their everyday life with their own eyes, whereas other Israelis disguise it with assumed normalcy. The members of the small community of Hebron Jews see themselves as fulfilling truly and faithfully the decrees of Judaism and Zionism, and therefore regard themselves as the privileged, chosen, and authentic representatives of the national movement. They live in history. Miriam Levinger expresses this idea:

> In Hebron, one can see the situation of the people of Israel exactly as it is. A small group of Jews surrounded by hostile people. I see the Jewish truth in its pure essence. Other places are in the same situation but with more makeup. Sometimes it is very hard to confront the truth in all its essence . . . But it is good. Nothing stands between the truth and us. (Aviezer 1985, 244)

Furthermore, in the eyes of the Hebron settlers, the entire Zionist project depends upon their own success. Since in Hebron one sees the raison d'être of Zionism in its purest form, what chances have Tel Aviv and Haifa once it falls? Hebron is the "heart," without which nothing holds importance. Betrayal of Hebron, claim the settlers, is, in a sense, patricide on the part of Israel: killing the moral source that renders meaning to the entire project and holds the lifeline of the Jewish people.

EXPLAINING GOLDSTEIN

As the Cave of Machpela is the holiest of places for the Jews in Hebron, the permission granted to the Muslims to share the space is a sty in their eye. When I joined a group of Jews praying in one of the halls of the building, the feeling of shame and rage became most apparent to me. When the muezzin on the tower turned on his loudspeaker and called the Muslims believers to prayer, the Jewish worshippers heard him and tried to continue their quiet prayer. What they were hearing, however, was the loud Arabic voice that made it impossible for them to concentrate. They started praying louder in a futile attempt to win this uneven contest. As they realized that their voices were no a match for the loudspeaker, tears formed in their eyes. The muezzin won the day, and he was able to compete successfully with the settlers only because the Israeli authorities allowed him to broadcast his religion, a fact that only accentuated the feelings of rage and insult felt by the Jewish worshippers. Such symbolic victories and defeats occur daily in Hebron, and greatly anger many of the Jews.

For the returning Jews, Hebron is a place of unbearable tension. On the one hand, it is a historical and religious center; on the other, it is demographically controlled by the "other" and geographically detached from Israeli urban centers. For the Jewish settlers, it is both "the center out there"[24] as well as the center of their everyday life. The huge gulf between "metaphorical Hebron" and "actual Hebron," Hebron as a symbolic center and Hebron as a poor endangered peripheral development town, creates the explosive atmosphere that fuels violent events.

Hebron settlers aim to close the gap eventually between the ideal and the actual, and to return Hebron to its former (Jewish) glory, to succeed in explaining the centrality of Hebron to their compatriots and to the rest of the world. Meanwhile, the idea that the murderers of Tarpat, who continue to murder the returning Jews, hold prayers at the place most sacred for Judaism while protected by Israeli soldiers is a difficult one for all Jewish residents of the area to swallow. Nonetheless, most will not endanger themselves and their community by employing violence to even scores. The majority, especially those associated with Gush Emunim and the teaching of Rabbi Kook the Elder, have a concept of delayed and prolonged salvation that enables them to face such discrepancies. Kiryat Arba, however, is a relatively large and pluralistic community, and some residents are eager to shorten the distance between daily reality and the divine plan to expedite salvation.

In February 1994, on the Jewish holiday of Purim, Baruch Goldstein, a physician living in Kiryat Arba, donned his army uniform with his officer's rank, took his rifle, entered the Cave of Machpela, and shot dead twenty-nine Muslim Arabs while they were praying. Once his rifle stopped firing, he was beaten to death. In the rage riots that followed, more Palestinians were killed. The event, which occurred several months after the signing of the Oslo Accords, shocked the Israeli public. Cries, and even political discussions, arose demanding the evacuation of the Jews from Hebron. In Kiryat Arba, Hebron, and the rest of the settlements, most of the settlers, especially the leaders, expressed their horror at the massacre, yet some of the more extreme groups supported it.

Goldstein's gravesite in Kiryat Arba, located in a garden dedicated to the memory of extremist Rabbi Meir Kahane, became a place of pilgrimage where visitors could wrap themselves in what was presented as the Baruch Goldstein's *talith*. After the assassination of Yitzhak Rabin, a young man vandalized the gravesite. After some legal deliberation, the site was removed by decree of the Israeli Supreme Court. However, among right-wing extremists, Goldstein is still considered a hero, and they even published a book in his memory.

Goldstein's extremist act is not typical of Gush Emunim supporters, and this book does not discuss his type of radicalism. The fact, however, that such a murderous act was committed in the Cave of Machpela is no accident. A symbolic analysis of the act can illustrate the meaning that Hebron holds for the Gush Emunim believers.[25]

The motif of revenge is crucial to understanding Goldstein's act. Goldstein, as a physician in Kiryat Arba, was among the first to arrive at scenes of terrorist attacks and witness their horrors. But the personal feeling of revenge was legitimized and supported by the broader narratives of Hebron, in which the Palestinians are guilty of the primordial crime of Tarpat, tantamount to the Holocaust. Goldstein's occupation as a physician was also an important issue in the creation of the myth and the symbolism of his act. The physician's task is to heal the body. This motif was expressed in graffiti that appeared on the walls of Kiryat Arba saying "There are many physicians in Hebron." In other words, the situation in Hebron, according to the settlers, is pathological—a disturbance in the natural order of the body of the nation that must be redressed and redeemed. The difference between settlers with different worldviews is that they have not reached an agreement on how long the healing may take and what types of "medicines" should be used.

The day of the incident, Purim, is the holiday of Jewish reversal. In the story of Esther, the decree to destroy all the Jews throughout the Persian Empire was reversed, and the Jews prevailed though cunning and resourcefulness. On that day, Israeli children don costumes and masquerade. Likewise, the interpretation goes, Goldstein donned his army officer uniform and entered the Muslim prayer hall undetained. Goldstein's supporters claim that his act saved Jews because the Hebron Arabs were planning a second Tarpat, and Goldstein foiled it. The logic of Purim, of the catastrophe that turned into salvation, is the logic of the Hebron settlers, as well as the logic of the Gush Emunim settlers as a whole.

The connection between Goldstein's murderous act and Jewish Hebron survival is, however, far more complex. Forty days after the massacre, the Palestinian Muslim Hamas committed its own massacre—the first of a long series of suicide bombings—declaring it a retaliation for Goldstein's act. It also mimicked that act. Following further suicide bombings and Israeli retaliation, the mutual trust needed to implement the Oslo Accords vanished. Thus, while the incident itself endangered the immediate future of Jews in Hebron, it led to a violent break in relations between Israel and the Palestinians, thus saving Jewish Hebron, at least for the time being.

The settlers of Hebron like to claim that the entire Zionist project is maintained by the same logic as their town, but that this basic fact cannot be discerned behind the modern secular disguises. The essential political question regarding Hebron is in what terms the place should be understood: as the center of centers and a true representation of the essence of Zionist Israel, as it wishes to be regarded; or as a peripheral development town, left in a limbo that occasionally reminds an indifferent Israel of its existence through outbursts of hatred and violence. The tragedies of late have contributed much to reinforce the first interpretation, while the political agreements implicitly promote the second. It is much too early to pass judgment. Perhaps it is always too early, for, in Hebron, every failure leads to a new success and every new building invites the possibility of a new Tarpat.

8

Gush Etzion and the Decline of Secular Zionist Mythology

In the story of Gush Emunim, a special place is reserved for Gush Etzion, located a few kilometers on the road to Hebron south of Jerusalem. The desperate stand of the four secluded settlements comprising the Gush during the 1948 Israeli War of Independence is one of the most heroic stories in Israeli history and folklore, on a par with the story of Tel Hai. Numerous mythic tales have arisen around this saga of struggle, massacre, and surrender that ended the very day before the declaration of Israeli independence. After the Six-Day War, six years prior to the emergence of Gush Emunim, the first village of Gush Etzion was rebuilt. The leaders of the return to Kfar Etzion were the orphan children of the warriors who had been killed defending the Gush nineteen years earlier.

For the leaders of Gush Emunim, the story of Gush Etzion was both emotionally moving and ideologically useful. Through Gush Etzion, they could connect their own narrative of sacred memory and return to the sacred soil of Judea to a consensually accepted heroic story. The fact that the original settlers of Kfar Etzion belonged to the national religious camp certainly helped, even if this was downplayed to gain wider national adherence to the myth. The founding meeting of Gush Emunim (April 1974) was held in Kfar Etzion, and many of the village's residents (though conspicuously, not all) became staunch supporters of the movement. One of them, Hanan Porat, was among the key leaders of Gush Emunim and became its foremost spokesperson.

Certain factors, however, prevented the fusion of Gush Emunim and the Gush Etzion myth. In settling in Shiloh or Kedumim, places that had no connection to modern Israeli history and myth, Gush Emunim marshaled justifications other than those of Zionist and Israeli heroism, as was described in previous chapters. Many Gush Etzion residents, on the other hand, were loath to endanger their most vital asset—the sympathy they held among the admiring Israeli-Jewish public—in order to further the interests of the divisive movement.

In what follows, I briefly describe the story of Gush Etzion, showing the connection it establishes between memory and place. I then discuss the problematic of this history for Gush Emunim and conclude with an exploration of the changes in the relations between Gush Etzion and the settlement project over the years.

BORN ORPHANS: THE STORY OF KFAR ETZION

Kfar Etzion was founded in 1943 as the third link in the chain of settlements in the Hebron Hills.[1] It was preceded by two short-lived attempts: Migdal Eder (1927–29) and El Ha-Har (1935–36). The founding group that settled there was Kvutzat Avraham, after the former chief rabbi of Palestine, Abraham-Itzhak HaCohen Kook, later to be hailed as the inspiration behind Gush Emunim. The settlers developed agriculture, raised livestock, and set up the Neve Ovadiah rest and convalescent home, which served as a center of religious culture. During the 1940s, three other settlements were established in the Etzion Bloc: Massuot Yitzhak (established in 1941), Ein Tsurim (1946), and Revadim (1947), the only secular community among them. In October 1947, Gush Etzion numbered 450 people.

Immediately after the United Nations declaration legitimizing a Jewish State on November 29, 1947, the neighboring Arabs launched an attack against Gush Etzion, which was, according to the partition decision, outside the borders of the Jewish State. Although its isolation from other Jewish settlement made it vulnerable, its strategic position on the route to Jerusalem made it crucial to the Jewish war effort. Key events in the War of Independence are linked with Gush Etzion, especially the Lamed Hei (Thirty-Five) platoon, annihilated on its way to relieve the besieged Gush Etzion. The last battle over Gush Etzion was fought on May 12–13, 1948, one day before the Israeli Declaration of Independence. The Arab Legion (i.e., the Jordanian army), assisted by villagers from the area, stormed the settlements of the bloc and forced their surrender. The Arab villagers massacred the Israeli fighters captured at Kfar Etzion—127 of them were killed that day while only 4 survived. The defenders of the other villages in the Gush became prisoners of war.

The awe felt by Israelis toward Gush Etzion was so great that the Knesset decreed the day of the fall of Kfar Etzion as the Day of Remembrance for all the slain of the Israeli Defense Forces. Prime Minister David Ben-Gurion wrote a hymn of praise to the epic story: "The episode of Gush Etzion is a great and awe-inspiring saga and the glory of the war of the Jews . . . Among the splendid heroism of our fighters from all corners of the land, the tremendous heroism of the defenders of Gush Etzion shines forth with a special light, and all those who took part in that glorious episode are assured of a share in the world-to-come and in the eternity of the people of Israel."[2] In 1952, the first book on the Etzion Bloc, *Siege in the Hills of Hebron* by Dov Knohl, was published. In the introduction to the English edition, Abba Eban, Israel's foremost diplomat, wrote, "The memory of these events is vivid in the mind of a grateful nation; and it will certainly be held in reverence wherever the saga of Israel's rebirth is told."[3]

The memory of Gush Etzion played an important role in the training programs of the religious youth movement Bnei Akiva and in other formal and informal educational frameworks. Two organizations were set up: "The Organization of the Survivors of Gush Etzion," devoted to providing social assistance to widows, and "The Organization of the Sons of Gush Etzion," directed at immortalizing the memory of the slain of the bloc and assisting in the education of their children. The latter organization published books and pamphlets by members of the Gush; kept the subject alive through conferences, radio programs, and journalism; and organized commemorative exhibitions and public assemblies.

Their mythic stature notwithstanding, the widows and orphans of Kfar Etzion had to find solutions to survive the harsh economic reality of postwar Israel. They remained together for a long period, ironically, living for some time in Giva't Aliya, formerly Jabeliya, a neighborhood near Jaffa, whose uprooted Arab population made its way to the Gaza Strip where they became refugees in the camp also called Jebaliya. The children of Kfar Etzion grew up in a community of widows and orphans and under the shadow of the great national myth. The connection of the children to their fathers and the destroyed village was nurtured through education and ritual.

On every Memorial Day for the Fallen, the sons of Kfar Etzion would make a pilgrimage to the Mount Herzl National Cemetery in Jerusalem to participate in the commemorative ceremony for the 240 slain of the Etzion Bloc. After the ceremony, the families made their way to places from which they could gaze from afar at the Lone Tree, an oak that was the only visible landmark of Kfar Etzion. Nili Gomeh (1988) relates, "On the day we left . . . the lorries stopped by the tree . . . From there we went on our way—a road which lasted nineteen years . . . To us, the children of Kfar Etzion and to our mothers, the tree was a symbol—a symbol of hope, a symbol of faith, a symbol of the certainty that the day would come when we would return to the place" (311). The annual reunions would end near Kibbutz Netiv Halamed-Hei, commemorating the convoy of the thirty-five soldiers wiped out on their way to the Gush. Gomeh continues her narrative: "Some stood in silence during those hours of contemplation and were overcome with a feeling of anger that the Arabs had subjugated us; in their hearts, they prayed for revenge and requital, a prayer mingled with the dim hope, almost a dream, that He who is enthroned in heaven would restore their stolen land to them" (311). This group of children who grew up together were, for the most part, conscripted into military service when the Six-Day War enabled them to first return and visit the place where their fathers fought and died.

THE RETURN

The return to Kfar Etzion took place six months after the end of the war. It was partly initiated by the "children," now in their twenties, and among right-wing activists who felt that Gush Etzion was the proper place from which to launch a massive campaign to populate the region of Judea with Jewish settlers. The Israeli government, lead by Levi Eshkol, declaring that the occupied territories are bargaining chips for future peace, was hesitant in granting its permission or support, but eventually complied, especially once they knew that the Kfar Etzion settlers were resolute to return in any case. Both the formal agreement on the action and the resoluteness to return regardless of formal approval became issues of future importance as the events of that period were compared to the actions of Gush Emunim.

The evening before the return, five Kfar Etzion widows told Hanan Porat, "We lost our husbands in Gush Etzion, and even though we have deep emotional connection to Gush Etzion we are not ready to lose our sons . . . All that happened in the War of Independence may repeat itself. You cannot undertake this adventure on the backs of our children." Porat reports that he was bewildered by the attack and tried to put their minds at rest.[4] This episode demonstrates the great traumatic affect of the events that had occurred at Gush Etzion.

The return itself, on September 28, 1967, was a ritualistic reversal of the evacuation twenty years earlier. The organizers commissioned busses, and Egged, the national bus company, complied by adding one of the original armored vehicles that had led convoys in 1948. The convoy began at the national military cemetery at Herzl Mount in Jerusalem, where the participants held a prayer, before starting south, stopping at the Tomb of Rachel and some of the famous battlegrounds on their way.

After the establishment of Kfar Etzion, other settlements soon followed. Alon Shvut was established in 1970, Rosh Tzurim in 1971, and Elazar in 1975. The region itself grew in other ways, as well. The religious kibbutz of Kfar Etzion currently has ninety families, and its economy is based mainly on agriculture (poultry and orchids) and light industry. A field school caters for visitors, specializing in "biblical tours" and presenting the heroic history of the Gush.

Gush Etzion can be partly understood as a community dedicated to the sacred national memory that renders its existence such a cherished and privileged status among Israelis. There are two important *lieux de mémoire* in the Gush, which serve as centers of pilgrimage and which pay respect to its dramatic history. The first is the Lone Tree itself, which stands in a plaza outside the entrance to the settlements, and the other is the hill of the final battle.

The oak tree, an object of longing for many years, has come to symbolize Gush Etzion, somewhat like the Cave of Machpela in Hebron. In the minds of the settlers, it functions differently because of the dialectics of exile and return. For the former community that perished in the war, it was one tree among many. Its unique status as *the* tree was due to its visibility from afar as a symbol of hope and as a constant reminder of their history.

The tree appears in the logo of most Gush Etzion institutions and is the object of various arts. Twenty years after the return to Kfar Etzion, a poetry contest was won by a song dedicated to the oak tree. In the four stanzas of the song, the history of the people of Israel was represented through four significant moments of time—the sacrifice of Isaac, the heroism of the Maccabees, the Bar Kochba revolt, and the fall of Kfar Etzion. The tree was presented as a stable and fixed entity, witness to the historical events that occurred around it. The eternal presence of the tree grants it sacred status as witness, attesting to the truthfulness of the Jewish claim. The battle at Gush Etzion is conjoined with other events of Jewish mythology, a move that, I shall claim, was to erode of its unique status.

The fetishization of the tree angered well-known Israeli writer Haim Be'er, who spoke of the "intense ritual worship" surrounding the tree. In his classic article, "Gush Emunim—Canaanites Who Wear Phylacteries" (1982), he reflected on some of the ritual practices regarding the tree:

> The tree became the center of a fervent cult. Experts were brought in and poured cement into its trunk, lest, heaven forbid, it should be broken in some storm. The buildings of the regional school built nearby were built lower than usual so that they should not, heaven forbid, block the view of the tree even for someone standing on the summit of Mount Ora in the Jerusalem Corridor. (Would they have acted with such sensitivity if they had dealt with people?) They printed its green silhouette on every sheet of writing paper, envelope, pamphlet, or book coming out of the place. And when they came to chose the name of a settlement—a name that would express their longings for the place for nineteen years—they chose a Canaanite name (Elon Moreh), belonging so closely to the primeval country where the loftiest sentiments were always projected onto trees and stones.

As it was transformed from an object of desire to a place of remembrance, the tree lost its living essence (its "treeness"), whatever made it a growing organism, and became a dead entity, doomed to stand forever in memory to the Gush history, and to become an eternal witness to future events that may occur nearby.

The other place commemorating the past heroics of Gush Etzion is the hill where the destroyed former kibbutz once stood. It is a memorial garden containing a museum of the history of Gush Etzion and a *Yizkor* (memorial) tent built on the ruins of the bunker of the fighters' headquarters. The *Yizkor* tent houses an audiovisual program, called "The People of the Mountain," that relates the history of the place, beginning with its ancient biblical history. The people of Gush Etzion thus stress that their presence there is not accidental, but a result of millennia of Jewish history and longing. Here they connect their story to the logic of Gush Emunim while the radical movement can depict its zealotry as a return of the kind presented by Gush Etzion.

THE POLITICS OF MEMORY AND THE MEANING OF RETURN

A resident of Kfar Etzion declared, "We returned to the Gush not out of feelings of revenge but from a determination that this is our home; we are returning to the soil and to our homeland, not only of our own parents but of the nation as a whole" (Ben-Pazi 1988, 76). The narrative of Gush Etzion can be framed in two perspectives that coexist both within the Israeli public as well as among the residents of Kfar Etzion themselves. One perspective, whose chief representative is Hanan Porat, understands the return to Kfar Etzion as an integral part of the larger return of the Jewish people to its biblical land, as best articulated by Gush Emunim; the other perspective, propagated by Yohanan Ben-Ya'akov, editor of the book *Gush Etzion: Fifty Years of Struggle and Creativity* (1978), distinguishes between the special status of the Gush Etzion settlement, which enjoys a wide consensus, and the messianic enterprise of settlement in Judea and Samaria.

For Hanan Porat (1988), Kfar Etzion is "a miniature example, which teaches us not about itself but about the settlement of the land of Israel at large." It is a "small place" that evokes the "large place," Israel, and embodies the Jewish-Zionist-Israeli metanarrative of exile and return. For this school of thought, the significantly situated Gush Etzion was not just a place of return, but a stage leading to the final Messianic redemption:

> What we, the children of Kfar Etzion, a small handful of friends weaving their dreams, have felt for nineteen years, ever since our home was destroyed; [what we have felt] about a single plot of land "on the way to Efrat—that is, Bethlehem"—if you multiply it by ten . . . by a hundred . . . by a thousand . . . by a million, you will have the yearning of the entire people for the whole land from the time its exalted House in Jerusalem was destroyed a thousand nine hundred years ago . . . Through it we may hear the song of the great act, through which the Lord of all worlds will set us on the path ascending to the House of the Lord: the whole people of Israel for the whole land of Israel, with, at its heart, our Jerusalem—the Temple of the King, the royal city. (11)

Ben-Ya'akov's more modest approach represents the historical position of the religious Kibbutz movement, which displayed restrained enthusiasm for the resettlement of Kfar Etzion. For him and many of his friends, with their return, the tragic circle has been closed; any further attempt to settle on contested land is open for discussion, but not as part of the Gush Etzion project:

> Our parents, the members of Kfar Etzion (May the Lord avenge their blood!), fell on the altar of the renewal of the State in defending Jerusalem, the holy city and capital of Israel. They fought under the command of the national leadership and fulfilled their duty to the nation. . . . It is therefore right and proper that the government of Israel should honor their memory and decide—as a nation—to rebuild their destroyed home out of respect for their heroism and self-sacrifice. . . . This claim is unique to Kfar Etzion. (Ben-Ya'akov 1998, 12)

The argument is fundamental to the connection between land and history in Israel. For Gush Emunim, the secular version of Zionism holds no special status, and its heroic deeds are no more deserving of commemoration than other events in Jewish history. The obligation to return to biblical sites, and to the land in general, is imperative and unrelated to acts of heroism of the last few decades. Conversely, Ben-Ya'akov echoes the national logic in his claiming that Gush Etzion should enjoy a special status because of its war history. His claims, however, were quickly discredited, not least by members of his own community.

Porat and his followers argued against the arbitrary restriction of Jewish history by the Zionist enterprise. The geographic area of the Etzion Bloc—between Hebron and Jerusalem—is considered the cradle of the Jewish people and is viewed in Jewish historiography and collective memory as the arena of the history of the ancient Hebrews in the land of Israel. On their journeys between Jerusalem and Hebron, the Patriarchs—Abraham, Isaac and, much later, David—performed deeds that became the constitutive experiences of the Hebrew nation. The region was the site of many other events in Jewish mythohistory, such as the Maccabean and Bar Kochba revolts. The Gush Emunim settlers regarded the restriction of significant history to the few years preceding 1948 as totally unacceptable, especially when suggested by their respected friends of the national religious camp. To their mind, the place was too steeped in ancient history to be left to the agents of recent memory.

In a scholarly article, David Ohana (2002), presents an additional argument that has some echoes in the history of the return to the Gush, though never in the discourse of the settlers themselves. If, he writes, the Jews are granted the right to return to villages ruined in the 1948 war, do

Palestinian refugees not enjoy the same right? If the cutoff line of 1948 is breached for Gush Etzion, then the Palestinian refugees have the right to return to their relinquished homes within the pre-1967 borders of Israel, as well. In other words, the use of the idiom of return is a slippery slope that may easily undermine Israeli moral claims. In this respect, Gush Etzion's claim, as formulated by Ben-Ya'akov, is politically more subversive than that promoting the return to biblical sites: if refugees are allowed to return to their *original* places from which they were evicted in their lifetime, Israel's case against the Palestinian right of return stands on shaky ground.[5]

In the period of uncertainty and public debate regarding the future of the territories, Porat attacked those settlers in Gush Etzion who thought of the Gush in terms of saving their own skin: "Let them have no doubt about it," he said. "Our fate is the same as that of the whole of Judea and Samaria. We have the capacity to contribute to the common struggle precisely because of the honor we enjoy."[6] What he meant was that, legitimacy claims not withstanding, all Jewish settlers in Yesha will find themselves in the same boat. The two intifadas were to strengthen his claim.

DIFFERENT LOGICS, SIMILAR FATE

Over the years, the uniqueness of Gush Etzion has eroded. The constituting memory of the War of Independence is slowly fading, and the children of Gush Etzion see little difference between themselves and the rest of the settlers' community. Originally, the region was to be connected to another region west of the Green Line, called Adulam. Over time, however, it became apparent that the "natural" place of Gush Etzion was as one link in the chain of Gush Emunim settlements on the mountain ridge.

Eighteen communities are currently in the administrative region of Gush Etzion, most of them with no connection to the founding myth of the War of Independence. The largest town is Beitar Ilit, named after the place of Bar Kochba's last stand against the Roman army. It has some twenty-one thousand residents and is a Haredi (ultra-Orthodox) community. The unofficial capital of the region is Efrat, which is seven thousand strong, whose name was taken from the description of the burial on the Matriarch Rachel in Genesis. Bat Ayin is a settlement of "born-again" Jews with Hasidic tendencies, considered by their Jewish neighbors to be somewhat eccentric and by their Palestinian neighbors to be highly volatile. On their Web site, these settlers present their goal as "building a Torah-abiding community that sustains itself by working the land based on the Torah. Jewish labor only."[7] There is a wide and growing range of settlements in the Gush, and it is no longer plausible to associate the chaotic present with the heroic War of Independence.

The great leveler connecting the Gush Etzion communities with the rest of the settlements is their common fate in encountering the two Palestinian intifadas. Gush Etzion is cut off from Jerusalem by Palestinian villages and the large refugee camp Daheiysha. The Palestinians were indifferent to Gush Etzion's relative claims to legitimacy, and the Gush's communities suffered their share of killed and injured. Israeli governments, on the other hand, were somewhat more committed to Gush Etzion than to other settlements; Yitzhak Rabin even claimed a difference between "security settlements" and "ideological settlements" and placed Gush Etzion among the former. A new road was built at huge expense, including tunnels and bridges, connecting the Gush with Jerusalem. Security reasons, however, along with demographic changes, determined that the uniqueness of the Gush Etzion story either would be forgotten or would lose its impact respective to other rationales.

The story of Gush Etzion holds important lessons for Gush Emunim and the changing concepts of time and space in Israel. The memory of the War of Independence, strong enough to propel the rebuilding of Kfar Etzion when huge-scale Gush Emunim settlement was still unimaginable, lost its impetus and was replaced by other types of justification. This is true of the memory of great wars in general: as the soldiers grow old or pass away, and newer wars and dead accumulate, the drama of the first great war fades into the distant past. Furthermore, in this case, Gush Emunim promoted alternative legitimating memories based on divine promise and ancient mythology rather than Zionist history. When Kfar Etzion was reestablished, few imagined that within Israeli society the memory of its War of Independence heroism could be displaced. Gush Emunim's vision swept away whatever it found on its path, leaving its own logic as the hegemonic, if not only, acceptable option.

As a fundamentalist religious movement, Gush Emunim could not appropriate the great myth of the 1948 war that established the secular state. To do so would involve accepting the claim that certain parts of the contested territories were privileged over others, which was unacceptable for the believers. Gush Etzion members, as religious Zionists, enacting the principle of the right of return, found it impossible to maintain their private myth. The pressure of Gush Emunim mythology, coupled with the demographic changes that occurred within Gush Etzion, undermined the force of one of the greatest myths of modern Israeli history. Israeli society lost one of its key heroic stories. As the Gush Emunim project "digested" Gush Etzion into its system, religious mythology won another battle over the declining secular Zionist ethos.

9

The Settlement of Ofra

Ritualizing Normalcy

In the Ofra's monthly *Et Ofra* (literally, the Pen/Time of Ofra), the last page is dedicated to local advertisements. In a random issue, one can find a blessing to resident Yehuda Etzion, known for his radicalism, that wishes him success in his messianic aspiration in "climbing the ladder of the House of David"; and an invitation by a cosmetician to visit her beauty parlor, citing the biblical phrase that actually upholds its antithesis: "not the lie of beauty." Which ad represents the *true* Ofra and the actual lore of the ideological settlements? The uncompromising, non-reflective fundamentalist statement or the whimsical, lighthearted invitation that uses the Bible freely in a mundane advertisement? In this chapter, I claim that both can coexist within the same community, and that their tense cohabitation and uneasy synthesis is the message, as well as the challenge, that the Gush Emunim settlement project encounters.

In this book's introduction, I presented the claim that Gush Emunim attempts to combine two sides of the great divide of the global world: on the one hand, it is a fundamentalist project that stands defiantly against the spirit of the day; on the other, it claims to be part and parcel, perhaps even the true representative, of Western modernity. Hebron accentuates rigid fundamentalism: while it is an extreme example of the overpowering force of collective memory, it is relatively unconcerned with connecting to the global world. The outside world, the believers would say, should accommodate itself to the sacred logic of Hebron, not vice versa. Noam Arnon, one of the leaders of Hebron and Kiryat Arba, expressed this to me clearly: "This is not a place that you come to in order to build a cottage and cultivate a garden. It is a place that is meant to articulate the fact that the people of Israel will not desert the city of the Patriarchs."

Elsewhere in Yesha, a cottage and a garden were exactly what many of the settlers wished for. Many were not dedicated to the idea of a Greater Israel, but grasped the opportunity, given them by the state, to improve their standard of living. Although they reside in the occupied territories, these settlers define themselves as normal Israelis and distance themselves from those living on the mountain ridge of Judea and Samaria, whom they define as religious fanatics. Although they are situated between the religious Gush Emunim and the more secular Israel, they have decided to declare themselves as belonging to the latter.

The dilemma between the global and fundamentalist perspectives is relevant to most Gush Emunim settlements, and, to explore it, I shall concentrate on one of them. Ofra tries to hold both sides of the globalization stick, or, to apply Tom Friedman's (2000) metaphor, to own the Lexus while cherishing the olive tree. I shall illustrate this through two modes of representation—the political joke and the ritual celebration—and conclude with a discussion of what it means to be a "normal fundamentalist."

WHY CHOOSE OFRA?

For a researcher interested in Gush Emunim, Ofra is not just a random choice. Ofra was established in 1975, several kilometers northeast of the large Palestinian town of Ramallah and some twenty kilometers north of Jerusalem.[1] It was the first Gush Emunim settlement and was established with tacit government consent. When I conducted my research there in 1993, it was home to 250 families, but the population has more than doubled since. Residents included many of the political and intellectual leaders of the movement, and it housed some of the settlers' main institutions, including the Yesha council and the monthly *Nekuda*. Some of the local residents were also prominent in the Jewish underground.[2] At every stage of Gush Emunim's political, ideological, or institutional history, Ofra has played an important role.

As the first Gush Emunim settlement, the population of the settlement is somewhat more diverse than that of other communal villages. Although the residents are national religious, they hold different standards of religious observance because their common denominator is political rather than religious. The settlement is also characterized by its rich public discourse, which is nuanced and displays self-awareness of the historical task confronting the settlement. The local monthly, *Et Ofra*, which has been published regularly since 1982, provides a valuable tool for examining the internal discourse of the village.

Unlike Hebron or Kfar Etzion and like all other Gush Emunim settlements, Ofra does not define its identity based on a binding sacred past. To be sure, the name "Ofra" does appear in the Bible, but the residents of Ofra do not see themselves as returning to a specific place and reviving its ancient glories. They feel free, therefore, to carve out their own identity and define for themselves what makes their act of settlement significant. Their rich internal discourse, of which this chapter can provide only a sample, can teach us on how the settlers construct the meaning of their newly found homes and balance the complex messages that make up their identity.

Ofra, then, is a place that has to negotiate its identity, and, thanks to its pioneering status and the abundance of leaders and writers among its residents, it is very articulate about it. Israeli authors and other visitors have not missed this, and Ofra has become the prototypical settlement to visit—in many ways, the window of the settlement project as a whole. I have mentioned the visits by Janet Aviad and David Grossman, who wondered if the settlements are still driven by zealotry and passion or have been institutionalized. Other well-known Israeli authors, such as Amos Oz and Hanoch Bartov, also chose Ofra as the prototypical settlement to visit. Significantly, the day after the Oslo Accords were revealed to the public, members of the Israeli Labor Party went to talk to the settlers and "naturally" came to Ofra.

Many Ofra residents are occupied with what they call the matters of the land of Israel; namely, leading and organizing existing and further settlements and defending their case in the media. The residents also take care of their own private homes, naturally. In the middle ground, between the occupation with national issues and the confines of the private homes, is the village public space, which nourishes its own activists, little known outside of the settlement. The known figures of Ofra are columnists in general newspapers, including the national ones, and, when they have something important to say to movement supporters, they publish in *Nekuda*. Local issues, however, are discussed in *Et Ofra*, and readers can learn much about the inner politics and problems of the community through this vista. Whereas *Nekuda* is the best source for the political and intellectual history of the settlements, *Et Ofra* can serve those interested in the social and cultural history of one, especially important, local community, trying to live a mundane life on the hills of Samaria.

The two public spaces, the national and the communal, complement each other while standing in positions of mutual criticism. The national discourse is dedicated to the success of the Gush Emunim project, while the communal discourse deals with the contours of everyday life. The very establishment of the community is a result of the success of the movement effort, and its continuing existence depends on the ability of the movement to reach its goal and obtain further resources. Every settlement has, however, its own problems that divert it from the common ideological purpose and consume energies that could have been used for national goals. The opposite is also true: the general interest can contradict communal interests. Recurrent demonstrations disrupt the village routine, and quick absorption of new settlers endangers its social fabric. Thriving communal life is an interest of the movement because it serves as proof that prosperous life in Yesha is a viable possibility, but, nevertheless, the ideological and the mundane, the national and the local, coexist with tense relations.

A COMMUNITY IN SEARCH OF IDENTITY

This tension is clearly seen in Ofra: total dedication to the ideas of the mother movement, coupled with the need to create a communal space that is considered to be mundane or normal. The settlement is supposed to be an exemplary model of how the Gush Emunim ideal can work, yet serve as a livable social group at the same time. In other words, it is to be both a symbol and a self-sustaining community. Achieving this is a great challenge, and the residents of Ofra, well aware of their pioneer status, view their communal decisions as affecting the rest of the settlement project and as a shining example for Israeli society. While they thrive to be a normal community with high moral values, they have yet to figure out exactly what being normal entails and what values should be promoted. Here is an example.

In the debate, current in many national religious communities, over separate classes for boys and girls in the local schools, Israel Harel objected strongly to the idea, maintaining that Ofra was a community whose residents were selected on their ideological merits. Thus, any attempt to modify its open religious character would alienate it from the rest of Israeli society and compromise its political goals.[3] To this, Rabbi Yonatan Balas angrily replied that "had Ofra chosen the path proposed in Harel's article, it would have remained a 'leading' settlement in trivial matters, such as its tax rate per square meter . . . Should we justify the building of such a society merely because it contributes to the settlement of Judea and Samaria?"[4] Whereas Harel demanded that Ofra remain within what he assumed to be the conventional bounds of Israeli normalcy, Balas suggested experimentation and further radicalization, even at the price of a schism with secular Israeli society. For him, the historical situation of Ofra calls for exemplary behavior in the religious realm.

Ofra has developed while trying to toe the fine line between these two positions: as a leader of a diverse movement including groups of various religious definitions united in a common political goal and as a cultural alternative that may attract some and alienate others. All Gush Emunim settlements have to encounter this dilemma. It invariably arises when deciding on separate classes for boys and girls in school, in establishing norms for women's public attire,[5] and, most importantly, in deciding who to accept for membership.

Meanwhile, Ofra encountered more mundane challenges, and *Et Ofra* records numerous examples of internal criticism that may cast doubt on Ofra's pretense of being an exemplary community. One is the neglect of guard duty, which is a crucial issue in a settlement located in the midst of a hostile environment. A letter to the magazine reads, "Yes, I mean you—you, who, instead of guarding me and my family while we sleep, prefer to stay warm at your wife's side and don't care that tomorrow our cold bodies will be carried off to the cemetery."[6] In his column, the community rabbi describes the problem of teenage vandalism. His "criminal chronicle of Ofra during the last month" refers to theft from the collection boxes in the synagogue, the breaking of windows, vandalizing of the security jeep, and even the desecration of the Israeli flag.[7] From my experience, and as reflected by *Et Ofra*, the settlers generally have succeeded in creating a vibrant and moral community, and the openness with which they discuss problems attests to that; the combination of a rich communal life and various problems with free riders and juvenile delinquency suggests that the people of Ofra have indeed created what many, in Israel and elsewhere, would consider to be a normal community.

THE IMPORTANCE OF HUMOR

Gush Emunim activists like to jest, especially about aspects of their political situation. Most of the jokes are aggressive attacks on their left-wing opponents, but at times it is possible to find humorous reflections on their own position in the world.[8] This use of humor, which is very common in Ofra and less common elsewhere in the settlements, can teach us about the intricacy of the community's existential position. Let us start with an example from Ofra's monthly, written by Hava Dinar. She describes the piles of garbage that lie around her village as though they were works of art:

> The next object worth notice is presented in the catalogue as "disperse objects striving for salvation" . . . At various distances from the central modular object are various objects dispersed seemingly at random (nothing is random!) . . . The message is clear: eternal disintegration with the environment . . . The messianic agonies of a people that sees its redemption before it shining like the morning dawn.[9]

The writer sarcastically criticizes the pollution of the public space, a problem well known in the settlements, which are almost constantly construction sites. Her claim is that the neglect of the public space is, in effect, a monument that the settlers are erecting in their environment. In her eyes, the fact that the settlement is supposed to reflect high ideals and serve as a model makes littering much more contemptible. She employs the unmistakable language of the true believers of Gush Emunim, hinting that perhaps the physical garbage is the true expression of the lofty words of redemption and salvation that the Gush Emunim believers utter so freely. She also expresses the idea that this use of the sacred language is perfectly legitimate, which is something that not all true believers may accept. Her sarcastic arrows are pointed not only toward the residents of Ofra, but also, in a subtle way, at the pomposity of religious language. It is also significant that a woman uses the words of the sacred texts so freely, which are mainly taught in advanced yeshivas attended exclusively by men. Hava Dinar can show proficiency in the use of religious language while demonstrating a critical distance from it.

Another woman, Tamar Spanier, uses nationalistic language to muse on Ofra's pretensions of leading the nation. She responds to the suggestion that each family will sew its name on a piece of cloth that will be pieced together to create a large quilt (a practice common in kibbutzim). She complains that her name is longer than that of the Levi family and notes that other families have even longer names. Her suggestion is for a computer program to divide the letters equally between families because, in an exemplary community such as Ofra, the values of mutual support and burden sharing are of the utmost importance. She concludes,

"In this act, we shall be, as always, a pioneering example to the people of Israel, and many settlements will walk in our path and be educated in our light. In any case and just to be sure, we decided to change our name to Shai."[10]

Uri Urbach, later to become the representative humorist of the national religious camp, began his satirical writing in Ofra. During one of Ofra's annual celebrations, he declared, "Ofra, our sister, may you grow to be thousands but no more than 150 families."[11] The first part of the sentence follows a traditional blessing. The second limits the blessing while hinting at the identity issues that beset the village: to fulfill its national goal the settlement should grow as much as possible, but to maintain its standard of living and communal nature it has to limit its population. Urbach offers his blessing for the village that the thousands supposed to reach Yesha will settle in elsewhere. Using humor, he expresses a very delicate issue in the life of the settlers: the larger the community grows, the less attractive it becomes, especially to its founders. Urbach's joke strikes precisely at the seam between the fundamentalist wish to settle the land and the urge to live in a prosperous and well-controlled community.

Another known humorist from Ofra is Haggai Segal, who participated in the Jewish Underground and wrote its story. He also writes short sketches about life in a settlement—presumably his own—some of which were compiled in a book called *Demo Settlement* (1992). This name, after the Israeli attempts to affect negotiation by creating "as if" settlements in the occupied territories, plays on the question of how real the settlements are. Are they actual living communities, as their residents claim, or only political statements, as rivals contend?

He describes a scenario in which a shopkeeper at the settlement decides to build a shack for his cardboard boxes, and the United States sends Israel a strong reprimand on building in the occupied territories. After the Arab countries, Europe, the United Nations, and the international media all take notice, the shopkeeper reluctantly decides to "withdraw" in order to save world peace. In this story, Segal tries to show how the settlers act in a fashion that can only be defined as normal, definitely more normal than the hysterical outside world that criticizes them for being fanatics. He claims that the settlers are actually on the side of the sane, and the radical fundamentalists are those who claim that a shack near a grocery is a threat to world peace and a violent act of occupation and colonialism directed against helpless Palestinians.

Reflections on their Palestinian neighbors are beset with humor. Commonly, the Palestinians are referred to as "our neighbors," without further elaboration, to hint sarcastically at the natural good relations that are supposed to exist between the sides. Ofra is sometimes called jestingly "Ein Yabroud heights," after the Arab village nearby, which is a joke that resonates both on national and on economic levels. A resident of Ofra complains that, residing on the edge of the settlement, she finds it difficult to participate in the village's social life, and she hears the muezzin of Ein Yabroud better than she hears the town's caller. "I have nothing against the Arabs," as she jokingly uses an idiom that was commonly used by anti-Semites: "My closest neighbors are Arabs."[12] In a satirical piece on the village council, a decision was made regarding the right of Arabs to fuel their cars in the gas station near Ofra: "Of course we should let them. How would they arrive home in time to throw stones at our cars without gas in their tanks?"[13] The same writer also suggested, "We must not allow into the village anyone that has a mustache yet does not wear a skullcap."[14]

Such jokes are inconceivable in Hebron and are uncommon in other settlements. In a place dedicated to a specific sacred memory such as Hebron, joking about the Arabs or on the founding myth of Tarpat is tantamount to joking about the Holocaust. In more homogeneous settlements, there are not many debates on issues of symbolic importance that give rise to political humor, and grasping the land of Israel and following the words of the Lord are not considered laughing matters. It can be said that the use of humor in Ofra is a response to the gravity of the issues. As a relatively pluralistic village of people that have gathered together for political and ideological common goals rather than out of religious agreements, many Ofra residents find their neighbors amusing or want to make sure that they will not be equated with some of the fanatics (or heretics) next door.

The best-known satirical writers of Gush Emunim come from Ofra. Most were not students of Merkaz HaRav and have always maintained a critical perspective toward the more radical true believers. Their connections with the wider Israeli society are critical to their identity, and humor is a way for them to express their belonging. The community of Ofra celebrates its humorists and encourages them to write and develop themselves; their existence serves as proof that the Ofra community shares their critical vision of radical fundamentalism with the rest of Israelis. Cultivating humor is, for Ofra's residents, a way both to stay within the confinements of the ideology and to glimpse it from the outside. If Jewish settlement in the West Bank is amusing, then it is not threatening, and all Israeli Jewish citizens, including the Ofra residents, may share a joke at the expense of religious fanatics.

RITUALIZING NORMALCY

The meaning of normalcy in Ofra can be investigated through an analysis of major rituals in which the settlement presents itself through a well-constructed narrative. Using ritual to examine how communities construct their world is a well-established anthropological practice (Kertzer 1988; Handelman 1990). Here I concentrate on a secular ritual that, while including some religious elements, is basically part of the emergent Israeli civil religion.[15] Local celebrations such as those described here, marking the anniversaries of the founding of agricultural and urban communities, are common in Israel; Ofra has followed that tradition.

The eighteenth anniversary of the founding of the settlement, in June 1993, was the most impressive celebration in the history of the settlement enterprise up to that day.[16] Eighteen is the numerological value of the letters of the Hebrew word *hai,* which means "life," and connotes hope and continuity. Questions were raised, however, about the point of celebrating that anniversary. Critics within the settlement inquired whether their leaders were doubtful that their village would survive to see a "real" anniversary—25, 50, 75, or 100 years—the milestones customarily observed in other, more secular, places in Israel. We see that the celebration was felt to accentuate deep survival anxieties that the settlers claimed not to have.

The event at Ofra began on a Saturday, with a conference of past and present residents. They discussed the community they had created as compared to the ideal they had envisioned. Problems such as education and delinquency were raised openly and discussed at this intimate gathering. These issues were not mentioned on the following Tuesday (June 8, 1993), when Ofra held its public celebration.

The invitations to the event noted Ofra's pioneering role in the Gush Emunim project. The motto "18 years of settlement in Samaria" asserted the founding of Ofra as a major event in the history of the land of Israel. As things turned out, the festivities were mainly local and regional; the vast majority of the hundreds of guests came from the neighboring settlements of the "Binyamin" regional council.

The evening began with greetings by dignitaries of the national, regional, or local level. They included a deputy minister, one of the two chief rabbis, and the head of the Jewish Agency. The importance of the official visitors should be understood in light of the legitimacy problems encountered by the settlement enterprise: speakers from the outside crowned Ofra with the leadership-pioneering image it sought and gave the event the appearance of a pilgrimage by representatives of the state of Israel to one of its symbolic centers. The fact that dignitaries representing official Israel were willing to participate in its celebration presented Ofra as a normal settlement.

The most problematic guest was the deputy minister of defense, Mordechai (Mota) Gur, who represented a government unsympathetic toward the settlers and their project and which would soon reach an agreement with the Palestinians that would jeopardize the Gush Emunim vision. His participation represented a dialectic of inclusion and exclusion. On the one hand, he was the representative of the state of Israel, which Gush Emunim theology holds to be sacred and which is the only political authority that can give the settlers a sense of belonging. On the other, most Ofra residents wanted to topple the government in which Gur served, and some even accused it of treason. The master of ceremonies endeavored to skirt the problem by referring to Gur's illustrious military career, culminating in his being the "liberator of the Old City of Jerusalem" in 1967 and later chief of staff of the Israeli Defense Forces. Gur himself tried to strengthen the consensual aspect of his public persona, referring to shared military experiences and security issues, and ignoring the tense relations between his hosts and the government.

The deputy minister was an accomplice in Ofra's self-representation as an apolitical, consensual entity, endorsed by all Israelis and the Israeli government, and an integral part of the heroic struggle of the Jewish people to return to its homeland. This narrative was reflected in the speeches and especially in the pageant that was the centerpiece of the evening. No mention was made of anything that might jeopardize the image the settlement sought to establish for itself—neither the rejection of the settlement enterprise by many Israelis nor the participation of some of Ofra's residents in the violent actions of the Jewish underground. Most obvious, the next-door neighbors, the Palestinian Arabs, were missing altogether. They had hardly any presence in the narrative and, needless to say, were not invited to participate in the celebration.

The pageant, written by a professional writer from outside the settlement, recounted Ofra's story according to its residents' wishes and in consonance with their ideological orientations. The same residents were also the actors, so that, in a sense, they were performing their own historical roles on stage. Remembrance rituals usually link a living community to dead ancestors; in this case, the participants themselves were the mythological heroes whose deeds were being reenacted in ritual. The pageant opened with a series of dramatic pronouncements:

> Ofra, the first settlement in the portion of [the tribe of] Benjamin. They were the first of the tribe of Benjamin, according to its families, Jericho and Beit El and Ofra.
>
> It is now 18 years since the beginning of the great settlement enterprise, part of the divine process of the return of the Jewish people to the inheritance of its fathers.
>
> Today is the year 5743, a year of the torments of the intifada and the ban on further construction.
>
> The current of renewed settlement, which began 18 [hai] years ago, will never cease flowing.
>
> Samaria lives [hai] and will live forever. Hai to Samaria, hai to Judea, hai to Ofra in Binyamin, hai to the people of Israel.[17]

This passage includes all the basic components of the Gush Emunim national mythology. The settlement project is a return to the golden age of the past set within a religious framework as part of the process of divine redemption. The enemies of the process are clearly defined as the Palestinians and the hostile Israeli government.

The celebratory mythic tone gave way to a catchy song composed especially for the event. The words, accompanied by a happy melody, were "Hai, hai, hai years my settlement has been alive [hai]; hai, hai, hai years it has lived in my heart." From there, the emphasis shifted from the ideological and mythical aspects of the project to focus on the lives of the residents. For most of the pageant, Ofra presented a version of what it considered to be its normal self.

As an acknowledged showcase of the settlement project, it is not surprising that the daily life of the community was presented through the eyes of a skeptical visitor. The pageant does not specify whether the visitor is a journalist, a sociologist, or an author writing about the settlement movement; it suffices that he comes from the outside and holds misguided conceptions and opinions regarding life in an ideological settlement. Through this heuristic trick, deconstructive and subversive criticism is countered and transformed into part of the play, even though the critical observer is carefully selective in his questions, never asking what most outside visitors ask, about the Palestinians outside the gates or the violent deeds committed by some of Ofra's residents.

He assumes he will meet messianic fanatics who are sacrificing their well-being on behalf of national goals, but learns gradually "to his obvious surprise," that life in Ofra is quite different from what he imagined. It is the children he meets who tell him the story. He opens with a question: "Kids, do you know what happened here many years ago? Joshua, for example, fought here. You like this place because of that, don't you?" He receives many different answers, all leading to the same conclusion:

> Joshua fought here? So what? That's why I should love this place? I love this place because there's so much room to play.

> I was born in a Communist country. I had no yearnings for Jerusalem. I was engaged in literature and art until eventually I came here. You know when I decided to stay? When I saw that people here leave their doors unlocked.

> Why did we come here? We kept moving from one settlement to another until finally we came back to the first, to Ofra. We liked it from the beginning.

This is an example of the dominant discourse in the pageant, whose role is to "normalize" the place. The overwhelming message is that the image of fundamentalist fanaticism is utterly false; Ofra is, first of all, a community that offers a high standard of living and good neighborly relations. This idea is transmitted in dialogue, song, and dance, as well as through overt statements. The normalcy of Ofra is unmistakable, but it is a ritualistic and constructed normalcy that is put on display. Rather than showing "life as usual," the pageant transforms the routine into an ideal that can counter the religious messianic obsession that is attributed to this settlement in particular and to Gush Emunim in general.

In the pageant, there is an intricate play between grand mythic statements, on the one hand, and the testimony of daily life, on the other. The narrators proclaim the important ideological statements in festive tones, while the Ofra residents, especially the children, ostensibly just chattering on stage, present the daily life in the settlement. The audience hears of life in Ofra "accidentally" through "overhearing" the children talk among themselves. The two messages are conveyed in a very careful mix: the construction of Ofra is a historical, even cosmological, event in the process of Jewish redemption; meanwhile, the community lives and prospers. The grand canonical statements encompass the pageant and give it direction, meaning, and symbolic value. The descriptions of everyday life are somewhat critical of the master narrative but remain well within accepted boundaries. The conflict between the two competing modes is presented as spurious. The settlement of Ofra, according to its residents, can contain both high ideals and mundane existence. It is simultaneously a key event in Jewish history and a pleasant place to raise children.

Let us return to the visitor, who is not just a passive learner: through his inquisitive stand, he is also a teacher. When he asks the children about Joshua, it is not a naive question: he is actually teaching them—and through them the audience gathered at Ofra—the deep meaning of the establishment of the village they claim to like for banal reasons. While they tell him of the small joys of life, he reminds them that they are living there for a reason. At the end of the pageant, he reaches a surprising conclusion for someone whose previous assumptions have not been borne out in the pageant dialogue: "We have been privileged to be a tool of the great process through which God has brought His people to redemption."

Ofra between Fundamentalism and Normalcy

The pageant was designed to convey several messages, some of them associated with the political situation of mid-1993. The Israeli government, the Palestinians, and the national and international media all contested Ofra's right to enjoy a "mundane life." They emphasized the denial of Palestinian rights and dismissed the settlements as "obstacles to peace." The violence that is always invested in the construction of "normal" enclaves is clearly visible in Ofra and other Jewish settlements in the occupied territories despite their attempts to hide and deny it. The celebration of normalcy came at a time when the legitimacy of everyday Jewish life in the occupied territories was especially threatened, and the Oslo Accords were just around the corner. The residents of Ofra felt a need to shout their normalcy for all to hear.

The pageant sanctifies both the divine process and the actual living community constituted by it. Ofra is defined—not much differently than

Israel as a whole—as a place that is at the same time old and new, part of mythology but leading a legitimate earthly life. The role of the ritual was to reflect and constitute normalcy where it was otherwise not to be found: in an isolated Jewish community within a predominantly Palestinian space. The ritual of normalcy was meant to enable a metaphorical leap that would detach Ofra from its immediate surroundings and tie it to the Jewish state across the Green Line.

In Gush Emunim ideology, the force that bonds the believers to the rest of the Jewish-Israeli nation is sacred memory—the affiliation with a united religious and ethnic group. But, as we have seen in previous chapters, Gush Emunim memory has become one of the most divisive forces, isolating the believers in their secluded enclave communities. Excessive faithfulness to Jewish memory, in the Gush Emunim version, threatens to marginalize the movement as fanatical and abnormal. The Ofra residents discovered that their strongest tie to their target audience is their everyday life; while few in Israel believe in divine redemption, most believe in the right to peaceful existence and a thriving community.

This does not mean, however, that the members of Gush Emunim are willing to abandon the belief system that renders meaning to their project. They demand their right to define their fundamentalism for themselves. Whereas external definitions present the settlement as a bastion of irrational messianic obsession, and internal criticism laments the lessened commitment to sacred memory, the ritual and the political joke chart a middle way. Their challenge, therefore, is one of compromise: to keep their national religious value while demonstrating its limits to themselves and others. They try to order the different components into bounded spaces where ideology reigns supreme and into other defined locations where the mundane is allowed and even encouraged. The ritual and the joke are mechanisms of constructing order within the contradictory components that construct fundamentalist lives. The message that the people of Ofra try to convey is that they are faithful to their movement and to the land of Israel, but will not compromise the autonomy of their community.

As the settlers aspire to be as normal as their fellow Israelis, they adapt definitions and standards taken from the Western world from which Israel takes its ideas of normality. A chain is thus established in which the settlers examine the secular Israeli society that examines the West for definitions of normalcy. The settlers' examination is ambivalent: even as they aspire to integrate into modern Israel and lament the attempts to label them as fundamentalists, as the ultimate others to Israeli normalcy, they remain sharply critical of that same normality. The ritual is a means to raise these issues and place Ofra within this baffling world.

At one point in the pageant, a child declared dramatically, "From this spot the Patriarch Abraham saw the entire land." His friend replied, "Once a kid told our kindergarten teacher, you know, when Abraham lived here we were still in Ramat Gan [a modern Israeli city]. Ha, ha, ha. But that was when we were still kids in kindergarten." The first child concluded, "But it is probably true. This is the place from which Abraham could have seen the entire land."

The first statement made Ofra the heir to a biblical past; the second used humor to burst the ideological bubble. The child's witticism distanced the past and expressed, in an unexpected way, that the biblical Patriarch, unlike Ramat Gan, is remote from here and now. He also showed how fundamentalist fanaticism, when carried to the extreme, could be funny and absurd even to "true believers," and what was probably more important, to their children. But the second child immediately "apologized" for his jest by noting that such talk was for preschoolers who didn't know better, and the first child then repeated his initial assertion. He was no longer as confident as before, though. Now the tale was "probably true" and Abraham could have seen the entire land, but he was not sure that he actually did so. This dialogue shows how sacred memory and fanaticism has limits when it faces against ridicule, but so does subversiveness.

Maintaining fundamentalist beliefs within a skeptical modern society is, as the people of Ofra have discovered, an ongoing project. The ability to convince their fellow Israelis that Ofra should remain where it now stands depends, to a large extent, on the ability of the settlers to balance the zealotry that fuels their drive to settle with thriving everyday life, which is what connects them to their compatriots.

10

The Trauma That Never Was

The Evacuation of Sinai

ON MOVING SANDS

As a young student, I researched the Movement to Stop the Withdrawal from Sinai, staying for some time in the doomed town of Yamit. In the final weeks before the town's final evacuation and destruction (April 1982), the municipal agencies, including the street cleaners, stopped functioning. Desert sand drifted in, blanketing the streets. Although I was never a supporter of the movement and agreed wholeheartedly with the peace treaty, the city slowly disappearing beneath the advancing desert was a metaphor that deeply touched the chords of one who was raised on the Zionist ethos of settlement. Like many other participants and onlookers, I felt that the central story of Zionism was being written (or erased) on the edge of the desert; though far away, Yamit seemed to be at the core of Zionist existence. Or was it?

In history as told by the settlers, the progressive victorious narrative is marred by two significant traumas: the evacuation and destruction of the settlement region of Yamit in the Sinai, and the repeat in the Gaza Strip settlements. In this chapter, I discuss the first event and its consequences, and return to the second in the last chapter.

The return of territory to Egypt following a peace agreement was proof that a broader evacuation of the West Bank settlements is also a viable option, and, indeed, it was immediately placed on the negotiation table. The fact that the government implementing the evacuation decision included the most ardent supporters of the settlers, such as Prime Minister Menachem Begin and Secretary of Defense Ariel Sharon, only increased the alarm. Their willingness to yield the settlements as part of a peace agreement was seen by the settlers as a capitulation by national leadership, as well as a personal and ideological betrayal. The withdrawal posed challenging symbolic missions for the settlers, who wished to halt further similar events. They could either explain why the remaining settlements were inherently different from Yamit and deserved a different fate or else marshal the experience to solicit support for their future struggles. In any case, they had to integrate this dramatic event into their understanding of history without undermining their concept of historic salvation.

All those involved in the struggle leading up to April 1982 understood that they were rehearsing for the grand show: the struggle over Judea and Samaria. In this chapter, I discuss the story of the settlement of Sinai, its evacuation, and the effect of this dramatic event on the movement. I present two modes of commemoration: the first is that of the secular settlers of the region, and the other is that of the Gush Emunim settlers. Finally, I inquire as to why the evacuation of Sinai has not become a major object of memory, neither for the Gush Emunim settlers nor for Israeli society at large.

The Settlements of Sinai

Based on agreements between the Ottoman Empire and the British rulers of Egypt, the Sinai was declared Egyptian territory. The Israeli troops that entered the region and reached the town of El Arish during the 1948 Israeli War of Independence were forced to withdraw under the terms of the interim agreements that ended that war. When, in the 1956 war, the Sinai was occupied by Israeli forces, Prime Minister David Ben-Gurion pronounced that, as Israel had now returned to Mount Sinai, the age of the Third Temple was dawning. Within a few months, however, Israel was forced again to evacuate its troops in exchange for a guarantee that the area would remain demilitarized. In the prelude to the 1967 war, Egypt renounced the agreement by closing the Straits of Tiran and the sea gates to the southern city of Eilat, and by moving its troops into the peninsula. In this war, Israel reoccupied the Sinai desert, this time demanding, with the support of the United States, full peace with Egypt in exchange for the lost territory. Minister of Defense Moshe Dayan went on to declare that he would rather keep the southern tip of the area, Sharm-el-Sheikh, than trade it for peace.

Israel then slowly began to settle the area. For most Israelis, Sinai was a recreational escape: long beaches, soft sand, scuba diving, hikes, and mountain climbing. The settlements that were erected were mostly on the northeastern shoreline, near the border of Israel. These settlements were an attempt to cut off the densely populated Palestinian Gaza Strip from any connection with Egypt and were erected with the thought that, if and when a peace agreement would be achieved, Israel would stand a better chance of holding on to the region closest to its borders.

As was the case with other settlement projects in Israel, the first to arrive were Nahal outposts. The Nahal is a military unit in which soldiers combine their military service with settlement. Eventually, they either stay to reside in the outpost or civilians arrive to replace them; in any case, the outpost is supposed to become "civilized" (as opposed to "militarized"). Neomi Shemer, the revered national poet, wrote a popular song about such an outpost, romanticizing the beauty that she saw there, which reminded her of the Zionist values of old. The romantic image of Sinai as a new Zionist frontier was strong, both in the minds of the planners of the region and among the new settlers.

The first civic agricultural settlement to be established there was Sadot in 1971, and the town of Yamit was built in 1975, reaching a few thousand residents by the early 1980s. The Yamit region also included some smaller kibbutzim and moshavim, and altogether some five thousand Israeli residents found their home in the Sinai region. All were secular settlements, independent of the religious Gush Emunim settlement project that had, meanwhile, developed in Judea and Samaria.

The 1973 Yom Kippur War was fought far away on the shores of the Suez Canal, but it soon set in motion events that had a profound effect on the fate of the region. Egyptian President Anwar Sadat arrived in Jerusalem in November 19, 1977, and, after lengthy negotiations, Israel and Egypt signed a peace treaty that required the removal of all Israeli presence from Sinai. The agreement passed through the Knesset after a heated debate that ruptured the dominant Likud Party. The ultra-Right party of Tehiya was formed and took a leading position in the struggle to halt the Israeli withdrawal. In the 1981 elections, the Tehiya Party received a disappointing 2.5 percent of the vote, sending only three members to parliament. This result signaled to the Israeli government, and to the Gush Emunim movement, that the Israeli public supported the government in its decision to trade Sinai for a peace agreement with Egypt, or that, in any case, they could not count on massive popular support to reverse the historical trend.

As the agreement was to be implemented, tensions around the settlement region grew. Gush Emunim followers began to move to Yamit and other settlements in the area. They erected some new settlements, such as Atzmona, and occupied empty and evacuated buildings in the town of Yamit and nearby settlements. Some early encounters with the army had occurred already in 1981, and the struggle intensified as the date of evacuation, April 1982, approached.

The Struggle to Stop the Withdrawal

Generally speaking, two large groups struggled against the withdrawal, each with its own interests, logic, and subdivisions.[1] The first group was the veteran residents of the region, mostly secular, who felt that the government had reneged on the promises it made when they chose to settle in the periphery.[2] The other was the population that streamed into the region in the period following the decision to evacuate, mostly as part of the Gush Emunim movement. After a certain period of collaboration, the joint struggle broke down: the veteran settlers reached a generous compensation agreement with the government and agreed to evacuate peacefully. The infuriated Gush Emunim settlers saw how the local residents, in order to improve their agreement with the government, had manipulated their struggle. By the last month, most of the regular residents of Yamit and the nearby villages had left in an orderly fashion, and the newly arrived protesters of Gush Emunim and their supporters were left practically alone to battle against the government and the army. Ironically, they were trying to save the homes of people who had already agreed to leave them.

Within the protesters' camp, most were hard-core Gush Emunim supporters. Joining them were the extremist Rabbi Meir Kahane and his followers, and a group of students headed by Tzachi Hanegbi (son of Geula Cohen, a Tehiya Party member of the Knesset), who later became, in another one of the many ironies of the story, Israel's Minister of Justice. The Gush Emunim settlers moved into the region by the hundreds, bringing with them the contents of their homes. Yeshiva students also arrived in the region with their rabbis. Some local residents joined hands with the newcomers. All of these groups crystallized in the Movement to

Stop the Withdrawal from Sinai, which, although an offshoot of Gush Emunim, concealed the origin of most of its activists so as to attract secular sympathizers.

Throughout the struggle, the question of legitimate violence against the army troubled the settlers. The young yeshiva students admired the army. Most were reserve soldiers themselves and, hence, were most reluctant to object violently to the evacuation. It was also widely assumed that a violent encounter with the army would be doomed to fail and would alienate the Israeli public, whose support was essential for even the slimmest chance of success. At one dramatic moment, Rabbi Ya'akov Ariel stood in front of the soldiers, calling on them to refuse the order to evacuate Jews from their homeland. His demand was not supported by the movement leaders and did not find an attentive ear among the soldiers.

This was not the only legal and moral issue involved in the struggle: another was the breaking into evacuated houses set for destruction. Leaders often distinguished between what was legal and what was legitimate. Hanan Porat compared the actions to running into a busy road to save a child: it is a legitimate and moral action, even if, technically speaking, it violated some laws. For him, saving a region of the land of Israel was a moral action on a par with saving lives, justifying infringement of Israeli law.

The slogan of the settlers was "There shall be no withdrawal." In support of the slogan, they performed actions such as planting crops that would bear fruit after the date of the evacuation. The movement's logo was a sliced map of Israel, illustrating the protesters' claim that they were stopping not only the evacuation of Sinai, but a domino effect that would inevitably lead to the collapse of Israel and the reversal of Zionism.[3] The withdrawal was presented as patently impossible, either because of changes in the international scene or because of divine intervention.[4] When I visited the Sinai settlement of Atzmona and insisted on an answer from a kind and patient settler as to what would happen in case of withdrawal, the settler finally responded, "You don't ask a soldier who is going to battle in which cemetery he wants to be buried."

A week before the evacuation date, the army blockaded the region and brought in troops, including female soldiers to evacuate the settler women. Rabbi Kahane's group was dragged out of a bunker where they had tied themselves to gas balloons and threatened to blow themselves up. Students led by Tzachi Hanegbi who had gathered atop a high monument that commemorated the dead of the Six-Day War were lowered by cranes. The majority of the protesters climbed the roofs of Yamit's buildings and clashed violently with the army. Using ladders, foam, and cages on cranes, the army wrestled them down and then removed them from the region. The houses of Yamit and the adjacent settlements were razed, and the site was returned to the Egyptians, as per agreement, on April 25, 1982.

As the resoluteness of the government and the army in implementing the agreement with Egypt became apparent, the focus shifted from the struggle itself to the way it would be remembered. The last days of Yamit were, in a sense, a presentation for the Israeli and international mass media, showing that any future evacuation of Jews from the land of Israel would be a difficult, if not impossible, project.[5]

REMEMBERING SINAI

The great failure of Yamit was followed by a process of soul searching.[6] Those who went to the region were proud of their stay there and felt that they had expressed the essence of their being through the struggle, although some reflected on problematic issues, such as the clash with the army and the final failure. The settlers then turned to the task of commemorating the event. Those who felt the threat to Jewish settlements in other regions sought to construct the evacuation as a national trauma, never to be repeated. The importance of remembering in Jewish history lent impetus to the commemorative project: remembering, reminding, and praying give the community rights to a certain territory, whereas forgetting leads to renunciation of those rights. According to Zionist ideology, one of the most important justifications for Jews' return to the land of Israel is the memory of their homeland—a memory they have preserved through the generations. At that time, the settlers, believing in the grand destiny of Israel and never trustful of Arabs' intentions to keep agreements, were confident that Israel would soon return to the region in a successful war, and that their remembering would grant them the right to revive the region.

As this book repeatedly stresses, Gush Emunim settlers are no strangers to the practice of commemoration; however, in the case of Yamit, they encountered a new challenge: how to retain and transmit to their children the memory of a region in which they held no physical presence and therefore could not settle or construct monuments. They sought to cast themselves as tragic heroes in a story whose components were at odds with the ethos of the settlers, such as the "betrayal" of the original settlers, who received money in exchange for homes and did not want to be "saved" by the movement, or the clashes with the army.

The commemorative practices had already been initiated during the evacuation. Uri Elitzur (1982) described how some of the leaders and youths of the movement infiltrated back into devastated Yamit hours after they were evacuated, declaring, "We hereby vow before God and Israel that we did not leave and will not leave, have not forgotten and will not forget, Yamit" (20). Year after year, the settlers' magazine *Nekuda* has mentioned Yamit and promised to remember and return. Here is one example:

> We, the residents of Yesha, were there three years ago. On our flesh we experienced the withdrawal, the destruction, and the uprootedness. On the roofs of Talmei-Yosef and Yamit, we took two vows: We shall return—even if the day is far off—to rebuild the greenhouses that were uprooted and the houses that were uprooted and destroyed. We vowed that Yamit shall not fall a second time.[7]

The motif of witnessing is central here: somewhat like witnesses to the Holocaust, those who experienced the traumatic event with their own bodies are the ones required to relate the experience to further generations. The sentence "Yamit shall not fall a second time" paraphrases a famous slogan regarding the last stand in Masada (Zerubavel 1995).[8] In the Zionist master narrative, that historical event represents the end of Jewish presence and sovereignty of the land in antiquity and the beginning of exile. Gush Emunim used Zionist building blocks in constructing its memory.

On the previous anniversary of the evacuation, *Nekuda* took its message from the Passover Haggada: "In each generation, man must see himself as if he came out of Egypt."[9] Although the settlers' movement sought to reinforce the memory of Yamit by evoking the Exodus, the symbolic value traditionally attached to Egypt may explain why the memory of Yamit has failed to have a lasting impact: As the memory of the Jewish people attaches positive connotations to the exodus from Egypt, and the Bible prohibits its return there, a movement—especially a religious one—that demands to return to a place currently regarded as "Egypt" must overcome deeply rooted symbolic concepts.

The memory of Yamit also took on an institutional expression. An organization called Shvut Sinai (Return to Sinai) was established, stating this as its goal: "[The organization] will follow in the footsteps of Gush Etzion that fell in battle in 1948. It will transform the trauma of eviction and destruction into an engine of renewal and resurrection; this time for all eternity."[10] In the region of Gush Katif, established in the Gaza Strip, some settlements were given names attesting to the desire of their residents to return to Sinai, such as Mitzpe Atzmona (Overlooking Atzmona) or Elei Sinai (Toward Sinai). Hanan Porat, always sensitive to the importance of memory, reported that in his house the memory of Yamit is raised in Saturday discussions and suggested the establishment of a memorial day for the destroyed settlements. His suggestion was not followed.

The yeshiva of Yamit was moved into a new building in Neve Dekalim in the Gaza Strip. The new concrete building was constructed like a giant Star of David with one point buried in the ground in remembrance of the destruction of the Yamit region settlements. Entering the yeshiva—a broken Star of David—one metaphorically enters the story of the destruction. At the entrance to the yeshiva, an artist, Zvi Gera, who was among the few secular supporters who moved to the region, created a sculpture to commemorate the event. The sculpture is a miniature model of the town of Yamit on the day of its destruction. The basic elements of the lost battle can be clearly seen: the shape of the one-story and two-story houses, the figures of the protesters on the roof, the huge monument, and the bunker where Rabbi Kahane and his supporters entrenched themselves. The human figures are faceless to symbolize the unity of wills.

The statue seeks to construct memory and thereby also to enforce forgetting. During the conflict, the roofs, the monument, and the bunker were the sites of three different groups: the religious settlers, the secular students, and the Kahane group, respectively. They suggested different strategies of struggle, and the relations among them were at times cooperative but, at others, tense and conflicting. The statue obliterates any hint of discord between the various groups that arrived at Yamit, while it omits mention of the uneasy—at times openly hostile—relationship with the local Yamit residents. After appropriating the town physically during the struggle, the movement now attempts to appropriate it symbolically. Another point of collective forgetting is the absence of the army. The settlers are standing on the roof for no apparent reason, and their protest is aimed at no one visible in the model—possibly at the sky? Thus, the event is portrayed as a cosmic disaster rather than the result of a political decision by the Israeli government. Although the settlers could not avoid the violent engagement with the army during their actual struggle, they do try to eliminate it from the representation of the event.

The lack of faces, internal conflict, and evacuation of the settlers by the army enables visitors to fill in the missing parts with their own emotions, memories, and recollections. More than a work of art, the sculpture is a map—it is built to guide visitors into the intricacies of the conflict as seen by the movement. A visitor who does not know the details, however, certainly needs a guide. Parents can bring their children and use the model to explain what happened in the final days of the conflict. When I visited the place, I joined a group of Yamit region evacuees who received explanations from an extremely deferential and respectful young female guide. She began by opening a book and reading the description supplied by an army officer of the evacuation. She sought to present the perspective of the "aggressor," symbolically incorporating his story with that of the evacuees. Her reassuring message was that the tragedy was a general Israeli one, not just that of the settlers alone.

To whom does the tragedy belong, and in what sense is it a tragedy at all? Many of the religious settlers do not remember the events with much anger, and the population of Israel did not take the events to heart, as I will elaborate on later. Furthermore, the veteran secular settlers of the region wanted nothing to do with Gush Emunim. They remember the region—if and when they remember—within their own communities, and religious settlers are not granted access to their practices and events, let alone to their inner memories. The statue in the yeshiva is a Gush Emunim *lieu de mémoire* and holds no interest for the former residents of Yamit, who in any case are hardly represented there. They, in turn, were angered by the invaders who, from their perspective, ruined their last few months in their beloved town, and thus are unlikely to endorse a sculpture that remembers the last days and obliterates all the rest.

Former Residents Remember Yamit

The two communities implicated in the struggle to stop the evacuation commemorated the event central to their identity as Israelis in radically different ways. Showing how the secular residents of Yamit and the vicinity remembered their ordeal can demonstrate the particular nature of Gush Emunim settlers' memory and their attachment to space—in this case, not "their" space. As these practices reflect on the fate of the former Zionist pioneers, whom the Gush Emunim settlers wished to emulate, they provide an important context illustrating the changing social values in which the new settlers function.

The "veteran" residents of Yamit were actually relatively new to the region, having arrived only some years before their evacuation. They arrived under the ideological auspices of the Zionist settlement ethos, having been sent by the state to inhabit and cultivate the desert and ensure Israeli rule on its periphery. They were hailed as embodying the national credo and as continuing the glorious tradition of the pioneers. Their presence on what, according to international law, was occupied territory, was not seen in Israel with the same ambivalence as that of the Gush Emunim settlements. The residents of the new region were mainly secular, and much of the theological discourse that accompanied the settlement of the West Bank was conspicuously missing. Since the town of Yamit was built to be a tourist resort, and its beaches were a haven for secular youngsters, the religious lingo was totally out of place. Three years before the town was founded, the vision of Yamit was presented as follows: "In its distance from Tel Aviv it is like Haifa, and with its completion there will be a triplet of great Mediterranean coastal cities in the land, 100 kilometers distant from each other. The distance between the planned city and the Suez Canal gives it importance, given the future amicable relations between Israel and its neighbors."[11]

The sound ideological base, the consensual political support, and the underlying planned logic of the Sinai settlements, all made the shock of the decision to evacuate that much greater. The settlers found themselves in a delicate situation as staunch Zionists: their loyalty to the state made them willing to evacuate in return for the chance of a lasting peace; they did, however, wish to receive compensation for their property, not to mention their years of hard work and dedication. Their struggle to receive what they considered a fair sum from the government endangered their good reputation as pioneers and forced them into an uneasy coalition with the religious and ultra-rightist Gush Emunim. Unlike the religious settlers, they were content to settle for compensation and leave the visitors to struggle on their own. However, the destruction of their homes engendered a severe, noticeable trauma.

Most of the former residents of the Yamit region dispersed throughout the country and no longer form a distinctive social group of evacuees. Some joined new communities that were established in the Negev desert, not far from the Egyptian border. The experience of one such village, Ein Habsor, was researched, described, and interpreted by Liav Sade (2000), an anthropologist resident. The village, situated near the Egyptian border, was populated by the former residents of various agricultural settlements of the Yamit region, who decided to reaffirm their commitment to Zionist values by starting a new agricultural settlement in the Negev. They first attempted to commemorate their past by naming their village Mavo Sinai (Entrance to Sinai) to remind them of their common origin. However, the National Naming Committee intervened, just as it did in the decisions regarding the Gush Emunim settlers (see chapter 3), and decided to name the village after the nearby stream: the Bsor. In this case, it was the secular that suffered discrimination: whereas the religious Gush Emunim settlements were allowed to adopt names commemorating the Yamit region, the secular settlers, who had lived there much longer, were allowed no such privilege. It may be that, in the Israeli mindset, memory today is solely associated with ideological religious believers. The roads in the village are named after destroyed villages.

The settlers of Ein Habsor were not obsessed with the idea of return to Sinai, but did want to preserve the remnants of their former existence, for their own nostalgic reasons and for the sake of their children. Some of their children received names of the settlements, such as Yamit or Dikla. The settlers also held annual celebrations in which they told their stories. There were two competing stories to tell: The first was of the former communities—a story that, apart from its common end, was divisive insofar as the residents of Ein Habsor came from different communities in the Yamit region. The second was the story of Ein Habsor itself, which was common to all and integrative in its nature. Sade shows how the narrative gradually changed from one annual celebration to the next and from the former story to the latter; with it, the meaning of Ein Habsor in the narrative changed—from a village dedicated to the commemoration of former communities to a village that consecrates its own history.

Over the years, the demographics of Ein Habsor have changed as new residents have arrived while some of the older ones have left. The unifying nature of the traumatic experience has disintegrated, and the interest in the nostalgic past has diminished. Eventually, the new village accumulated its own history that competed with the stories of the "good old days" in the Yamit region. If the village that housed the "survivors" of the Yamit experience failed to guard the memory, other places had even less chance of success. The memory of evacuation has gradually waned and, apart from rare appearances in the media, it is rarely told among the Israeli public.

The slipping of the Yamit story into social oblivion is not accidental. It was difficult for Israeli society to make the transformation from a mind-set of war, which legitimated settlements on contested grounds, to a mind-set of peace and cooperation, which entailed the evacuation of those same settlements. As a result, the secular pioneers, the most cherished sons of the Zionist state, felt betrayed while simultaneously implicated in the "crime" of betrayal through their agreement to accept compensation. Ironically, the evacuees from Sinai found themselves as pioneers in a different sense: the greatest symbol of the privatization process that, from the mid-1980s, engulfed the country was the use of land for profit rather than for agriculture. Postideological Israel does not wish to remember the initial moment of this momentous transformation, when villagers received money for their land, and a basically agricultural region was destroyed through a state decision. Consequently, the residents of Ein Habsor received no assistance from the state in their attempt to preserve their cherished memory. As the Israeli ethos changed, and ideological settlement was gradually becoming a subversive practice, the uniqueness of the Gush Emunim phenomenon became even more apparent.

Lessons from Sinai

The ideological settlers of Gush Emunim wanted to transform the tragedy of Sinai into a national trauma that would influence any future evacuation agreement that Israel might consider. Just as they failed to stop the evacuation, however, they failed to control its social and political meanings. Although arguments against evacuating settlements do exist, including the risk of possible violence on the part of radical settlers, the memory of Yamit broadcasts no vibes of fear or worry. For the settlers, the fact that an Israeli government—and a rightist one at that—could decide on withdrawing from territory and evacuating Jewish settlements with the full support—or at least indifference—of the Israeli public, and that the whole affair might be soon forgotten, was indeed, a sobering lesson. The settlers also learned that they stood to lose not only the battle for their homes, but also the place of their settlement project in Israeli memory and history. They were to receive the same lessons in the implementation of the disengagement plan in August 2005. The ability of an Israeli government to decide upon and efficiently carry out such a large-scale evacuation attested to the little impact that the memory of

Yamit had on the minds of Israelis. Rarely is it possible to assess the success of a memory project and declare it a total failure; Yamit is one such example.

Why and in what sense was the Yamit struggle forgotten? Why did the destruction of houses and flourishing settlements fail to leave a lasting mark on the Israeli public and have only limited effects on the settlers themselves? First and foremost, the agreement with Egypt withstood the test of time and, while it is still a "cold peace," characterized by distrust and recurring crisis, it is generally considered to be a success. The predictions of the settlers regarding the forthcoming betrayal of the Egyptians did not materialize, and the revisionist sentiments regarding Sinai had little ground on which to flourish. The settlers could not hope for popular support for a movement to return to Sinai, and their longing became more nostalgic than political. The withdrawal from territories and evacuation of settlements in return for lasting peace with an Arab nation was not an example that Gush Emunim leaders could draw upon to elicit support for their cause.

The settlers found it difficult to recuperate from the "betrayal" of the veteran settlers of the region. While the settlers fought for the survival of the settlement region, its residents were willing to be evacuated for what they considered ample monetary compensation and were only manipulating the movement to better their agreement with the Israeli government. Gush Emunim protestors were found to be more attached to the territory than were the "unthankful" people they were fighting for, who readily sold their rights. The Gush Emunim settlers often hear the claim that most of the people of Israel do not want them fighting on its behalf and do not appreciate their sacrifice. This sense of solitude was nowhere more apparent than in the case of Sinai. Again, as this message was not one that the settlers wished to accentuate in their dialogue with the Israeli public, the myth of Yamit was marginalized.

The fact that the story of Yamit became a private affair of the radical national religious faction blocked any attempts at granting it wide national meaning. Furthermore, the Israeli public understood that the settlers were using the media to construct a national trauma. While it was accepted that the settlers were indeed grieving, it was apparent that the entire event was, at least in part, manufactured for media purposes. In the case of Yamit, unlike in Yesha, the settlers were not fighting for their actual homes. To be sure, they did refer to the houses they entered, or the mobile homes that they placed in the desert, as their *homes*. Their presentation, however, was hardly convincing: they had other, more sub-stantial homes in their home settlements, while the veteran settlers were willing to evacuate their places of residence, which had far more right to be called homes. When the soldiers who carried out the evacuation were interviewed, they expressed anger at the settlers for using the loaded symbol of "home": they said that the settlers actually stole their mobile homes from military camps, as the unit symbols were still visible on the sides of the mobile homes.[12]

New issues soon took center stage of Israeli public opinion, pushing aside the memory of Yamit. Within two months, Israel was at war in Lebanon—a war that created its own bitter memories—so any plans to entrench Yamit's evacuation as a traumatic memory in the hearts of Israelis had to be postponed indefinitely. The new war ironically accen-tuated the gains of Israeli's decision to evacuate Sinai: Egypt chose to sit on the sidelines, keeping its part of the agreement. The war also countered the claim that Israel would be weakened by the withdrawal and would continue to withdraw.[13]

The symbolic nature of the territory that was forsaken also had much to do with the inability to install a potent memory. During the struggle, the leaders of Gush Emunim, especially the rabbis, took pains to prove that Sinai—or at least the Yamit region—was indeed part of the land of Israel, but their claims were only partly convincing. Desert—especially the Sinai desert—is associated in the minds of Jews with wandering to reach the Promised Land, not with a territory that actually belongs to people. It is a liminal space on the edge of the Promised Land, and hos-tile terrain in which the Jews are not expected to stay for long.[14] As men-tioned before, Egypt is a place the Jews leave, a place connected to exile and slavery, not a place to which Jews wish to return. Settler Hava Pinhas-Cohen (1996), wondering how it was possible to part from Sinai, reached the following profound conclusion: "This is a place whose myths con-nect it to non-place, to wandering without burial" (43).

As the memory of the evacuation faded away, it gave rise to two op-posing positions vis-à-vis the project of Gush Emunim.[15] The leaders and activists of the movement debated what went wrong, and Yoel Bin-Nun concluded that they had failed to capture the hearts of the people. In his mind, better preparation and a more intensive socialization of the Israeli masses would have yielded better results; the cognitive distance between the settlers and their audience led to the failure. On the opposite side, others arriving at the same diagnosis derived a radically different prognosis. They concluded that it was futile to attempt to convince the Israeli public of the correctness of their views. They sought to bring about cataclysmic change by blowing up the mosques on the Temple Mount. Although this idea preceded the events of Yamit, and the struggle over Yamit actually postponed the operational plans, their motivation grew once it became evident that they could not count on the government and people of Israel for support. As the activists of the Jewish underground put it, when they realized that they could not achieve their goals by evolution, they opted for revolution (Segal 1988).

Both responses attest to the problems that the movement encountered in trying to memorialize Yamit. The divided perspectives limited the educational potential of the case. The settlers could not agree on the lessons to be learned from the trauma: should they, as part of Israeli society, turn their attention to education and communication; or should they assume that the larger society, immersed in the shallow pleasures of modernity and consumerism, abandoned them to fight on their own with all the means at their disposal.

Many individual settlers hold strong memories of their experiences in Sinai. While thousands passed through Yamit during the months of struggle, some hundreds persisted and made the struggle a part of their identity. They were usually those who, at the time, could afford to move there or could not afford, politically and morally, to abstain. Some belonged to the ideological hard core, dedicated to the struggle over every piece of land, moving to any place they felt to be endangered. Others were young couples or families not yet entrenched in the world of work and the community, and who could afford to spend a long period in the Yamit region. They formed a network of friends that kept the memory of the struggle alive, at least among themselves, though they could not pass it on to the rest of Israeli society. For them, the memory is indeed a painful one that has haunted them for decades. I visited a family in Gush Etzion that had pictures of Yamit on the walls, a tree from the region in their backyard, and a plastic bag with sand from Yamit hanging on their wall. Twenty years after the events, Sara Drukman used the strongest possible imagery in recollecting the experience: "The most awful moment for me—the moment that is carved in memory—was the moment when I saw through the windows of my home soldiers coming with helmets and shields. The first association in my mind was of the Holocaust."[16]

What is most salient in the memory of those who went to Sinai is the communal feelings of the last weeks, when the secular Yamit population had, for the most part, accepted the compensation and left to find a new life elsewhere. A religious atmosphere pervaded, bringing, if only temporarily, new life to the dying town. The few secular residents that remained in their hometown to the end were frustrated to see their town change before their eyes, but the religious settlers felt that they had created the sacred ambience they had been searching for: rabbinic classes, peaceful Saturdays, and a strong sense of communalism and purpose. These memories temper the bitter ones of struggle against the army and the traumatic scenes of destruction. The invitation for the tenth anniversary of the evacuation read "Ten years after the evacuation, and it seems as though it was yesterday's dream. We shall gather by the sea and the sand to remember Yamit, Sinai, and the settlements, and—especially— to be together with the same people."

The struggle over Yamit took place on Israel's geographic periphery. Visitors, among them members of the Knesset, were surprised to find it less than two hours' drive from Tel Aviv and Jerusalem, as they imagined it beyond their grasp. At the time, however, the Yamit region seemed symbolically and ideologically central: the struggle there was over the core values of Israeli society, the great divide between Right and Left, the value of settlement versus the fruits of peace, or perhaps between the remnants of Zionism and the growing specter of post-Zionism. In hindsight, it seems that the drama was both symbolically and geographically marginal—after a brief intense struggle, Yamit was practically forgotten. For the Gush Emunim settlers, the lesson was that Israeli society has its own agendas, and the defense of settlements in peripheral locations might not be one of them.

11

Terrorism and Feminism

The Case of Rechalim

DEATH AND COMMEMORATION IN THE HILLS OF SAMARIA

Feminism among the national religious camp, especially the Gush Emunim settlers, is a revolution within a revolution. As the camp has undergone dramatic changes, achievements, and tragedies, women, in a precarious situation in the mostly men-led movement, have started to assert their power. I shall explore the challenge to gender relations among the settlers, and especially its built-in limitations, through an elaborate test case in which a settler woman was killed and commemorated.

On October 27, 1991, Palestinian terrorists fired on a bus leaving the settlement of Shiloh on its way to a large political rally in Tel Aviv. The bus driver, Yitzhak Rofeh, and one of the passengers, Rachel Druk, were killed, and several children were injured. In the months following the event, some dozens of women took it upon themselves to establish a new settlement at the site of the murder in commemoration of their dead friend, Rachel, mother of seven from Shiloh. The settlement was to be called Rechalim (literally, "Rachels"). This was the first time that a Jewish settlement in the West Bank had been engineered, conceived, and led solely by women.

The events at Rechalim followed three years of the Palestinian First Intifada, and the friction between the two populations was intense. Research has shown that, in the early 1990s, among the residents of the ideological settlements, 73 percent of the men and 53 percent of the children encountered Palestinian acts of violence at an average of once a week or more (Gutman 1992). This escalation of violence occurred at a time when the settlements were attempting to expand with the support of a rightist government. The routine disturbances of life in the settlements were perceived as a real threat to the future prospects of development. Retaliation, deterrence, and confidence boosting became paramount factors in settler leadership considerations.

Rachel Druk's funeral at Shiloh, the first in the young settlement's history, was subdued and well controlled. Immediately afterward, the mourners, accompanied by sympathizers from other nearby settlements, went to the curve in the road where the attack had occurred, demanding what they defined as a "fitting Zionist response": namely, the establishment of a new Jewish settlement on that spot. The settlers tried to establish their presence, as the Israeli army surrounded their illegal settlement, awaiting the government's decision to evacuate them. The settlers, using their political influence and capitalizing on popular outrage at the attack, were allowed to stay for the customary week of mourning and then for the traditional month, as well. After that, the government decided to allow the settlers to extend their stay indefinitely. Their intention was to expand the memorial site into a settlement called Rechalim, named after the woman who had been killed, as well as after Rachel Weiss, who had perished three years earlier with her three children in a Palestinian terrorist attack near Jericho.

The site was located near the main road of Samaria, 100 meters away from the actual scene of the murder. At first, it consisted of mobile homes and, later, of two large tents: one served as a kitchen, study room, and makeshift synagogue; the other was used for lodging and major events. An overturned army helmet held the perpetual flame burning in memory of the victims. A month after the events, a huge stone monument was erected bearing biblical inscriptions referring to Isaac and Rachel.

While a group was being formed to organize the permanent community of the settlement, temporary solutions were devised. Surrounding settlements and educational institutions took turns sending women by day and men by night to maintain the site. An informal college, named after the bus driver, Yitzhak Rofeh, was also established at the site. Neighboring settlements provided food and other supplies for those who stayed there.

For a year, the site constituted a symbolic center of the Jewish settlements in the region that participated in its upkeep. Many of the ceremonial and organizational activities conducted during the year were held there, such as the lighting of Hanukkah candles, the planting of trees on Tu Bishvat (the New Year for Trees), and the annual Samaria march on Lag ba-Omer. The most dedicated among the settlers chose to perform their personal rites of passage, such as circumcision of their babies, at Rechalim. In short, during that year, Rechalim became the social, political, and ritual center for the West Bank Jewish settler community. However, the envisaged settlement, which in the settlers' words was to become "another twinkling star over the hills of Samaria," did not materialize at that time. After the elections of 1992, a new Labor government promised to freeze the development of settlements in the occupied territories. Only in the late 1990s, after another change in government, was the settlement eventually established.

FUNDAMENTALISM, GUSH EMUNIM, AND GENDER

At face value, Rechalim can be seen as a rare case of feminism within a fundamentalist movement. It is feminist in the strict and limited sense that women assumed leadership roles, initiated the establishment of a joint project, and proudly displayed their achievements in the public sphere. However, feminism is a complex and multifaceted ideology with various contradictory definitions. Fundamentalism is usually associated with the reassertion of patriarchy and the reestablishment of traditional gender roles. In this case, women engendered role reversal by appropriating the quintessential male role of their movement: settling the land. This raises intriguing issues. National religious women have indeed initiated, and to a large extent successfully, a totally new way of regarding gender roles within their community. A most impressive feminist revolution is currently under way, focusing mainly on the study of holy texts. The struggle over Rechalim took place on the threshold of a decade of radical change and, in a sense, preempted what was to follow. From a historical perspective, the establishing of Rechalim can be conceived as an embryonic feminist revolt that was suppressed before it had the chance to develop.

Fundamentalism can be conceived as a traditionalist response to modern culture, modernist ideas, and the rise of science.[1] Feminism, accompanied by the weakening of the traditional family, is one of the most significant "evils" encountered in fundamentalist thought and politics. While appealing to both genders, religious movements are usually male led, maintain a strongly gendered division of labor, and may even be conceived as patriarchal protest movements. Recently, scholars have begun to realize how gender ridden the rhetoric of fundamentalism is in its aspiration for a physical and conceptual separation of the genders.

One may add that the defiant nature of fundamentalism calls for a reassertion of the self and therefore tends to be strongly affiliated with maleness and machismo. In the fundamentalist ideal, the role of the woman is confined to the home, and "good mothering" has become the most important standard of evaluation. The restriction of the place and role of women to the private sphere within the nuclear family, understood by today's scholars as a historical construct, is elevated, in fundamentalist ideology, to mythical and sacred proportions.

In some respects, however, fundamentalism can also empower women. Fundamentalism thrives where the women's labor market situation offers limited possibilities. While it establishes and legitimates women's inferior status, fundamentalism also aids women in their efforts to "domesticate" men. Many women agree enthusiastically with the anti-modernist, profamily fundamentalist ideology and view themselves as equal partners in furthering the movement's goals.

In national fundamentalist movements (mainly in Islam), gendered imagery is applied to the nation as a whole. The nation is often symbolized as a woman at the mercy of strangers, and freeing her is part of a process of masculinization. Feminism, in the sense of freeing women from their socially and symbolically assigned traditional role, is conceived as morally wrong for both religious and nationalistic reasons because it challenges both the divine order and national virility. Therefore, fundamentalist men active in liberation movements expect the women fighting at their side to return to the traditional lifestyle once the battle is won, whereas women find it difficult to retain the achievements of their emancipation.

Many of the aforementioned motifs are concordant with the concepts of femininity in Gush Emunim and in the national religious camp in general. Due to the relative socioeconomic affluence of the group and the state, the situation of these women is a far cry from that of Islamic women and is closer to that of the women in Christian fundamentalist groups in North America. There is, however, a crucial difference here, too: whereas women's issues, in particular abortion, have been most significant in the history of American fundamentalism, the struggle over territories and settlements greatly overshadows all other issues in the Israeli case.

Research does indicate some significant similarities between the situation of the national religious women and those of fundamentalist women elsewhere. Institutes of higher religious education, as well as many primary and secondary schools, are gender segregated. Studies conducted within Israeli religious educational institutions for girls (*ulpanot*) have shown that gendered socialization is still the norm, and this is reflected both in the curriculum and in the accounts given by the girls themselves (Rapoport, Penso, and Garb 1994). Within the Gush Emunim camp, the political leadership of the early days was uniformly male, and the religious authority of rabbis, which is constantly increasing in influence, excluded women entirely.

The role fulfilled by women in the radical rightist movement is in accordance with the concept of the "republican woman"; namely, the woman, who through her reproductive role, as educator of children and keeper of the household, constitutes the backbone of the national ethos.[2] It is widely accepted that women's contribution to the national endeavor consists in their wholehearted fulfillment of their female role. But the traditional role of women is granted special meaning in the settlement project because, in essence, it is a project of private and national home building. As a woman settler told a reporter from *Nekuda,*

> Without the heroism of women to build on, when we lived a family per room in army camps, we would never have reached the mobile homes, the temporary houses, and—finally—settled homes. Mothers and children turned the struggle into something real and serious [. . .] in actuality, we, more than others, determine the nation's policy by giving our support behind the scenes to those around us, to grow, develop, contribute, and build. (Arzieli 1987)

As in other nationalist and revolutionary movements, women were enthusiastic participants in the Gush Emunim project, impelling their husbands toward increased radicalism. Research by Israeli political scientist Yael Yishai (1996) has shown that religious women are among the most extreme elements among the various right-wing political groups in Israeli society today, even more than their spouses.

Feminism has become, through the years, one of the most outstanding issues on the agenda of both the settlers and of the national religious camp in general. The most significant change lay in allowing women to study the sacred texts, mainly the Gemara. In a religious community, accessibility to the holy texts is the most esteemed intellectual asset, and hence it conditions and legitimates social hierarchies. Although the national religious community was never as gender segregated as the ultra-Orthodox community, men have always occupied the most essential religious roles, and women have been excluded from leadership positions in this realm. Allowing formal or informal education for women, therefore, constitutes a direct threat to the established order and is harshly criticized by some rabbis and halfheartedly endorsed by others. Rabbi Ya'akov Shilat (1999), for example, pointed out that a woman cannot study the Gemara without encountering contradictions within the text because the Gemara reflects on the pointlessness of teaching women.

Studying the sacred texts is an important example of a more comprehensive transformation in gender relations. As anthropologist Tamar El-Or (2002) has noted in her work on religious women's literacy, religious feminism in Israel is a rare nonviolent revolution, which has so far led to radical change with minimal direct confrontation. Surprisingly, it has not (yet) been accompanied by one of the most noted consequences of feminism around the world, which alarms fundamentalists: namely, a decline in fertility. Family values are still highly respected by Israeli religious women, and a newspaper report on the subject, titled "Children Are Happiness, But So Is a Career," written by a religious woman,[3] reflects the persistence of these values in face of the changes taking place that are fueled by a growing awareness of feminist issues.

Women express anger and anguish at being excluded from direct encounter with the religious texts that determine their sense of self. The title of El-Or's book on this phenomenon, *Next Year I Will Know More* (2002), is taken from a statement by one of her female interviewees who claimed that it was inconceivable that next Passover she would know only what she knew last Passover. Similarly, Bambi Sheleg (2001), a national religious journalist, articulates her inner drive to learn, describes her process of revelation, and admits regretfully and with apparent anger, "I shall never be able to overcome the huge gap that was created between myself and he who learned Gemara from the age of 10" (147). She concludes, "Full partnership in the Torah and in life will transform us all, women and men alike, to be richer in spirit and deeds" (153).

The feminist revolution has recently sprouted new institutions of higher education for women, as well. A religious feminist organization, Kolekh (Your Voice), has also been established that organizes popular conferences. An exhibition at the entrance to one of these conferences (2001) presented the synagogue from the women's perspective: all that could be seen was the partitioning wall and some fragments of the rich world perpetually screened from the women. The exhibition represents what will most likely be the next stage of the religious feminist revolution: changes in traditions and religious norms that currently determine the inferior place of women.

Hana Kehat (2001), a leading figure in the religious feminist revolution, has written, "The feminine issue is the national-religious society's current 'hot' story and only the grief for those killed on the roads of Yesha overshadows it" (33). In what follows, these two issues collide and merge.

The Women of Rechalim: A Feminist Challenge?

From the outset, women played a dominant role in both the organization and the management of the protest, as well as in the occupation of the Rechalim site. According to the semimythical story told by the women settlers, during the first days after the killing, the men felt that further protest would be futile and preferred not to confront the Israeli troops. It was the women who decided to persevere until a decision regarding a new settlement was reached. Practically and symbolically, the women filled the void left by the men.

The organizing group, called the Women of Rechalim, was comprised mainly of religious women, married and with children, from the more established ideological settlements of Gush Emunim. They were veterans of Gush Emunim activities and well connected with the elite group, some through family relations. Most were wage earners, some in the organizations established in the wake of Gush Emunim, such as the settlement organization Amanah (Treaty).

After years of struggling against governments and enduring the bumpy ride of establishing their previous settlements, a general feeling of déjà vu permeated the experience of Rechalim. Some of the women who visited Rechalim, whether during their turn on duty or as passersby, rejoiced at the opportunity to relive some of their experiences in earlier Gush Emunim events, including the establishment of their own home settlements. In Rechalim's visitors' book, one can find nostalgic entries such as this: "In the best tradition of Gush Emunim: all serious beginnings are in wintertime. Again it is cold and rainy: just like in Sabastia."

However, the leadership group, though thrilled by their own activities, expressed frustration and disappointment that, eighteen years after the establishment of the first settlement at Sabastia, the same tactics had to be used again. In any case, the image of Sabastia as the ultimate act of defiance against the government was not evoked in speaking of the act of settlement. The settler women did not wish their act to be understood merely as homage to past movement heroics, partially because they did not care to promote an agenda claiming that whatever men could do, they could do better. Neither was the act of terrorism in itself sufficient to provide the women with an explanation for their decision to dwell in the barren hills of Samaria in midwinter. To be sure, for the settlers, the act of settling needed no rationalization; however, the act, in which women took it upon themselves to erect a settlement in response to the killing of a friend, did require explanation and evoked discussions. Was the event a feminist act of defiance and liberation?[4]

To onlookers, such as the journalists who visited the site, Rechalim was seen as a feminist act par excellence. The women took upon themselves the movement's quintessential practice of settlement, which can be interpreted as a masculine act of erection and penetration. The men were recruited to bring food and take care of the homes and children while the women situated themselves "at the front" or "on the battlefield." In a sense, the women did what the men had been doing in Israeli society at large: they appropriated the key symbol of settlement from the men and made it their own.

Before we attach a feminist definition to the acts of Rechalim, two caveats should be borne in mind. First, this was not the first time that women found themselves in such a situation; the Jewish settlement in Arab-populated Hebron, for example, was initiated and carried out by women. The advantages of employing women in such activities have little to do with feminist sensitivities, but can rather be understood as a cynical manipulation of the stereotypical gender images in Israeli society. The settlers assume (rightly) that Israeli soldiers will find it more difficult to evacuate women than men. Furthermore, femininity bears images of peaceful existence and established households; the settlers send women with their children to confront soldiers to illustrate how well rooted the settlers are in their newly established homes. Not that the women of Gush Emunim are any less devoted to the cause than the men; typically, the women are even more militant. There are, however, clear strategic advantages in sending women to perform settlement duties. Thus, the act of placing women front stage in Rechalim may have had less to do with feminist interests and motivations than with capitalizing on advantages stemming from established gender stereotypes.

A second point is that the Women of Rechalim never defined or regarded themselves as feminist. They claimed that, whereas feminists held negative attitudes and destructive goals, they held positive attitudes and creative goals. Rather than challenging the national religious gender regime, they insisted their acts were actually reinforcing it. They regarded themselves as Jewish and Zionist women and mothers fulfilling their maternal role of protecting their children, as defined by the dominant discourse. They did not formulate a critical perspective on their gender situation, neither within their community nor in their households.

The site itself displayed traditional feminine motifs. The women took pride in their cleaning and cooking abilities and in their competence in tending to all male visitors who visited. The older women taught the younger ones how to sew and kept a watchful eye on their "proper" feminine behavior. In a film they made about their adventure, the women are shown cleaning the mobile home and preparing soup for the male visitors. Among the entries in the visitors' book, one visitor expresses admiration for the women, noting that "the talent in overcoming the little everyday troubles, in cleaning and nursing what tomorrow will again need repairing, without forgetting the larger goal of building the future and drawing power from that vision—that is the talent of righteous women." The republican mother could hardly find better advocates than the Women of Rechalim and their supporters.

Their antifeminist stance was further stressed by their construction of the significant "other." The left-wing group Women in Black was chosen by the Women of Rechalim as epitomizing the feminist and leftist antithesis. This group of women stood every Friday afternoon (when, according to traditional conventions, they were supposed to be at home preparing for the Sabbath), dressed in black, while holding signs bearing a single message: "Stop the occupation!" Women in Black, though small in number, threatened the Israeli imagery of maternity and nationalism, as evidenced by the chauvinist and sexist remarks by many passersby (Helman and Rapoport 1997). Conversely, Rechalim was intended to present in the public sphere the very maternal values that the Women in Black rejected. When asked about their motivations, the Women of Rechalim explained that, as a fellow woman and mother had been the victim, they felt it their sacred duty to provide a fitting response. They were, according to their definition, protecting their children, which they regarded as the quintessential role of women.

Here we see how maternal thinking can evolve into a multilayered and self-contradictory concept. Looming large before them was the idea of collective national defense. The terrorist act was conceived as a threat to all Israeli children, whether directly, by endangering them and their parents, or by threatening their rights to live on the land. Women were thus called upon to leave their households and rush to the rescue. They took for granted that women possess an intuitive understanding and reaction to dangers threatening the safety of their families. Thus, the Women of Rechalim claimed that they spontaneously gathered at the site, spurred on by virtue of their feminine essence. Collectivizing their concern, however, meant abandoning their actual homes to embrace the metaphorical collective: the national family. For them, a Jewish mother's essence is to nurture the community and Jewish continuity rather than selfishly tend her own private family and home.

An additional aspect of "responsible motherhood" is apparent here, even if it was not raised by the women settlers themselves and was shrugged off as a nonissue when evoked by others. In moving to a contested area, parents make decisions that affect, and sometimes endanger, the lives of their children. The settlers pay a heavy price for their ideology, both with their own lives and with the lives of those they hold dear and who depend on them. The settlers claim, though, that all Jews who choose to live in Israel share this danger and that the rewards of living in the sacred land more than compensate for the hardship. The terrorist act opened an abyss of existential fear that had to be closed for the settlement project to continue.

The dramatic events of Rechalim can be partly understood as a response to a mortal threat—not only to physical existence, but to the image and identity of responsible parenthood. Consequently, the self-definition of the Women of Rechalim could only be a traditional one because it was their capabilities and roles as responsible mothers that were being threatened. They had to overcome and suppress the disturbing thoughts that their settlement project might fail and that they were incapable of securing the safety of their loved ones in the place they had chosen of their own free will.

The choice between a patriarchal and a feminist interpretation of the events cannot be determined based on the declarations of the agents alone. Although regarding the Women of Rechalim as feminists would conflict with their self-definition and might be seen as an imposition of an external perspective, such a definition may be justified in the context of the feminist challenge of the following years. The behavior of the Women of Rechalim might be perceived as subversive to the established, taken-for-granted, patriarchal order, even if that order were not overtly aware of it at the time. Thus, following the implicit challenge to patriarchal roles in Rechalim, the reestablishment and reproduction of those roles were put to the test for both genders.

RACHEL AS THE JEWISH *MATER DOLOROSA*

The naming of the settlement itself can illuminate how gender relations were reinstated and reaffirmed in Rechalim, while exemplifying how the Gush Emunim community—as opposed to Israelis in general—remembers and commemorates violent death. The memory of Rachel Druk and the tragic circumstances of her death were apparently insufficient to bestow profound meaning on the new site. According to the established tradition of naming villages after fallen soldiers and deceased leaders, a settlement called, for example, Kfar Druk (Druk Village) would have fit the symbolic geography of Zionism. The settlers, however, chose to give their settlement a name with more historic and mythical resonance.[5] Rachel Druk and Rachel Weiss were conceived not merely as individual women who died for a cause, but also as incarnations of nationalism and maternity, both strongly associated with the biblical name Rachel. Significantly, the slogan chosen by the female actors was "We are all Rechalim."

The choice of Rachel, the mythical mother, inserted the events into a traditional, patriarchal, and nationalistic narrative. Of all biblical names, Rachel has the most gendered connotations. Etymologically, the name comes from "ewe" or "sheep," the primary capital of the biblical man, as well as the most common sacrifice. Rachel was the beloved woman for whom Jacob worked for fourteen years. She died fulfilling her wish to bear her spouse a second son, and her midwife consoled her in words that may sound horrifically insensitive to modern ears: "Fear not; thou shalt have this son also" (Genesis 35:17). She was buried on the road to Bethlehem and is the only one of the four Matriarchs who, according to the Bible, is not buried in the Cave of Machpela in Hebron.

In the context of the Babylonian exile, the prophet Jeremiah related God's promise to Rachel, urging the weeping woman to "restrain thy voice from weeping, and thine eyes from tears; for . . . thy children shall return to their borders (Jeremiah 31:16–17). Not only is her unique status as mother of the nation evoked here, but also her place of death, on the road, in a location enabling her to oversee and encounter both exile and return.

The people of Israel significantly refer to themselves as the "Children of Rachel" (for example, see Kaufman 1991), a term not fully substantiated by the biblical narrative: Judah was the son of Leah, not Rachel, and Sarah and Rebecca are more clearly the genealogical mothers of the mytho-nation. The story of Rachel, however, touches on a more profound meaning of maternity and its connection to the continuing national existence between homeland and exile.

The place traditionally known as Rachel's Tomb has for centuries served as a pilgrimage site for barren women and still serves as a major fertility shrine. Anthropologist Susan Starr Sered (1989) examined records left by pilgrims during the 1940s and found several exemplary statements; for example, "Rachel, Rachel, mother of the Israeli Nation, for how much longer will the tears of Israel be shed in vain? Arise, arise from your sleep" (33). Starr Sered concludes, "The themes that 'took off' at Rachel's Tomb in the 1940s—fertility, nationhood, the return of the exiles, the Holocaust—are intrinsically and dramatically linked to Rachel's biography as it is described in the Bible and Midrashic literature. Rachel, in the Jewish tradition, is the mater dolorosa" (37). For the religious settlers, Rachel held special significance. They regarded themselves as returning to the actual places of the biblical stories and felt that the prophecy of returning to Rachel's grave had been fulfilled. Gush Emunim leader Hanan Porat employed the image of Rachel extensively, claiming that the evacuation of Judea and Samaria was tantamount to spitting in her face. With the Palestinian revolt and the ensuing dangers, Rachel's Tomb became a fortress, raising criticism regarding the dissonance between her feeble, tender, motherly image and the shape of her shrine.

In the context of the early 1990s, the two semiotic meanings linked with the figure of Rachel—her role as mother of the nation, and her death on the road, where she weeps and waits for the people of Israel to return from exile—have not engendered subversive feminist thought. Rather, they reinforce the link between traditional maternal values and Zionist nationalism: the people return to their homeland, where the mythical mother was buried.

Apart from the two dead settler women Rachel Druk and Rachel Weiss, another "Rachel" was readily evoked: the renowned poet Rachel Blustein, known simply as Rachel, whose poems are among the most popular in Israel and are often set to music. This Rachel lived in a celebrated pioneering collective settlement on the shores of the Sea of Galilee. She died childless in 1931. Her poems reflected her yearning for a child, relating

to the experience of Rachel the Matriarch. The Rechalim settlers cited
one such poem in their pamphlet: "Her blood flows in mine / Her voice
sings in me / Rachel shepherdess of Lavan's herd / Rachel, the mother of
mothers." This is the greatest expansion of the symbol: all Rachels, all
Jewish women throughout history, share the same blood and voice, the
same essence—they are all, first and foremost, potentially or actually,
mothers.

The decision to name the settlement Rechalim silenced any potential
for a feminist discourse. Femininity, motherhood, nationality, settlement, and religion, were all "explained" through the romantic symbol
of Rachel. Gender issues were controlled so as to neutralize any threat to
the basic premises of daily life and keep attention focused on the main
goal of settlement building.

RECONSTRUCTING HAPPINESS

Feminism is linked to a subversive reading of texts, whereas the Women
of Rechalim merely performed according to the script they had received,
shaped through years of Gush Emunim testing and application.

As presented earlier, in chapter 6, Gush Emunim commemorative practices follow a structural pattern. By the early 1990s, constructing a new
settlement in response to terrorism had become a standardized, ritual-
ized practice, well integrated in the narrative structure of bereavement.
Death was framed within an encompassing plot, which led to a defiant act
of settlement supposedly to be followed by the establishment of a flourishing village. This is an uplifting narrative, which serves as a blueprint
for similar events, with the happy end predetermined by the story's ritualistic nature. In the case of Rechalim, this institutionalized form of behavior was the vehicle that reconstituted the established gendered order.

The narrative of Rechalim—namely, the story of death and revival in
the land of Israel—was presented as a metaphor for the entire Gush
Emunim settlement project, and the Zionist project as well. The site was
established as a showcase where the well-known components of the Jewish drama were reenacted: great defeat and tragedy, followed by national
and religious heroic persistence, culminating in a victorious return to the
original site. Rechalim was conceived as a ritual of revitalization.

Only a few weeks after the terrorist attack, the spirit on the site changed
dramatically from grief and anger to joy and jubilation. An entry in the
visitors' book reflects the transformation explicitly: an adolescent girl from

Ofra contributed a poem, culminating with a famous line from the official Yizkor for the fallen Israeli soldiers: "and there is much sorrow inside / and from the great sorrow emerge tears of joy / yes, of joy / because there is life in this place [. . .] / and I tell myself / blessed are the people that know how to arise / that out of death awaken to life [. . .] / blessed be the dead who through their death commanded us / life!" In a dialectical process, the meanings of the commemorative site were transformed and assimilated into the narrative structure of other such events. In a pamphlet distributed at one of their meetings, the Women of Rechalim told their admirers how their story should be related: "What started as a spontaneous vigil following the murder of Rachel Druk and Yitzhak Rofeh became a fact in the settlement landscape of the land of Israel." Joy and satisfaction, not shock and bereavement, were the desired and required emotional responses from visitors. When the children of neighboring settlements made pilgrimages to the site, they were greeted with happy music; it was not what one would expect to find at a memorial site. All symbols of solemnity were either suppressed or secluded in one of the tents.

The film that the women made about Rechalim relates a similar story. It opens with the sound of gunshots, followed by scenes of the bus and the two victims. From there, it moves on to reveal a pastoral landscape and the heroic story of the Women of Rechalim. The movie ends on an optimistic note, with the women's smiling faces and the promise that another twinkling star will soon shine over the hills of Samaria.

With the change in the solemn atmosphere came a redefinition of the heroes. In place of the slain man and woman came the Women of Rechalim, who were elevated to a mythical status. Through their resolve to fulfill the demands of the sacred tradition and create life out of death, they became the reason for the story. They were hailed as heroines and in public events were invited time and again to retell their story, which became part of the lore of the settlers' community. They became potential political leaders and made (unsuccessful) attempts to create a broad women's rightist movement. Their standing as heroines, however, was dependent on their acting according to the established script and, hence, was valid only until the time that *their* story reached a satisfactory conclusion and a new story began. Until then, the women held center stage; later, another social group would hold the symbolic position of leadership. The position of temporary hero was filled each time anew, in a modular fashion, by different agents from within the settlers' camp. Becoming a hero and leader was, therefore, conditional upon accepting the normative system as a whole. In other words, the unchanging hero was the settler's narrative, whereas those who translated it to action were only heroes for the day.

Once the narrative moved toward what was considered the happy ending, gender issues disappeared from the discourse, and feminism ceased to count. Tradition safely embraced the potentially subversive events, and the "rightful order" was restored. In actual fact, it was never seriously threatened, though men and women alike caught a glimpse of a potentially different order slowly taking the form of a feminist revolution with no violence and little confrontation.

The story of Rachel Druk, as told by the settlers, cannot be understood on its own. Her life and violent death were appropriated by the movement and the ideology, and she acquired a symbolic life after her physical death. Her actual life was placed within broader schemes of signification focusing on the name Rachel and the meaning of maternity, and on the reenactment of a consecrated plot, with a prescribed and uplifting ending. Whereas the concrete image of a woman can serve a feminist cause, the mythical image of Rachel could only support the existing patriarchal order. The patriarchal mechanisms of control were, at that time, still strong enough to dull the radical edge of the dramatic events. Hence, the Women of Rechalim found themselves in a golden cage: they were hailed as heroes of the day, but could not use their position to challenge gender relations within their camp, nor did they show any desire to do so.

Research on religious women today concentrates on literacy—on how women appropriate the sacred texts and comprehend them in subversive ways. In the case of Rechalim, the women left the interpretation of religious texts to the men while concentrating on appropriation of the all-too-important commemorative text. They did not rewrite the script, but were content merely to play the leading role temporarily. Later in the decade, they turned their attention to radical appropriation and alteration of other identity-forming texts.

THE SETTLERS' CULTURE OF COMMEMORATION

The Gush Emunim practices of commemoration revealed in Rechalim are different in many respects from other Israeli commemorations. Let us consider the name Rechalim. In chapter 6, two Israeli communities,

Kiryat Shmona and Giva't Brenner, are mentioned: both commemorate through their name a person or event that embodies a national idea. Kiryat Shmona commemorates a specific group of eight, with Yosef Trumpeldor as its leader, and Giva't Brenner is a tribute to a famous author murdered by Arabs. Rechalim, representing Gush Emunim commemoration, is different: it commemorates all the Rachels—actually all of the Jewish heroic mothers, of all generations. The figure of Rachel Druk, as important as it may be, did not have enough symbolic weight to carry the name of a place in the Holy Land, and the settlers returned frantically to the Bible and Jewish history for support for the name. To put it differently, if the woman's name had been Suzanne or Barbara, or even a nonbiblical Hebrew name, she would not have "received" a settlement named after her.[6]

Terrorism is an act designed to rupture everyday life and change historical dynamics. Gush Emunim members encounter the challenge by restating and reinstating the logic that brought them to Judea and Samaria. When a woman is killed, the settlers use the event to revive the figure of the Matriarch Rachel, who awaits, weeping at the roadside for their return. In response to the violent act, which reflects the insoluble problems of the present, the settlers return to what they consider to be endless truths. Returning ritualistically to the old axioms of the past certainly makes Gush Emunim fundamentalism a conservative phenomenon and limits the ability of women to improve their situation, but it also places all tragedies within a meaningful narrative and enables the continuation, sometimes even the thriving, of Jewish settlements under what many would consider impossible hardship.

The settlers appropriate the names of their dead for the sake of their struggle, as was done with Rachel Druk. This may seem insensitive, but for a community of believers it is self-evident. Parents of the children killed participate in demonstrations, claiming that their children would have wanted them to be there and would have participated themselves had they been alive. Most eulogies to settlers who have been killed include words such as these: He died so that we will be able to rebuild Jewish Hebron/return to Shechem/hike in our land, etc. The individual settler, risking his (or her) life, at least knows that his memory will not be abandoned and that his friends will commemorate him in a manner that he sees as respectful and in accordance with his belief system. He or she will be connected to the land of Israel in death as much as in life.

Rachel Druk was not only commemorated for all eternity; she was also politicized. Her memory belongs to her community, but not to the

rest of Israeli society. The opponents of the settlement project are outraged by what they consider the sacrilegious manipulation of the sacred
symbols of bereavement. Through their unique political commemoration, the settlers sectorialize bereavement. Their grief and agony, which
should, apparently, link them to their compatriots, actually serve to distance and isolate them. While the new Israeli heroes are the victims of
terrorist acts, the settlers, who suffer more than others, do not enjoy the
unreserved sympathy of other Israelis. This is the price that the settlers
pay for their form of commemoration and for their burning desire to
establish "another twinkling star over the hills of Samaria."

12

Growing Up Radical

The Emergence of the "Biblical Sabra"

THE EMERGING SECOND-GENERATION SETTLER

The future of the settlement project depends on the choices and orientations of the second generation of settlers. What will the first Jewish children born in Judea and Samaria be like? How will the environment of the settlements—whether it be the contact with the Land of the Bible and the spirit of sanctity or the violent surroundings and the plight of the Palestinians—affect the next generation? Shall they be faithful to the ideas of their parents that brought them there? Will they be more willing to negotiate and compromise? What kind of religiosity should we expect from a Jew born and raised in Hebron or Shiloh? These are some of the important research questions that come to mind regarding the sons and daughters of the Gush Emunim settlers. In the past decade, as a second generation of settlers first appeared and left its mark, we are starting to receive some, albeit partial, answers.

Similar questions regarding the sons and daughters were raised earlier in Zionist history in the case of the pioneers of the second and third *aliyas* (Zionist immigrations), who arrived in Palestine as young adults. The pioneers were intrigued to learn about the nature of the future first generation to be born in the new land, free of the impact of exile. To what extent did the mystique of the new land, its connection to the greatness of the biblical stories, and the mythical productivity attributed to the soil make a difference?

The new generation, known in Israel by the nickname *sabras*, fulfilled some expectations and foiled others.[1] In general, they conformed to the ethos of their parents and channeled their energies into military excellence. The sabras, as a generational group, have always been a minority in the prestate Jewish community, among the many young immigrants and children of groups not dedicated to the *halutz* (pioneer) ideal. The sabras have been considered a young aristocracy, however, and have developed a unique subculture that has been mimicked by many. In the Israeli War of Independence, the sabra generation paid a heavy toll in casualties, which the parents who had decided to immigrate to Israel felt guilty about. During the 1950s, the percentage of sabras in society further diminished with the mass immigration to Israel. Nevertheless, in examining the culture of the young Israeli state, the place of the sabras is paramount because most of the popular music, literary works, and plays in the first decades of Israeli history—especially those dealing with questions of bereavement and memory—were either created by or about this group.

Within the wider phenomenon of the halutz-sabra relationship, the case of the kibbutzim, often compared to Gush Emunim settlements, is most relevant. The sons and grandsons of the first kibbutz builders did not always continue the vision of their parents: many left for the cities, and others were instrumental in the privatization that totally transformed the nature of the kibbutz.[2] One reason for this may be that, whereas the parents participated in the thrilling adventure of battling odds to create new institutions according to grand designs, the children were born into established and thriving communities, with little to challenge their energies. The memories of the pioneering generation fueled quests for self-fulfillment in novel ways that turned out to be destructive to the basic premises of the kibbutz. Furthermore, while the parents were occupied with their thrilling national adventures, their children grew up virtually parentless, which had severe consequences for their future and especially for their commitment to the kibbutz ideal. Here, Gush Emunim settlers differ insofar that familial values were and are of paramount importance to them (as is invariably the case in fundamentalist families).

In this chapter, I consider the emergence of the young generation, aptly called in a pioneering research the "biblical sabras" (Kniel 2004). The young growing up in the settlements are, using the term that sociologist Carl Mannheim (1959) uses in discussing the concept of generational groups, a sociological generation. They are a relatively large strata of youth growing up in unique historical circumstances and with shared agents of socialization. They live in secluded ideological communities, with large families, usually with both parents working, recurrent encounters with Palestinian violence, and constant social and political drama. Their most important educational motif is dedication to the land of Israel, instilled through schools, informal education, hikes, and social pressure. The children participate in demonstrations, including violent ones, and are, as a matter of course, included in the political universe of their parents.

The most substantial component in the emergence of the new generation is, to my mind, the treatment of the settlements as a "conventional home." In Gush Emunim terminology, as exemplified in previous chapters, the term *home* is used for a wide range of situations, at times abstract and metaphysical. It is common to hear the settlers saying that they will not leave a contested place because it is their "home" even when they reside elsewhere. For the young settlers, the settlements are home in a more concrete and literal sense. They grew up there and know of no other place they can call home. The import of the fusion of the home of national destiny with the home of private memories has yet to dawn upon many of the settlers' opponents, who claim that the "new settlers" should return to their "true" home on the other side of the Green Line. The commitment of the young settlers to the places where they live is based on religious principles and extensive socialization regarding the meaning of home, as well as on actual childhood experiences. Thus, their claim to be natives has to be judged somewhat differently than that of their parents.

The experience of Gush Emunim, however, affected the children in unexpected ways. While their parents feel obliged to fulfill the demands of God and Jewish history, the children grew up in the freedom of relatively lawless frontiers. Some Israeli laws were either irrelevant or unenforceable in the vicinity of the young settlers. For example, though it is not formally acknowledged, Israeli traffic laws are no more than a polite suggestion for Yesha settlers and, at times, not even that. They drive faster than the allowed limits either because of the hostile surroundings or out of a sense of adventure. They usually will not buckle up, also because it is important for them to be able to leave their cars quickly. The chance of encountering a police officer enforcing traffic laws in Judea and Samaria is minimal, and, actually, the very idea is ludicrous. Law enforcement officers are treated with suspicion in the settlements: there is a very low crime rate within the tight communities of believers and a high sense of solidarity in face of the outside world. Furthermore, defiance of authority is part of the Gush Emunim ethos.

Another effect that cannot be easily measured is that of fear and the stories of violent death. Each and every child in the ideological settlements has experienced Palestinian hostility, either through the stories of his or her family and friends or, more likely, through direct encounter. Many children in Yesha lost friends in the Second Intifada. The Jewish children of the Gaza Strip have slept with the fear of makeshift Palestinian missiles that once fell on their villages at an average rate of three per day and of infiltrations of their settlements, usually foiled by the large army guarding them. This ordeal was one of the reasons given to justify their evacuation.

In this atmosphere, the children internalize the air of lawlessness, coupled with a fear for their lives that is transformed into bravery and recklessness. Thus, in recent years, issues of drugs and juvenile delinquency —phenomena very rare in past Jewish religious communities—have surfaced in the settlements.[3] The local social workers and educators, who only lately admitted and began to debate the problems, attribute the deviant juvenile behavior to the lawlessness present in their lives and the constant uncertainty regarding their future. Rabbi Eitan Eckerstein, manager of a home for delinquent children, explained,

> There are places in Yesha where an atmosphere of the Wild West reigns, and all is permitted. They drive without safety belts and drive fast, carry guns, and live above the law. This atmosphere is conducive to drug users, as they do not fear the law. For this reason, the boys will use drugs in the villages rather than in the city. Among the youth of the hills there is sometimes an atmosphere of "eat and drink because tomorrow we die." There could also be a challenge gap: the parents came with many challenges and went all the way for their ideology, while their children grow up with their only challenge—buying designers clothes at Zara. (Reichner 2001a, 63)

Most youngsters do not turn to delinquency, but rather try to maneuver around their parents' ideology. Like the sabras before them, they show a complex mix of conformity and rebellion. They wish to be as radical and defiant as their parents, and they admire the zeal and achievements of their elders. As their parents took them on thrilling adventures that included struggles against the soldiers and police, evasion of roadblocks, and marches through Arab fields and towns, the rebellious character of the youth found enough outlets within the confines of the established Gush Emunim project. They search, however, for ways to mark their own place in history and to step out of the more traditional modes of behavior that they still detect in their parents. Within the bounds of their loyalty to the ideas of Greater Israel, they try to innovate. Apart from the fact that the adults that they are rebelling against are considered rebellious themselves, their rebellion is not much different from that of other youth groups.

The young settlers compare themselves to secular Israeli youth affected by global trends, Western consumerism, and Far Eastern philosophy. Gush Emunim settlers left the large Israeli cities in order to reside in secluded religious settlements, thus isolating their children from other Israeli groups. Their fundamentalism also implied a disdain toward trends originating in what they considered the corrupt West. The settler children, growing up from birth in isolation from the rest of Israeli society and attending secluded schools and, often, yeshivas, mainly meet other religious children and youngsters. This contradicts one of the most important dicta of Gush Emunim and the national religious camp—their stated commitment to national unity and presumption to serve as a bridge between religious and secular Jews.

The place to meet secular youth is the army. Religious youth enter the army with great motivation and reach high ranks. The motivation is, obviously, the result of intense nationalist socialization, but also reflects the attempts of the youth to meet Israelis of other camps. Another popular Israeli trend that has been eagerly adopted by religious youth is long journeys of adventure and self-discovery to South America and the Far East. Religious youth, however, are among the more controlled and conformist of the young Israeli partygoers: they refrain from drug parties in the Far East and are not found in the trendiest nightclubs because these youth are, after all, the product of a normative religious system that has instilled strong values of moderation and conformity (Y. Sheleg 2000, 59).

Yair Sheleg (2000), in his book on changes in the Israeli religious communities, had this to say about national religious youth:

> Recent years have witnessed, throughout the country, and especially in the large cities, a new breed of religious youth, who have internalized essential elements of the secular leisure culture in a manner not acceptable in previous generations: they go with their secular friends to pubs . . . ; study film and television; return to mixed swimming and mixed dancing . . . ; and are seen openly cuddling their dates; sometimes they even date secular girls. (54)

I shall not explore here the vast array of options encountered by the religious youth from the settlements: within each of the large settler families, different children choose their own individual paths. Although the relative uniformity of experience has great effect, it does not determine the directions that the youngsters pick. In what follows, I concentrate on one of the most prominent options chosen among the second-generation settlers: the emergence of the "youth of the hills," which is associated with a phenomenon we may term, though not with absolute accuracy, the privatization of the settlement project. This does not include all of the young age groups, nor is the term "youth of the hills" strictly defined. It does, however, help us understand the developmental logic of the settlements and facilitates the discussion that is developed at the end of the chapter, regarding the changing nature of home, space, and place in the settlers' new ethos.

The Emergence of the Private Settlement

Almost invariably, the new generation to emerge from the settlements tends to hold similar or more radical rightist positions than those of its parents, and the ideal of settling the land and resisting any attempt at territorial compromise is paramount in their identity. While, politically, we see a clear continuation of their parents' philosophy, the religious picture is more complex: some may not keep their religious faith, some tend to become more observant, and many experiment among Jewish religious options. Sometimes, all this wide variety may be found within the same family. Like their parents, the young settlers search for ways to express their political stand and promote the camp's political goals. They do so, however, in an environment already changed by various processes—among them, the existence of already established Jewish settlements.

The appearance of the youth of the hills is the most important and salient sociological phenomenon to emerge among the settlers in recent years. Young settlers try to expand the Jewish settlement by leaving the established villages and capturing a hill somewhere in Judea and Samaria. Some such outposts are extensions of more veteran settlements, whereas others are in totally new locations far away. Sometimes, they merely try to build a new settlement in the Gush Emunim tradition, but often this is coupled with an attempt to experiment with alternative lifestyles. Some of these places are named after settlers who have been killed: an example is Bnei-Tal, named after a couple killed near Ofra (the victims were the son of ultra-rightist leader Rabbi Meir Kahane, and his wife). Others receive the name of the initiator, such as "the hill of Skali," expressing the experiential nature of the site. Others are named after the coordinates or the altitude of the specific hill, such as hill 777. Those that are near established settlements receive names that define them as neighborhoods or extensions, such as Tekoah D and South Itzhar. One such outpost is called West-West Bat Ayin, reflecting the expansionist pretenses of the small settlement Bat Ayin. Some outposts have only a few young male settlers, but most have few young families, as well. Because of religious restrictions, young single women do not live in these spots.

The new outposts can be understood as responses to the restrictions of the Oslo Accords and the limitations imposed by various Israeli governments constrained by international pressure. The young simply find a hill and settle there, whether or not permitted by the government or their elders. As the Gush Emunim settlement project has grown more defensive and protective, and come under greater international scrutiny, the young who settle on the hills take the initiative. Currently, they are the most dynamic phenomenon emerging from the settlers' camp.

The outposts on the hills are, in a sense, an accommodation to general trends that affect young people in Israel today and transform the nation as a whole. As Israeli society undergoes a process of economic and cultural privatization (see this book's concluding chapter), so do the settlers. It is no longer the political movement that decides collectively where and when to place a new Jewish dot on the map, but rather private individuals who want to fulfill a dream and ask no one for permission. The motivations are self-fulfillment and personal freedom. When I visited a farm in the Judean hills, the owner explained to me that he owns the land—several square kilometers—and, even if Israel chooses to withdraw, Arafat and the Palestinian authority would have to deal with him personally.

The Israeli government has been somewhat ambivalent toward the phenomenon of the privatization of the outposts: it clearly violates Israeli law, and, at times, soldiers (who are accompanied by the media) sent to evacuate these outposts encounter violence, with hundreds of other youth joining in. Other government agencies, however, are meanwhile helping to establish more outposts, either though direct monetary assistance or by constructing the infrastructure, such as roads or connections to water and electricity.

The ambivalence that Gush Emunim displays toward the youth of the hills and the illegal outposts marks the boundaries of the settler project and serves as a buffer that protects, legitimates, and normalizes the more established settlements. Much of the Israeli press and left-wing movement energy is invested in discovering where the young settlers have decided to settle next. The evacuation of settlers, when it occurs, will be focused on the outposts, which are manned by energetic youth who struggle with and wear out the soldiers. The few clashes (the results of which in any case are ineffectual, since the settlers return immediately afterward) make the public consider the evacuation of the more established settlements as a nearly impossible task. The labeling of the new outposts as "illegal" implies that the other settlements are indeed legal, which is a status that few outside of Israel would be ready to grant. The ambivalence of the right-wing government that supports the outposts it declares as illegal while deploying troops to evict them is not surprising: the struggle over the outposts is a buffer for the struggle over the entire settlement project, which, according to right-wing politicians and activists in Israel, is a buffer for the struggle over the existence of Israel.

The father figure of the outposts is Avri Ran, a man in his fifties, who grew up in a secular kibbutz, turned religious, and, in the early 1990s, went to live in the settlement of Itamar in Samaria. The relatively tranquil life there did not suit him, so he moved to one of the unoccupied hills near the village. He called his outpost "the hills of the world" (*Gevaot Olam*), where he manufactures diary products distributed under that label throughout Israel. He has ten children. Some are married; others live on the same ranch in other buildings. About twenty young men, admirers of Ran, pass through to work on the ranch.

For the nearby Palestinian village of Yanon, the new outpost has spelled disaster: Ran and his men, waving guns and walking dogs, visit the village often. They hike through it, show up at night, damage property, and get into violent encounters. Eventually, most residents of Yanon left for relatives in nearby villages, and peace activists from Israel and other places around the world arrived to try to reassert some security and revive the village.

The story of Ran is well known, not only because he is notorious in the region of Samaria, both among Jews and Arabs, but also because his case reached the Israeli courts, where he was tried twice.[4] In the first case, he allegedly broke the nose of a peace activist. The other case involved the detainment and beating of an Israeli Arab who had entered his ranch as part of his job as a construction worker. Ran approached the Arab, who was held by his men, and allegedly said, "You stinking Arab, how dare you enter a Jewish place! Your place is not here. Your place is six feet under." Ran was eventually acquitted, and the court criticized the police for not conducting the investigation properly.

The case of Avri Ran is not typical of the youth of the hills, because he does not belong to their age group; nevertheless, Ran serves as a role model for many, and his case demonstrates many of the characteristics of the phenomenon. First, it attests to the radical privatization of the settlement project as Jewish presence is established in new territories by the whims of eccentric individuals. Second, it reflects the intense hostility toward the Arabs, which is not camouflaged by ideological lingo and not restricted to the Palestinians of the occupied territories. Third, in the outposts, Israeli law is considered little more than a courteous recommendation, and respect for state institutions is practically nonexistent. Ran's admirers among the youth of the hills display several other characteristics that will now be discussed.

THE FLOWER CHILDREN OF THE HILLS

Some distinctions regarding second-generation settlers have to be made at this point. The term "youth of the hills" is now used indiscriminately in Israel to connote every type of encounter with young radical settlers. The term describes both those who actually live in the new outposts on the hills and those who join in to confront the soldiers when they arrive to evacuate the outposts, even if those youth are not residents of the place. By extension, the term is used for settler youth in general, though it may lose much of its explanatory power in the process. Even with regard to the outposts mushrooming on the hills, some are simply new settlements in the making, whose residents work hand in hand with the veteran establishment in an attempt to make their presence permanent. In such cases, the young settlers have internalized the teachings of their parents and show remarkable conformity, both in their political actions and in their lifestyle. While the term "the youth of the hills" is applied to them, it is not certain that this is helpful, because it is too inclusive.

Those I will describe here are the young settlers who complement their settlement activity with a radical drive against all forms of establishment, including the bourgeois homes of their parents. It should be said that there are also great differences between various regions and individual outposts: those in Samaria tend to be more militant and politically oriented, whereas those in Judea represent attempts to construct new lifestyles and profess to be disinterested in politics. The difference is marked by the presence of cell phones: the Samaria youth use them extensively in political struggles, whereas the Judea youth make a point of not having any.

Bearing these differences in mind, here is how one of the young settlers explained his mission: "To work the land, to harvest olives, to ride freely on horses. This is part of what it means to show who is the landlord around here; not to hide inside the settlements but to step out of the settlement. All the space is ours; that is the idea of the hills. That is the trend of a salvation that is not exilic" (Shafran 2002, 22). His comment combines the free spirit of experimenting youth and the nationalist motif of controlling the territory. The well-known theme of the new Jew, free as the wind on the plains of the national terrain, is relived here. The irony of the situation is that those who in this phase are credited with the role of exilic Jews are the Gush Emunim settlers who choose to stay within the confines of their established villages, and who, not long before, blamed the rest of the Israeli society for being exilic. This new Jew is a far cry from the prototypical settler: the ideal of riding freely on horseback and working the land was never propagated by the Gush Emunim ideology, let alone theology. That part was taken from New Age ideologies of returning to nature that have lately become common in Israeli society and abound among the young settlers; it has more to do with Far Eastern philosophy than with mainstream Judaism.

The youth, who grew up as part of the Gush Emunim project of returning to the authentic, take their quest in new directions, searching for authenticity in the same territory but with different means. Their sense of authenticity is carved from the array of religious options currently offered to Israeli youth. Whereas Gush Emunim preferred the benefits of modern life, many of the youth of the hills search for everyday authenticity, which for them means simple lives and traditional occupations. Many of them raise livestock and eschew electric appliances. When I visited one such outpost, a young settler emerged from a cave, approached me, took out a flute, and started playing, making a point of performing his "authenticity" for the visitor.

These enthusiastic youth elicit ambivalent feelings among their elders, who recognize the zeal that they had when they were younger and cannot criticize the love of the land that the young express. They are, however, worried about antinomian tendencies left unchecked and uncontrolled. In their own fashion and according to their interpretation, the Gush

Emunim followers were orthodox in their religion and extremely loyal to the state and its institutions, endowing them with sanctity. They are worried that in these respects their children will not follow in their footsteps. The residents of some of the outposts defy practically all groups and organizations that have a say regarding the future of the territories. They are considered illegal and thus oppose the government, but they also defy the decrees and requests of the settlers' leadership (the Yesha council). The radical youth see themselves as people that cannot be bought, unlike the Yesha council, which may sacrifice the outposts in order to save the more established settlements. This, again, is highly ironic with respect to the veteran Gush Emunim leadership: the revolutionaries of yesterday find themselves as the traditional establishment of today.

The case of largest and best known of these outposts, which was endorsed by the settlers, teaches us much about the differing attitudes of the settler establishment toward the mushrooming outposts. Migron was listed among the outposts marked for evacuation, and the settlers embarked upon a struggle against the government, claiming that the outpost was wrongly classified. Uri Elitzur (2003), editor of *Nekuda,* wrote in an editorial, "Migron is a watershed and let there be no illusions. This is not an outpost or a ranch, but a settlement by all accounts. Forty-three families, old people and young, women and children" (3). The veteran Gush Emunim establishment distinguished between the outposts of the youth of the hills, with which they had a tense relationship, and the few outposts that were a direct continuation of the established Gush Emunim struggle and may become full-fledged settlements. Apparently, the loners, with their flutes, guitars, and sheep in the hills, are not considered as having this potential. Hence, the Gush Emunim settlers do not see them as a continuation of their project.

Shlomo Kniel (2004), who conducted a survey of the youth of the hills, summarized the differences between them and the first-generation of Gush Emunim settlers. The new settlers are not committed to the teachings of Rabbi Kook the Elder like their parents, and their love of the land is not mediated by a metahistorical theology. As they are local born, they do not need elaborate rationalizations to create attachment to the land. For the young, the settlement is a privatized spiritual effort rather than something that must be done as a group. Thus, the new settlers adapt themselves to the individualistic tendencies in Israeli society. They are not organized under an umbrella organization that represents them to the authorities, and therefore negotiation and compromise become more difficult. Physical work, especially traditional—meaning "biblical"—occupations, is part of their ideology and becomes part of their striving for authenticity, much unlike their middle-class parents. A further difference is their criticism of the Israeli state and institutions: as the youth do not have an elaborate metahistory, the state does not enjoy the sacred status that it enjoyed under Rabbi Kook's teachings. Unlike their parents, the youth, who grew up in a relatively rich and powerful Israel, do not see the establishment and existence of the state as a metahistorical miracle. They also grew up in an age of withdrawals and concessions made by various governments and heard their parents criticize state actions. It would be an exaggeration to say that they regard the state as enemy, but its mystical aura is clearly lacking.

This new generation brings with it a different conception of religiosity and spirituality, inspired mainly by "Dancing Rabbi" Shlomo Carlebach, who died in 1993, leaving a rich musical legacy, with many religious singers distributing his Hasidic gospel. After his death, dozens of "Carlebach minyans" appeared across the country, where it became the hegemonic musical taste of the religious young generation. As Rabbi Carlebach adopted motifs from the flower children of the 1960s, the young settlers have much in common with that generation: hostility to any establishment, ridicule of the parents' generation, the desire to commune with nature, a craving for freedom, and an affinity for Eastern spirituality.

The youth of the hills also dress according to the "dress code" of the 1960s—the young women in long, colorful dresses and the men with wide skullcaps. An onlooker commented, "They look as if they inherited the wardrobe of the creators of the movie *Hair*." The two central components of the 1960s generation that have no place in the hills of Judea and Samaria are sexual promiscuity (which is beginning to appear elsewhere among national religious youth) and pacifism.

While their political convictions are unrelenting, their self-definition is as nonpolitical believers interested only in spirituality. Their Carlebach-inspired songs of loving the Lord are much less political and defiant than the overtly political songs shouted by their parents during their settlement adventures. Some of the young settlers live in the hills of Judea and Samaria because of the freedom that it allows them, which would be impossible elsewhere in Israel. They recognize no border, not only because of the political ideology and theology of Greater Israel, but because their spirituality recognizes no limits. One of them said, "We are totally nonpolitical. We don't read newspapers; we do not know where the Green

Line lies. The land does not belong to anyone. She returns love to whoever gives her love."[5]

The Place of the Arabs

The interaction between the youth of the hills and the Palestinians is radically different from that of their parents, and, accordingly, their attitudes toward their hostile neighbors differ. Unlike their parents, who arrived not knowing what to expect, the young settlers were born into a situation of conflict and hold neither hope nor interest in good relations with the Arabs. For them, the Palestinians are those who murdered their friends and would annihilate them, given the chance. Thus, the youth of the hills show greater hostility toward the Arabs than did their parents, with one possible mitigating factor: searching for authenticity, the young settlers sometimes find it among the Arabs and hence express respect and admiration when they do. However, most of today's Palestinians do not correspond to the authentic standards set by the young settlers, and, in any case, this is not enough to override other factors.

The hostility toward the Arabs was depicted by anthropologist Chen Bram in a paper presented at a sociological conference.[6] Working as a tour guide with a yeshiva, he had the chance to observe the behavior of national religious youth, many from the settlements, as they encountered Arabs. The tours were within the Green Line, either through Arab residential areas (for example, Jaffa or Jerusalem) or in Arab places that hold a symbolic presence (a sheikh's tomb). The young hikers displayed hostility whenever they encountered signs of an Arab presence, even though the Arabs present were Israeli citizens. They took a large flag everywhere to show their symbolic appropriation of the place, displaying that, for them, the entire land was a contested frontier and a battleground between the two groups.

The conflict with the neighbors has little of the elaborate ideological rationalization and debate that characterized the Gush Emunim project. Arabs are not allowed near the new outposts, nor do they build the settler homes as they did in the established settlements. This is possible because of the modest lifestyle: living in mobile homes, shacks, tents, or caves, the youth of the hills do not need intensive labor to build their homes and can do without cheap Palestinian labor. Stressing their individuality, the youth of the hills have no collective need to compromise feelings of hate or racism with anyone. Their militant posture is a constant threat to the local Palestinians, and therefore the proliferation of the outposts marks vast areas into which Palestinian residential areas cannot expand.

For the portion of the youth of the hills that tries to innovate and forge a new identity, the connection to Arab existence on the land is more ambivalent. The young settlers, obsessed with the concept of Jewish authenticity, use a mishmash of influences from around the world—Indian, American, and even Arab. They are attached to the secular youth, meeting with them in alternative spiritual "happenings" that have proliferated in Israel over the past decade. By their definition, they are reaching their authentic roots in a more profound manner than did their parents, and that also entails a different attitude toward the Arabs. As a young musician said,

> Music transcends borders, it is above controversies . . . but the *darbuka* [an Arabic drum] and the flute are not Arab instruments. Patriarch Abraham and Miriam the prophet played them, and they belong to the culture of the Land of Israel. It should be said to the credit of the Arabs that they preserved the authenticity from which we distanced ourselves when we left the Land of Israel. Now we return to the roots that once were ours.[7]

Again we see the recurrent Gush Emunim orientalist motif that respects the Arabs for their alleged dedication to authenticity. When a reporter visited one such hill, he noticed that the settlers did not hate the Arab as such, but only as a national enemy: "The thing that they hate about the Arab is his hatred of the Jews." One of his interviewees even said, "I prefer that Arabs live here and not Jews like those of Efrat [a large settlement in the Gush Etzion region]. The Arabs at least respect the land." The declared apolitical nature of the youth of the hills encouraged the reporter to think that perhaps they could coexist with the Arabs as two groups who love and work the land and encounter similar problems with water and livestock. Elsewhere in his article, however, he cited the settlers commenting on the lack of authenticity among the young Arabs they encounter, who have already succumbed to the trends of the corrupt West.[8] Once the Arabs lose their "authentic charms," they are of no further interest to the young settlers.

Notwithstanding their search for authenticity, the youth of the hills represent the most extreme relation with the Palestinian Arabs. The youth have no interest in teaching the Arabs and do not care for theological explanations for their existence. Consequently, the battle over the territories is being gradually redefined—in a sense reduced—by the settlers to one of power and exclusion. This is an important way in which the youth of the hills transform the project of their parents. I next present another transformation of great importance: the concept of home.

THE HOMELESS YOUTH

Gush Emunim was an attempt by national religious Israelis to create a personal and national home in the frontier lands of Judea and Samaria. For various reasons explained previously (for example, see chapter 3), the Gush Emunim settlers had vested interests in building successful homes and had the resources to accomplish that goal. The attacks from the outside—be it the political struggle with left-wing Israelis or the physical threats by Palestinians—made the protective home ever more appealing.

Children, obviously, are an integral part of the symbolic construction of the Gush Emunim home. By taking them to live in harsh conditions on new settlements, insisting that they grow up in the settlements, and bringing them to demonstrations, Gush Emunim parents showed that the settlements are a "true home"; that is, a place where children can be raised and are the object of interest and affection. Whenever a new settlement was erected, among the first actions performed were walking the children and the babies in carriages, drying laundry, and establishing makeshift classes for the young. This was a way of declaring to an imagined eye that an "instant home" had been created. The children are a crucial part of the story of Gush Emunim settlement; furthermore, they were the "elements" that could legitimate calling the settlements "homes" rather than "political demonstrations."

As these children grew up, some of them chose to construct a new type of settlement: the outpost. In a sense, the youth of the hills have learned their lesson well: like their parents, they wish to construct a new home on a new hill and to continue moving to the next frontier. Gush Emunim has created in many of its youth a restless mind that keeps searching for new homes, never wishing to be tied down. The home that the youth of the hills construct is a mobile one characterized by its fluidity. They have internalized the Gush Emunim concept that the entire land is home. But the bourgeois dream of the parental generation—to create a stable and enduring settlement that will find its place on the settlement map of Israel—has been replaced by other dreams. The outposts, manned by individuals, are not Gush Emunim's joint projects, and the backing of the settlement organizations is either ambivalent or nonexistent. The display of a ritualistic version of peaceful familial and communal life is not part of the show that the youth of the hills present to the nearby Palestinians and the Israeli public. Rather than children, laundry, and Torah classes, the new outposts present frightening dogs guarding their perimeter.

The youth of the hills took the idea propagated by Gush Emunim—that all the land of Israel is home—to its extreme. Home, for them, is more of an ephemeral concept to be acted upon whenever and wherever it accords with the wishes of the individual, who is the self-appointed representative of the national will. Whereas their parents declared that their struggle for home was a constraint forced upon them by uncaring or misunderstanding governments and the dire realities of the national conflict, the youth of the hills see home as a constant struggle, always temporal, and constantly moving. They are settlers who, like many other youngsters, fear to settle down.

There are many ironies in the emergence of these youth. Perhaps most striking is that the Gush Emunim settlements, seen as a wild off-shoot of the Zionist urge to settle in the frontier land, turned out to be suffocating enclaves for the youth growing up in them. When the Gush Emunim settlers set out, they were seen as celebrating their freedom through song and dance on the windswept barren hills. Their religiously orthodox and socially bourgeois normative values were spotted at the time by academic observers, but, seen in contrast with the exuberant youth, the organized nature of the Gush Emunim phenomenon becomes much more apparent. The youth have surprised their parents in the same way that their parents took Israeli society by surprise: by showing that the frontiers of Judea and Samaria can be the venue for new sociopolitical adventures.

The concept of the lack of borders, so strong among the youth of the hills, is shaped by the Gush Emunim notion of Greater Israel; the idea, however, is turned on its head. Although many Israelis see Gush Emunim as a lawless group that takes no heed of the state's laws, the movement's leaders always actually stressed that their goal has been the opposite—to see Israeli law implemented on all the land of Israel. According to the settlers' narrative, they did not seek a lawless land, nor did they partici-pate in constructing one, but rather found themselves drawn into pre-carious situations as the state either failed or refused to implement its laws and protect them as citizens. For ideological reasons, their children who roam the hills have a disdain for borders. If the parents wished to transform the territories where they settled into an integral part of the state of Israel, the youth choose to problematize the concept of the state. Unlike their parents, their wish is to unsettle Israel rather than to settle its land according to historical conventions that lead back to the pioneering past. While their parents wanted to create homes, they wish to "de-home" Israel. For them, the land of Israel in its entirety is a frontier, a playground where they can experiment with their identity and find their way, outside of the established institutions transmitted to them by their parents.

The youth of the hills are a strong critical voice within the Gush Emunim settlement project, respected for their devotion and zeal and yet, for their elders, quite worrisome because the youth have not yet assumed leadership positions or even organized substantially. The traditional, older generation still leads the community through its struggles and enjoys general respect and legitimation. The question for the future is whether what we see today is merely a whim of overenthusiastic youth who will eventually settle down and somehow channel their revolutionary energies into more institutionalized patterns. Perhaps, though, we are witnessing a partial rethinking of the most basic concept in Gush Emunim settlers' ethos: that of home.

The emergence the youth of the hills arose in a particular context: the aftermath of the Oslo Accords. The settlers found themselves confined to their settlements as the territory handed to the Palestinian Authority began to enclose them, and terrorism curtailed their ability to move freely around the land they define as theirs. The appearance of the rebellious youth can be partly interpreted as a cry for openness and freedom in a situation of steadily constricting boundaries. The children, who grew up in intoxicating free spaces, found ways to burst out of the confines forced on them by historical contingencies. The energies of Gush Emunim found surprising new ways of expression, even if they were not to the liking of the traditional leadership.

Settling behind the Green Line—currently meaning also behind fences and walls—is no longer an attractive economic proposition for Israelis wishing to improve their standard of living. As the Israeli society distances itself from Yesha, the youth that grew up in the wake of Gush Emunim project are the troops—possibly the only ones left—of the ideological settlers of tomorrow. Although it is still too early to fully understand the nature of the generation that will undoubtedly hold the fort for the Gush Emunim settlements—the first studies of the sabras only appeared in the 1980s—the importance of this phenomenon cannot be overstated. With this in mind, we shall now turn to the concluding chapter, which analyzes the great transformation in the lives of the settlers over the last decade and a half, starting with the Oslo Accords and ending with the construction of a wall that isolates the settlers in their beloved land.

13

Settling in the Hearts of the Nation

Gush Emunim in Times of Crisis

GUSH EMUNIM: BETWEEN SUCCESS AND FAILURE

In my closing chapter, I return to the question I posed at the outset: has Gush Emunim succeeded in settling in the hearts of Israelis? I conclude that, although Gush Emunim succeeded impressively in settling the land, it failed to convince most Israelis that Judea and Samaria are indeed the national homeland that must never be forsaken or forgotten. This has been proven on many occasions, never more clearly than in the disengagement plan and the relative disinterestedness of Israelis at the dismantlement of Jewish communities and the destruction of settlements. The residents of Israeli cities, development towns, and kibbutzim, even those tending politically to the Right, generally do not accord Hebron or Shiloh a status superior to their own place of residence. As opinion polls consistently show, most Israelis are willing to cede most of the territories and dismantle many of the settlements under appropriate circumstances. The settlers' failure has been a paradigmatic one: it did not result from faulty decision making or an inefficient public relations mechanism, but is inherent in the situation of a fundamentalist movement in a modern, mostly secular, society.

In other words, there are no longer open and available hearts in which to settle, and maybe there never were. When Gush Emunim started out, observers such as Ian Lustick (1991) wrote that the stalemate between the two, roughly equal, forces of the Right and the Left froze Israel in a "permanent temporal" position.[1] Now, most Israelis, including right-wingers, are prepared to evacuate large parts of the occupied territories, but the presence of militant settlers in large numbers, as well as other vested Israeli interests, impede such action. Is this situation a great success or a great failure on the part of Gush Emunim? The believers themselves are not certain.

In recent years, when the allegiance of the Israelis was put to the test, the settlers gained a few victories and experienced some great setbacks. In this concluding chapter, I provide four examples—milestones in Israeli history—that have changed the lives of Gush Emunim settlers and show how these examples define the place of Gush Emunim in relation to the rest of Israeli society. The first is the Oslo Accords, the second is Yitzhak Rabin's assassination, the third is the El-Aqsa Intifada (aka the Second Intifada) that resulted in the construction of a wall sealing off the West Bank from the rest of Israel, and the fourth is the disengagement plan and its implementation. After explaining how these historical events reflect on the situation of the ideological settlers, I conclude with how social changes in Israeli society have affected the settlers and their project.

The Settlements in the Wake of the Oslo Accords: Fish in a Shrinking Pond

In 1982, when the settlers were some twenty thousand strong, Peace Now launched one of its numerous campaigns against them, claiming that they would soon reach the one hundred thousand mark, at which point the Israeli occupation of the West Bank would become a fait accompli for all eternity. Meron Benvenisti provoked the peace activists by claiming that it was already too late. The settlers soon made this argument obsolete: by the 1990s, their number easily passed the mark set by Peace Now and, by the end of the decade, they passed the two hundred thousand mark. The question debated by Peace Now and Benvenisti, however, was not put to rest: is the trend reversible? Can the settlers be "de-settled," their demographic strength notwithstanding?

The Oslo Accords were a step in that direction, launching a dramatic period that continues today. The settlement project grew exponentially prior to the agreement and, surprisingly, following its partial implementation. Thus, the settlers had become a well-established and highly organized community, relatively sure of its own viability, with a demographic mass and the resources, experience, and motivation to engage in a long battle for its existence. When the Israeli government, headed by Yitzhak Rabin, signed the Oslo Accords with the Palestine Liberation Organization, headed by Yasser Arafat, the settlers' long-standing fear materialized: an Israeli government that would be lured by the promise of peace to sign an agreement with the Palestinians at their expense. The settlers opposed the Rabin government and mounted demonstrations even before the agreement was announced, and the pace and intensity of these protests grew increasingly bitter and hateful. The beginning of the Palestinian suicide attacks provided further impetus for the demonstrations.

The Oslo Accords, negotiated in secret and signed on the White House lawn in Washington, established an official and legitimate Palestinian presence in the territories that was headed by Yasser Arafat, with whom, until then, Israeli citizens were prohibited to speak. In the first stage, the Palestinian Authority was to receive parts of the Gaza Strip and the area around the town of Jericho. At a later stage, the Palestinians were to receive control of the large towns, including most of the Palestinian population. The treaty's implementation engendered a complex land regime: areas designated by the letter A were to be under full Palestinian control; area B was transferred to Palestinian civil control, but left under Israel security control; and area C, including all Jewish settlements, remained under Israeli rule. The Palestinian police force was given light arms to assume control and combat local militias. Some of the most delicate issues, such as the future of Jerusalem, the right of return of the Palestinian refugees, and the future of the Jewish settlements, were left for future deliberations.

Following the agreement, Israel enjoyed a period of economic prosperity and great improvement in its international standing. With the successful absorption of more than a million immigrants from the former Soviet Union, the peace agreement with Jordan, and improving relations with Arab states and Europe, the Oslo Accords seemed at first to pay high dividends. Gradually, though, the agreement collapsed, either because of its inherent flaws, the violent actions of extremists on both sides, or the inability of the leadership and people of both sides to develop the mutual trust needed for its implementation. The eruption of Palestinian terrorism led to an Israeli backlash, including restrictions on Palestinian movement within the territories. Soon to follow were the collapse of the Palestinian economy and eventually the El-Aqsa Intifada. The entry of Israeli forces into major Palestinian cities in March 2002 can be seen as the final mark of the collapse of the Oslo Accords.

Obviously, the settlers totally opposed the agreement from its outset. They expressed their ideological and pragmatic opposition through political struggle and violent demonstrations. Ideologically, they claimed that an Israeli government, regardless of the majority it may enjoy, had no right to end the dream of a Greater Israel by ceding land and sovereignty to non-Jews. They demanded a Jewish—rather than a civil—majority in the Knesset for approval of such a move, but also made it clear that even this would not be enough to satisfy them. Daniella Weiss of Kedumim claimed that the true poll on the future of the territories should be held among all Jews that ever lived. While the settlers voiced their opposition to the agreement in terms of the alleged dangers the agreement posed for the future of Israel, the new arrangements also threatened their future development and even the existence of the settlements. They lost much of the land reserves that they believed should be theirs, and a Palestinian armed presence, legitimated by the Israeli government, appeared at their doorstep.

In settlers' discourse, the Oslo Accords were the ultimate catastrophe, idiocy, and tragedy. All subsequent terror was attributed to the accords, and the settlers considered those involved in achieving the agreement as unfit for further political decision making and often refer to them as the "Oslo criminals." Many refer to the Second Intifada as the "Oslo Intifada." The settlers see the failure of the Oslo Accords as self-evident and a warning for the future—not for themselves, who assessed the dangers correctly, but to the rest of Israeli society. Assuming a consensus on the untrustworthiness of the Palestinians, who received such generous gifts at Oslo, the settlers ask the Israeli peace camp to reconsider its position and claim that the fate of the Oslo Accords has proven how right they were all along.[2]

The Oslo Accords were the greatest political failure of Gush Emunim and its followers. For the first time since the initiation of the movement (with the partial exception of the evacuation from Sinai), a decision significantly affecting them was reached that was not in their favor, despite all the political leverage at their disposal. The project of Gush Emunim was geared to encounter this moment of truth, and, when it arrived, it became clear that the movement had not settled in the hearts of people sufficiently to ensure the future of its project. To add insult to injury, after the assassination of Yitzhak Rabin, all Israeli prime ministers, regardless of party affiliation, either endorsed the Oslo Accords or suggested alternative withdrawal plans. The settlers regarded a series of Israeli prime ministers as traitors to the nation, and extreme factions of the religious Right discussed the proper Jewish punishment those leaders should receive for their alleged crimes.

The settlers undertook three steps in response: First, they initiated a prolonged political battle, recruiting all the resources and support they could muster. Second, they occupied all the land that they could before it fell into Palestinian hands. The outposts discussed in the previous chapter, were, in part, a response to these new conditions. Third, the ideological settlements relaxed their screening processes in order to attract as many Israelis as possible to move to Yesha.[3] The alertness of the settlers did halt a possible collapse of their project, stabilized their position, and, with government "compensation," even enabled growth and development.

Although the damage of the Oslo Accords to the settlement project and the settlers themselves is plain enough, the agreement had a far more profound impact on the basic tenants of Gush Emunim. Gush Emunim is a movement dedicated to sacred remembrance, whereas the Oslo Accords were based on mutual forgetting. They were constructed on the premise that the two sides, the Israelis and the Palestinians, should put aside ancient animosities and historical territorial claims, and focus on the demographic facts of the present. The Palestinians were required to accept the existence of Israel, forsaking their demands for its annihilation that were based on their memory of the *Nakbah,* their 1948 catastrophe (that is, their displacement). The Israelis were required to accept that the borders of their state would be determined by political possibilities rather than religious and historical rights. Historical scores that both sides promised never to forget needed to be put aside. The mutually required forgetting did not mean that the two sides would forsake their national dreams, but rather that maximalist aspirations would not receive political articulation, nor serve as a blueprint for the future.

The logic of Oslo as a regime of forgetting is expressed in the administrative names—A, B, and C—given to regions in the contested territories, as opposed to the biblical names assigned those territories by the Gush Emunim settlers. The strength of the new names, and the political reality and the security situation that they have implied, are such that even the settlers have begun using them. The Oslo Accords, though only partly implemented, have imprinted their logic on the area and, in a sense, have "bureaucratized" the sacred land. Whereas the settlers could make a strong case for the area of Judea and Samaria as the heart of the historic land of Israel, they now had to convince others that an area designated "C" should not be changed to one called "A." Furthermore, according to the accords, the reason for a region's remaining in Israeli hands was the current Israeli settlement presence rather than its historical connection to the Jewish past. The accords hampered the ideological settlers' ability to present their case using their own discursive tools. Consequently, the settlers (apart from the Yesha rabbis) ceased using their preferred language promoting the Jewish return to the sacred land and resorted instead to complaints about how the Palestinians were not keeping their end of the bargain, and warning that further implementation of the agreement would endanger the lives of Israelis on both sides of the Green Line.

Two examples of the existential shift in the status of the settlements following the Oslo Accords are the construction of bypass roads and fences around the villages, both discussed in another context in chapter 6. From the outset of their project, the ideological settlers demanded that Israeli actual and symbolic presence be instantiated everywhere in the land of Israel, including in the heart of large Palestinian towns. In fact, this was never accomplished: except for Hebron, settlements were established outside Palestinian towns. Sometimes the distance from Palestinians was a factor in luring fearful potential residents to move to them. Nevertheless, the presence of settlers driving on the roads through the towns was considered symbolically and practically important in showing who the true owners of the land were. The implementation of the Oslo Accords established roadblocks manned by armed Palestinian policemen; thus, settlers driving through Palestinian towns might encounter hostile armed forces. While the construction of bypass roads was welcomed by many as a safe solution enabling the growth and development of the settlements, others lamented it as abandoning the demands for a Jewish presence everywhere. The exclusive Jewish roads built with immense government funding were a declaration by the Israeli government that some places would not return to Israeli rule and were not even to be visited; in using these roads, the settlers accepted—albeit reluctantly—this new reality.

For ideological reasons, for years many settlers chose not to build fences around their villages. They claimed that Palestinian infiltrators could easily find their way around or through fences, and that physical obstacles transmit the message that the Jews are afraid, thereby encouraging further Palestinian violence. Another rationale was that fences indicated the borders and limited the growth of the settlements. As the Palestinians received territories near the settlements and acquired more weapons, one settlement after the other opted for costly electronic fences. This symbolizes the deep meaning of the Oslo Accords, which is the confinement of the settlements as secluded and isolated islands within an alien sea.

The designation of bureaucratic names and the installation of bypass roads and electronic fences are part of a larger picture: the decision about Israeli borders. Gush Emunim's vision of gradually settling everywhere on the land and bringing it under total Israeli rule was curtailed, delegitimated, and made practically impossible to implement. The Oslo Accords entailed a decision on an issue that Israeli governments had long avoided answering: the future of the occupied territories. The decision went against the Gush Emunim plan.

In their initial stages, the settlements were seen by their creators and residents as pioneering, avant-garde posts, presaging the mass arrival of Jews in Judea and Samaria. Although they did not say so explicitly, the Oslo Accords meant that the Israeli government regarded the existing settlements as the last to be built, while the presence of the Palestinian Authority in the territories assured that establishment of further settlements would become extremely difficult. The agreement, signed at the White House, involved a superpower as guarantor, thus further increasing international surveillance of the occupied territories. Although the number of Israeli settlers has doubled since the accords, the number of settlements has remained almost unchanged.

As a result of the accords, the symbolic status of the settlements changed practically overnight: no longer pioneer posts in a frontier land, they became forsaken outposts on a dangerous periphery. Instead of leading the way, they became a problem requiring protection and costly maintenance. Elyakim Haetzni, of Kiryat Arba, suggested a metaphor for the actions of Rabin's government: instead of removing the fish from the pond, the government removed the water and left the fish to dehydrate. He meant that, although the Israeli government did not evacuate the Jewish settlements—a momentous task not stipulated by the Oslo Accords—it created an environment in which it is difficult to survive, let alone thrive.

Some of the settlements—mainly the secluded secular ones—have almost collapsed following the accords and the subsequent rise in terrorism, while others—mainly the religious ones—have, to the surprise of many, survived and thrived. Gush Emunim ideology has proved to be a powerful incentive to settle, even in the harsh realities created by an unfavorable government. Israeli governments of all colors did not cease moral and financial assistance to the settlers, and some provided massive assistance, raising allegations that their policy undermined the spirit of the accords. Nonetheless, the accords forced the settlements to re-evaluate their symbolic position. The ideological system that gave meaning to the settlers' existence had to be redefined because they were no longer seen as pioneers in a project of Judaization of the land. The settlements are still dear to the hearts of those committed to a continued Jewish presence in the land of the Bible, and to those who have faith in the settlements' potential to revive their historical role through currently unforeseeable historical transformations. For the time being, however, they are becoming increasingly costly to maintain in terms of human sacrifice and financial cost and in terms of Israel's standing in the international community. The settlers' greatest fear is that, once the Israeli water is removed from the pond and the Palestinian water pours in, the next step will be to remove the fish.

THE SETTLERS REACT TO RABIN'S ASSASSINATION

On November 4, 1995, Israeli Prime Minister Yitzhak Rabin was assassinated in Tel Aviv, at the end of a mass demonstration in support of the Oslo Accords. His assassin, Yigael Amir, though not a Yesha settler, was a frequent visitor to the settlements and an active participant in heated arguments regarding the Oslo Accords and possible courses of action against the Rabin government. While awaiting trial, in which he was sentenced to life in prison, the argument raged regarding whether he truly represented the national religious camp and the Israeli Right. If Yigael Amir was a child of the Gush Emunim revolution, this would have severe implications for the basic teachings and institutions of the national religious camp. If, on the other hand, he acted alone and was not inspired by the teachings and the internal logic of the camp, Gush Emunim could preserve its claims regarding the morality of the settlement project.[4] The interpretation of Rabin's assassination was, therefore, crucial for ascertaining the place of the Gush Emunim identity among the myriad of Israeli identities.

Following the assassination, Gush Emunim activists deliberated about whether the national religious education was to blame for the deed. The answers oscillated between two extremes. Some claimed that the murderer acted alone and that the camp could not be held responsible for the one disciple who strayed. Thus, Rabbi Mordechay Greenberg, head of the Kerem Beyavneh Yeshiva, where Amir had studied, said, "The man did indeed study in our yeshiva, but I tell you that we do not raise such crops. . . . I don't know from where this man got this madness. . . . Madness is a matter for psychologists, not educators. We are educators."[5] Others examined Amir's biography and mentioned his Mizrahi origin, his black (ultra-Orthodox) skullcap, and his childhood and adolescence in the secular city of Herzliya as evidence that he was not truly a member of their camp.

There were also attempts to blame the victim, and the settlers are avid consumers of conspiracy theories on the assassination. They wonder who else had an interest in Rabin's death and scrutinize every detail of that fateful night. After the assassination, there were disclosures of a mole that the Israeli security forces had planted in the extreme right-wing factions. Avishay Raviv, whose operative name was "Champagne," was among the leaders of the extremists who protested against Rabin while he was supplying information—which turned out to be useless—about his friends. While Raviv is all but forgotten by the Israeli public, and in Rabin's commemorations is hardly mentioned, the settlers regard him as a crucial figure in the story. Numerous theories and reports, including some published in the respectable *Nekuda,* tie him to the murder.[6] The settlers seek to convey the message that the assassination could have been prevented; thus, they share less of the blame and are actually victims of persecution. Still others place the blame elsewhere, claiming that the Israeli secular Left has used the opportunity to attack the settlement project. They claim that public soul-searching on the part of the national religious camp would only play into the hands of the Left. A week after the assassination, Israel Harel said, "This week, all the wearers of knitted skullcaps, all of religious Zionism, and especially religious education in all its varieties, sit on the bench of the accused."[7]

On the other hand, some voices from within the national religious camp demanded fuller acceptance of responsibility and placed the blame at the camp's doorstep. Some called the settlers to intensive soul-searching and claimed that Amir was indeed a product of the system of thought that gave rise to the settlement project.[8] Professor Aviezer Ravitzky, for example, mentioned that all three Jewish ideological murders in Israel's recent history emerged from the same camp.[9] Rabbi Yehuda Amital, of Gush Etzion, claimed,

> As painful as it may be, the desecration of the name of God is manifold in this case. For the deed was done by one who considers himself religious, and as justification for his acts he cites mitzvoth of the Torah. I heard the

words of the murderer in court. He had nothing new to say. Every word
that he uttered was heard more than once over the last year in the circles
of religious Zionism in the written and electronic media.[10]

Yoel Bin-Nun, attentive as ever to the implications of the assassination
for his demand that the Gush Emunim project settle in Israelis' hearts,
was even more radical in his claims against his friends. Consequently,
he was ostracized by his own community of Ofra, was obliged to employ
bodyguards, and eventually left for another settlement, Alon Shvut.

After the assassination, the settlements, and with them most institutions of the national religious camp, came under severe attack. The Bnei
Akiva youth movement and the Yeshivot Hesder were said to be incu-
bators of radical nationalist feelings, and even Ban Ilan University, where
Yigael Amir had studied (law, of all subjects), generally considered as a
moderate counterforce to Gush Emunim zeal, was subjected to criticism
(Ravitzky 2000). As the national religious camp came under attack, it
responded by withdrawing to itself, lamenting bitterly that its members
were all unjustly blamed for the deeds of one individual. It could be said
that the defensiveness of the national religious camp curtailed further
possibilities for soul-searching and reflection.

Although the settlers' mainstream institutions did not demand that
Amir's sentence be revoked or that he should be released ahead of time,
they did fight for his friends who were accused as accomplices. Amir had
confided to a young woman, Maragalit Har-Shefi, from the settlement of
Beit El, who failed to report his plans to the authorities and did nothing
to stop him. She claimed that she did not realize his determination. The
settlers infuriated many when they backed her vehemently and celebrated
her release after she had served a short jail sentence. By backing her
claims, they were, in a sense, proclaiming that none within their camp
shared the responsibility and blame for Amir's deed.

The first *Nekuda* issue to appear after the assassination included a
picture of the funeral and contained a carefully worded obituary by the
Yesha council and the editorial board, depicting Rabin as "Prime Minister and Minister of Defense, Chief of Staff in the Six-Day War and liberator of Jerusalem." Neither his peace initiative nor the context of the
assassination was mentioned. The illustrious career of Rabin enabled
the settlers to identify with some components of his biography while constructing the story of his death in a way convenient for them.

Rabin's assassination was a major trauma for Israeli society, and he is commemorated extensively through a special memorial day and by sites and institutions named after him throughout the country. This commemoration raises many questions and issues, mainly related to the fissures within Israeli society and the divisive policies of the slain prime minister. Sociologist Vered Vinitzki-Saroussi (2002) referred to Rabin's commemoration as fragmented memory; that is, Rabin is remembered in different times and places in light of contesting narratives.[11]

The settlers are ambivalent, if not outright hostile, to Rabin's commemoration, as it is practiced in Israel. Many do not commemorate Rabin's assassination because Rabin, as chief among the "Oslo criminals," committed, in their mind, unforgivable crimes against the Jewish land and people. Others, horrified by the crime against the head of the state they held sacred and committed to the idea of Jewish unity, find other reasons not to participate. They claim that the commemoration has been usurped by their rivals from the Israeli peace camp, and hence Rabin's memory serves to legitimate the Oslo Accords. In other words, for the national religious camp, let alone the ideological settlers, if Rabin was dangerous in life, he is even more dangerous in death. Some settlers claimed that they wished to join in the mourning because they had great respect for Rabin as a warrior, but were turned away. Furthermore, the national religious camp, with its elaborate culture of commemoration, shows disdain and skepticism toward the attempts of the Israeli peace camp at commemoration. They claim that Rabin has no legacy in the true sense of the word, no written corpus to be proud of, and the commemoration of one who is unworthy should be deplored by all dedicated to Jewish memory and Israeli culture.

According to the peace camp, the myth of Rabin is of a man of war who was most important in establishing the occupation regime, yet "saw the light" and led the way to peace, paying the ultimate price for his decision. The settlers cannot join this narrative without renouncing their convictions because it places them in the role of unenlightened warmongers. For them, Rabin represents a tragic mistake by a deluded faction of the Jewish people rendered delirious by the prospects of peace and unable to see the truth before its eyes. Commemorating Rabin is unthinkable because the settlers do not want to display the slightest appearance of legitimating the narrative that his life represents for their opponents.

All of this should not, however, blur the fact that Rabin's death was a watershed event in the history of the Gush Emunim settlers, even if they are reluctant to admit it. The idea of settling in the hearts of Israelis was constituted upon a concept of moral superiority and a privileged understanding of the public good. Amir's radical act proclaimed that he did not believe in the ability to convince the rest of the people through peaceful means and therefore resorted to murder. Once the destructive potential of a believer in Greater Israel was (once again) revealed, the ability of other believers, never as radical as he, to serve as educators of the nation was diminished. Thus, the ability of the national religious camp to make moral claims on behalf of authentic Judaism and Zionism suffered a fatal blow.

The tone of the articles in *Nekuda* has changed drastically following Rabin's assassination.[12] Elaborate theological discussions have ceased, and an atmosphere of practicality has suffused this flagship journal. Although attacks on the government and discussions regarding the future continue, there is, as Aviezer Ravitzky (2000, 155) has noted, a theological silence. Spiritual leaders are weary of writing, and the followers are less interested in reading, about how secular Israel is a stage in the process toward salvation and about how they can detect the divine reasoning that others cannot. This silence is reflected in various fields. For example, Zipora Luria, editor of *Dimui* (Image), a new journal for national religious artistic expression, told a researcher that after the Oslo Accords she received an abundance of plays, stories, and movie scripts that dealt with the new, frightening situation. It all stopped "on that awful day," when Rabin was assassinated (Shenkar 2004, 321). It suddenly seemed that the Gush Emunim settlers had little left to say to the rest of the Israeli people, and the Israeli public—especially the liberal Left—never very attentive to claims of divine promise and historical rights, was in no mood to listen.

The Rabin assassination is considered by many Israelis as one of the greatest traumas of their lives—a life-shattering event personally and a watershed event in Israeli history—especially for those born after the 1973 Yom Kippur War. The Gush Emunim settlers were hostile to Rabin's government from the outset and are ambivalent, at best, with respect to his commemoration. For them, the 1990s brought greater traumas. However, as they attributed sacred status to the state, Rabin's assassination might have had significant delayed ripple effects throughout the Gush Emunim community that were on a par with the Oslo Accords and the experience of withstanding extensive terrorist attacks. For the settlers, Rabin's assassination is a deep trauma in the sense that afterward, even if those involved do not care to admit it, the Gush Emunim project can never regain the vision and moral zeal it held before.

THE RETURN OF THE BORDER

In the years since the outbreak of the El-Aqsa Intifada in October 2000, the defining Israeli experience has been the suicide terrorist attack, occurring in public places such as buses, shopping malls, and restaurants.[13] Israeli public behavior has changed, both in terms of actual practices and symbolic meanings. At the peak period of terrorist attacks, Israelis entering public places looked suspiciously at their neighbors while alert for sources of possible danger. Distrust was institutionalized in the structural organization of Israeli public space: since terrorists may disguise themselves, no social category is exempt from suspicion and physical search. New categories began to undermine classic Israeli ethnic and religious divisions: the terrorism did not discriminate between Ashkenazi and Mizrahi origins, and it targeted religious and secular Israelis alike. It also hit tourists, guest workers, and Israeli Palestinians, including those in the same "imagined community" defined by common fate and risks rather than its common goal and purpose. In this Israel, victimhood defines belonging, which is not a new sensation in Jewish history. This, however, is a far cry from the ethnocentric world that Gush Emunim supporters dream of, even if it does push Israelis toward Gush Emunim's preferred hawkish policies.

Gush Emunim set out to define the nature of "true" Israeli identity and connect it to "Emunim"; namely, to loyalty to the decrees of Jewish history. Terrorism has its own ways of defining what is important in determining identity. While the Gush Emunim leaders were trying to decipher what it means to be Israeli, so were the Palestinian terrorists, who wanted to decipher and then target normal Israeli life, which, they claimed, was built on their misery. As the ability to go shopping or take a bus became a declared act of bravery and a national achievement, the banality of normal life became consecrated. For a certain period, Israelis realized that they had had a rather pleasant "normal life" all along, consisting of simple everyday actions. On the makeshift monument that was dedicated to the twenty-one youngsters, mostly immigrants from the former Soviet Union, killed in Tel Aviv while waiting to enter a dance club, the caption in Russian says, "This is our home," while the caption in Hebrew reads, "We shall not stop dancing." Israelis began to demand rights so commonplace that they did not realize that they had once enjoyed them: to walk the streets, sit in a café, and go dancing on Saturday night. The Israeli government received unequivocal messages that the Israeli public wanted a return to normalcy.

The terrorist acts in Israeli cities have delayed peace talks and discredited possible Palestinian partners, thus reinforcing the position of the Israeli Right, including the Gush Emunim settlers. The settlers were content, at times even jubilant, to see the Israeli army do what they had recommended all along: reconquer the Palestinian cities. But terrorist acts also cruelly redefined for Israelis what they considered a "home" worth fighting for, and it was not Hebron and Shiloh, and definitely not the Gaza Strip. Walking the path of Abraham and King David and settling the score of Tarpat have never been more distant from the Israeli agenda. The settlers have found themselves in a confusing cycle of victory and loss: while their claims that they are not the main reason for Palestinian rage and that the Palestinians are not worthy partners for negotiation have received credibility, their project of defining Judea and Samaria as the true Jewish home has either been discredited or simply become irrelevant. This is one respect in which the Second Intifada unsettled the basic ethos of Gush Emunim.

A more threatening prospect was the building of the fence and the wall. After several attempts to subjugate the Palestinians through armed force proved only partly successful, the Israeli government resorted to constructing a physical obstacle around the territories in order to keep out terrorists. The fence expressed the widely held feeling that there is little chance for reconciliation with the Palestinians in the near future, and that a temporal solution must entail disengagement between the two national groups. The fence follows the Green Line very loosely and, according to suggested plans, will encompass the large settlements near the Israeli Coastal Plain in the occupied territories. The portions built thus far have been catastrophic for the livelihood of tens of thousands of Palestinians, who have been cut off from their fields, schools, friends, and family.[14] Consequently, the issue of the fence reached Israeli and international courts and alerted civil rights organizations. Some marginal Israeli left-wing groups protest the construction of the fence, but most Israelis feel that it is a wise, if tardy, decision, and that the Palestinians' troubles were brought on themselves through their terrorist tactics. Few, however, discuss the meaning of the fence for the Gush Emunim project, which shows how irrelevant the project has become in the wake of the intifada.

Those in Israel who support the concept of the fence debate its location: should it follow the Green Line, in sovereign Israeli territory, or should it extend deep into Judea and Samaria in order to engulf Jewish settlements and annex areas to Israel? The Israeli government has made great efforts to include the large nonideological settlements nearer the Green Line, such as Ariel, within the region protected by the fence. According to all concerned, the ideological settlements on the mountain ridge of Judea and Samaria will remain on the other side of the fence. The right-wing government claims that the fence is only a security measure and not a statement regarding the future borders of Israel. However, it is clear to all that states do not construct such massive obstacles within their territory except to use them to demarcate what belongs to them and what does not. It is hard to think of a more salient expression of the statement that Judea and Samaria are not part of the state of Israel. Gush Emunim settlers, at the end of a difficult decade, have received yet another slap in the face.

The wall engulfs the West Bank and is supposed to lock in the Palestinians and monitor their entrance to Israel. It is by far the largest public construction project undertaken by the state of Israel since 1967 (if one does not include the construction of the settlements, now hidden beyond the fence). The fence constitutes a decision between two versions of Israeli normalcy: one sees the achievement of grand national aspirations as the center of Israeli existence, whereas the other places everyday life, security, and the economic well-being of most Israelis at the center. The idea of Greater Israel, and the settlers that embody it, has been readily sacrificed in order to return normalcy to the suicide-bombed cities of the Israeli Coastal Plain. The terror within Israeli cities, which seemingly blurred the difference between the two sides of the Green Line, produced the most visible sign of detachment from the territories. The settlers, along with their nemesis, the Palestinians, have been left to coexist or codestruct, hidden from sight behind a wall.

The settlers claim that the wall will not protect Israel, that the Palestinians will use it to connive murderous plans while hidden from the gaze of Israeli security forces, and that the Palestinians will find ways of passing over, under, or around it. In general, the voice of the settlers is hardly heard because of the delicate situation in which they find themselves, especially after the fence has proved its efficiency in stopping terrorist attacks on the Israeli Coastal Plain cities and in returning "normal" life to most Israelis. Their struggle to include their own settlements inside the fence, as well as their agreement to build fences around their homes, undermine their claim that the physical barrier should not be built at all.[15]

Although the settlers understand the symbolic meaning of the fence all too well, they can hardly afford to alienate their target public by objecting to its construction. Instead, they wield their political power to widen the territory included within the walls. Arie Heskin (2004, 75), of Tekoah, wrote in *Nekuda,* "Despite the danger of the fence, we cannot fight against its construction. We must struggle so that the maximum area of the land of Israel, the maximum number of settlements, the maximum number of settlers will be included within the side that stays under Israeli rule." He went on to suggest that an eastern wall should be built including the Jordan Valley and all the hilltop ideological settlements. He admitted that such a wall would evoke anger around the world, but was optimistic regarding the chances of convincing the Israeli public and government of its necessity. Instead of fighting for the traditional Gush Emunim position—for Israeli presence and control over the entire land—Heskin suggested accepting the inevitable and making the most of it.

The wall forebodes deterioration for the settlements left on its other side. It is safe to assume that Israelis would prefer to build their homes and open their businesses in places protected from terrorism and not in settlements that the government has all but declared cannot be effectively protected. The Palestinian terrorists have already targeted the settlers as their prime objective, and, once the rest of Israel is sealed off, they will have greater motivation to concentrate their efforts against their relatively unprotected traditional enemies. Heskin expressed his worries:

> Most of us are afraid of the dynamics that may develop once the fence is finished. The terror blocked by the fence will be diverted to our settlements enclosed beyond it, and while the terror will increase, the motivation of the public to back the protection of our villages by soldiers will decrease. We may see [mothers] . . . asking why their sons must guard a small group of settlers, as—so they will claim—guarding the Yesha settlements on the east no longer protects North Tel Aviv, now that the fence protects it. . . . A dynamic of desertion may develop. (75)

While all of this does not amount to the end of the settlement project, it does portend difficult days ahead. The settlers are no strangers to hardship, and their ideology teaches them to expect it and even to prosper from the motivation that it raises. The settlements may even thrive under the new conditions, especially as Israeli governments will feel the need to compensate them for the hardship they endure and will continue to use them in the battle against the Palestinians. However, the settlers' attempts to settle in the hearts of the nation have received a severe blow, indeed, from which they are unlikely to recover.

THE DISENGAGEMENT PLAN

The most dramatic issue on the Israeli political agenda of 2004–2005 was the struggle over the disengagement plan and its eventual implementation. The national religious camp was totally committed, recruited, and absorbed in the struggle; the rest of Israeli population remained interested bystanders. While some have supported the settlers' cause and others have opposed it, few outside of the settlers' camp have acted upon their convictions and actually done anything. The apathy of the Israeli public facing the settlement destruction was another sobering slap in the face for the settlers and their diminishing cadre of supporters.

Israeli Prime Minister Ariel Sharon was considered godfather of the settlement project in general and of the Katif bloc (Gush Katif) settlements in the Gaza Strip in particular. He decided to evacuate all Israeli military personnel and civilians from Gaza, as well as four isolated settlements in northern Samaria. Sharon presented his plan in a speech at an economic conference in the city of Herzlia in December 2003, immediately triggering a political crisis. His motivations for acting against his previous convictions were never explained fully. He may have been trying to buy time before international pressure would force Israeli withdrawal under unfavorable conditions. Probably the hardship of the army, fighting a guerilla war for years in the Gaza Strip while defending secluded settlements, was also an important factor. In a sense, Israel was unilaterally shortening its lines of conflict with the Palestinians, and the settlers, yesterday's pioneers, were demanded to pay the price.

As the plan moved through Israeli parliamentary channels, right-wing parties resigned from Sharon's coalition government and his own Likud Party was on the verge of disintegration. (It did split in the wake of the evacuation.) Sharon initiated a plebiscite within his party, which he lost, yet moved on with his plan regardless. The Israeli Labor Party stepped in to stabilize Sharon's coalition and enable the plan to proceed. Meanwhile, the Gush Katif settlers and their supporters debated strategies and took their protest to the streets in various ways (Roth 2005).

The choice of strategy and symbolism reflects the situation of the settlers vis-à-vis the rest of Israeli society after thirty years of settlement. Two of the main tenants of Gush Emunim ideology, used repetitively in the past, were rarely raised. The claim that Gush Katif and the Gaza Strip are part of Greater Israel, while self-evident to the settlers, was not evoked because the claim was considered to be ineffective and even counterproductive in the discourse with the mainly secular Israeli society, especially after the Oslo Accords and the Second Intifada.

Second, Jewish history was also left out of the picture. The Gaza Strip was, in any case, devoid of useful Jewish memories and in biblical times was the land of the Philistines. The relative weakness of traditional Gush Emunim reasoning was not unlike the situation that hampered Gush Emunim's struggle in Yamit twenty-three years before; the failed Yamit experience was another historical event hardly mentioned for reasons elaborated on chapter 10.

As the settlers found their life achievement collapsing before their eyes, many resorted to the most extreme symbolism: the Holocaust. Some placed an orange Star of David on their chest, equating their own fate with that of the Holocaust victims, and insinuating a comparison, at times even making a direct comparison, between Sharon and the Nazi leadership and between the Israeli and German soldiers. At face value, comparing the two historical events seems both ludicrous and horrific, as many critics soon pointed out: after all, the Gush Katif evacuees were handsomely compensated and on their way to a state-sponsored new life somewhere else in Israeli suburbia rather than anything remotely resembling Auschwitz. They received the democratic right to protest their eviction, again unlike European Jews in the Nazi era. Why many did choose the loaded and clearly counterproductive symbolism of the Holocaust is, however, worth contemplating. For the messianic-religious settlers, the delay in national salvation caused by decisions by a national Israeli government was an inexplicable and unforgivable crime. The Jewish presence in parts of the land of Israel was destroyed through—according to the settlers—no visible necessity. As they saw it, as communities vanished and a region declared *Judenrein* (German: free of Jews), the Holocaust metaphor was poignant and valid.[16]

The choice of orange for the Star of David shows a certain reluctance in choosing the yellow used by the Nazis, but also a connection to the color picked by followers of Viktor Yushenko in the Ukraine struggle for democracy at the same time. It was also the color of the Gush Katif council and therefore a logical choice. While the Holocaust symbolism was harshly criticized by many, including from within the settler's camp, the orange color became the trademark of the struggle. Cars of supporters were decorated with orange ribbons, as were Israeli flags, and the political camp itself was nicknamed "the oranges." As long as the color was dominant in Israeli streets, it seemed as though Gush Katif had a popular presence and a chance of survival. Rabbi Shlomo Aviner, using language resembling that used in the reverence of religious artifacts such as phylacteries, called on the supporters to wear orange:

> Please, wear an orange ribbon day and night, on your hand and on your coat, on your belt, on the antenna of your car, and on all the windows at your house. Wear an orange shirt, wear an orange skullcap, give orange to your friends, give orange to everyone, color the state orange. This is how we declare, "Our land, our land, you are ours forever! Do not worry our land, we love you. We did everything for you and we shall do more. . . . They do not let us speak, they do not let us express ourselves, so we paint. . . . We use the color of the smiling sun, because we love everybody."[17]

The salience of the color and its symbolism was such that whoever did not sympathize with the cause refrained that year from wearing orange so as not to be suspected of belonging to the "wrong" political camp. Since the right wing had appropriated orange, their opponents quickly grabbed the opportunity to reappropriate Israel's national colors—the blue and white—for their cause. While Sharon continued with his plan, the Israeli symbolic sphere was bubbling with new ideas and representations.

Regarding other political strategies, the settlers found themselves in an awkward dilemma. Displaying their zeal and sense of historical moment, they threatened to bring Israel to a standstill, claiming that while some Israelis were experiencing momentous tragedy the rest should not be allowed to continue with their normal life. Blocking main highways and planting fake bombs in crowded places did much to erode popular support for the settlers' cause; on the other hand, protesting quietly had little effect either. The trope they felt could win the day was "love," so they appropriated a slogan taken from Israeli sports: "We have love and it will prevail." Offering love and threatening violence interchangeably did much to baffle Israeli public opinion, expose the settlers' tactics as manipulative, and undermine their credibility.

Since history and metahistory failed as ample reasons to halt the withdrawal, the settlers discovered that their everyday life and plight were their strongest assets. The media and Internet became major weapons as some settlers documented their lives and shared them with the Israeli public. Each of the important media in Israel had its favorite Gush Katif resident, expressing his or her thoughts, doubts, hope, and despair while facing eminent evacuation. The responses, especially in Internet talkbacks, were diverse and heated. Some supported the settlers and sympathized with the writers, whereas others were rude and offensive, responding sarcastically with the likes of "We are deeply touched, now get the hell out of there." Settler leaders who posted their comments discovered for the first time and to their surprise how much popular hatred, and not only support, was directed toward the settlers.

In the final weeks before the evacuation, mystical tales of miracles at Gush Katif were told and retold. They were even published in a book that began with a statement associating current events with biblical times: "Great miracles, such as those happening today in Gush Katif, have not happened to the people of Israel since the day we went into exile" (Yefet 2005). Rabbi Mordechay Eliyahu, of Safad, who infiltrated the besieged region, marveled on a prime-time television show how the five thousand shells that landed on Gush Katif in five years had harmed very few Jews, and, when a house was directly hit, three Arab workers inside were killed while the Jewish homeowners were spared. The rabbi explained that such miracles show that God favors the place and will not allow it to perish. His point was lost on the interviewers, not only because of its racist undertones, but also because of the heavy human toll that had been exacted among the settlers and the soldiers guarding them. They mentioned that five thousand shells hardly qualify as an argument against evacuation.

The rabbi's words show how, as the actual Gush Katif was slipping away from physical existence, it was already entering the realm of folklore and popular imagination. In reviewing the aforementioned book, a critic mentions that the forthcoming evacuation is not mentioned at all: "This forgetting is not accidental. One may say that this is a deliberate step, transforming Gush Katif in the minds of the readers into a territory that cannot be 'detached,' because it is already not within the natural order of things."[18]

Weeks before the evacuation, an important showdown occurred in Kfar Maimon, a religious moshav (agricultural community) some miles outside the Gaza Strip. Tens of thousands of "orange" supporters gathered there to display their strength and force the government to change policy. At one dramatic point, the leaders had to decide on whether to protest quietly and than disperse, or march to Gush Katif, inevitably clashing with the Israeli army encircling them and bringing the conflict to new, probably violent, heights. After a heated debate, they opted for dispersal, justifying their decision in their desire to preserve national unity.

In all probability, the Kfar Maimon resolution had little practical consequence: it is most unlikely that the protestors could have changed the course of events had they actually marched to Gush Katif against the resolute security forces that would have encountered them. The debate and decision were, however, important in enabling the settlers to save face and maintain their ideological convictions. According to their narrative, only their unreciprocated commitment to national unity and their moral inhibitions stopped them from saving the besieged region. Later, the settlers were able to maintain the argument with a veiled threat that, next time, the decision would be reversed. Whereas the Gush Katif evacuation glaringly exhibited the settlers' weakness, the Kfar Maimon events enabled them to insist that they actually had a choice in the matter. Their relative inactivity and refraining from confrontation in what they defined as a major historical watershed led to feelings of remorse and guilt that, in turn, led to heightened violence in the encounters that followed after the fall of Gush Katif.

The settlements were evacuated within a few days in August 2005. The relative ease with which the complicated maneuver was conducted was much mentioned in the media: most of the settlers' resistance was passive, and the male and female soldiers showed great consideration and remarkable patience in dismantling possible points of contention. The army's roadblocks prevented many demonstrators from arriving and stifled any possible flames. The civil war scenario threatened by the settlers did not materialize.

The nature of the encounter between the soldiers and the settlers was revealing. Before the events, the soldiers received training and rationales in order to withstand the mental stress of facing the settlers. They were to deaden their senses, or at least their reactions, and absorb passively whatever logical arguments or foul language the settlers would throw at them. Their only response was to refer the settlers to the decisions of the political authorities. To the annoyance and open anger of the settlers, their attempts to persuade their interlocutors met an impenetrable blockade, without responding subjects on whom they could exercise their discursive strategies.

In response, the settlers attempted to "reindividualize" the soldiers standing in front of them—they wanted the soldiers to see themselves as being responsible for their actions. They called specific male and female soldiers by name, alternately luring and threatening them. They sobbed to the troops that the soldiers were war criminals hiding behind anonymity like the Nazis before them. Women settlers threatened female soldiers that, as divine punishment for their deeds, they would be barren. It became clear, however, that the loyalty of the soldiers to their units and army was as resolute as that of the settlers to their cause.

After the evacuation, some of the settlers were left without a place to stay, either for the short term or as a permanent solution. They blamed the Disengagement Office, yet part of the fault fell on their ideological refusal to look to the future while struggling for the survival of their settlements. This was an intricate issue involving the complex intermingling of private and public homes in the settlers' worldview. Taking care of their own affairs—for example, where they would work, their children would study, their possessions would be moved after the evacuation—seemed to them a betrayal of their comrades, not to mention an act of disbelief in the possibility of divine intervention on their behalf. All evacuees suffered in the process, but the more ideologically minded ones suffered more because it was against their most entrenched beliefs to somehow alleviate their problems.

As the settlers were looking for a new life elsewhere in Israel while their homes were bulldozed, one last struggle ensued: to save their synagogues from destruction. In a reversal of their former decision, and under the pressure of settlers and rabbis in Israel and abroad, it was decided that the synagogues be declared sacred buildings and left in the hands of the Palestinians. Among the ruins of the region, the surviving synagogues were seen as a hinge for a hope of return, not unlike the famous tree of Gush Etzion. Some of the political and spiritual leaders of the camp expressed this sentiment explicitly, trying desperately to save a glimpse of hope from the total destruction they saw before them. The cycle of Jewish memory was left with physical markers on which to evolve, and a new sacred goal was set: to redeem the synagogues and pray in them once more. This was not to be: once the Palestinians received the buildings, the synagogues were not saved from desecration and eventual destruction. Whether the ruins will retain some symbolic importance is a matter for the future. Meanwhile, the Yesha council defiantly did not change its name: the acronym of Judea, Samaria, and Gaza still holds, even though the Jewish settlement region of Gaza no longer exists. The name commemorates the "amputated limb" and offers a glimpse of hope for the future.

Yoel Bin-Nun, speaking almost a year before the actual evacuation, claimed that the Gush Katif settlements had already been evacuated. He was referring to his known phrase about the project not settling in the hearts of the nation: for him, the fact that a sovereign Israeli government could decide on withdrawal while the Israeli nation quietly accepted the decision meant that the project had failed. The actual physical evacuation was just a technicality. Next I discuss some of the reasons for the settlers' failure to settle in the hearts of Israelis, as expressed time and again in the years between the Oslo Accords and the disengagement plan.

WHY HAVE THE SETTLERS NOT SETTLED IN THE HEARTS OF PEOPLE?

The four historical events described here—the Oslo Accords, the Rabin assassination, the Second Intifada, and the disengagement plan—are very different from one another. The first was a government decision to initiate a diplomatic process, the second was the act of a right-wing extremist in reaction to that process, the third was an eruption of Palestinian rage, and the fourth was a unilateral decision by an Israeli leader—yet they all demonstrate the uneasy and conflicted nature of the relationship between the Gush Emunim settlers and the rest of Israeli society. Israeli society, including its right wing, which seemingly supports the settlers, clearly has other agendas, some contradicting that of Gush Emunim. Those agendas existed prior to the Oslo Accords, but resurfaced with greater urgency in the years to follow.

Even among its group of origin, the national religious camp, a certain backlash occurred. All along, this camp held a wide range of political goals; after all, the ideological settlers number some tens of thousands while the larger religious community numbers over ten times as many. Most religious Zionists live in big cities around the country, and there are numerous religious agricultural settlements (kibbutzim and moshavim) on the western side of the Green Line. Even within the West Bank, larger communities (notably Efrat) contain religious critics of Gush Emunim.

Most national religious Israelis have family members and friends living in the settlements to whom they feel obligated and committed. Nevertheless, they hold a variety of views on the social and national role of their camp and Israel's future borders. Members of the larger community complained that the radical movement had usurped the national religious agenda, damaged other causes and, in general, alienated the Israeli secular public toward the camp.

In the 2004 Passover edition of the national religious daily newspaper *Hatzofe,* columnist Hanoch Daum presented what he saw as the nine problems confronting the national religious sector at the moment.[19] The first was the West Bank settlers' lack of pragmatism, their unwillingness to compromise, and their distancing themselves from the people. Those who reach for everything are often left with nothing, warned Daum, echoing criticism leveled at Gush Emunim by the Left. Tellingly, the other eight problems he mentions are unrelated to the issue of territories and settlements.[20] His article demonstrates the varied agenda of the national religious camp. The question of the settlements is only one among many, and even here the settlers' position has come under attack. In other words, Gush Emunim's project of settling in the hearts of people has only partially succeeded even within the camp that would seem to support it unquestionably—those for which, according to Ehud Sprinzak (1981), Gush Emunim was "the tip of the iceberg."

The claim regarding Gush Emunim settlers' fall from favor and their gradual marginalization and isolation may be contested: after all, they still receive more than their share of the budgets, various government offices help them directly and indirectly, and they manifest a constant presence in the Israeli media. Their organizational capabilities and their commitment to the cause may compensate for their lack in numbers, and their opponents find it difficult to outmaneuver them. The recurrent crises they have endured since 1992 were not a product of the success of the Israeli peace camp, but resulted from the growing resistance of the Palestinians and the structural changes in Israeli society and politics.

The transformation that has affected Israeli society is the rapid shift from socialist to capitalist principles that occurred both in social values and in economic structure. To be sure, Israel was never a socialist state in the mold of the Soviet bloc; it was, nevertheless, constructed on values of social justice and equality that were borrowed from the socialist movements of Europe and became institutionalized in strong labor unions and a developed welfare state. While strong individualistic tendencies always existed in Zionism and in Israeli society, and were represented by large political parties and influential thinkers, the pioneering collectivist ethos, represented by the ruling Labor Party, held hegemonic positions in politics and culture. The strength of these values can be attributed partly to a socialist heritage, partly to traditional Jewish solidarity, and partly to the effects of the perennial conflict with the Palestinians and the Arab states that enhanced the need for social sacrifice and national unity.[21]

While Israel has indeed enjoyed relative social equality, various aspects of the social and cultural order have come under severe criticism. The collectivist ideology, with its strong unifying urge, encountered problems in integrating Jewish "others": the Haredim were left outside the Zionist national camp, while Mizrahi Jews were absorbed into society in a way that marginalized them, ignored their cultural heritage, and promoted economic inequalities. Thus, the social and cultural order, grounded in a Zionist and collectivist ideology, was criticized as ethnocentric. Other criticisms were leveled at the centralist state, monopolist economy, and collectivist ethos, which were claimed to stifle civil liberties and limit initiative.

Historical and sociological developments transformed the structural characteristics in Israeli society. The Six-Day War brought new prosperity that enhanced demands for more openness and greater personal freedom. The costly Yom Kippur War, on the other hand, brought dependence on foreign markets, which opened up Israeli trade further and caused attrition of collectivist values. The pioneering elite that had governed Israel to that point was discredited by the failures of the war (mainly their failures in leadership and foresight) and the disclosure of corruption. Menachem Begin's government, established in 1977 and based on the Likud Party, included a faction of the "new liberals," who appointed the finance minister from among their ranks. Israel was now set on its way to becoming a capitalist state with an individualist ethos—a process sealed by the national emergency economic plan of 1985, under the national unity government, which included the Likud Party and the former socialist Labor Party, both now committed to the principles of capitalist market economy. The socialist ethos of the early years of the state was discredited, which in turn fueled further privatization.

In other societies undergoing similar processes, the new middle class formed social movements and nongovernmental organizations that battled the process of globalization and the social ills of swift privatization, forcing capitalist firms to take some account of social concerns. In the

Israeli case, the two important social movements to emerge from the new social class—Gush Emunim and Peace Now—turned their attention to questions of boundaries and settlement and did not counter the economic and social transformations in Israeli society.

Although the political and economic interests in maintaining control of the territories were strong, the changing economic climate in Israel was, as sociologists claim, conducive to attempts at peace. The Israeli business elite grew in power because of the structural changes in the Israeli economy. Seeking an improved economic environment and better standing in the world economy, they pressured governments to reach an accommodation with the Palestinians. The Oslo Accords provided strong economic incentives, linking Israel to global markets; accordingly, the accords were seen in Israel as a peace initiative by and for the rich and powerful, and hence were viewed with suspicion among the Jewish lower classes.[22]

In this historical context, Gush Emunim sought to further its agenda of a Greater Israel, loyalty to Jewish tradition, and revival of the Zionist collectivist ethos. To be sure, Gush Emunim leaders were well aware of the situation in which they operated: they presented their communal village as an attempt to bring Zionist settlement forms, dominated until then by the collectivist kibbutz and moshav, up to date in the postsocialist era; they struggled to improve the economic conditions of those who thought of joining them and marketed their settlements by using capitalist incentives; and they suggested their project as one of the remedies to the ills of modern life and tried to connect with alienated modern man's search for authenticity. Basically, however, their project of memory, return, and collectivistic values swam against the prevailing currents, and, over time, the contradictions between their ethos and the newly emerging Israeli social and economic order became evident. The processes of globalization, liberalization, and privatization made the Gush Emunim commodity one among many, with advantages and disadvantages for Israeli consumers. It could not hope to obliterate other options by the strength of its commitment.

Gush Emunim offered national solidarity and personal sacrifice to a society that was undergoing rapid privatization—a society that sought personal and national security and that legitimated individual gratification. A linguistic neologism marks the social transformation and illustrates the difficulties faced by Gush Emunim's logic in a changing society. In the 1970s, a new slang term entered Israeli language and imagination:

the "freier." A *freier* is someone who loses a deal or is manipulated by others—for example, by paying too much for goods or services or missing an easy opportunity. In everyday speech, Israelis take pride in not being freiers or mock others for belonging to that category. Israeli commercials use the idiom intensively, claiming that one who does not consume their product is a freier. While many cultures have similar idioms (for example "sucker" or "wimp" in the United States), and terms that express self-assertion and mock weakness are prevalent in macho Mediterranean cultures, the Israeli freier is somewhat different: it is a novel invention that has emerged in a society that had consecrated pioneering and self-sacrifice and held to a strong socialistic ethos.[23]

Enduring hardship and living humbly for the sake of the collective future, once hailed as pioneering, is today often ridiculed as a sign of the freier. It is revealing to see how rationalizations of nationally acclaimed acts have changed their meaning: Once, youth were enticed into prestigious army units under the ethos of national sacrifice; today, the recruits' motivation is as high as ever, but the rationalization is self-fulfillment and meaningful army service. Once, settlement in the periphery was considered a contribution to Israeli security; today, it is promoted through promises of better housing, clean air, and beautiful scenery. Under the culture of the freier, voluntary acts of self-sacrifice for the collective good may still be found, but are becoming harder to legitimate.

The appearance of "don't be a freier" as a major component of Israeli identity poses a dilemma for the ideological settlers: on the one hand, they can claim that they remain pioneers in a society that has forsaken such values and even praise themselves for being the freiers of Israeli society. They must then totally change Israeli values, lest they become objects of ridicule. On the other hand, they can downplay their collectivist ideology and try to convince others that those who bet their future on the hills of Judea and Samaria are not freiers, but sound investors.

The Gush Emunim settlers have used both strategies with varying success. In Hebron, they accentuate their ideological zeal, and, while admitting that the Jewish residents endure hardship and danger, proclaim that this is compensated for by their contribution to the nation and active participation in the redemptive process. For those uninterested in ideological matters, other, larger settlements, closer to the Israeli metropolitan centers, have been marketed through capitalistic strategies stressing the low cost of housing and their proximity to Israeli centers of population, commerce, and entertainment. There, residents are encouraged to feel that they are part of the "normal" Israel of the Coastal Plain rather than those seen as radical fanatics on the hills. Most of the settlements on the mountain range, however, have tried to balance both tendencies in order to maintain the Hebronian zeal while connecting to Israeli society at large. The case of Ofra in chapter 9 focused on the intricate balance between being a pioneer and not being a freier.

Being concomitantly collectivists and individualists, pioneers and freiers (perhaps Zionists and post-Zionists), left the settlement project susceptible to attacks on all sides. While the ideological settlements were criticized for being too radical and uncompromising, and hence out of touch with the flow of history, the more radical settlers claimed that the established Gush Emunim settlers compromised their principles in a futile attempt to please Israeli and global public opinion, an option alien and hostile to the process of redemption. Among fundamentalist movements around the world, the phenomenon of being attacked concomitantly for being both too extreme and too moderate is well known. This is associated with what sociologist Peter Berger (1979) called the "heretical imperative." To survive and thrive in a modern world, believers need to adopt aspects of modernity selectively. They use modern media, often use advanced weapons, and, where such a regime exists, join in the open atmosphere of democracy and free press. Modern technology and institutions are usually accompanied by modernist culture that infiltrates the believers' ranks. The fundamentalists are always, therefore, betwixt and between, balancing strict religious dicta with the lures of modern life.[24] That is true even among groups that succeed in constructing a secluded enclave, such as the Jewish ultra-Orthodox, and is inevitable in communities that cherish their good relations with secular co-nationals, such as the ideological settlers of Gush Emunim.

The settlers failed to settle in people's hearts because they proposed a vision that ran counter to dominant trends in the society in which they functioned and on whose support they depend. They offered collectivism in an age of individualism, traditional commitment in times of personal self-fulfillment, sanctification of place in an age of cyberspace and easy territorial mobility, and memory in an era of forgetting. Furthermore, with one leg in the global world to which they claimed to belong, and which they see themselves as representing against the Arab-Muslim world, they were somewhat ambivalent toward their fundamentalist principles insofar as they stood against the encroachment of Western modernity and global influences.

The social transformation of Israeli society did offer the settler project some advantages, however. The move toward a capitalist ethos and privatization weakened the Israeli state, thus enabling a committed and well-organized group to advance its goals. From its early stages, the movement skillfully used conflicts and inconsistencies within Israeli governments, and the lack of a clear-cut policy toward them, to advance their cause. The rise of the movement, therefore, coincided with and benefited from the demise of authoritative national leadership in Israel. The existence of Gush Emunim would have been inconceivable in the early days of the state, when, by exercising the principle of *mamlachtiut* (roughly translated as "statism"), Ben-Gurion crushed autonomous organization from both the political Right and the Left. In the case of the disengagement plan, we see that, when the state exerts its power, the settlers find themselves helpless to shift the historical tide. For most of the Gush Emunim settlers' history, however, they have thrived on the weakness of the Israeli political leadership.

In a sense, the ideological settlers are well adapted to the demands of a capitalist market. Their zeal, entrepreneurship, and organization give them considerable advantages over their adversaries. In its attempts to organize and recruit, the Israeli peace camp finds itself in a far more difficult situation: while the settlers can at least rely on their camp to rally for battle, the peace camp struggles for support among the secular upper middle class, which has a distaste for attending anonymous mass demonstrations, let alone coming into physical contact with the settlers. Potential peace camp supporters do not want to be considered freiers, wrestling the settlers while the rest of Israeli society gets a free-ride peace and its benefits. As no one else can organize a strong coalition, the settlers' organization and dedication give them the edge.

Although the Gush Katif experience has shown that it is indeed possible, it is still difficult to see at the moment an Israeli government willing to battle each and every illegal outpost, let alone established settlements, especially when there are numerous settlers among the ranks of the decision makers and top bureaucrats. The critics of the settlement project claim that, since a growing number of Israelis appreciate the damage caused by the settlements, their eventual evacuation is just a matter of time; but they fail to explain how such recognition will be transformed into the sustained action required to uproot years of settlement on the part of a powerful, well-organized group. It has turned out that the settlers do not need to settle in the hearts of people to survive: they need only ensure that no one else will settle in the hearts of the nation, and, in a privatized society, other ideological groups find themselves in the same trap as Gush Emunim.

As Ariel Sharon's plan to disengage from the Gaza Strip gained force, the settlers decided on a dramatic demonstration symbolizing the connection of the Gaza Strip to the rest of Israel. They called on their supporters to join hands in a chain stretching from Nisanit in the Gaza Strip to Eastern Jerusalem. Between one hundred thousand and two hundred thousand people participated in one of the most impressive peaceful demonstrations in Israel's history, hailed with appreciation from all sides of the political map. Veteran Gush Emunim leader Uri Elitzur wrote,

> What can I say, friends, the excitement was great. We felt that we did a huge thing. Exactly at seven, we started to sing *Hatikva* ["The Hope," Israel's national anthem]. The people started to sing based on the clock: "When you hear the beginning of the news on the radio start singing." In the front lines, we were somewhat like a flock without a shepherd, like a choir without a conductor, but by the time we reached the line "toward east," everyone was singing at the top of their voice and holding hands, and you knew that along ninety kilometers people were standing and singing with you word for word.[25]

Elitzur marveled at the way the demonstration expressed togetherness: everyone was singing together, symbolizing a powerful "imagined community." He mentioned that all were impressed by the demonstration, praising the settlers for their achievement. For him, that was cause for worry: it meant that the demonstration was not threatening enough. Elitzur, along with others, touched on two important points: first, the recruitment of the national religious camp was close to total, regardless of the camp's multiple agendas; and, second, practically no one else joined in, and the knitted-skullcapped believers stood on the roads alone, either passively admired or totally neglected by those whose lives and souls they sought to save. The isolation of the national religious camp was never as apparent as at the moment of one of their most cherished triumphs, when they held hands to sing the Israeli anthem.

EPILOGUE: SETTLING ELSEWHERE

This book is about constructing and reconstructing a national and personal home. While the settlers build their home in Judea and Samaria, in a sense they are also redefining the homes of all Israeli Jews and non-Jews —even those, like me, who choose not to join them. I conclude with two personal episodes, describing my encounters with religious settlers: one at their home and the other near mine.

On one winter day in 1992, I joined a couple of Peace Now activists on their way to examine—you may say spy on—Gush Emunim settlements. I was in the midst of my doctoral research on the two opposing movements and oscillated between both. On that day, my academic gaze was focused on the peace movement activists, just as their gaze was focused on their adversaries from Gush Emunim. The Peace Now duo consisted of a young man and a young woman, whose role was to count the number of new constructions in old and new settlements and inform the Israeli general public. The idea behind the counting project was somewhat naive: that once the Israeli public learned what its government was doing with its tax money, an outcry would arise and halt the advancement of the settlement project. As we now know, that was not the case: Peace Now's strategies failed to settle in Israelis' hearts just like those of their adversaries.

The duo hired a minivan, and its driver, while not a member or supporter of Peace Now, tried his best to show genuine interest in view of their findings. The fourth person in the minivan was me, an anthropologist in a very awkward position. Doing comparative research on both groups, I was concerned about a possible encounter with my interviewees of the previous day. Not that I kept the topic of my research a secret, but I felt that it was unwise to accentuate my good connections on both sides to the activists of the two ideologically opposed movements. I was worried that the settlers would be disappointed to see me travel with a group dedicated to uprooting them from their homes; likewise, my Peace Now friends would undoubtedly raise their eyebrows at my familiarity with their foes. Luckily for me, the couple I was with dreaded a possible encounter with the settlers as much as I did and thus evaded them whenever possible. Their assignment was to count the settlers' houses, not to engage in a dialogue with the settlers, which might easily regress into violence, as had nearly occurred on previous occasions.

At the end of a long day of traveling the roads of Samaria, learning of the growing power of the settlement project, the small and tired group was on its way back through the settlement of Shiloh. Suddenly, a strong and authoritative voice was heard: "Stop!" Our driver stopped the car instinctively. The three of us, perhaps the driver as well, immediately felt that he should not have done so. However, once the minivan had stopped, it seemed that starting to drive away would signal alarm and panic, and perhaps even end in a chase. Thus, we waited anxiously and quietly in the car, tense while trying to display calm, as a man approached us. He looked like the quintessential settler, if ever there was one: he wore an army coat (*dubon* in Hebrew) over a flannel shirt and had a wild red beard, a huge smile, and held a little girl in his arms. As he reached the car, he poked his smiling head through the driver's window and looked around. Did he understand that the group was a Peace Now crew, scared by his presence and wishing only that he go away? If he did, he did not show it. He turned to the driver and asked him, "How much for your car?"

The only one in the car who was snapped out of this tense posture by this innocent (or was it innocent?) question was the driver. He was relieved to find himself on solid ground and launched into an enthusiastic discussion of cars, prices, engines, and transmissions. I was wondering at the time whether it were possible to conceive of a settler buying a vehicle carrying the crew intent on evicting him from his home. The heated, yet friendly, discussion went on for several minutes, and the two parted as friends, exchanging phone numbers. Our small group returned to Jerusalem. As I sat down to write my field notes, I did not include this event, which, at the time, I felt was inconsequential. I later returned to that encounter and reflected on its meaning.

The settler from Shiloh was telling me, so I felt, something important about the meaning of belonging. That was his way of conveying to the skeptic visitors that he was at home. The surprising insight about the encounter was that there was nothing surprising or extraordinary about it: similar banal encounters occur in Israel innumerable times daily. Israelis tend to be obtrusive and to ask perfect strangers in chance encounters whether their car is for sale and for how much. In other words, what the settler was saying to the visitors was "This is Israel," and the "correct" behavior, therefore, should be to act accordingly. This was the exact opposite of the message that the Peace Now activists were trying to convey. For them, struggling to dislocate the occupied territories from Israel, his utterance held a threatening, yet allusively subtle, message. A violent argument regarding the rights of Jews and Palestinians and the status of divine commandments would have been more reassuring because it would have reflected the boundaries between Gush Emunim and Peace Now and marked the two sides of the Green Line separating "Israel" from its "occupied territories."

I cannot guarantee that the Shiloh settler would agree with my interpretation, yet his awareness of my reflections is inconsequential. Either manipulatively or naively, through early socialization or later accommodation, he deciphered (whether correctly or not) the trope of "being Israeli" and enacted it in the face of those who—by their very appearance—announced to him that he is not "at home." His declaration was that his being at home is so taken for granted that it needs no declaration. Erving Goffman (1959) distinguished between messages that we give and messages that we give off. The settler did not tell the visitors in so many words that he was home, but the subtext of his behavior made it clear that he saw himself as beyond the trivial issue of arguing to whom the land belonged.

The two sides danced a delicate dance of inclusion and exclusion. The Peace Now duo embarked on a project that declared that the occupied territories are only in temporal possession of Israel and will return to their "true" status as outside of Israel, whereas the settler made the point that Samaria, including himself, is part and parcel of the entity called Israel. They wanted his home; he replied by asking to buy their car. Within a few months, however, things were to change: new elections brought Yitzhak Rabin to power, with the Oslo Accords soon to follow, threatening, perhaps even destroying, the settlers' sense of home. Ironically, it was the ideology of the activists of Peace Now, looking pathetically out of place in their encounter with the confident settler, that became relevant because their agenda of "de-homing" the settlements became the official policy of the Israeli government.

I reside in Midreshet Ben-Gurion, a small village in the middle of the Negev desert, almost an hour's drive from the nearest large city, Beer Sheva. The tomb of Israel's first prime minister, David Ben-Gurion, with its view of the Zin Valley, is our famous tourist attraction. Ben-Gurion chose to be buried in the Negev, rather than at the Mount Herzl National Cemetery in Jerusalem, because of his devotion to the concept of pioneering (*halutziut*). In 1953, as acting prime minister, he moved to Kibbutz Sede Boker in the Negev, wishing that many more, especially youths, would follow in his footsteps. This was not to be: Israelis preferred to live in the crowded Coastal Plain, and the Negev, more than half of Israel's territory, was left relatively unpopulated and underdeveloped. The pioneering zeal of Gush Emunim increased the neglect of the Negev, as funds and population that could have helped in the south were diverted eastward. Ben-Gurion's vision of a blooming desert is seldom discussed today, forgotten by most Zionists and criticized by environmentalists.

In 2001, we received our own "Gush Emunim settlement": a group of young religious families, mostly second-generation settlers, decided to build their home near our village. Since the local authorities were slow (as always in this region) with formal approvals and connections to utilities, the resourceful settlers used the experience gained in the hills of Judea and Samaria and brought mobile homes. This was a Gush Emunim settlement par excellence, apart from the fact that Gush Emunim does not exist anymore as an organization and the location was inside the Green Line.

The newcomers were received by the veteran Jewish residents of the Negev with mixed feelings: On the one hand, all agreed on the importance of bringing young Jewish residents to the Negev, and the left wingers among us were pleased that it came at the expense of the West Bank settlements. On the other hand, many worried that the religious settlers would initiate a process that would transform the secular nature of the region. The fact that the new village was called Merchav Am did not help put our worries to rest: it commemorated the slain Israeli extreme Right minister Rechavam Ze'evi, who preached the removal of Arabs from the land of Israel.

The discourse around the new settlement made ironic use of the powerful idiom of "return." Gush Emunim defined its project as a return to the heart of the land of Israel, while several young couples now "returned," in the sense that the Israeli Left would use it, to inside the Green Line. The group felt a need to apologize to their fellow settlers, explaining that, while they are committed the Greater Israel concept, the Negev was also an important part of the land (Reichner 2001b). After the grand celebrations of the establishment of the new settlement, one of the distinguished visitors, Israel Harel, published an article in the *Haaretz* daily newspaper. Harel, of Ofra, was the entrepreneur behind some of Gush Emunim's most important institutions, such as the monthly *Nekuda* and the Yesha council. In his article, he explained the purpose of the new settlement: to bring the pioneering spirit to the Negev and to control the Arab Bedouins, who, claiming rights to the Negev lands, settle wherever they can, thus endangering the Jewish dominance of the region.[26]

I read Harel's article with great concern. Suddenly, Judea and Samaria were becoming inconveniently close, actually next door. I was, in a sense, insulted: proud of living a five-minute walk from Ben-Gurion's tomb, I was not going to allow the newcomers to teach me what pioneering really means and appropriate one of the only sources of symbolic capital that life in the Negev offers (for what it is worth in the age of the freier). Harel reflected a major Gush Emunim theme: telling others what Zionist values actually represent. Although I never considered myself a great pioneer, the newcomers' pretensions, as expressed by Harel, had a condescending flavor.

More important, the idea of transforming the Negev into a new Yesha was, for me, a frightening prospect. Harel did not differentiate between the angry Palestinians of his region and the Negev Bedouins, who are the poorest and most deprived of Israeli citizens: many live in shanty towns, unrecognized by the state, without running water or electricity. The prospects of a Bedouin intifada are prominent, and Harel's attitude could serve as a dangerous spark in an explosive situation. For Harel, the Bedouins were a national enemy, either actually or potentially, whereas, for me, they were, first and foremost, deprived Israeli citizens. I wrote a letter to *Haaretz,* congratulating the newcomers and inviting them to participate in the activities of the Negev community, but asking them to denounce the ideas expressed by Harel and to refrain from reproducing the catastrophic relations between Jews and Palestinians in the relatively peaceful Negev region.[27]

Reflecting on my fears of Harel's vision being implemented in the Negev area, I understood something of my own sense of home, perhaps informed by a sensitivity that comes from my research. Many people do not want this or that neighbor to move into their vicinity, and the American saying "There goes the neighborhood" resonates well elsewhere, as well. Secular middle-class Israelis, however, are more concerned with lower-class and ultra-Orthodox (not to mention Arab) neighbors than with national religious ones. The national religious are considered good neighbors for various reasons, such as their high economic status and their aspiration to coexist peacefully with secular Jews. The threat that I felt was not from Merchav Am's religiosity, but rather from its assumed Gush Emunim ideology of confrontation as expressed by Harel.

The Gush Emunim home is a political and national one meant to achieve a collective goal while providing security for, and ensuring the well-being of, its members. It is conceived as part of a long and mainly tragic history of homes shattered by outside forces and of families destroyed. For Gush Emunim, the personal is the national and the private is the collective. As expressed by Harel, the residents of Merchav Am did not arrive to enjoy the desert surroundings or to construct peaceful neighborly relations with other groups in their vicinity: like the Jews in Hebron or Ofra, they were on a mission, and, for Harel, a true Zionist should never lose touch with national goals. After the partial success and partial failure of the attempt to symbolically transform and reinvent Judea and Samaria, other areas in Israel, perhaps more convenient and inviting, were to follow. Since I define my home (maybe mistakenly, as Harel would claim) as a private one, not constructed in order to push Bedouins out or to Judaize space, I felt that my concept of home was threatened.

Meanwhile, both Harel's hopes and my fears did not materialize, and Merchav Am is well integrated in the region. Not reading *Haaretz*, most Merchav Am residents were unaware of the argument, and, while maintaining their right-wing views and at times expressing them, they did their best to promote friendly relations, and some even found work in the Ben-Gurion Heritage Institute. One of the residents turned to his former neighbors on the pages of *Nekuda*, trying to convince them to join him in the Negev. He enlightened his friends to the fact that the Bedouin issue is complex, and in any case, has little to do with his arrival. In his words,

> Settlement for settlement sake, settlement in order to make the desert bloom, will only do good for religious Zionism, which is often portrayed, regretfully, as settling only in areas of conflict. Widespread religious Zionist settlement in the Negev will prove that religious Zionism settles everywhere, even in the most remote places, out of a true and honest vision of the return of the people of Israel to its land. Sometimes we need to remind ourselves that, although we settle the land in spite of the conflict with the Arabs, we do not settle because of it. (Gotlib 2004, 54)

I was somewhat reassured about my home in the Negev, even though in Israel "home" is always contested territory. The young religious families of Merchav Am went about defining their concept of home between the tradition of Gush Emunim and the demands of the new environment; and Israel Harel went back to his home in Ofra and to his daily struggle for national survival and salvation. Again I received a glimpse of what Gush Emunim's "being at home" means. I could only wish that they could achieve it without "de-settling" and "de-homing" others, both Israelis and Palestinians.

Appendix:
Historical Time Line

1967

June—During the Six-Day War, Israel occupies Eastern Jerusalem, the West Bank, the Golan Heights, the Gaza Strip, and Sinai. The debate over what should be done with these territories commences almost immediately.

September—Kfar Etzion, the first Jewish settlement in the occupied territories, is built.

1968

April—The first Jewish settlers arrive at Hebron to celebrate the Passover and remain in the city.

1970

March—The Israeli Knesset decides to establish Kiryat Arba near Hebron.

1973

October—The Yom Kippur War is fought, leading to a crisis of trust regarding the Israeli government and army, followed by diplomatic negotiations over the future of the occupied territories.

1974

April—Gush Emunim is established as a political movement.

June—The Alon Moreh group makes the first attempt to settle in Samaria.

1975

Yamit, the main town in the Jewish settlement area in northern Sinai, is built.

April—Ofra, a Gush Emunim settlement north of Jerusalem, is established.

December—The eighth attempt to settle in Samaria. The government concedes to the Kadum compromise, allowing the settlers to remain in Samaria.

1977

May—In a political upheaval, Menachem Begin and the Likud Party form a right-wing government. Begin's first statement: "There will be many Alon Morehs."

November—Egypt's president Anwar Sadat visits Jerusalem, and peace talks begin between Egypt and Israel.

1978

November—The Camp David Accords are signed, and Israel commits to withdrawal from Sinai.

1979

April—In Hebron, women from Kiryat Arba enter Beit Hadassah, thus marking the start of the Jewish settlement within the city.

1980

January—Yehoshua Saloma, a yeshiva student in Kiryat Arba, is the first settler there killed by Palestinians.

May—Six settlers are killed in an attack on Beit Hadassah.

June—The first attacks by the Jewish underground injure Palestinian heads of municipalities.

1982

April—Israel's withdrawal from Sinai leads to clashes between the army and the Gush Emunim settlers.

June—The Lebanon War begins.

1984

April—The members of the Jewish underground are caught and brought to trial.

1987

November—The First Intifada begins.

1988

April—A hike by settlers through the Palestinian village of Beita El ends with two Palestinians and one Jewish girl being killed.

1992
June—Yitzhak Rabin and the Labor Party come to power in Israel.

1993
September—Yitzhak Rabin, Yasser Arafat (leader of the Palestine Liberation Organization), and U.S. President Bill Clinton sign the Oslo Accords in Washington, D.C.

1994
February—Baruch Goldstein murders twenty-nine Muslims praying at the Cave of Machpela in Hebron.
March—The first Palestinian suicide attack in Israel occurs in Tel Aviv.

1995
November—Prime Minister Yitzhak Rabin is assassinated.

1996
September—Prime Minister Binyamin Netanyahu decides to open the Western Wall tunnel, and riots ensue throughout the West Bank.

1997
January—The Hebron agreement is signed.

2000
September—The Second Intifada begins.

2003
December—Prime Minister Ariel Sharon presents his plan to evacuate the Jewish settlements from the Gaza Strip unilaterally.

2004
May—The Likud Party holds a plebiscite on the Gaza Strip disengagement plan. Tali Hatuel and her four daughters are murdered.

2005
August—In the disengagement from Gaza and north Samaria, Jewish settlers are evacuated from twenty-two settlements and their villages are destroyed.

Notes

1. Tali Hatuel's grieving parents displayed their disbelief in their daughter's convictions: wishing to visit the graves in safety, they brought the family to be buried in their home city of Ashkelon, not in the Gaza Strip.

2. Israeli "occupied territories" included Sinai and currently the Golan Heights. This book concentrates on Judea, Samaria, and the Gaza Strip because of its focus on Gush Emunim and the ideological settlers. The Sinai settlements are discussed in chapter 10. Israel also occupied and annexed the eastern part of Jerusalem and therefore, technically and morally, that area is seen by many as part of "the occupied territories." The internal Israeli status and social dynamics of these areas are, however, very different and raise a separate set of questions. Therefore, without declaring any political statement, they are not discussed in this book.

3. In concentrating on this group, I follow the work of Gideon Aran, who dubbed them "the Kookists" and claimed convincingly that they possess unique characteristics. He concentrated mainly on the first phases of the movement, which he examined at the time through participant observation. I arrived later, and the group that I focus on is somewhat wider. On the boundaries of the group, see Aran (1991).

4. Again, not counting, as some critical scholars would, the Jewish population in Eastern Jerusalem, numbering approximately another two hundred thousand.

5. For an article of his explaining his position, see Bin-Nun (1992).

6. There is a massive body of work on globalization. For some concluding statements, see della Porta (1999), Guidry, Kennedy, and Zald (2000), Lechner and Boli (2000), and Schuerken (2003).

7. For different conceptualizations of the transformation of Israeli society, see Eisenstadt (1985), Roniger and Feige (1992), and Kimmerling (2001).

8. Published in English. Interestingly, Epstein was a doctoral student of Kimmerling's.

9. For some examples, see Morris (1987), Pappe (1995), Silberstein (1999), and Nimni (2003).

10. The project was published in Hebrew.

11. I have conducted forty interviews of Gush Emunim leaders and followers in total, along with numerous ethnographic interviews.

CHAPTER 1

1. For detailed examples and explanation, see Kimmerling (1984). See also Ram (1999).

2. The interview appeared in the daily newspaper *Maariv,* May 12, 1967.

3. Elaboration of the argument for keeping, annexing, and settling the territories occupied in the Six-Day War can be found in Shimoni (1995) and Naor (2001).

4. This claim was made, for example, by Meron Benvenisti 1995. It is also part of the discussion of Israel—and the 1967 occupied territories—in terms of a colonial project. For example, see Shafir (1985).

5. For the case made by the Israeli peace camp, see Hall-Cathala (1990) and Kaminer (1996).

6. On the importance of the Six-Day War in the movement's ethos, see Aran (1988).

7. On the movement for Greater Israel, see Issak (1976).

8. On Gush Etzion, see Ohana (2002), and, on Hebron, see Feige (2001a) and Neuman (2004). The events of Gush Etzion and Hebron are presented in chapters 7 and 8 of this book.

9. For periodization of Gush Emunim, leading up to the late 1980s, see Aran (1991) and Gorny (1994).

10. On Gush Emunim and the withdrawal from Sinai, see Aran and Feige (1987). See also chapter 10 of this book.

11. The story of the group was told by one of its members (Segal 1988). See also Medoff (1986), Sprinzak (1991), and Garb (2004).

12. The question of settler violence and vigilantism, and especially its connection to democratic principles and commitment, has interested many researchers. See Weisburd (1989), Sprinzak (1993), and Yanovski and Weiman (1998).

13. I discuss the Goldstein massacre in chapter 7 and the implication of the Oslo Accords and the assassination of Rabin in chapter 12.

14. See chapter 6 on the effect of terrorism and chapter 12 on the "youth of the hills."

15. The enrichment of the analysis is also compatible with changes in social movement theory, especially the emergence of the resource mobilization theory. It claims that, although grievances are commonplace at any given time, the opportunity to articulate them in the political field is conditioned on prior organization and resources and should be the main object of research. For some of the main statements of the theory, see Zald and Ash (1966), Tilly (1978), and Jenkins (1983).

16. This point is made most explicitly by Ravitzky (1996).

17. On the figure and writings of Rabbi Kook, see Hertzberg (1975) and Avineri (1981).

18. Ravitzky states his claims in public speeches. His logic is presented in *Messianism, Zionism, and Jewish Religious Radicalism* (1996).

19. The recurrent choice of Ofra of all places is explained in chapter 9. Grossman's book was translated into English; however, I found the translation from Hebrew somewhat lacking and made some alterations.

20. On the national religious soldiers, see Cohen (1997).

21. The group is named Hardalniks, an acronym for National Religious Haredim.

22. On the extreme Right in Israel, see Sprinzak (1991).

23. On this perspective, see Kaminer (1996) and Ophir (2001).

CHAPTER 2

1. Much has been written on the importance of collective memory to Zionism. For example, see Zerubavel (1995), Wistrich and Ohana (1995), and the articles in *Israel Studies* 7, no. 1 (2002).

2. *Nekuda* 59 (1983):17.

3. The literature on nationalism and territoriality is vast. Most important in this respect are the works of Anthony Smith regarding the ethnic origins of the nation. See Smith (1986, 2001) and Guibernau and Hutchinson (2004).

4. Best portrayed by Yerushalmi (1982).

5. On the role of the Bible in the Israeli civil religion, see Liebman and Don-Yehiya (1983) and Aran (1993).

6. On the meaning of exile and its negation in Zionist thought, see Eisen (1986) and Neusner (1988).

7. Don-Yehiya (1993) has written on the negation of the exile in religious Zionism and has devoted some attention to the Gush Emunim case.

8. Quoted in *From Israeli Culture to the Ways of Israel* 1:11, in 1979 in Jerusalem.

9. For further examples of use of the exilic idiom, and especially the memory of the Holocaust, see chapter 7 on Hebron.

10. Much has been written on Israeli myths. For some examples, see the volume edited by Wistrich and Ohana (1995). See also Zerubavel (1995).

11. Kimmerling (1983, 1989) noted the importance of the frontier in both Israel and the United States.

12. "General lines for prayers for Independence Day," *Et Ofra* 123 (1991):1–3.

13. Edna Lomsky-Feder (2004), on the other hand, shows how the war was normalized into the life stories of Israelis. She claims that Israelis expect to participate in combat during their lifetime. Hence, it is usually a less traumatic experience than onlookers believe it to be.

14. Haim Sabato was enraged at Rosenthal's interpretation, in my opinion rightly so. Sabato's book is a rich account of war seen from the standpoint of a religious soldier. Other soldiers attested to their identification with the manner in which Sabato represented the war. Rosenthal's insights, even if not convincing in this case, are quite accurate regarding the war writing of the national religious camp as a whole.

15. Quoted in *Artzi* 3 (1983):5.

16. Quoted in *Artzi* 3 (1983):22–23.

17. I find Shmuel Noah Eisenstadt's (1999) concept of multiple modernities to be of much use here. Eisenstadt claims that clashes between Western modernity and fundamentalism or among various civilizations are actually representations of multiple versions of modernities. Gush Emunim insists on their being modern, and Eisenstadt's formulation questions what is their interpretation is of the concept. In any case, it is still well within the boundaries of the phenomenon.

18. On the fundamentalist enclave and a comparative view of types of fundamentalism, see Almond, Appleby, and Sivan (2003).

Chapter 3

1. On Zionism and territory, see Kimmerling (1983) and Kelleman (1993).

2. On the concept and implementation of the communal village, see Appleboim and Newman (1989).

3. "With Yoel Bin-Nun," *Gushpanka* 26 (1990):8–9.

4. On the question of naming places, changing names, and establishing maps, see Monmenier (1993) and Wood (1993).

5. On naming places in Israel, see Kliot (1996). On the transformation of the map after 1948, see Slymowicz (1998) and Benvenisti (2000).

6. See also Segal and Weizman (2003) and Weizman (2007).

7. This point was also made by author Amos Oz (1983) in his celebrated visit to Ofra.

8. As I detail in chapters 7 and 13, the settlers have resorted to fences in re-action to the growing dangers of Palestinian terrorism.

9. The importance of the desert and the barren land in the Israeli ethos is well acknowledged. Yael Zerubavel (2004) discusses the duality of the desert as a void to be replaced and as a liminal place to be cherished.

10. Dean MacCannell (1973) has made the same point regarding the tourist industry.

11. "Yitzhar—it is not only teachers" (*Shelcha BeAmana* 7 [1989]:11).

CHAPTER 4

1. The literature on the subject in Hebrew is voluminous. For some refer-ences in English, see Kimmerling (1983), Ben-David (1997), and H. Grossman (2004). On archaeology, probably the best researched of these practices, see Liebman and Don-Yehiya (1983).

2. Their responses are attached at the end of his article.

3. The Jews of Hebron, whose story is told in chapter 7, are certain that they have returned to the "right place" and therefore have no reservations about holding *Purim Demukaffin,* with the accord of their rabbis.

4. The issue of the Haredim and archaeology is too complex to discuss here. For example, the Haredim are interested in the research of *mikves* (ritual baths) around Israel to settle halakhic questions.

5. See Yoel Elitzur (1980a) on the case of Beit El and its region.

6. For recent developments in this subject, see El-Or (2002). For further exposition of the question of gender among the settlers, see chapter 11.

7. On Israeli national archaeology, see A. Elon (1994), Silberman (1994), Ben-Yehuda (1995), Zerubavel (1995), Shavit (1997), Feige (2001b), Abu el-Haj (2002), and Hallote and Joffe (2002). On archaeology and nationalism in gen-eral, see Kohl and Fawcett (1995), Diaz-Andreu and Champion (1996), Kohl (1998), and Meskell (1998).

8. For example, see Finkelstein and Silberman (2001). For a much more radical stand, not accepted by Israeli scholars, see Whitelam (1996).

9. On the presentation of archaeology within the annual meetings of the Israeli Exploration Society, see Feige (2001b).

10. On this historical phenomenon, see Silberman (1982).

11. Zelkin is a resident of Efrat, a large town in the Gush Etzion region.

12. An interesting comparison can be made with Yigael Yadin's excavation of Masada, where, according to Nachman Ben-Yehuda (2001), he manipulated the facts to fit the myth.

13. This sentence is taken from the volume of abstracts from the conference.

14. The unique Israeli idiom of *gibbush* has been analyzed by Tamar Katriel (1988).

15. The quote is taken from a letter published in the Samaria council bulletin *Mirosh Hahar* (From the Top of the Mountain) 35, no. 16 (1993). The information disclosed was based on Erlich (1987).

16. Typically, left-wing speakers will not enter into discussion with the settlers regarding the actual historical evidence. Their claim, as expressed in one of Peace Now's slogans, was that the lives of the children are more important than the graves of the Patriarchs, and therefore the discussion as to the exact location of Joseph's Tomb is irrelevant.

17. *Lecha Beamana* (Yours in Amana; the bulletin of Amana, the Gush Emunim settlement organization) 14–15 (1991):12.

Chapter 5

1. On the Palestinian peasant as a national symbol, see Sweedenburg (1990).

2. On the Arabs in Zionist ideology, see Yadgar (2003).

3. The Israeli Arabs number currently about one million. They received citizenship right after the establishment of the state. On their history, situation, and identity issues, see Rabinowitz (1997) and Yiftachel (2000).

4. On the theory of Israeli ethnocracy, see Yiftachel (2006).

5. It is interesting to note that the support of a "Jewish majority" was first presented by Yitzhak Rabin himself, and later strengthened in the election campaign of Ehud Barak, both leaders of the Labor Party.

6. The Palestinians have described their battle in Jenin, in which they claimed that the Israeli Defense Forces committed a massacre, as "Jeningrad" (after Stalingrad) and as their Masada or Warsaw Ghetto revolt. Thus, they have appropriated Israeli myths to tell their side of the story to the world.

7. *BaMachane,* April 20, 1999.

Chapter 6

1. "David Rosenfeld, Eli Presman," *Nekuda* 45 (1982):2.

2. On Jewish vigilantism, see Weisburd and Vinitzky (1984) and Weisburd (1989).

3. On the Jewish underground, see Medoff (1986), Segal (1988), and Garb (2004).

4. These figures and the following ones are taken from a special issue of the daily newspaper *Haaretz,* September 26, 2003, dedicated to the cost of the settlements. On the numbers and the stories of the dead in terrorist actions, presented from the viewpoint of the settlers, see the "Israeli War Against Terror" Web site, www.israel-wat.com/parent_eng.htm.

5. The name mimics the formal name given to the Lebanon War: the War for the Peace of Galilee. On the Israeli Left and the Second Intifada, see Ophir (2001).

6. The event usually mentioned is the *Yizkor* book of 1911 dedicated to the dead of the Second Aliya.

7. On the Akeda and the Israeli ethos of sacrifice, see Sivan (1991) and Miron (1992).

8. "In memory of Rabbi Biran: so we can tell our children," *Yours in Amana* 21 (1992):12.

9. The story of Chomesh, including the citations, is taken from Nadav Shragai, "Once this was heaven," *Haaretz*, July 23, 2004. See also Dolev (2003).

CHAPTER 7

1. For a written history of the Jewish new settlements of Hebron and Kiryat Arba, see Segal (1988). For two accounts in Hebrew, see Sharvit (1985) and Huberman (2002b).

2. "An interview with Rabanit Levinger," *Hevruta* 3 (1986):27.

3. "Is Kiryat Arba the same as Hebron?" *Hevruta* 3 (1986):12.

4. "Purity in the Cave," *Hevruta* 4 (1986):19.

5. *Yediot Hamatnas* [bulletin], 1988.

6. The literature on this subject is vast. For two examples, see Weingrod (1990) and Ben-Ari and Bilu (1997).

7. *Haaretz*, June 18, 2004.

8. For a detailed account of the events of Tarpat, see Segev (2001).

9. *Haaretz*, May 28, 1979.

10. *Hevruta* 8 (1986).

11. *Yedion* 62 (1989).

12. For several examples among many, see Don-Yehiya (1993), Segev (1993), and Feldman (2002).

13. For some time, the soldiers guarded the entrance to the Jewish section of Hebron from a high post called the Eagle's Nest. The Jewish residents demanded that the name be changed because it reminded them the name of Hitler's fortress in the Alps. After the soldiers were informed of the meaning of the name, they changed it to one more favorable to the settlers: the Shield of Abraham.

14. *The words of the women of Hadassah* [pamphlet], 1979, 134.

15. *Maariv*, Passover edition, 1969.

16. *Nekuda* 17 (1980).

17. *Hevruta* 3 (1986).

18. Ehud Ashri, *Haaretz*, December 25, 2005.

19. *Nekuda* 69 (1984).

20. *Hevruta* 3 (1986).

21. For the use of these terms in anthropology, see Herzfeld (1991).

22. *Nekuda* 177 (1994):23.

23. *Nekuda* 176 (1994):60.

24. In the terms formulated by Turner (1978).

25. An analysis of the symbolic aspects of the Goldstein massacre was suggested by Paine (1995a).

CHAPTER 8

1. For the history of the return to Gush Etzion, I depended greatly on Ohana (2002). For a historical account by one of residents of Kfar Etzion, see Ben-Ya'akov (1998).

2. David Ben-Gurion, "Gathering of released prisoners," March 29, 1949, Ben-Gurion Archive, Sede Boker. The full citation can be found in Ohana (2002, 148).

3. Abba Eban, introduction to Knohl (1952, 11–12).

4. The event is described in Huberman (2002a, 35).

5. This point is enhanced by the demographic realities within the space of the Gush. Similar to other Jewish settlements within the Gush Emunim project, the remembrance of Jewish history entails the *forgetting* of Arab past and present. Not unlike the Hebron case, in the eyes of the Gush Etzion settlers the local Arabs, through their violence against the former peaceful Jewish community, have lost any legitimacy they had to the place. Ironically, among the Gush Etzion villages, an Arab village called Beit Iskaria was left. The name, given to the village by the local Arabs, commemorates the biblical prophet Zechariah, who the local Arabs believe is buried there—a belief that is not shared by the Jews. However, in this rare reversal of fortunes, the Jewish settlers base their legitimacy on recent history, whereas the Palestinians have a village named after a biblical figure.

6. "A lighthouse of Torah and work: Some questions for Hanan Porat," *Gush-panka* 43 (1992):15.

7. See the Gush Etzion Web site, www.gush-etzion.org.il.

CHAPTER 9

1. On the history of Ofra, see Huberman (2002c).

2. Yehuda Etzion was one of the leaders and intellectual inspirations, Haggai Segal was a participant and wrote the book on the group (*Dear Brothers*, 1988), and his then neighbor in Ofra, Rabbi Yoel Bin-Nun, was the one to oppose the group most strongly.

3. *Et Ofra* 68 (1986).

4. *Et Ofra* 69 (1986):7.

5. The question dealt with the permissibility of wearing trousers rather than a long skirt, and whether married women may appear in public without a hat or other head covering.

6. *Et Ofra* 87 (1986):10.

7. *Et Ofra* 136 (1992):1

8. On fundamentalism and humor, see Aran (1995).

9. *Et Ofra* 107 (1990):15–16.

10. *Et Ofra* 111 (1990):19.

11. *Et Ofra* 71 (1986):18.

12. *Et Ofra* 101 (1989):22.

13. *Et Ofra* 161 (1995):27.

14. *Et Ofra* 139 (1993):26–27.

15. A term coined by Bellah (1967) and applied to Israel by Liebman and Don-Yehiya (1983).

16. Since then, another major ceremony was held, making Ofra's twenty-fifth anniversary.

17. I used two sources for this and the next citations: the original manuscript of the pageant and the actual performance, which I taped. For the rare discrepancy, I preferred the taped information.

CHAPTER 10

1. The history of the struggle was presented mainly in books in Hebrew by participants in the movement (Segal 1999). For a sociological account, also in Hebrew, see Aran (1985). For various aspects of the withdrawal, see the *Journal of Applied Behavioral Science* 23, no. 1 (1987), and, on the movement itself, Aran and Feige (1987).

2. When he reached power, Prime Minister Menachem Begin stated that, after he retired, he wished to reside in one of the Yamit region settlements. To his embarrassment, he was often reminded of his declaration.

3. On the question of Zionist reversal in Yamit, see Kimmerling (1987).

4. See *Nekuda* 41 (March 1982). The picture on the cover is of Benni Katzover, leader of the movement, working in a field, and the caption reads "There will not be a withdrawal."

5. On the crucial role of the media in Sinai, see Wolfsfeld (1984).

6. See *Nekuda* 59 (1982).

7. "The vows that we made," *Nekuda* 86 (1995):5.

8. The line was taken from a famous poem by Yitzhak Lamdan (1927).

9. *Nekuda* 72 (1994).

10. "Shvut Sinai," *Nekuda* 43 (1982):21.

11. The document is cited in Segal (1999, 7).

12. Edna Pe'er, "Attentive ear, from the journal of a broadcaster," *Maariv*, February 19, 1982.

13. This claim resurfaced numerous times in Israeli history, including in the wake of the withdrawal from Lebanon and during the deliberations over retreating from the Gaza Strip.

14. On the meanings of the desert in the Israeli ethos, especially as liminal space, see Zerubavel (2004).

15. This point was developed by Aran (1985).

16. *Nekuda* 250 (2004), an issue dedicated to commemorate twenty years after the withdrawal from Yamit (p. 35).

CHAPTER 11

1. On fundamentalism and gender, see Hardacre (1993) and Hawley (1994).

2. On the concept of "republican woman," see Yuval-Davis (1997).

3. Bambi Sheleg, "Children are happiness, but so is a career," *Kol Hair*, October 21, 1994.

4. The issue of Rechalim and feminism is discussed in El-Or and Aran (1995). For another examination of the gender issue in the settlements, see Neuman (2004).

5. Near Rachel Druk's home village of Shiloh, a new neighborhood was built, later becoming a distinct settlement. Its name is Shvut Rachel (the Return of Rachel). Once again, rather than commemorating their actual friend, the settlers chose to connect to the mythical Rachel.

6. More probably, she could have "received" a neighborhood named after her within a settlement.

CHAPTER 12

1. On the Sabra generation, see Almog (2000).

2. On the transformation of the kibbutz society, see Ben-Rafael (1997).

3. Yet it is also currently appearing among ultra-Orthodox youth.

4. Aviv Lavi, "When Ran gets angry," *Haaretz*, March 19, 1994.

5. Jakob (Jackie) Levi, "This is how I stopped to fear and started to love the youth of the hills," *Yediot Aharonot*, April 26, 2004.

6. Chen Bram, "Walking the land: The footsteps of the youth of the hills." Paper presented at the Israeli Sociological Association Meeting, Beit Berl, February 4, 2003.

7. *Haaretz*, September 26, 2003, 63

8. Levi, "This is how I stopped."

CHAPTER 13

1. See chapter 2.

2. While a few left-wing activists have reconsidered their position, most have maintained their convictions. They blame the settlers for the collapse of the Oslo Accords, and some see the Second Intifada as an Israeli struggle to keep the set-

tlements. They have promoted new peace initiatives in collaboration with Palestinian leaders in an attempt to demonstrate the possibility of advancing on the basis of the Oslo Accords. However, the peace camp has indeed entered a prolonged crisis after Oslo, when its cause was adopted by Israeli government. Thus, after the agreement's collapse, the peace camp was considered as holding misguided assumptions regarding their possible peace partners.

3. For a discussion of the adaptations from the settlers' perspective, see Shvut (2002b).

4. The same argument followed other violent events such as the actions of the Jewish underground and the massacre committed by Baruch Goldstein in Hebron (see Segal 1988).

5. *Hatzofe*, November 6 1995. For a broad presentation of the different perspectives in the national religious camp, see Sorek (2004).

6. Shlomo Filber (1995) suggested such a theory. According to his interpretation, the agency in charge of Rabin's safety wanted to simulate an assassination of the prime minister in order to turn the public against the Right. They used Raviv, who was supposed to lure Amir into perpetrating this act while the bullets in Amir's gun were replaced with blanks, but for some reason the second part of the plan failed. Based on his analysis of the behavior of the security men after the assassination, Filber claimed to have found circumstantial evidence for his theory.

7. In "Document: Soul-searching conference," *Nekuda* 190 (1995):61.

8. Before the assassination, Bar Ilan University used the picture of its student Yigael Amir in a public relations booklet and neglected to remove the picture afterward. This was, in all probability, an honest mistake. It is, however, noticeable that before the assassination Amir was considered a representative figure and a notable success by the religious university.

9. In Shlomit Baum, "Our public is not to blame," *Hatzofe*, December 8, 1995. He referred to the murder of peace activist Emil Grunzweig in 1983, the Goldstein massacre, and the Rabin assassination.

10. In "Document: Soul-searching conference," 59.

11. For other discussions of Rabin's commemoration, see Feige (2000) and Peri (2000).

12. Note that the first editor of *Nekuda*, Israel Harel, stepped down at the same time.

13. The El-Aqsa Intifada has not yet been comprehensively researched and placed in historical perspective. The first Israeli book on the subject was *The Seventh War* (2004), by Harel and Isacharoff.

14. The meaning of the wall to the Palestinians is discussed in Lagerquist (2004).

15. On the struggle and its inner paradoxes, see Roth (2005).

16. Another Israeli social group that uses the Holocaust metaphor freely is the more extreme of the Haredim (ultra-Orthodox), who place the enlightenment,

secularization, mass consumption, the Nazi Holocaust, and Zionism in the same historical basket. In their worldview, whereas the Nazis destroyed the Jewish body, Jewish nationalism has destroyed the spirit and soul.

17. *Beahava Ube'emunah* [In Love and Belief], 518, 2005 (a pamphlet distributed at synagogues).

18. Noam Seri, *Haaretz* Review of Books, August 2005, 2.

19. Hanoch Daum, "Entrance," *Hatzofe,* April 2, 2004.

20. He lamented that the yeshivas put too much emphasis on studying the Gemara rather than on other texts or on their students' creativity; the hostility confronted by religious feminism; the lack of popular support for the religious members of Knesset, whom, he claimed, are the most industrious and efficient in Israeli Parliament; the disdain for and mistrust of mass communication; the difficulty for single women to find husbands in a community that creates separate educational frameworks; the accelerated creation of new educational frameworks at the expense of older ones; the lack of consumption of the modern culture increasingly created by religious artists; and the militaristic admiration of generals and the army.

21. On Israeli society during its formative years, see Eisenstadt (1967) and Horowitz and Lissak (1978).

22. On the connection between the peace initiatives and Israel's changing economy, see Shafir and Peled (2000).

23. On the freier, see Roniger and Feige (1992).

24. On fundamentalism today, see Marty and Appleby (1991, 1992), Armstrong (2000), and Almond, Appleby, and Sivan (2003).

25. *Yediot Aharonot,* July 30, 2004.

26. Israel Harel, "There is nothing finer than your modest holiday," *Haaretz,* November 8, 2001.

27. Michael Feige, "Yesha is there, not here," *Haaretz,* November 18, 2001.

References

WORKS IN HEBREW

Appleboim, Levia, and David Newman. 1989. *Between village and suburb: New forms of settlements in Israel.* Rehovot: Center for Rural and Urban Settlement.

Aran, Gideon. 1985. *The Land of Israel between religion and politics: The movement to stop the withdrawal from Sinai.* Jerusalem: Jerusalem Institute for Israel Studies.

———. 1987. *From religious Zionism to Zionist religion: The roots and culture of Gush Emunim.* PhD diss., Hebrew University of Jerusalem.

Arend, Aharon. 1998. *Research chapters about Independence Day.* Ramat Gan: Bar Ilan University Press.

Ariel, Israel. 1988. *The Land of Israel border atlas according to halakhic sources.* Jerusalem: Cana.

Arzieli, Dvorah. 1987. Look for the woman. *Nekuda* 154:24–25.

Aviezer, Yishai, ed. 1985. *The Book of Haggai.* Kiryat Arba-Hebron: Haggai Foundation.

Aviner, Shlomo. 1980. Killing the Messiah Ben-Yosef. *Nekuda* 11:10–11.

———. 1990. *Shu't* [Questions and answers] *intifada.* Beit El.

Avisar, Oded, ed. 1970. *The Book of Hebron.* Jerusalem: Keter.

Azaryahu, Maoz. 1995. *State cults: Celebrating independence and commemorating the fallen in Israel—1948–1956.* Sede Boker Campus: Ben-Gurion Research Center.

Be'er, Haim. 1982. Gush Emunim: Canaanites who wear phylacteries. *Davar,* October 15, 1982.

Ben-Pazi, Rina, ed. 1988. *Like in the beginning.* Beit El.

Ben-Ya'akov, Yohanan, ed. 1978. *Gush Etzion: Fifty years of struggle and creativity.* Alon-Shvut: Yad Shapira.

———. 1998. The sons have returned to their place. *Gushpanka* 7:12.

Benvenisti, Meron. 1992. The wretchedness of academia. *Haaretz*, April 10, 1992.

Benvenisti, Meron, ed. 2002. *The morning after: The era of peace—No utopia.* Jerusalem: Carmel.

Be'ri, Rabbi Dan. 1985. Autonomy to the land of Israel Arabs. *Nekuda* 87:10–11.

Bin-Nun, Yoel. 1985. The altar on Mt. Ebal. In *Before Efraim, Binyamin, and Menashe,* ed. Ze'ev Ehrlich, 137–62. Ofra.

———. 1992. We have not settled in the hearts. *Nekuda* 158:30–31.

———. 1994. Interview in *Thinking it over: Conflicts in Israeli public thought,* by Yona Hadari-Ramage, 84–109. Ramat Efa'al: Yad Tabenkin.

Deutch, Hayuta. 2002. Two keys, one gate. *Nekuda* 255:60.

Dolev, Meira. 2001. The house in Alon Moreh. *Nekuda* 251:2–3.

———. 2003. A settlement at the edge. *Nekuda* 260:30–39.

Elitzur, Yoel. 1980a. When Purim should be celebrated in Beit El and the army camps around it. *Tehumin* 1:109–19.

———. 1980b. Those are the names. *Nekuda* 10:3–12.

———. 1982. Is Lebanon also the Land of Israel? *Nekuda* 48:10–13.

———. 1985. Those are the names: Correct names for the holy places in the land of Israel as a Zionist mission. In *Before Efraim, Binyamin, and Menashe,* ed. Ze'ev Ehrlich, 19–22. Ofra.

———. 1988. The time of Purim in the city of Lod. *Tehumin* 9:367–80.

Elitzur, Uri. 1982. A promise in front of the ruins. *Nekuda* 43:20–22.

———. 2003. Migron and Hertzelia. *Nekuda* 267:3.

Elon, Emuna. 1988. *Fatchi's treasure.* Beit El.

Erlich, Ze'ev. 1987. The Tomb of Joseph. *Judea and Samaria* 1:153–62.

Erlich, Ze'ev, ed. 1985. *Before Efraim, Binyamin, and Menashe.* Ofra.

Eshel, Ya'akov. 1992. The wells of hatred. *Nekuda* 158:7–9.

Feige, Michael. 1996. *Social movements, hegemony and political myth: A comparative study of Gush Emunim and Peace Now.* PhD diss., Hebrew University of Jerusalem.

———. 2000. Yitzhak Rabin: His commemoration and the commemoration of his commemoration. In *Contested memory: Myth, nation and democracy,* ed. Lev Grinberg, 39–64. Beer Sheva: Humphrey Institute for Social Research.

———. 2002. *One space, two places: Gush Emunim, Peace Now and the construction of Israeli space.* Jerusalem: Magnes.

Filber, Shlomo. 1995. Demo bullets. *Nekuda* 190:11–14.

Filber, Ya'akov. 1989. *The morning light* [Ayelet HaShahar]. Jerusalem: Rabbi Kook Institute.

Fruman, Menachem. 1993. Only men of truth, men of religion, can settle the conflict. *Nekuda* 165:40–43.

Garb, Yoni. 2004. Messianism, antinomism and power in religious Zionism: The case of the "Jewish underground." In *The religious Zionism: An era of change—Studies in memory of Zvulun Hamer,* ed. Asher Cohen and Israel Harel, 323–63. Jerusalem: Bialik Institute.

Goldberg, Giora, and Efraim Ben-Zadok. 1983. Regionalism and a territorial rift: Jewish settlement in occupied territories. *State, Government and International Relations* [Medina, Mimshal VeYechasim Beinleumim] 21:69–94.

Gomeh, Nili. 1988. And they shall no longer be taken from their land. *Amudim* 438.

Gotlib, Daniel. 2004. Come to the Negev as well. *Nekuda* 272:53–55.

Gutman, Irit. 1992. The attitudes and functioning of children in Samaria in the context of their level of exposure to violence. *Research of Judea and Samaria* 2:377–87.

Hantshke, David. 1996. The eternity of Israel is not reliant on the eternity of Zionism. *Nekuda* 188:28–30.

Harel, Amos, and Avi Isacharoff. 2004. *The seventh war.* Tel Aviv: Yidioth Ahronoth.

Hareven, Shulamit. 1977. Sociological model against reality. *In the Diaspora* [Bitfutzot HaGola] 79/80:104–8.

Harnoi, Meir. 1995. *The settlers.* Jerusalem: Maariv.

Heskin, Arie. 2004. Define the eastern fence. *Nekuda* 269:74–76.

Huberman, Haggai. 2002a. Kfar Etzion: Pioneer of settlement in Judea and Samaria. In *Ascent to the mountain: Renewal of Jewish settlement in Judea and Samaria,* ed. Avraham Shvut, 31–36. Beit El.

———. 2002b. Kiryat Arba-Hebron: Pioneers of urban settlement in Judea and Samaria—Erasing the shame of Tarpat. In *Ascent to the Mountain: Renewal of Jewish Settlement in Judea and Samaria,* ed. Avraham Shvut, 37–46. Beit El.

———. 2002c. Ofra from a working village to a settlement. In *Ascent to the mountain: Renewal of Jewish settlement in Judea and Samaria,* ed. Avraham Shvut, 61–66. Beit El.

Kedar, Mira. 1999. *Back and forth.* Jerusalem: Keter.

———. 2002. Clouded mirror. *Nekuda* 252:48–49.

Kehat, Hannah. 2001. Woman's status and Torah studies in the Orthodox society. In *Will you listen to my voice? Representations of women in Israeli culture,* ed. Yael Etzmon, 355–64. Jerusalem: Kibbutz Meuhad and Van-Leer.

Kimmerling, Baruch. 2003. Sociology in crisis. *Sociology: Bulletin of the Israeli Sociological Association* 28:1–2.

Kniel, Shlomo. 2004. The settlers of the hill: The biblical sabra? A pilot study of the hill settlers in Judea and Samaria. In *The religious Zionism: An era of change—Studies in memory of Zvulun Hamer,* ed. Asher Cohen and Israel Harel, 533–58. Jerusalem: Bialik Institute.

Knohl, Dov. 1952. *Siege in the hills of Hebron.* Jerusalem: Jewish Agency.

Lamdan, Yitzhak. 1927. *Masada.* Tel Aviv: Hedim.

Maudlinger, Moshe. 1987. *The Land of Shekhem.* Alon Moreh: Itzuv Shalem and Midreshet Shomron.

Melamed, Z. 1988. A new stage in the redemption process. *Nekuda* 119:10–11.

Miron, Dan. 1992. *Facing the silent brother: Essays on the poetry of the War of Independence.* Jerusalem: Keter.

Naor, A. 1988. From Chmielnitzki to Beita. *Nekuda* 120:16.

Naor, Arie. 2001. *Greater Israel: Theology and policy.* Haifa: Haifa University Press and Zmora-Bitan.

Odea, Janet. 1977. Gush Emunim: Roots and ambivalence. *In the Diaspora* [Bitfutzot HaGola] 79/80:95–103.

Ophir, Adi, ed. 2001. *Real time: Al-Aqsa Intifada and the Israeli Left.* Jerusalem: Keter.

Ortner, Nathan. 1988. Purim in the city of Lod. *Tehumin* 9:341–66.

Pinchas-Cohen, Chava. 1996. There the end meets the beginning. *Nekuda* 188: 42–43, 66.

Porat, Hanan. 1975. Eye in eye they shall see the return of the Lord to Zion. *Ptachim* 32:3–12.

———. 1988. *I am looking for Anat.* Beit El.

Ravitzky, Aviezer. 1991. Place markers for Zion: The evolution of an idea. In *The land of Israel in medieval Jewish thought,* ed. Moshe Halamish and Aviezer Ravitzky, 1–39. Jerusalem: Yad Ben-Zvi.

Reichner, Elyashiv. 2001a. Drugs in the settlements. *Nekuda* 250:58–64.

———. 2001b. Settling in the Negev. *Nekuda* 247:26–33.

Rosen, Rabbi Yosef. 1974. *Sacred sights in the mirror of the old sages* [Chazal]. Jerusalem: Zur Ot.

Rosenthal, Robik. 2001. Three war diaries. *New Land* [Eretz Hadasha] 3:40–47.

Roth, Anat. 2005. *The secret of its strength: The Yesha Council and its campaign against the security fence and the disengagement plan.* Jerusalem: Israeli Democracy Institute.

Sabato, Haim. 1999. *Teum kavanot* [Adjusting sights]. Tel Aviv: Yediot Aharonot.

Sade, Liav. 2000. *Ein HaBsor as a memorial community to the Sinai settlements.* Master's thesis, Ben-Gurion University.

Salmon, Yosef. 2004. Renew our days as of old: A Zionist myth. In *Myths in Judaism,* ed. Ithamar Gruenwald and Moshe Idel, 207–22. Jerusalem: Zalman Shazar Center for Jewish History.

Segal, Haggai. 1992. *Demo settlement.* Beit El.

———. 1999. *Yamit, the end: The struggle to stop the withdrawal in Sinai.* Beit El.

Schwartz, Dov. 1997. *The land of reality and imagination.* Tel Aviv: Am Oved.

Shafat, Gershon. 1995. *Gush Emunim: The story behind the scenes.* Beit El.

Shafran, Dvir. 2002. We the youth of the hills. *Nekuda* 257:18–27.

Sharvit, Yosef. 1985. The history of the new settlement in Hebron. In *Book of Haggai,* ed. Yishai Aviezer, 145–78. Kiryat Arba: Haggai Foundation and Nir Kiryat Arba Yeshiva.

Sheleg, Bambi. 2001. The new women of Torah. In *The inner split,* ed. Robik Rosenthal, 142–53. Tel Aviv: Yediot Aharonot.

Sheleg, Yair. 1986. Achieving rest [Hamenucha VeHaNachala]. *Nekuda* 94:19.

———. 2000. *The new religious Jews: Recent developments among observant Jews in Israel.* Jerusalem: Keter.

Shenkar, Yael. 2004. We have no creators: A national religious community constructs its artists. In *The religious Zionism: An era of change—Studies in memory of Zvulun Hamer,* ed. Asher Cohen and Israel Harel, 283–322. Jerusalem: Bialik Institution.

Shilat, Rabbi Ya'akov. 1999. Bitter feminism is the enemy of the Halakha. *Panim* 11:135.

Shilat, Rabbi Yitzhak. 1988. The fear to use force comes from moral weakness. *Nekuda* 119:48–49.

Shvut, Avraham. 2002a. The temporal center as an element in the process of settlement development in Judea and Samaria. In *Ascent to the mountain: Renewal of Jewish settlement in Judea and Samaria,* ed. Avraham Shvut, 175–83. Beit El.

———. 2002b. The Jewish settlement in Judea and Samaria facing the Oslo process. In *Ascent to the mountain: Renewal of Jewish settlement in Judea and Samaria,* ed. Avraham Shvut, 189–96. Beit El.

Simon, Moshe. 1986. The State of Israel is alienated to the Land of Israel. *Nekuda* 100:44–45.

Sivan, Emmanuel. 1991. *The 1948 generation: Myth, profile and memory.* Tel Aviv: Ma'rachot.

Smooha, Sami. 1986. Four models and another model. *Politika* 15:61–63.

Sorek, Yoav. 1997. A window the Mediterranean Sea. *Nekuda* 208:74–75.

———. 2002. There is no place for two people. *Nekuda* 256:42–43.

———. 2004. A shattering moment: National Zionism confronts Rabin's assassination. In *The religious Zionism: An era of change—Studies in memory of Zvulun Hamer,* ed. Asher Cohen and Israel Harel, 457–532. Jerusalem: Bialik Institute.

Yanovski, Yitzhak, and Gabriel Weiman. 1998. Lines in Nekuda: Settlers attitudes to democracy and law in Israel in the settlers' newspaper *Nekuda. Megamot* 39:191–215.

Yefet, Eric. 2005. *On miracles: Stories from Gush Katif.* Nezarim.

Yishai, Yael. 1996. Woman of force and woman of sword. In *State and religion in Israel,* ed. Dana Arieli-Horowitz, 53–84. Jerusalem: Center for Jewish Pluralism.

Waldman, Rabbi Eliezer. 1980. The song of Joshua. *Nekuda* 4:3.

Wasserman, Rabbi Abraham. 2001. Defense against settlement. *Nekuda* 249:54–55.

Weiss, Daniella. 1986. 3650 days of struggle and construction. *Nekuda* 120:37.

Weiss, Hillel. 1994. Secular Zionism is departing from Masada (and from Zionism). *Nekuda* 178:45–46.

Weizman, Eyal, and Rafi Segal. 2002. The mountain settlements: Principles of building in heights. *Studio Art Magazine* 134:44–53.

Zelkin, Mordechai. 1994. With the book: The study of Judea and Samaria. *Kathedra* 71:150–54.

Zerubavel, Yael. 2004. The wilderness as a mythical space and as a memorial site in Hebrew culture. In *Myths in Judaism,* ed. Ithamar Gruenwald and Moshe Idel, 223–36. Jerusalem: Zalman Shazar Center for Jewish History.

Zeruya, Chaim. 1980. The right to hate. *Nekuda* 15:12.

Zilberkland, Orli. 2002. We have an abusive father. *Nekuda* 254:36–40.

WORKS IN ENGLISH

Abu el-Haj, Nadia. 2002. *Facts on the ground: Archaeological practice and territorial self-fashioning in Israeli society.* Chicago: University of Chicago Press.

Almog, Oz. 2000. *The sabra: The creation of the new Jew.* Berkeley: University of California Press.

Almond, Gabriel A., R. Scott Appleby, and Emmanuel Sivan. 2003. *Strong religion: The rise of fundamentalism around the world.* Chicago: University of Chicago Press.

Aran, Gideon. 1986. The beginning of the road from religious Zionism to Zionist religion. *Studies in Contemporary Jewry* 2:402–28.

———. 1988. A mystic-messianic interpretation of modern Israeli history: The Six-Day War as a key event in the development of the original religious culture of Gush Emunim. *Studies in Contemporary Judaism* 4:263–75.

———. 1991. Jewish Zionist fundamentalism: The bloc of the faithful in Israel. In *Fundamentalism observed,* ed. Martin E. Marty and R. Scott Appleby, 265–344. Chicago: University of Chicago Press.

———. 1993. Return to the scripture in modern Israel. *Bibliothèque de l'Ecole des Hautes Etudes, Section des Sciences Religieuses* 99:101–31.

———. 1995. What's so funny about fundamentalism? In *Fundamentalisms comprehended,* ed. Martin E. Marty and R. Scott Appleby, 321–53. Chicago: University of Chicago Press.

Aran, Gideon, and Michael Feige. 1987. The movement to stop the withdrawal in Sinai: A sociological perspective. *Journal of Applied Behavioral Science* 23:73–88.

Armstrong, Karen. 2000. *The battle for God.* New York: Ballantine.

Aronoff, Myron J. 1986. Establishing authority: The memorialization of Jabotinsky and the burial of the Bar Kokhba bones in Israel under the Likud. In *The frailty of authority,* ed. Myron J. Aronoff. New Brunswick, NJ: Transaction.

Aviad, Janet. 1991. The messianism of Gush Emunim. *Studies in Contemporary Jewry* 7:197–213.

Avineri, Shlomo. 1981. *The making of modern Zionism: The intellectual origins of the Jewish State.* New York: Basic.

Barber, Benjamin R. 1995. *Jihad vs. McWorld.* New York: Times.

Bellah, Robert N. 1967. Civil religion in America. *Daedalus* 96:1–21.

Ben-Ari, Eyal, and Yoram Bilu. 1997. Saints' sanctuaries in Israeli development towns: On a mechanism of urban transformation. In *Grasping land: Space and place in contemporary Israeli discourse and experience,* ed. Eyal Ben-Ari and Yoram Bilu, 61–84. Albany: State University of New York Press.

Ben-David, Orit. 1997. Tiyul (Hike) as an act of consecration of space. In *Grasping land: Space and place in contemporary Israeli discourse and experience,* ed. Eyal Ben-Ari and Yoram Bilu, 129–46. Albany: State University of New York.

Ben-Rafael, Eliezer. 1997. *Crisis and transformation: The kibbutz at century's end.* Albany: State University of New York Press.

Ben-Yehuda, Nachman. 1995. *The Masada myth: Collective memory and myth-making in Israel.* Madison: University of Wisconsin Press.

———. 2001. *Betrayal and treason: Violation of trust and loyalty.* Boulder, CO: Westview.

Benvenisti, Meron. 1995. *Intimate enemies: Jews and Arabs in a shared land.* Berkley: University of California Press.

———. 2000. *Sacred landscape: The buried history of the Holy Land since 1948.* Berkeley: University of California Press.

Berger, Peter. 1979. *The heretical imperative: Contemporary possibilities of religious affirmation.* Garden City, NY: Anchor.

Berman, Marshall. 1982. *All that is solid melts into air: The experience of modernity.* New York: Simon and Schuster.

Castels, Manuel. 1996. *The rise of the network society.* Malden, MA: Blackwell.

Cohen, Stuart A. 1997. *The scroll or the sword? Dilemmas of religion and military service in Israel.* London: Harwood.

Connerton, Paul. 1989. *How societies remember.* Cambridge: Cambridge University Press.

della Porta, Donatella, Haspeter Kriesi, and Dieter Rucht, eds. 1999. *Social movements in a globalizing world.* New York: St. Martin's.

Diaz-Andreu, Margarita, and Timothy Champion, eds. 1996. *Nationalism and archaeology in Europe.* Boulder, CO: Westview.

Don-Yehiya, Eliezer. 1992. The negation of galut in religious Zionism. *Modern Zionism* 12:129–55.

———. 1993. Memory and political culture: Israeli society and the Holocaust. *Studies in Contemporary Jewry* 9:139–62.

Eisen, Arnold M. 1986. *Galut: Modern Jewish reflections on homelessness and homecoming.* Bloomington: Indiana University Press.

Eisenstadt, Shmuel Noah. 1967. *Israeli society.* London: Weidenfeld and Nicolson.

———. 1985. *The transformation of Israeli society: An essay in interpretation.* London: Weidenfeld and Nicolson.

———. 1999. *Fundamentalism, sectarianism and revolution: The Jacobin dimension of modernity.* Cambridge Cultural Social Studies. Cambridge: Cambridge University Press.

Elon, Amos. 1994. Politics and archaeology. *New York Review of Books,* September 22, 1994, 14–18.

El-Or, Tamar. 2002. *Next year I will know more: Literacy and identity among young orthodox women in Israel.* Detroit: Wayne State University Press.

El-Or, Tamar, and Gideon Aran. 1995. Giving birth to a settlement. *Gender and Society* 9:60–78.

Epstein, Alek D. 2004. The decline of Israeli sociology. *Azure* 16:78–108.

Feige, Michael. 2001a. Jewish settlement of Hebron: The place and the other. *GeoJournal* 53:323–33.

———. 2001b. Identity, ritual and pilgrimage: The meetings of the Israeli Exploration Society. In *Divergent Jewish cultures,* ed. Deborah Dash Moore and S. Ilan Troen, 87–106. New Haven: Yale University Press.

Feldman, Jackie. 2002. Marking the boundaries of the enclave: Defining the Israeli collective through the Poland "experience." *Israeli Studies* 7:84–114.

Finkelstein, Israel, and Neil Asher Silberman. 2001. *The Bible unearthed: Archaeology's new vision of ancient Israel and the origin of its sacred texts.* New York: Free Press.

Friedman, Thomas L. 2000. *The Lexus and the olive tree.* New York: Farrar, Straus and Giroux.

Giddens, Anthony. 1990. *The consequences of modernity.* Stanford: Stanford University Press.

Goffman, Erving. 1959. *The presentation of self in everyday life.* New York: Doubleday Anchor.

Gorny, Yosef. 1994. *The State of Israel in Jewish public thought: The quest for collective identity.* New York: New York University Press.

Gramsci, Antonio. 1971. *Selections from the prison notebook.* London: Lawrence and Wishart.

Grossman, David. 1988. *The yellow wind.* Translated from the Hebrew by Haim Watzman. New York: Delta.

Grossman, Haim. 2004. War as child's play: Patriotic games in the British Mandate and Israel. *Israel Studies* 9:1–30.

Guidry, John A., Michael D. Kennedy, and Mayer N. Zald, eds. 2000. *Globalization and social movements: Culture, power and the transnational public sphere.* Ann Arbor: University of Michigan Press.

Guibernau, Montserrat, and John Hutchinson, eds. 2004. *History and national destiny: Ethnosymbolism and its critics.* Oxford: Blackwell.

Hall-Cathala, David. 1990. *The peace movement in Israel: 1967–1987.* London: Macmillan.

Hallote, Rachel S., and Alexander H. Joffe. 2002. The politics of Israeli archaeology: Between "nationalism" and "science" in the age of the second republic. *Israel Studies* 7:83–116.

Handelman, Don. 1990. *Models and mirrors: Towards an anthropology of public events.* Cambridge: Cambridge University Press.

Handelman, Don, and Elihu Katz. 1990. State ceremonies of Israel: Remembrance Day and Independence Day. In *Models and mirrors: Towards an anthropology of public events,* ed. Don Handelman, 191–233. Cambridge: Cambridge University Press.

Hardacre, Helen. 1993. The impact of fundamentalism on women, the family and interpersonal relations. In *Fundamentalism and the state,* ed. Martin E. Marty and R. Scott Appleby, 129–50. Chicago: University of Chicago Press.

Harvey, David. 1989. *The condition of post-modernity: An inquiry into the origins of cultural change.* Cambridge, UK: Blackwell.

Hawley, John Stratton, ed. 1994. *Fundamentalism and gender.* New York: Oxford University Press.

Helman, Sara, and Tamar Rapoport. 1997. Women in black: Changing Israeli gender and socio-economic order. *British Journal of Sociology* 48:682–700.

Hertzberg, Arthur. 1975. *The Zionist idea.* Westport, CT: Greenwood.

Herzfeld, Michael. 1991. *A place in history: Social and monumental time in a Cretan town.* Princeton: Princeton University Press.

Horowitz, Dan, and Moshe Lissak. 1978. *Origins of the Israeli polity: Palestine under the Mandate.* Chicago: University of Chicago Press.

Huntington, Samuel P. 1996. *The clash of civilizations and the remaking of world order.* New York: Simon and Schuster.

Isaak, Rael Jean. 1976. *Israel divided: Ideological politics in the Jewish State.* Baltimore: Johns Hopkins University Press.

Jackson, J. B. 1980. *The necessity for ruins.* Amherst: University of Massachusetts Press.

Jenkins, Craig J. 1983. Resource mobilization theory and the study of social movements. *Annual Review of Sociology* 9:527–53.

Kaminer, Reuven. 1996. *The politics of protest: The Israeli peace movement and the Palestinian Intifada.* Brighton, UK: Sussex Academic Press.

Katriel, Tamar. 1988. "Gibush": A study in Israeli cultural semantics. *Anthropological Linguistics* 30:199–213.

Katz, Saul. 1985. The Israeli teacher guide. *Annals of Tourism Research* 12:49–72.

Kaufman, Debra Renee. 1991. *Rachel's daughters: Newly orthodox Jewish women.* New Brunswick, NJ: Rutgers University Press.

Kelleman, Aharon. 1993. *Society and settlement: Jewish Land of Israel in the twentieth century.* New York: State University of New York Press.

Kempinski, Aharon. 1986. Joshua's altar: An Iron Age I watchtower. *Biblical Archaeology Review* 12:42, 44–49.

Kertzer, David I. 1988. *Ritual, politics, and power.* New Haven: Yale University Press.

Kimmerling, Baruch. 1983. *Zionism and territory.* Berkeley: University of California Press.

———. 1984. Between the primordial and civil definition of the collective identity: The state of Israel of Eretz Israel. In *Comparative social dynamics,* ed. Erik Cohen, Moshe Lissak, and Uri Almagor. Boulder, CO: Westview.

———. 1987. Exchanging territories for peace: A macrosociological approach. *Journal of Applied Behavioral Science* 23:13–34.

———. 1989. Boundaries and frontiers of the Israeli control system. In *The Israeli state and society: Boundaries and frontiers,* ed. Baruch Kimmerling, 265–84. Albany: State University of New York Press.

———. 2001. *The invention and decline of Israeliness: State, society and the military.* Berkeley: University of California Press.

Kohl, Philip L. 1998. Nationalism and archaeology: On the construction of nations and the reconstruction of the remote past. *Annual Review of Anthropology* 27:223–46.

Kohl, Philip L., and Clare Fawcett, eds. 1995. *Nationalism, politics and the practice of archaeology.* Cambridge: Cambridge University Press.

Kliot, Nurit. 1996. Place names as a manifestation of culture and politics: The Israeli context. In *The mosaic of Israeli geography,* ed. Yehuda Gradus and Gabriel Lipshitz, 247–52. Beer Sheva: Ben-Gurion University Press.

Lagerquist, Peter. 2004. Fencing the last sky: Excavating Palestine after Israel's "separation wall." *Journal of Palestinian Studies* 33:5–35.

Lechner, Frank. J., and John Boli, eds. 2000. *The globalization reader.* Malden, MA: Blackwell.

Liebman, Charles. 1993. The myth of defeat: The memory of the Yom Kippur War in Israeli society. *Middle Eastern Studies* 29:399–418.

Liebman, Charles, and Eliezer Don-Yehiya. 1983. *Civil religion in Israel.* Berkeley: University of California Press.

Lomsky-Feder, Edna. 2004. Life stories, war, and veterans: On the social distribution of memories. *Ethos* 32:82–109.

Lustick, Ian. 1991. *For the land and the Lord: Jewish fundamentalism in Israel.* New York: Council on Foreign Relations.

———. 1993. *Unsettled states, disputed lands.* Ithaca, NY: Cornell University Press.

MacCannell, Dean. 1973. Staged authenticity: Arrangements of social space in tourist settings. *American Journal of Sociology* 79:589–603.

Marty, Martin E., and R. Scott Appleby, eds. 1991. *Fundamentalism observed.* Chicago: University of Chicago Press.

———. 1992. *The glory and the power: The fundamentalist challenge to the modern world.* Boston: Beacon.

Medoff, Rafael 1986. Gush Emunim and the question of Jewish counterterror. *Middle East Review* 18:17–24.

Mannheim, Karl. 1959. The problem of generations. In *Essays on the sociology of knowledge,* 276–322. London: Routledge and Kegan Paul.

Meskell, Lynn, ed. 1998. *Archaeology under fire: Nationalism, politics and heritage in the Eastern Mediterranean and Middle East.* London: Routledge.

Monmenier, Mark S. 1993. *How to lie with maps.* Chicago: Chicago University Press.

Morris, Benny. 1987. *The birth of the Palestinian refugee problem.* Cambridge: Cambridge University Press.

———. 1993. *Israel's border wars 1949–1956: Arab infiltration, Israeli retaliation, and the countdown to the Suez War.* Oxford: Clarendon.

Neuman, Tamara. 2004. Maternal "anti-politics" in the formation of Hebron's Jewish enclave. *Journal of Palestinian Studies* 33:51–70.

Neusner, Jacob. 1988. *Self-fulfilling prophecy: Exile and return in the history of Judaism.* Atlanta: Scholars Press.

Newman, David, ed. 1985. *The impact of Gush Emunim.* London: Croom Helm.

Nimni, Ephraim, ed. 2003. *The challenge of post-Zionism: Alternatives to Israeli fundamentalist politics.* London: Zed.

Nora, Pierre. 1989. Between memory and history: Les lieux de mémoire. *Representations* 26:7–25.

Ohana, David. 2002. Kfar Etzion: The community of memory and the myth of return. *Israel Studies* 7:145–74.

Oz, Amos. 1983. *In the Land of Israel,* trans. Maurie Goldberg-Bartura. New York: Harcourt Brace Jovanovich.

Paine, Robert. 1995a. Behind the Hebron massacre, 1994. *Anthropology Today* 11:8–15.

———. 1995b. Topophilia, Zionism and certainty: Making a place out of the space that became Israel again. In *The pursuit of certainty,* ed. Wendy James. New York: Routledge.

Pappe, Ilan. 1995. Critique and agenda: The post-Zionist scholars in Israel. *History and Memory* 7:66–90.

Peri, Yoram, ed. 2000. *The assassination of Yitzhak Rabin.* Stanford: Stanford University Press

Rabinowitz, Dani. 1997. *Overlooking Nazareth: The ethnography of exclusion in Galilee.* Cambridge: Cambridge University Press.

Ram, Uri. 1995. *The changing agenda of Israeli sociology: Theory, ideology, identity.* New York: State University of New York Press.

———. 2007. *The globalization of Israel: McWorld in Tel Aviv, jihad in Jerusalem.* New York: Routledge.

Rapoport, Tamar, Anat Penso, and Yoni Garb. 1994. Contribution to the collective by religious-Zionist adolescent girls. *British Journal of Sociology of Education* 15:375–88.

Ravitzky, Aviezer. 1996. *Messianism, Zionism, and Jewish religious radicalism.* Translated by Michael Swirsky and Jonathan Chipman. Chicago Studies in the History of Judaism. Chicago: University of Chicago Press.

———. 2000. Let us search our path: Religious Zionism after the assassination. In *The assassination of Yitzhak Rabin,* ed. Yoram Peri, 141–62. Stanford: Stanford University Press.

Ritzer, George. 1993. *The McDonaldization of society: An investigation into the changing character of contemporary social life.* Thousand Oaks, CA: Pine Forge.

Roniger, Luis, and Michael Feige. 1992. From pioneer to freier: The changing models of generalized exchange in Israel. *European Journal of Sociology* 33: 280–307.

Sabato, Haim. 2003. *Adjusting sights.* Translated by Hillel Halkin. New Milford, CT: Toby.

Schuerken, Ulrika. 2003. The sociological and anthropological study of globalization and localization. *Current Sociology* 51:209–22.

Segal, Haggai. 1988. *Dear brothers: The West Bank Jewish underground.* New York: Beit Shamai.

Segal, Rafi, and Eyal Weizman. 2003. *A civilian occupation: The politics of Israeli architecture.* New York: Storefront for Art and Architecture.

Segev, Tom. 1993. *The seventh million: The Israelis and the Holocaust.* New York: Hill and Wang.

———. 2001. *One Palestine, complete: Jews and Arabs under the British Mandate.* London: Abacus.

Sered, Susan Starr. 1989. Rachel's Tomb: Societal liminality and the revitalization of a shrine. *Religion* 19:27–40.

Shafir, Gershon. 1985. Institutional and spontaneous settlement drives: Did Gush Emunim make a difference? In *The Impact of Gush Emunim,* ed. David Newman, 153–71. London: Croom Helm.

———. 1996. *Land, labor and the origins of the Israeli-Palestinian conflict, 1882–1914.* Berkeley: University of California Press.

Shafir, Gershon, and Yoav Peled, eds. 2000. *The new Israel: Peacemaking and liberalization.* Boulder, CO: Westview.

Shamgar-Handelman, Leah. 1986. *Israeli war widows: Beyond the glory of heroism.* South Hadley, MA: Bergin and Garvey.

Shavit, Ya'akov. 1997. Archaeology, political culture and culture in Israel. In *The archaeology of Israel: Constructing the past, interpreting the present,* ed. Neil

Asher Silberman and David Small, 48–62. *Journal for the Study of the Old Testament* supplement series, no. 237. Sheffield, UK: Sheffield Academic Press.

Shimoni, Gideon. 1995. *The Zionist ideology.* Hanover, NH: Brandeis University Press.

Shohat, Ella. 1998. Sepharadim in Israel: Zionism from the standpoint of its Jewish victims. *Social Text* 19–20:1–35.

Silberman, Neil Asher. 1982. *Digging for God and country.* New York: Knopf.

———. 1994. *A prophet from amongst you: The life of Yigael Yadin—Soldier, scholar, and mythmaker of modern Israel.* Reading, MA: Addison-Wesley.

Silberstein, Laurence J. 1999. *The Postzionism debates: Knowledge and power in Israeli culture.* New York: Routledge.

Slymowicz, Suzan. 1998. *The object of memory: Arabs and Jews narrate the Palestinian village.* Philadelphia: University of Pennsylvania Press.

Smelser, Neil. 1962. *Theory of collective behavior.* New York: Free Press.

Smith, Anthony. 1986. *The ethnic origins of the nation.* Oxford: Blackwell.

———. 2001. *Nationalism: Theory, ideology, history.* Cambridge, UK: Polity.

Sprinzak, Ehud. 1981. Gush Emunim: The iceberg model of political extremism. *Jerusalem Quarterly* 21:28–47.

———. 1991. *The ascendance of Israel's radical Right.* New York: Oxford University Press.

———. 1993. Elite illegalism in Israel and the question of democracy. In *Israeli democracy under stress,* ed. Ehud Sprinzak and Larry Diamond, 173–98. London: Lynne Riener.

Sweedenburg, Ted. 1990. The Palestinian peasant as a national signifier. *Anthropological Quarterly* 63:18–30.

Tilly, Charles. 1978. *From mobilization to revolution.* Reading, MA: Addison Wesley.

Turner, Victor. 1978. The center out there: Pilgrim's goal. *History of Religion* 12: 191–230.

Yadgar, Yaacov. 2003. Between "the Arab" and "the Religious Rightist": "Significant others" in the construction of Jewish-Israeli national identity. *Nationalism and Ethnic Politics* 9:52–74.

Yerushalmi, Yosef Hayim. 1982. *Zakhor: Jewish history and Jewish memory.* Seattle: University of Washington Press.

Yiftachel, Oren. 2006. *Ethnocracy: Land and identity politics in Israel/Palestine.* Philadelphia: University of Pennsylvania Press.

Yuval-Davis, Nira. 1997. *Gender and nation.* London: Sage.

Vinitzki-Saroussi, Vered. 2002. Commemorating a difficult past: Yitzhak Rabin's memorials. *American Sociological Review* 67:30–51.

Waxman, Chaim. 1985. Political and social attitudes of Americans among the settlers in the territories. In *The impact of Gush Emunim,* ed. David Newman, 200–220. London: Croom Helm.

Weingrod, Alex. 1990. *The saint of Beersheba.* SUNY Series in Israeli Studies. Albany: State University of New York Press.

———. 1995. Dry bones: Nationalism and symbolism in contemporary Israel. *Anthropology Today* 11:7–12.

Weisburd, David. 1989. *Jewish settler violence: Deviance as social reaction.* University Park: Pennsylvania State University.

Weisburd, David, and Elin Waring. 1985. Settlement motivation in the Gush Emunim movement: Comparing bonds of altruism and self-interest. In *The impact of Gush Emunim,* ed. David Newman, 183–99. London: Croom Helm.

Weisburd, David, and Vered Vinitzky. 1984. Vigilantism as rational social control: The case of the Gush Emunim settlers. In *Cross currents in Israeli culture and politics,* ed. Myron J. Aronoff. New Brunswick, NJ: Transaction.

Weizman, Eyal. 2007. *Hollow land: Israel's architecture of occupation.* London: Verso.

Whitelam, Keith W. 1996. *The invention of ancient Israel.* London: Routledge.

Wistrich, Robert, and David Ohana, eds. 1995. *The shaping of Israeli identity: Myth, memory and trauma.* London: Frank Cass.

Wolfsfeld, Gadi. 1984. Yamit: Protest and media. *Jerusalem Quarterly* 31:130–44.

———. 1987. Protest and the removal of Yamit: Ostentatious political action. *Journal of Applied Behavioral Science* 23:103–16.

Wood, Denis. 1993. *The power of maps.* London: Routledge.

Zald, Mayer N., and Roberta Ash. 1966. Social movement organization: Growth, decay and change. *Social Forces* 44:327–41.

Zertal, Adam. 1986. How can Kempinski be so wrong! *Biblical Archaeology Review* 12:43, 49–53.

Zertal, Idith, and Akiva Eldar. 2007. *Lords of the land: The war over Israel's settlements in the occupied territories 1967–2007.* New York: Nation.

Zerubavel, Yael. 1995. *Recovered roots: Memory and the making of national tradition.* Chicago: University of Chicago Press.

———. 2003. Female images in a state of war: The Israeli war widows in fiction and film. In *Landscaping the human garden,* ed. Amir Weiner, 236–57. Stanford: Stanford University Press.

Index

Italicized page numbers indicate photographs in the gallery, which begins following page 130.

www.ingramcontent.com/pod-product-compliance
Lightning Source LLC
Chambersburg PA
CBHW070739210226
39545CB00063B/118/J